The international politics
of the Middle East

Manchester University Press

The international politics of the Middle East

Second edition

Raymond Hinnebusch

Manchester University Press

The right of Raymond Hinnebusch to be identified as the author of
this work has been asserted by him in accordance with the
Copyright, Designs and Patents Act 1988.

First edition published 2003 by Manchester University Press

This edition published 2015 by Manchester University Press
Altrincham Street, Manchester M1 7JA, UK
www.manchesteruniversitypress.co.uk

British Library Cataloguing-in-Publication Data
A catalogue record for this book is available from the British Library

Library of Congress Cataloging-in-Publication Data applied for

ISBN   978 0 7190 9975 5 hardback
ISBN   978 0 7190 9525 2 paperback

This edition first published 2015

Typeset 10/12 Sabon by
Servis Filmsetting Ltd, Stockport, Cheshire
Printed in Great Britain by
Bell and Bain Ltd, Glasgow

To Yuki

Contents

Preface

This second edition of *The International Politics of the Middle East* comes after multiple watershed events in the region made the need for a fully revised and updated volume ever more pressing. The first edition ended with the 9/11 attacks on the US. What followed was massive US intervention in Afghanistan and Iraq, a failed attempt to establish hegemony over the region that destabilised it and pre-cipitated major changes in the regional power balance. Then, a decade later, the Arab Uprising further spread this instability, again reshuffling the cards in the regional deck. The book has been exten-sively updated and enlarged to take account of these and other developments in the region. In addition, the interaction between theory and empirical realities of the region has been further under-lined, particularly with the addition of a conclusion assessing the role of IR theory in understanding MENA and the relevance of the MENA experience for IR theory. A glossary of international relations terms is added to assist in the grasp of the IR theoretical side of the book.

Abbreviations

AKP	Justice and Development Party (Turkey)
ARAMCO	Arabian-American Oil Company
AWACS	Airborne Warning and Control System
bpd	barrels per day
CENTO	Central Treaty Organization
CIA	Central Intelligence Organization (US)
GAFTA	Greater Arab Free Trade Area
GCC	Gulf Co-operation Council
GDP	gross domestic product
GNP	gross national product
Hamas	Movement of the Islamic Resistance
HS	historical sociology
HST	Hegemonic Stability Theory
IFIs	International Financial Institutions
IMF	International Monetary Fund
IPC	Iraq Petroleum Company
IR	International Relations (discipline)
IS	International Society (approach to IR)
ISIS	Islamic State of Iraq and Syria
KDP	Kurdish Democratic Party
KRG	Kurdish Regional Government (Iraq)
LDCs	Less Developed Countries
MENA	Middle East/North Africa (region)
NATO	North Atlantic Treaty Organisation
NIC	newly industrialised country
OIC	Organisation of the Islamic Conference
OPEC	Organisation of Petroleum Exporting Countries
PA	Palestinian Authority

PKK	Kurdish Workers Party
PLO	Palestine Liberation Organisation
RPP	Republican Peoples Party (Turkish)
SAVAK	Iran's secret police under the Shah
TNCs	Transnational Corporations
UAR	United Arab Republic
UN	United Nations
UNEF	United Nations Emergency Force (in Sinai)
UNSC	United Nations Security Council
USSR	Union of Soviet Socialist Republics
WMD	weapons of mass destruction

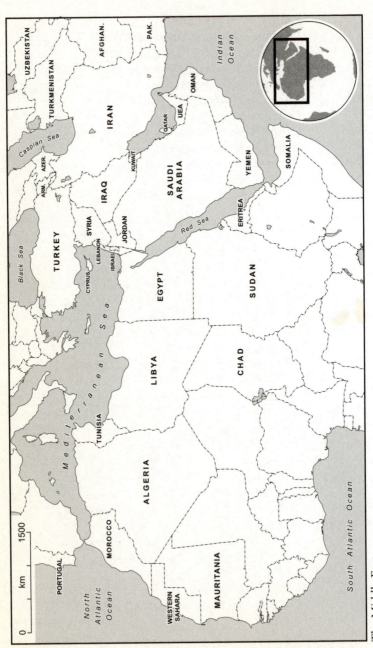

The Middle East

1

Introduction to the international politics of the Middle East

This book and the study of the Middle East

This study takes the Middle East to be constituted around an Arab core, with a shared identity but fragmented into multiple territorial states; the core is flanked by a periphery of non-Arab states – Turkey, Iran and Israel – which are an integral part of the region's conflicts and its balance of power (Cantori and Spiegel 1970; Ismael 1986: 5–13). Because the Middle East's unique features defy analyses based on any one conceptual approach to international relations, this study will deploy a combination of several to capture its complex reality.

The book's approach to understanding Middle East/North Africa (MENA) international politics might be called 'complex realism'. It starts with realist basics since Middle Eastern policy-makers are quintessential realists, preoccupied with the threats that are so pervasive in MENA. The Middle East is arguably the epi-centre of world crisis, chronically war-prone and the site of the world's most protracted conflicts: it is the region where the anarchy and insecurity seen by the realist school of international politics as the main feature of states systems remains most in evidence. The book therefore accepts the realist claim that insecurity generates struggles for power and that state foreign policy seeks to counter security threats, first of all, to regime survival, but also to state interests such as sovereignty and territorial integrity. Because it specialises in explaining the central aspects of international politics – power, war, alliances, international order – realism offers unique insights into the dynamics of *inter-state relations* in the region.

Yet several realist assumptions are problematic in MENA. First, realism assumes the formation of *cohesive Westphalian states* pursuing agreed 'national interests' but this can be misleading in MENA where many states are so fragmented and their sovereignty so compromised by dependency that their foreign policies might reflect regime interests but not 'national' interests; and whether MENA states approximate realist 'rational actors' is highly contingent on a process of state formation that is very much incomplete. Second, realism's assumption that conflict is chiefly the by-product of a states system's *anarchy* misses the main causes of the Middle East's exceptional war and instability, namely the peculiar historical construction of the regional system under imperialism, which left behind a misfit between identity and territory that built irredentism into the system. Third, neo-realism's assumption that states' international behaviour is chiefly determined by the inter-state system is inadequate to understand the Middle East; rather the 'environment' in which MENA states operate is multi-layered, with realism's inter-state system embedded in a global hierarchy and in regional trans-state identities. Finally, while the international system is, for realism, largely unchanging, except for the distribution of power among states, in MENA the ever-changing relative weight of these levels continually alters the dynamics of regional politics.

Thus, while realism gives important insights into the dynamics of the *regional inter-state system,* with its balance of (material) power among states, to understand the other dimensions of the regional system, we need to bring in other theories. Marxist-inspired 'structuralism' identifies the *place of the MENA system in the global hierarchy,* namely in the economic periphery, dependent on the international capitalist core. It shows how the region's penetrated client states behave quite differently from fully sovereign states. Constructivists help us understand *the trans-state level* where *identity* matters: in the Middle East, sub- and supra-state identities compete with state identity, inspire trans-state movements and constrain purely state-centric behaviour. Constructivism's insistence that systemic structures are not just material configurations of power and wealth and include the cultural norms that derive from *identity* helps us to understand how the region's powerful supra-state identities lead to a unique contestation of state sovereignty. The ideas of *historical sociology* (HS) on state formation and particularly how states and state systems are mutually constitutive, offer indispensable insights into change in the regional system: not just how the system shapes the nature of the states but also how the *kind of states* – their levels of state formation – that dominate a system shapes its dynamics. Finally, we need, with Foreign Policy Analysis, to open the black box of *decision-making* for, as realists themselves acknowledge, how states respond to environmental pressures is a product of internal leadership and policy processes.

The following lays out the book's framework of analysis, identifying the main issues to be treated and approaches that will be deployed in subsequent chapters; the order in which these issues are discussed begins with the most macro and proceeds to the more micro, then returns to the macro level.

Core–periphery relations: MENA in the world hierarchy

According to structuralist analysis, the world system is not, as realism imagines, a pure anarchy, but has features of a hierarchy, with the global hegemon at the top and regions such as MENA located toward the bottom. The Middle East, once an independent civilisation headed by its own great power, the Ottoman empire, was turned, under imperialism, into a periphery of the Western dominated world system. This resulted, in the view of structuralism, from the drive of the 'hegemon' of the time, the UK, to force open non-capitalist economies and incorporate them into the world capitalist system as peripheries of the Western core (Callinicos 2009; Wallerstein 1974). Thereafter, nationalism forced a certain retreat by Western imperialism but, even after nominal independence, MENA, as the location of both Israel and of the world's concentrated petroleum reserves, remained an exceptional magnet for external intervention, led by the subsequent American hegemon, which, in turn, kept anti-imperialist nationalism alive long after de-colonisation. The region remains, as Brown (1984) argues, a uniquely 'penetrated system'.

A starting point for understanding the persistence of highly unequal core–periphery relations, even after the retreat of imperial armies from the region, is Galtung's (1971) 'structural model of imperialism'. In his view, two mechanisms sustain penetration by the Western 'core': (1) the core created and left behind client elites and classes that have an interest in dependent relations and (2) regional states were linked to the core, in feudal-like north–south relations, while horizontal (south–south) relations were shattered.

Indeed, imperialism's fragmentation of the Middle East into a multitude of weak states dependent on core states for security against each other, and its division of the formerly existing regional market into small economies exporting primary products to the core and dependent on manufacturing imports from it, approximates Galtung's model. According to Moon (1995), the effect of such a structure on the foreign policy-making of dependent states is to create a 'constrained consensus' from the overlap of local elites' economic interests, worldviews (through Western education) and threat perceptions (fear of radical movements) with those of core elites. As a result, rather than *balancing against* intrusive external power, as realism might expect, dependent elites typically '*bandwagon*' *with* a global patron to contain more immediate regional or domestic threats. Although a hierarchy, this structure is not a relation of command, but, rather, a patron–client system in which, however asymmetric, there is always an *exchange* in which the patron supplies resources and protection and the client gives political support. This sharply limits the autonomy of the client, which, in major crises, must support its patron, regardless of the wishes of regional populations; but there is otherwise always room for bargaining with the patron, particularly when, as during the Cold War, clients could threaten to switch patrons.

Indeed, core–periphery relations merely set the outside parameters within which Middle East regional politics are conducted. Moreover, far from being static, they are constantly contested and have regularly stimulated anti-imperialist movements, which, where they took state power, attempted to restructure these relations. Whether nationalist states can do this, however, depends on systemic structures. When there is a hegemonic power (UK, US) able to 'lay down the law' on behalf of the world capitalist system (in the Middle East ensuring core access to cheap energy), and especially if the regional system is simultaneously divided (the usual condition as Galtung details), external powers can exploit local rivalries to sustain their penetration of the region. Conversely, when the core was split, as under Cold War bi-polarity, nationalist states were able to exploit superpower rivalry to win protection, aid and arms from the number-two state, the USSR, enabling them to pursue nationalist foreign policies and dilute economic dependency. Moreover, as Thompson (1970) has shown, the Middle East is a partial exception to Galtung's feudal model in that, while fragmented economically and politically, it enjoys trans-state cultural unity which nationalist states have exploited to mobilise regional solidarity against the core. Thus, the conjuncture of the Cold War and the spread of Pan-Arabism allowed Nasser's Egypt to sufficiently roll back imperialist influence to establish a relatively autonomous regional system. Briefly, Galtung's normal global structure was turned on its head, with the core split and the MENA periphery united. Additionally, in the rise of the Organisation of Petroleum Exporting Countries (OPEC), south–south solidarity produced exceptional financial power that, while failing ultimately to raise the region from the economic periphery, arguably transformed the position of the swing oil producer, Saudi Arabia, from dependence into asymmetric interdependence.

However, favourable conditions for regional autonomy were, particularly with the end of the oil boom and Cold War, largely reversed. The West's restored ability to intervene militarily (e.g. in two wars against Iraq) and impose economic sanctions and loan conditionality revived key features of the age of imperialism at the expense of regional autonomy. As such, although structuralism expects on-going challenges to the core–periphery structure, it is pessimistic about the effectiveness of agency by regional actors to restructure the system in which they are embedded. Nevertheless, no analysis of the international politics of the region can be convincing that does not take account of the impact of the on-going struggle for regional autonomy from external control.

Between identity and sovereignty: the flawed construction of the regional system

If there is one thing that distinguishes the Middle East states system it is the powerful role of non-state identities. In the Westphalian states system, on which the Middle East regional system was ostensibly modelled, the principle of state sovereignty is usually accompanied by a rough correspondence of identity and territory. The consequent 'nation-state' provides the basis of the state's legitimacy and underlies acceptance of the norm of sovereignty. This correspondence is assumed by realists to make possible a relative consensus on the national interest that is thought to shape a state's foreign policy.

In the Middle East, however, imperialism's arbitrary imposition of state boundaries produced a substantial incongruence between territory and identity, with the result that loyalty to the state has been contested by sub-state and supra-state identities. One result was weak states debilitated by enduring legitimacy deficits. Territory-identity incongruence also built *irredentism* into the fabric of the system: in many states, the trans-state connections of sub-state groups and dissatisfaction with borders generated protracted conflicts which spilled over in state–sub-state or inter-state wars, e.g. the role of the Kurds in conflicts between Turkey and Syria, Iran and Iraq. Equally important, as constructivist analysis showed (Barnett 1998), Pan-Arab norms deriving from a shared supra-state identity became as important in shaping Arab state behaviour as the distribution of material power stressed by realism. State leaders were at least partially socialised into *roles*: a proper Arab state defends regional autonomy from the West, promotes the Palestine cause and co-operates with other Arab states for the common interest. Pan-Islam holds to similar norms. The contradiction between the global norm of sovereignty, in which state interests are legitimately the priority of foreign policy, and the regional norms of Pan-Arabism or Pan-Islam, which expect these interests to be compatible with the values of the indigenous supra-state identity community, have caught Arab foreign policy-making elites, in Korany's (1988: 165) words, between the logics of *raison d'état* and of *'raison de la nation'*. While they have tenaciously defended the sovereignty of their individual states, legitimacy at home has depended on their foreign policies appearing to respect Arab–Islamic norms. For more ambitious states, supra-state identity presented the opportunity to assert regional leadership by championing Pan-Arab or Islamic causes.

While this 'dualism' is a constant, the relative balance between supra-state identity and state sovereignty has evolved – been 'constructed' in the view of constructivists – over time by the interactions of states and the actions of state-builders, and, at least until recently, in favour of the latter (Barnett 1998). Several forces interacted to define this evolution. Imperialism and the creation of Israel stimulated Pan-Arabism movements crossing state boundaries, which created conditions for competition between states over Pan-Arab leadership. Although Pan-Arabism enjoined co-operation among Arab states it was, ironically, constructed out of this competition for Pan-Arab leadership. Nasser's disproportionate ability to mobilise trans-state support in this contest allowed the assertion of Egyptian hegemony in the region and Cairo's construction of a 'Pan-Arab regime' which constrained the sovereign right of states to seek security outside regional collective arrangements. At the same time, however, this competition stimulated state elites' defence of sovereignty through anti-hegemonic (anti-Cairo) balancing and encouraged state formation aiming to immunise states from trans-state ideological penetration. The rivalries of Arab leaders, expressed in disagreements over Arabism and unleashing the Pan-Arab 'outbidding' that brought on the disastrous 1967 defeat by Israel, helped 'de-construct' the Pan-Arab regime. Thereafter, the regularity of war and much increased insecurity greatly accelerated the impulse of the individual Arab states to fall back on self-help and power balancing, while trans-state rent flows released by the oil boom helped consolidate states, making them much less vulnerable to Pan-Arab or Islamic ideological penetration. Although attempts were made to agree on a form of Arabism, defined in Arab summits, which was compatible with sovereignty, the divergent routes Arab states took to protect themselves from war and to exit from it 'deconstructed' Pan-Arab constraints on reason of state. A surge in Islamic identity precipitated by the Iranian revolution increasingly manifested itself at the grassroots of MENA societies, but at the state level Islamic solidarity, albeit institutionalised in the Islamic Conference Organisation, was unable to substitute for Arabism as a basis of inter-Arab order. Rather, as realism expects, heightened insecurity moved the system toward the Westphalian model in the 1980s, but this evolution, far from inevitable, was a 'constructed' outcome of internal state-building and of inter-state relations and, to this day, is far from complete. Indeed, as a result of the weakening of many regional states from legitimacy erosion in the 1990s, accelerated by destruction of the Iraqi state in the US invasion of 2003 and by the Arab Uprising of the next decade, trans-state Islamist movements, increasingly polarised along Sunni–Shia lines, appeared to capture the loyalties of many of the putative citizens of regional states; but, this contributed to regional fragmentation rather than regional order. No analysis of the Middle East can succeed without taking account of the constantly mutating identity-sovereignty dynamic that constitutes the regional system.

The dynamics of the inter-state system: the struggle for power

According to neo-realism, the state *system*'s 'anarchy' imposes security-maximising behaviour on all states. MENA states operate in a particularly 'anarchic' regional system, with border conflicts and irredentism built in at its formation and containing two of the world's most durable conflict centres, the Arab–Israeli and the Gulf arenas, where war is a regular occurrence. As such, for realists, constructivists greatly underestimate the role of power and violence in regional politics; indeed, as realists expect, security threats do appear to be the first priority of foreign policy-makers and power balancing against such threats is pervasive in the region. The strategic importance or vulnerability of a state's geographical location shapes the main threats and opportunities it faces and contiguity typically makes neighbours the most salient threat to most states.

There is, however, considerable variation in balancing strategies. According to Walt (1987), states respond to threat by 'power balancing' and most adopt a 'defensive realist' accumulation of sufficient military power and alliance partners to deter an aggressor. In realism, however, power matters for behaviour. Weaker states are more likely to concentrate on defending their sovereignty, and instead of self-help balancing, may seek protection by 'bandwagoning' with an external great power; where states are so weak that the major immediate threat is from internal opposition, they may seek support from such a patron to deal with both internal and regional threats – what Steven David (1991) called 'omnibalancing'. On the other hand, states with greater power resources (wealth, population, size, social coherence) are likely to have more ambitious and activist foreign policies, consistent with an 'offensive realist' (Mearsheimer 2001) pursuit of regional hegemony, which they see as the only sure key to security. Such hegemony requires not only material but also 'soft' power derived from a credible claim to act for wider regional interests. The non-Arab states have generally enjoyed more material assets, notably Turkey and Iran, from their size and historic coherence, and Israel from its special external connections, but have often lacked soft power; among the Arab states, Egypt by virtue of its population, centrality, cohesion and soft power, has always been the potential Arab hegemon but Iraq also made a bid after Egypt relinquished the role. These states have periodically sought regional hegemony, often under the

banner of a supra-state ideology (Pan-Arabism, Pan-Islam) enabling them to speak for wider regional interests. While 'offensive
realism' appears to attribute agency to aspirant regional hegemons,
their bids for hegemony have regularly come up against opposition
from both regional rivals and the global hegemons, and therefore
have regularly proved temporary, often de-railed by war.

Realism further argues that the pervasive balancing behaviour of
states constitutes an equilibrium mechanism – a balance of power –
that both tends to preserve the states system against revisionist
challenges and becomes a norm of behaviour. Rustow (1984: 598)
argues that 'while many Middle Eastern countries individually
nurse expansionist or hegemonic ambitions, all of them collectively, by their preference for the weaker side and their readiness
to shift alignments regardless of ideology, offer strong support for
the status quo'. Similarly, Alan Taylor (1982) identified classic
patterns of power balancing in the region. Walt, whose classic
study, *The Origin of Alliances* (1987) systematically applied realism to the region, also argued that realist rules held in MENA in
spite of the special feature of the Arab state system, namely shared
Arab identity: he showed that, even at the height of Pan-Arabism,
which enjoined inter-Arab co-operation, Arab states widely balanced against each other and specifically against Egyptian hegemony. However, importantly, while this balancing took the form
of rival alliances, the threat Arab states posed to each other, as
constructivist scholar Michael Barnett (1998) pointed out, was *not
military*, as realists expect, but rather attempts to de-legitimise and
thereby subvert the rival regime via discourse wars, and balancing
similarly took the form of defending one's own nationalist legitimacy, not the *military balancing* expected by realism. In the longer
term, balancing was manifest in domestic state-building efforts to
make regimes less permeable to ideological subversion. In time,
Pan-Arab trans-state movements, having failed to overthrow the
state system, gradually declined: states had outlived their main non-
state challengers.

In reality, realism's supposedly self-balancing mechanism depends
on state actors adhering to the reason of state deemed rational in
the realist tradition: by adopting 'realistic' goals (subordinating
ideology to the realities of the power balance) and by increasing
capabilities or striking alliances to counter threats. That balancing
practices were in actual fact pervasive in the Middle East is for

realism entirely expected, not simply because of insecurity but also because regimes that play by realist rules are successful and imitated and regimes that violate them tend to suffer disaster and are replaced: thus, the pursuit of domestically driven ideological policies to the neglect of the power balance, notably the Pan-Arab outbidding on the eve of the 1967 Arab–Israeli war or Islamic Iran's attempt to export revolution, led to military disasters (Stein 1993; Taylor 1982), and stimulated the subsequent rise of new leaders that pursued more 'realist' policies taking account of the balance of power. The state system itself therefore tends to 'socialise' its constituent parts into playing by 'realist' rules, not only balancing against threats but prudently matching their goals to their capabilities (Waltz 1979: 74–77).

Once ideological revisionism is replaced by pragmatic geopolitics, the balance of power, other things being equal, is more likely to be stable. However, as MENA states throughout the region were consolidated during the 1970s and 1980s, this very state strengthening enhanced the potential threat each posed to the other. With domestic opposition more manageable, states could mobilise the support and resources to build up their power and, if they wished, pursue external ambitions. Arms races generated a highly militarised region, creating an intense security dilemma that, in turn, shaped states into similar 'national security' states. Designed to ward off external threats, they actually generated a 'Hobbesian' system of high insecurity for all: the system shaped the units into similar moulds, which reproduced the system.

Regional order therefore became dependent on the balance of power but, unfortunately, this balance proved widely unstable. Power imbalances were built into the regional system by the arbitrary boundary drawing that created non-viable or mini-states (around oil wells – Kuwait or as buffers – Jordan) alongside large neighbours dissatisfied by these boundaries. Also, the unevenness of state formation meant states consolidated earlier, notably the non-Arab states, had a power advantage over the later-developing Arab states. The power balance was also repeatedly upset by the rapid differential growth in the relative power of certain states owing to their exceptional access to oil revenues and/or foreign aid and hence to arms deliveries from external powers. Thus, Israel and Iraq achieved power superiority over neighbours, providing the occasion – when combined with irredentist leaderships – for, altogether, four wars: Israel's 1967 pre-emptive war, its 1982 invasion of Lebanon and Iraq's two Gulf wars. In the end, power balances were restored, but only after very costly wars: balancing preserved the system but did not keep the peace.

Bringing in history: variations in the MENA states system

Historical sociology (HS) occupies a bridging space between the tri-layered character of the MENA system and the states that make it up, between structure and agency. Neo-realists see states systems as an unchanging anarchy that shapes state units into uniform moulds, specifically ones with the capabilities to balance against external threat. This one way direction of causality is remedied by HS's demonstration that, historically, states and state systems *co-constitute* each other in a circular feedback; for example, in historical periods where, as Tilly famously argued, war makes the state and the state makes war, a realist-like system may be co-constituted; but, as Buzan and Weaver (2003) point out, pre-modern states with little capacity to make war constitute a quite different kind of system. Neo-realism's ahistorical insensitivity to such *variations* in states systems is also remedied by HS's demonstration that they vary over time, and, in particular, that in non-Westphalian systems, as Ruggie (1983) notes, states have been subjected, not just to inter-state rivalry but also to forces above and below the states system.

This is, indeed, currently the case in MENA where the regional states system is subordinated within a global hierarchy and embedded in a trans-state arena and where state-system co-constitution and system dynamics is thus extremely complex. Specifically, variations in the dynamics of the regional system have been determined by *relative levels of state formation*: when regional states are weak, they are readily penetrated by both trans-state and global forces, and are likely to be buffeted between the two; only consolidated states can defend their sovereignty against these forces while power balancing against each other, thus constituting a realist world. On the other hand, state consolidation itself has depended on extracting material resources from the global level and achieving legitimacy in the trans-state one.

In MENA states and state systems have co-constituted each other in several identifiable *historical stages*, with the trajectory of the region described by a bell-shaped curve in which state formation first rose and declined and with it the potency of other levels to affect states' behaviour. In each stage, the nature of regional politics was palpably different. Thus in the first decade after independence (1945–55) most Arab states were ruled by weak landed-tribal oligarchies while the second decade (1955–67) was one of middle class political mobilisation and Pan-Arab revolution that ushered in praetorian instability. Weak states made for global subordination in period one and trans-state penetration in period two; political competition largely took the form of legitimacy wars and subversion between states aligned with the core and states/movements promoting Arab autonomy against imperialism. In a third stage, apparent from the 1970s to the 1990s, in a reaction to earlier state weakness and under the impact of war, and enabled by oil rent, there was an increased, albeit incomplete, state consolidation, driving an approximation of the realist model. This period saw the rise of quite durable neo-patrimonial regimes, less domestically unstable and less permeable to trans-state subversion than hitherto; yet these states now made, through their arms races and wars, a regional system fraught with insecurity, in which they power balanced against threats from neighbours. Since states were at the top of their formation curve, the core great powers were less able to penetrate them or affect their decision-making than hitherto.

In the next two decades (1990–2010), however, state consolidation declined, particularly in the Arab republics where the overdevelopment and over-militarisation of states exceeded their economic bases, leading to economic crises and economic liberalisation that required favouring investors and also an opening up to and renewed dependency on the West. This drove the exclusion of popular constituencies and stimulated the rise of trans-state Islamic opposition that undermined domestic stability. States, now highly penetrated by the core of the global hierarchy, 'omni-balanced' with the US hegemon to get resources and protection from interlocked regional/internal threats. The Arab Uprising beginning in 2010, in good part a reaction to states' loss of autonomy to the global core, further weakened them, making them much more permeable to competitive trans-state interference by rival identity movements and aspirant regional and global powers. Unravelling of states' formation ended in a return to a system wherein the Arab republics were again buffeted by global and trans-state forces at the expense of Westphalian sovereignty; from actors in regional politics, they turned into arenas of regional competition.

States and foreign policy

Realism has limits in understanding state behaviour in MENA. The state cannot be assumed, as realism does, to be a unitary actor responding chiefly to system-level determinants (external threats and opportunities). Indeed, where this model of the state does not hold, foreign policy may be more immediately shaped by domestic conflict or may sacrifice state interests to supra-state ideological causes. Neo-classical realism (Lobell 2009) acknowledges that one cannot deduce state behaviour from the systemic structure (particularly given its multi-layered complexity in MENA), and thus *how* states respond to external threats and opportunities varies according to internal factors, including elite perceptions and the capacity of institutions. However, even neo-classical realism still tends to see external actors as the main security threats and sees threats as objective and fairly self evident, with the main variation in state behaviour being whether they are able to effectively perceive and balance against threats – neither over- nor under-reacting to them; and it is still ultimately a state's capabilities that determine its ambitions and performance.

However, as constructivism insists, threats are not self evident, and even more powerful neighbours, unless elites construct relations as ones of enmity, may not be threats: it is identity that determines which states are 'friends' and 'enemies'; identity is itself, however, fluid, constructed and highly contested in the domestic political arena (Barnett 1998). When in MENA the same states have differently constructed their identities, their foreign policies have radically changed; thus, both Iraq and Iran changed from clients to challengers of the West after their revolutions generated new anti-imperialist identities. As regards institutions, HS points to the importance of levels of state formation: where regimes are institutionally consolidated society is a source of resources and support mobilisable for the conduct of assertive foreign policies; where it is unconsolidated, it is source of *internal* threats, productive – as one version of realism, that of Steven David (1991), acknowledges – of 'omni-balancing', wherein regimes seek the support of an external patron. Thus, to understand states' foreign policies requires analysing how state and identity formation affects foreign policy.

State formation

Analysis of a state's formation is, for several reasons, crucial in understanding its international behaviour. First, whatever the constraints put on states by their systemic environment, there is never only one possible response to it. Thus, while some states challenge the status quo, others support it; indeed, the same states may change from supporters to challengers. This points to how the *initial composition of regimes*, notably whether their dominant social forces are essentially satisfied or dissatisfied, locks states into differential (status quo or revisionist) reactions to the system. This, in turn, is shaped by such factors as whether or not, at its formation, a state's boundaries satisfied its identity and whether the dominant social forces incorporated into the regime were of privileged or plebeian origin. This differentiation tended, especially in the 1960s, to be associated with particular *regime types* since where *monarchies* survived, their ruling coalitions were privileged, pro-Western and status quo; *republics* rose to power in revolt against the status quo and incorporated plebeian dissatisfied social forces, hence were initially revisionist. Once set on a particular tangent, subsequent evolution is 'path dependent': although changes in the composition of the ruling coalition are bound to alter a state's original policy bias and although systemic pressures may deflect it from its course, initial – revisionist v. status quo – foreign policy directions proved rather durable.

Second, Middle East states, new and artificial, started off so fragmented, unstable and permeable to trans-state forces that realism's unitary rational actor confronting an external chess board could not be assumed and is only one possible product of a contingent state formation process. Indeed, the dominant models of Middle East foreign policy analysis assume low state formation: the 'leader-dominant model' views authoritarian leaders as free of institutional constraints, hence able to translate their personal idiosyncrasies into policy (Clapham 1977); alternatively, what might be called the 'domestic vulnerability model' (Calvert 1986; David 1991) assumes that unstable regimes, facing greater threats at home than abroad, adopt belligerent or rhetorical foreign policies to appease domestic nationalist opinion or seek the protection of an external patron against threats from their own populations. In both cases foreign policy rationality is, from a realist perspective, sacrificed. Neither model is adequate, however: even durable authoritarian regimes face domestic constraints and, particularly in the Middle East, even domestically unstable states must attend to external enemies. Indeed, because their strength determines whether the region's states become actors in or victims of their 'rough neighbourhood', both internal and external threats spurred significant efforts to consolidate states and there is evidence that this, at a certain period, endowed decision-making elites with greater autonomy to make rational decisions and greater capacity to implement them. As such, in explaining states' foreign policy behaviour, it is necessary to differentiate their *levels* of state formation. In summary, the direction and the effectiveness of Middle East states' foreign policies are intimately connected with their internal formation.

However, foreign policy behaviour can only be adequately explained as the product of an *interaction* between the state's domestic features and the states system in which it operates. Thus, while state formation – specifically, the social composition of the ruling coalition – determines what a state *wishes* or *tries* to do, it is the system level, as realism observes – i.e. the balance of power – that determines what it *can* effectively do (although of course, a state's power position vis-à-vis external rivals depends in part on its level of state formation at home). Over the long run, a state's systemic power position tends to *reinforce or divert* its foreign policies from the original direction built-in by its formation.

The decision-making process

While state formation biases state responses in certain (status quo or revisionist) directions, it by no means wholly determines them and to understand the foreign policy behaviour of any given state, it is necessary to open the black box of decision-making, hence to benefit from the traditions of *foreign policy analysis*.

MENA foreign policy-makers, in trying to maximise their autonomy and security, must balance between conflicting determinants at three different levels: (1) geopolitical threats and opportunities concentrated in the regional environment; (2) the need to maintain domestic legitimacy (by representing identity and protecting autonomy); and (3) the need to acquire international resources and protection, for which states may well become dependent on the global core. In attempting to balance these pressures, elites face potential contradictions: most notably, responsiveness to domestic demands for autonomy from the West clashes with states' dependency on core powers. Foreign policy decisions are a product of elites' calculations of where the main threats and opportunities are located and where the main resources to counter threats are accessible – at the levels of global great powers, regional rivals or domestic opposition.

However, there are always likely to be several possible rational choices in any given situation and elites' perceptions of rationality are shaped by the identity embodied in a state's *foreign policy role* (Holsti 1970). To the extent elites are socialised into such roles, they give foreign policy some consistency over time. Moreover, where elites disagree over policy, choices will be determined by the power distribution among them and their various constituencies as structured by the state's governing institutions. The interests and differential weight carried in the policy process by such con-stituencies as public opinion, business, the military and the dip-lomatic corps will bias the direction of choices. The rationality of choices also will be shaped by the degree to which the structure of decision-making allows a balance between elite autonomy and cohesion, on the one hand, and openness to input and accountabil-ity, on the other. Finally, the personality, values and perceptions of the top leader are an immediate determinant of choices while the skills and policy instruments at their disposal help determine the outcomes of policy implementation.

Explaining conflict and order

The character of the regional order is the product of its original external imposition and the collective interactions and conflicts of the states that contest or defend it over time. That order, in turn, shapes the character and behaviour of its parts, the states.

Roots of conflict and war

Conflict was literally built into the Middle East regional system, but not simply because of the anarchy of a states system, as neo-realism holds. Rather, it was the external imposition of a very flawed system that generated at least four durable sources of conflict: the struggle against imperialist control, the frustration of identity by the arbitrary imposition of borders, the struggle over Palestine and the struggle over control of the region's oil. The irredentism and revisionism fostered by these conflicts became pervasive in Middle Eastern societies and when the power machineries of different states were captured by social forces or identity groups on opposing sides of these issues, conflict was institutionalised at the inter-state level – taking in extreme cases, the form of war. Conflict took exacerbated forms in the cases of settler states, with their built-in expansionary impulses (Israel); artificial states, with their built-in identity frustration (Iraq); and revolutionary states with their built-in ambition to export their revolutions (Nasserist Egypt, Khomeini's Iran) – all of which have been disproportionately involved in regional wars, especially where, as periodically has happened, they have bid for regional hegemony. Once, as a result, war became a recurring feature of the regional system and states were entangled in the security dilemma, wherein the attempt of each to protect itself only made it a greater threat to its neighbours, a Hobbesian-like system was, indeed, 'constructed'. Such a system (with its insecurity and power imbalances) arguably becomes, itself, a source of war. Moreover, in the decade of the 2000s, the US, in its attempt to defend its faltering hegemony in the region, became a source of war and insecurity. Today, there is not a single state that has not come to feel a military threat from one or more of its neighbours or from the US. While the Middle East's conflicts chiefly originate in societal-level reactions to the flawed architecture of the region, once differential reactions are institutionalised in inter-state rivalry and war becomes pervasive, then, as realism expects, the security dilemma increasingly shapes regional relations, motivates the consolidation of states, and forces state elites to follow 'reason of state'. When, however, state formation is rudimentary or regresses, it is not states' military threats to each other, but sub/trans-state threats to regimes and the use of these threats by states against each other that are the main source of regional conflict.

The problem of order building

Order in states systems may be built on shared identity and norms where an 'international society' is emerging (Bull 1995). Constructivists have charted the fate of the Middle East's first indigenous attempt to create a regional order, Nasser's Pan-Arab 'regime'. Rooted in the Arab world's common identity, this 'regime' enjoined co-operation, enforced by Egyptian hegemony, against shared threats and external domination while limiting inter-Arab conflict to ideological rivalry (Barnett 1998; Sela 1998). Pan-Arabism helped establish a relatively autonomous regional system, but had no mechanism for bridging the Arab–non-Arab gap. It was, indeed, based on a certain 'enmity' for the non-Arab 'Others' in the region. Nor could it reconstruct the regional economic interdependencies snapped by the imposition of state boundaries under imperialism that could have generated networks of shared trans-state regional interests. Moreover, because Egyptian hegemony threatened other states, it induced anti-hegemonic balancing which undermined Pan-Arab solidarity and encouraged nationalist outbidding; this led, inadvertently, to war, the de-construction of Arabism, much increased insecurity, and states' increasing resort to sovereign self-help. The nascent Arab 'international society' started unravelling.

Where a system of states shares little more than mutual security vulnerability, the default mechanism for sustaining order is the balance of power, a built-in equilibrium mechanism, in neo-realist thinking, that tends to preserve the system, even in the absence of shared norms. Indeed, all these tendencies became operative in the Middle East as insecurity-inducing wars became regular occurrences, stimulating the rise of national security states and the replacement of ideology by reason of state in foreign policy formulation. Alliance formation and power balancing blunted the ambitions of hegemonic powers and, while this often failed to keep the peace, it did preserve the states system. The system, thus, shaped its parts for survival in a dangerous environment and they, in seeking to preserve themselves, became agents of system maintenance, much as neo-realism anticipates (Waltz 1979: 74–77). This dynamic pushed the region toward a classic 'Westphalian' system in which power overshadowed shared (Arab) norms as the main determinant of state behaviour and regional order.

In liberal (or 'pluralist') thinking, order results from the taming of the power struggle through complex interdependence, which facilitates construction of a contractual 'international regime' (Keohane and Nye 1977). Interdependence is fostered by trans-state economic ties and interests; is associated with the rise of internationalist coalitions inside states, which see peace as essential to joining world markets (Solingen 1998); and may be reinforced by democratisation which deters war through increased ideological homogeneity, internal constraints on leadership and the trans-state interactions of open societies (Doyle 1995). In these conditions, international regimes are both more readily constructed and adhered to and have, in the West, created a 'zone of peace' (Singer and Wildavsky 1996). In the Middle East, however, realist solutions to the problem of order remain more relevant than elsewhere because, as Yaniv (1987) argues, trans-national norms restraining inter-state conduct are the least institutionalised there. This, in turn, is arguably because the conditions which liberals expect to generate power-taming norms – democratic cultures and economic interdependence – are absent or weak in the region. Economic dependence on the core states and autarky-seeking neo-mercantilist reactions against dependence both stunted the regional economic interdependence which liberalism expects to generate shared interests in the peaceful resolution of conflicts. To be sure, economic liberalisation has increased the influence of internationalist-minded *infitah* bourgeoisies in several states. However, as realism argues, only when threat declines does the pursuit of economic gain displace security at the top of state agendas. This is reflected in the fact that even the region's few democratic states are no more pacific than their authoritarian counterparts; indeed the most pacific states are authoritarian monarchies, both Western dependent and status quo, while the most belligerent state also has the most democratic regime, namely Israel, which has attacked its neighbours, including semi-democratic Lebanon, more often than any other regional state; more important, seemingly, than regime type was Israel's dissatisfaction with its borders, the identity incompatibilities that generated mutual insecurity between it and its Arab neighbours and the power imbalance between them.

In hegemonic stability theory (Hinnebusch 2006), one way to overcome the inability of states under anarchy to co-operate, even where they might all benefit, is for a hegemon to impose an 'international regime' – a set of rules and consultation practices. While the rules are shaped by and benefit the interests of the hegemon, the international regime also delivers sufficient 'public goods' – facilitating trade, keeping the peace – to benefit other states and reconcile them to its hegemony. However, bids by regional states for hegemony were consistently defeated by anti-hegemonic balancing by regional states or by US intervention. US efforts in the 1990–2010 period to impose a 'Pax Americana' in MENA proved elusive. Far from delivering public goods (notably a solution to the Arab–Israeli conflict), the US became a partisan player in the region and

a source of war (e.g. against Iraq) that intensified instability, undermined US legitimacy and precipitated balancing against it, partly
by states but more so by trans-state Islamic movements. With the
outbreak of the Arab Uprising, the remnants of regional order fell
into tatters, with economic dependencies, the Arab League and the
US hegemon all seeming impotent to contain regional dis-order and
the insecurity that drives 'realist' behaviour. As long as the region's
high-profile conflicts continue to generate insecurity, no spread of
the 'zone of peace' will soon re-write the now-dominant realist
rules of Middle East international politics.

Complex realism in action: nesting three theoretical traditions in the case of Gulf international relations

The extra explanatory power gained by combining approaches that
this book advocates can be illustrated by a case study of Gulf international politics: 'complex realism' most immediately explains the
regional power struggle but must be 'nested' – located within – a
constructivist context, which, itself, must be nested in the broader
context established by structuralism.

Structuralism explains the origins of the Gulf's conflict-prone
condition. It was British imperialism's drawing of arbitrary boundaries, its construction of artificial states suffering legitimacy deficits
and the creation of super-rich oil mini-states alongside large dissatisfied regional powers that built insecurity into the structure of
the system. As the same time, imperialism left behind client elites,
with precarious domestic legitimacy, which naturally looked to
Britain and later the US for protection in this environment. As long,
however, as the main powers, Iran, Iraq and Saudi Arabia were
ruled by status quo pro-Western monarchies, British hegemony
was sufficient to mute built-in regional instability (Alnasrawi 1991;
Hinnebusch 2011); but this was not to last.

Constructivist analysis, exemplified in the work of Adib-
Moghaddam (2009), explains the translation of systemic structural insecurity into perceived security threats. As against realists,
constructivists argue that anarchy is what states make of it and in
the Gulf anarchy moved from a 'Lockean' form in which status
quo states, accepting each others' legitimacy, limited their rivalry,
toward a 'Hobbesian' one in which the power struggle was more
unlimited. As built-in instability spawned revolutionary movements

overthrowing the status quo monarchies in Iran and Iraq, nationalist and revolutionary regimes arose, promoting their legitimacy by constructing the 'Other' as enemies. The Iraqi and Iranian regimes constructed radical Arab nationalist and revolutionary Islamic identities that not only denied the legitimacy of the monarchies but also posed the 'Other' as enemy, leading to the Iran–Iraq war.

Realist analysis *assumes* rather than problematises the state rivalries and insecurity which structuralism and constructivism explain; however, it provides a more thorough analysis of the *behavioural consequences* of this insecurity than they do. Gause (2010) provides a complex form of realist analysis of the Gulf regional sub-system. It is tri-polar, with rival powers, Iran, Iraq and Saudi Arabia, trapped in a security dilemma, exacerbated by the fact that seizure of contested territory could bring oil riches. While these powers, as conventional realists would expect, balanced against each others' armies through alliances and arms races, Gause argues that the *greater threat* they faced from each other was *internal* subversion and that the main instruments used in the power struggle were ideational. Regimes manipulated trans-national identities – Arab, Kurdish, Shii, Sunni – to mobilise support across state borders against each other. Further, the Gulf monarchies faced ideological threats from the appeals to their populations of both Ba'thist Arab nationalism and Iran's revolutionary Islam. Fortunately for them, Iraq and Iran debilitated each other in the first Gulf War. Insecurity drove Saudi Arabia and the smaller Gulf states together in the Gulf Co-operation Council and, seeing the threat from Iranian ideological subversion as more immediate than that of Iraqi armies, supported Iraq against Iran. The monarchies also increasingly bandwagoned with the US to balance Iran and Iraq. With the enervation of Iraqi power in two US wars against Saddam Hussein's regime, the US had to increasingly counter Iran by itself, deeply penetrating the region. Saudi Arabia and Iran balanced each other by exploiting the Sunni–Shia divide to construct sectarian animosities that spilled out over the whole region, with Iraq after 2003 a main site of their sectarian proxy war. Through their behaviour, therefore, the states reproduced the insecure system they had inherited from imperialism.

Conflict in the Gulf can, thus, only be adequately understood by a multivariate analysis combining data from the domains of structuralism, constructivism and realism; indeed, to fully understand the behaviour of a particular state at a particular time, one also would need to add in data on its unique state formation and decision-making process.

Organisation of the book

This book will survey the international relations of the Middle East through an examination of three of its central aspects or problems. (1) *The emergence of a unique regional system*, itself a product of core–periphery relations (treated in chapter 2) and the conflict of identity and sovereignty (examined in chapter 3). (2) *The determinants of Middle Eastern states' international behaviour*: chapter 4 examines state formation and chapter 5 the foreign policy process in the Middle East; chapter 6 uses comparative analysis to elucidate how the interaction between the system level and particular state formation paths shapes similarities and differences in states' international behaviour. (3) *Patterns of state behaviour: war and order*: chapter 7 examines regional wars, alliance making and attempts to create regional order and how these have impacted on the structure of the regional system; chapter 8 assesses the impact of the American world hegemon's drive to establish a Pax Americana in the region in the 1990–2010 period; chapter 9 examines the impact of the Arab Uprising on regional politics: how it has both debilitated some key state actors and drawn others into a struggle to affect the outcome. Finally, the conclusion reprises the arguments and evidence to adumbrate the lessons of the MENA case for IR theory.

2

Core and periphery: the international system and the Middle East

The Middle East has been profoundly shaped by the international system, or more precisely, the great powers, which dominate its developed 'core'. The nineteenth-century expansion of capitalism and imperialism into the region reflected a combination of superior Western technological, market and military power which penetrated and eventually reduced the Middle East to an economic periphery of the core and imposed a very flawed Western-style state system on it. Even after independence, Western capitalism continued to penetrate the Middle East: the region's strategic transit routes, oil resources, the creation of Israel, a Western bridgehead, and the relative power vacuum issuing from regional fragmentation – all continued to draw in external powers.

Leon Carl Brown (1984: 3–5, 16–18) has argued that the Middle East became a *penetrated system*, one subject to exceptional influence and intervention from the outside but which could not be fully subordinated or absorbed. Fred Halliday (1988) observes that, from the time of the 'Eastern question', great power competition over the Middle East has been more enduring than in any other Third World region. As Brown stresses, local players have always tried to manipulate such rivalry for their own agendas. But equally, imperialism's fragmentation of the region into rival states often harbouring irredentist grievances against each other, its implantation of client elites and new class structures against local resistance and the creation and military enforcement of the state of Israel have kept the region divided and dependent on external powers. Moreover, when there has been a hegemon on the world scene, it has tended to dominate the region on behalf of a relatively united 'core'. The first of these hegemons, Great

Britain, came near to imposing an imperial order in the Middle East (Brown 1984: 112–139). After the interval of bi-polarity, in which the Arab world attained considerable autonomy, the sole American hegemon attempted to establish a Pax Americana in the region. The result, according to Barry Buzan (1991), is that the Islamic Middle East is the only classical civilisation that has not managed to re-establish itself as a significant world actor since the [formal] retreat of Western empires.

As Sadeq al-Azm has noted, the Arabs and Muslims, viewing themselves as a historically great nation and bearers of God's true religion, find it hard to accept their domination by the West (Talhami 1997). As such, external intervention and its often damaging consequences has stimulated an on-going reaction manifested in nationalist and Islamic movements, in the rise of revisionist states, and in the attempts of regional states to assert autonomy and to restructure dependency relationships. To many Arabs and Muslims, the struggle with imperialism, far from being mere history, has continued into recent times, as imperialism reinvented itself in new forms. The Middle East has become the one world region where anti-imperialist nationalism, obsolete elsewhere, remains alive and where an indigenous ideology, Islam, provides a worldview still resistant to West-centric globalisation. This dynamic explains much of the international politics of the region.

The age of imperialism and the imposition of the Middle East states system

The first major expression of Western expansion into the region was the growing threat to the Ottoman empire, ultimately ending in the transformation of the regional system from a universal multinational empire to a system of states ostensibly meant to represent separate nationalities. While local rulers were by no means passive in this process, they were increasingly likely, in the face of superior Western power, to become victims or clients rather than autonomous actors.

Ottoman Turkey: from supra-national empire to defensive modernisation

The Ottoman system was the antithesis of the European nation-state system. It was a patrimonial empire headed by a Sultan-Caliph whose rule was legitimated by the implementation of the Islamic law, the outward sign of the supra-national Islamic *umma*. The ruling elite's multinational origins reflected the universalistic aspect of the state: Greeks were prominent in the bureaucracy; janissaries (slave soldiers) of Christian origin rose to top military and political office, while in the provinces Turkish landed notables and Arab religious leaders (*ulama*) linked state and society. The quarters of trading cities, peasant villages, tribes and a mosaic of religious minorities were self-contained communities enjoying autonomy under their own leaders. The empire embraced Christians in the Balkans, Turks in Anatolia, and Arabs in the Fertile Crescent, Egypt and North Africa.

Ethnic nationalism was a foreign concept. While semi-independent territorial states sometimes emerged in the provinces when the imperial centre weakened, since the boundaries of such units fluctuated with the power of the time, there was usually little popular identification with them. Rather, people identified themselves as Muslims (or members of a religious minority 'millet') and as inhabitants of some sub-state 'little community'. They were regarded by the rulers as *ra'aya* (flocks) to be both protected and fleeced, not politically active citizens ready to defend a nation. Foreign policy was 'imperial': the Ottomans regarded the West as *Dar al-harb* – the sphere of war – against which the Sultan waged jihad (holy war) in continual expansion. However, once a balance of power was established with the West, 'normal' diplomatic relations between sovereign states emerged (Ahmad 1993: 15–23; Keyder 1987: 7–23; Mansfield 1991: 23–34).

By the 1700s, the Ottoman empire was in decline. Its economy was being enervated by Western economic encirclement and penetration. In capturing the East–West trade routes, the West diverted the economic surplus on which Ottoman civilisation had been built; subsequently, the penetration of Western manufactures undermined traditional industries (Bromley 1994: 46–85; Issawi 1982: 138–155; Owen 1981: 3–9, 92). Western military encroachment was constant, beginning with Russian advances on the northern frontiers. Internal disintegration, which allowed local Muslim warlords to carve out semi-independent principalities – most notably Muhammad Ali in Egypt – was hastened by the rise of nationalist movements among Christian minorities in the Balkans, beginning with the Greek war of independence, spreading thereafter to the Slavic peoples.

The Ottoman response to this threat was 'defensive modernisation'. Reforming sultans and viziers promoted selective change, chiefly military modernisation – enough to reinforce without disrupting the traditional order. But military modernisation required or led to broader changes: bureaucratic centralisation, improved tax collection, conscription and modern education to train modern officials. The result was the rise of a small modern middle class affected by Western ideas of nationalism and democracy. Military officers, as the first to be educated and entrusted with the mission of Ottoman defence against the West, made up the vanguard of the early modernising nationalist groups. Middle-class opinion came to see the survival of the empire as dependent on a constitutional system, which would allow the creation of a citizenry with political rights, and hence a stake in the defence of the empire. At the turn of the nineteenth century, the Young Turk Movement, looking for radical solutions to reverse the empire's decline, led the Revolution of 1909, which forced a constitution and parliament on the Sultan.

Ultimately Ottoman modernisation failed. The costs of modernisation led to foreign debt, giving Western bankers leverage over the Ottoman state. This took an extreme form in semi-independent Egypt where the Muhammad Ali dynasty's debt led to British and French control over Egyptian finances and eventually the British occupation of the country. In the remaining Ottoman domains, debt repayment became a heavy drain on the economic base of the empire. At the political level, the reformers failed to create a new participant community. With the bulk of the masses still encapsulated in 'traditional' communities, they were handicapped by a narrow social base and soon split between 'democrats' and 'authoritarian-nationalists' who believed democracy would only empower traditional leaders. The modernisation of political identity – the construction of an identity that could mobilise the empire's diverse groups against the external threat – proved an insurmountable task. The first attempt – to replace Islam with Ottomanism, a secular loyalty that cut across ethnic and religion diversity – was limited in appeal to the educated Muslim elite; it failed to attract the Christian minorities who were turning to ethnic nationalism while for the Muslim masses, alienated by the taxes and conscription imposed by the modernisers, it was no substitute for identification with the Islamic *umma*. Ultimately, the Young Turk elite turned to linguistic based nationalism – Turkification – but this was incompatible with a multinational state and, fatally, it split the two main – and predominantly Muslim – peoples of the empire, the Arabs and Turks. This allowed the British to engineer the World War I Arab revolt that contributed to the collapse of the empire (Ahmad 1993: 23–45; Bromley 1994: 53–55; Brown 1984: 21–81; Keyder 1987: 25–69; Mansfield 1991: 35–84, 114–135, 149–166).

Formation of the post-Ottoman successor states
The collapse of the empire opened the way for the establishment of a Western-style states system in the region: boundaries were drawn, for the most part by Western imperial powers, but indigenous forces attempted to fill the vacuum as well and their success or failure put Middle Eastern states on very different paths.

In the Turkish-speaking Anatolian heartland of the empire, Mustafa Kemal Ataturk, a military hero of the collapsed empire, revived the Young Turk movement and the remnants of the Ottoman army and bureaucracy and initiated a relatively successful adaptation to the Western nation-state system. Ataturk nationally mobilised the emerging Turkish nation to fight off Western and Greek designs on Anatolia. He then invested the vast nationalist legitimacy won in this war of independence in the establishment of a secular Turkish national republic. Identity was based on a combination of ethnicity/language (Turkish) and territory (residents of Anatolia) (Ahmad 1993: 46–71; Owen 1992: 26–31). In the absence of an indigenous bourgeoisie, Ataturk launched statist economic modernisation that laid the foundations of economic independence. He defended Turkish autonomy in foreign policy by playing off the great powers, Bolshevik Russia, Britain, France and Germany, while avoiding entanglements in their rivalries (Keyder 1987: 71–115). In Iran, Reza Shah Pahlavi attempted to imitate Ataturk as a nationalist moderniser, although Iran was less developed and subject to the rival influences of Russia and Britain which controlled its oil.

In the Arab world, no smooth adaptation to independent statehood was possible. Only in the Arabian Peninsula did Arab independence survive: in the northern mountainous part of Yemen and also in the arid heartland and Hijaz where an indigenous state-builder, Ibn Saud, used Islamic identity to forge a new state. Elsewhere, the Arab world fell victim to creeping conquest and occupation. The piecemeal dismemberment of the Arabic-speaking

Ottoman realms by the British and French, begun decades before World War I, with Algeria (1830s), Egypt (1880s), Tunisia (1881) and Morocco (1912), was crowned by the post-war establishment of 'mandates' in the Fertile Crescent.

In the process of imperial competition and boundary drawing, the Arab world was fragmented into a multitude of small states that were bound to be politically and militarily weak. This was all the more so because these states fitted very imperfectly with indigenous identity. While some such as Egypt and Morocco had traditional roots, others were seen by people as artificial: notably in historic Syria, which was dismembered into four mini-states: Syria, Lebanon, Palestine and Jordan. The natural post-imperial loyalties were still those most familiar from the Ottoman era, that is, to the small group (tribe, sect, village) or to Islam rather than to the newly created territorial states, few of which were regarded as nation-states by their inhabitants. It was in Palestine, however, than imperialism left its most enduring mark. There, Zionist settler colonialism under British imperial auspices sparked a struggle over the land, leading eventually to the uprooting of the native Palestinian population. The collapse of the (Ottoman) state that had embodied the Islamic *umma*, discontent with the new 'artificial' boundaries, and the colonisation of Palestine spurred the emergence of the Arab nationalist movement which preached the doctrine that the Arabs (roughly defined as Arabic speakers) constituted a nation entitled to an independent state or, if several states, that these ought to be grouped in an Arab confederation. Arabism was seen as a solution to the modernisation of identity in the Arab core of the region but it was, of course, at odds with the Western states system being imposed there.

The imposition of the state system was paralleled by the fragmentation and more thorough incorporation of the regional economy into the world capitalist system as part of the 'periphery': the role of the new states in the world division of labour was that of primary product exporters and importers of manufactured goods. Thus, Egypt became a plantation producing cotton for Europe's textile industries; later began the exploitation of local oil reserves by Western oil companies to fuel industrialisation in the West (Amin 1978). At the same time, imperialism completed the formation of an Arab ruling class. In the more settled societies, private ownership of land accorded to urban notables and tribal chiefs consolidated a large landed magnate class while turning formerly independent peasants into tenants; in the more tribal societies, certain tribal leaders were co-opted and given a stake in the newly discovered oil wealth. A 'comprador' class of international traders was enriched as middlemen between the West and the local economy. Limited modernisation – the spread of urbanisation, infrastructure, education and the most rudimentary industrialisation – left traditional society relatively untouched outside the big cities (Amin 1978: 1–50; Ayubi 1995: 86–99; Bromley 1994: 62–85).

State apparatuses were also implanted in the new states. A political elite recruited from the new upper classes wavered between collaboration with imperialist power and leading independence movements against it. The personnel of the military and bureaucratic machinery needed to establish order was recruited from and expanded a state-dependent middle class. The legitimacy of the new ruling elites depended on their ability to win full independence from their imperial patrons, but everywhere they were either perceived as clients of imperialism or were, in one way or another, discredited by nationalist failures: in Egypt it was the failure of the Wafd to get the British out, in Syria, the loss of the Palestine war which discredited the first generation ruling elite. In essence, imperialism both created and then helped de-legitimise the new state establishments almost from their birth (Ayubi 1995: 99–133; Owen 1992: 8–23).

The first reaction against this deformation of the region was the rise of rival ideological movements each offering different solutions to its multi-sided crisis: the national problem, the legitimacy crisis and the challenges of economic backwardness and dependence. Liberal nationalism, which first dominated elite circles (1900–1920s), advocated the adoption of the Western formula – secular democratic states, capitalist economies – as the key to national strength; but, embraced chiefly by the new upper classes, it declined as their failures cost them ideological hegemony. Reacting against liberalism was an Islamic resurgence in the 1930s, beginning with the rise of the Muslim Brothers in Egypt, which insisted that a return to Islamic practices held the key to strength; but the movement failed to achieve hegemony among the rising educated middle class. Simultaneously, communist and socialist movements captured the loyalties of many intellectuals and parts of the small industrial working class. In the first decades after World War II, as regional states won political independence but failed to achieve political strength, the Arab nationalist movement was captured by the new middle class, radicalised, and turned against the ruling dynasties and oligarchies. This Pan-Arabism, combining a more radical and illiberal nationalism with demands for Arab unity and populist social reform, achieved ideological hegemony among both the new middle class and mobilising sections of the masses (Hourani 1970; Khadduri 1970; Sharabi 1970).

The fragility of upper-class-based regimes and the Arab nationalist mobilisation of the middle class against them ushered in two decades of political instability (1945–67) expressed by military coups and the rise of radical parties. The military overthrew monarchies and oligarchies across the region but, except in Nasser's Egypt, could not consolidate stable states until the 1970s. Lacking traditional or democratic legitimacy, these precarious republics sought it through Arab nationalist ideology, pursuing Pan-Arab unionist projects, challenging Western influence and championing the Palestine cause. However, the failure of unity schemes and the 1967 defeat by Israel shattered the ideological hegemony of Arab nationalism, depriving the populist republics of a secure basis of legitimacy. This prepared the way for the revival of an alternative supra-state ideology, political Islam, which, like Arabism, conditioned regime legitimacy on defence of regional autonomy against Western domination.

De-colonisation and the Cold War

De-colonisation and the bi-polar Cold War between the US and the USSR transformed the terms of international penetration in the Middle East. To be sure, given the exceptional concentration of Western interests there – oil, transit routes and the protection of Israel – the Western great powers had no intention of leaving the region in the wake of Arab political independence. The Cold War actually raised the stakes, as the USSR was perceived to challenge the West's regional interests. Indeed, the Cold War began when the Truman Doctrine, responding to Soviet pressures for a share of Iranian oil and access to the Turkish straits, extended Western protection to these states. Thereafter 'containment' of Soviet communism's 'threat' to the region drove US and Western policy. In this contest, oil, Israel and 'containment' were intimately linked: the Soviets had to be denied control of Middle East oil through which they could strangle Western Europe but Western support of Israel inflamed pro-Soviet sentiment in the region and increased the threat to oil.

As direct imperialist control in the region faltered after World War II, nationalist movements and regimes sought to fill the gap and exploit Soviet power as a counter to the West. In these conditions, the Western powers had to find new, subtler ways of protecting their interests than hitherto but, at least initially, their efforts proved largely counterproductive. The unfolding of the relation between the great powers and the region during the Cold War will be explored below through an analysis of the two main regional attempts to restructure a more equal relation with the 'core', namely: (1) the rise and fall of Nasserite Pan-Arabism and (2) the rise and containment of OPEC.

The Arab nationalist decade and the retreat of the West (1956–67)
By the early 1950s, most Arab states were nominally independent. But they remained subordinated to the old imperial powers owing to the continued rule of client elites needing Western protection from domestic threats and the economic dependency of the region on the West. Moreover, the ex-colonial powers retained the ability to intervene militarily if their interests were threatened, facilitated by their possession of bases in and treaties with many regional states. The British and French sought to retain their bases and, as the perceived Soviet threat increased, the US joined them in an effort to establish a new pro-Western regional order: the Tripartite Declaration of May 1950 guaranteed the Arab–Israeli status quo and made arms deliveries conditional on an Arab–Israeli peace, while the project for a regional security organisation – what would become the Baghdad Pact and the Central Treaty Organisation (CENTO) – aimed at harnessing regional states to the containment of the Soviet Union.

The first watershed in the contest between great power dominance and regional autonomy was the rise of Gamal Abdul Nasser who challenged Western control over the area in the name of Arab nationalism. Nasser's starting point was his drive to throw off British domination of Egypt, in particular its continued military presence in the Suez Canal zone. The West needed Egypt if its Middle East security arrangements were to be accepted and Egypt first tried to use this leverage to negotiate a British evacuation. However, influenced by the rise of the non-aligned movement, Nasser came to view the proposed anti-Soviet pact as a neo-imperialist effort to establish indirect Western control. It would entangle the region in the Cold War and possibly make it a battlefield, as it had damagingly been made in the previous two world wars. Egypt was also alienated by the West's refusal to sell Egypt arms needed for security against an activist Israel or provide aid unless it made peace with Israel and joined the proposed pact (Gerges 1994: 21–25). As such, Egypt put forth an alternative to the West's plans, a project for a collective Arab security pact within the framework of the Arab League.

Nuri al-Said of Iraq led the pro-Western forces which believed the West too strong to resist and that Western alignment could be traded for aid and concessions on Israel. Chafing at Egyptian domination of the Arab League, aware of the proximity of the Soviet 'threat', and seeking to capitalise on his close British connection, Nuri proposed that Arab security be realised through links to the West and to the 'northern tier' of Turkey and Iran. Egypt would, however, accept no such alignment as long as British forces remained in the Suez Canal zone and Nasser insisted the Arab states collectively reject pro-Western pacts unless they could be made compatible with de-colonisation and a settlement with Israel involving major Israeli concessions on borders and repatriation of the Palestinian refugees. The Arab League agreed and stipulated that no alliance should be concluded outside the Arab collective security pact. When Iraq joined the Baghdad Pact without winning Western support against Israel, it was perceived to have broken Arab ranks (Barnett 1998: 103–120; Maddy-Weitzman 1993: 147–154).

Ironically, the British-led Western drive to create the Baghdad Pact invited, rather than contained Soviet penetration (Evron 1973: 129–172). Since the Soviets' interest in 'leaping over' the wall of Western 'containment' coincided with that of the emerging Arab nationalist regimes seeking to evade pressures to join the pact, Moscow was willing to provide generous economic aid and arms to substitute for that which the West was making conditional on treaties, bases and an Israeli peace (Telhami 1990: 58–62). The catalyst of an emerging new alignment between Moscow and Arab nationalism was Israel's 1955 raid on Egyptian positions in Gaza; this was perceived in Cairo as punishment for its obstruction of the pact and came at a time when Egypt was being denied Western arms while

French supplies to Israel threatened to upset the balance of power. Egypt, therefore, successfully sought arms from the East – as well as new markets for its cotton for which prices in the West were declining. This opened the door to Soviet penetration of the region. The Czech arms deal was decisive in swinging the region against the Baghdad Pact since it demonstrated the option of obtaining arms while avoiding Western domination. The breaking of the Western arms embargo, seen as a great victory over imperialism in the Arab world, began Nasser's rise as a Pan-Arab hero. It put pro-Western regimes under such enormous pressure from domestic nationalist sentiment orchestrated from Cairo that conservative elites in Jordan and Lebanon did not dare join the Baghdad Pact despite their desire for Western protection and Arab nationalists were brought into the ruling coalition in Syria, which aligned with Nasser (Barnett 1998: 115–120; Cremeans 1963: ch. 6; Gerges 1994: 21–25; Walt 1987: 61–62).

The US Under Secretary of State Dulles, seeing the world in starkly bi-polar terms, viewed small powers as natural clients and Arab non-alignment as creating a power vacuum the Soviets would fill. Although Dulles tried to distance the US from European imperialism and recognised that support for Israel was a major liability in winning over the Arabs, he did not appreciate the extent to which Arab fears of Israel and desire for real independence were more important to rising nationalist opinion than any remote Soviet threat (Brown 1984: 176; Gerges 1994: 50–51). He wavered between an impulse to punish Egypt for its obstruction of Western plans and fear that this would drive the country into Soviet arms. Although he entertained the notion that Nasser might be a credible alternative to communism, who could be enticed away from a Soviet alignment with economic aid, in the end, he opted to punish him for obstructing the pact by withholding aid for the building of the Aswan High Dam. In this way, Dulles unwittingly unleashed a chain of events that unravelled Western control of the region. Nasser's response was to nationalise the Suez Canal and claim the transit dues to finance the Dam. This reinforced the view of Britain and France that Nasser was a mortal threat to their remaining positions in the Arab world. The nationalisation of the Canal unleashed such a tide of Pan-Arab support that even the pro-Western Arab states were forced to applaud it in front of domestic opinion. Nuri warned that Nasser's appeal was putting the stability of the Iraqi pillar of the pro-Western order at risk and France was alarmed by Nasser's encouragement of rebellion in Algeria. A sign of the new post-imperialist climate was British realisation that Western public opinion would not accept a reoccupation of Egypt; but the Hitler analogy that British Prime Minister Eden applied to Nasser convinced him Egyptians would welcome Nasser's removal in a quick strike and allow a friendly leader to be put in power. The British–French–Israeli tripartite invasion failed in part because the superpowers opposed it: the Soviets threatened war while the US, fearing it would endanger the pro-Western states that guarded the oil and turn the Arabs to the Soviets, applied economic pressure on its own allies to withdraw. The outcome transformed the region. Nasser was now the unrivalled hero of Arab nationalism, Egypt and Syria, now recipients of Soviet arms and aid, were de-aligned from the Western camp, and the remaining influence of the old imperial states was destroyed. The colonial era was decisively superseded by a new bi-polar era that allowed greater independence to small states (Barnett 1998: 123–129; Cremeans 1963: ch. 6; Gerges 1994: 47–71; Ionides 1960: ch. 8; Love 1969).

As Britain's influence collapsed while Nasser's burgeoned, Washington perceived a growing threat of collaboration between Nasserism and communism. The US responded with the Eisenhower Doctrine, which offered support to Middle Eastern states supposedly threatened by communism but was, in fact, the doctrinal justification for an American attempt to contain Arab nationalism. The Jordan crisis of 1957, the doctrine's first test, provided one model for confronting Nasser's attempts to roll back Western influence in the Arab world. In that crisis, the elected Arab nationalist Nabulsi government and its military allies initially forced King Hussein into the pro-Egyptian camp and threatened to curb royal power. However, King Hussein rejected the Arab subsidies needed to substitute for the Western ones that kept Jordan aligned with the West and carried out a royal coup against his own government; he benefited from US support and Israel's warning that it would intervene against any Arab threat to Jordan. Thereafter, Jordan's Western subsidy was restored. Jordan's client status was starkly exposed but the episode showed that nationalist opinion could be defeated by a combination of external support and royal dictatorship. Jordan's restoration of its Western alignment was paralleled by growing Saudi alarm at a similar pro-Nasser mobilisation of nationalist opinion in Arabia. This allowed the US to sponsor a new 'King's Alliance' pitting Iraq, Jordan and Saudi Arabia against republican Egypt and Syria (Cremeans 1963: ch. 7; Gerges 1994: 79–90; Ionides 1960: ch. 16; Walt 1987: 67–71).

The Jordanian approach did not, however, prove effective when applied in Syria. Washington, alarmed at the potential of communism there, gave backing to conservative politicians and encouraged Turkish and Iraqi pressures and plots against Syria's nationalist government. However, the USSR warned Turkey, Nasser sent token troops to bolster Syria, and aroused nationalist opinion further marginalised Syria's remaining conservative politicians. Even conservative Arab governments disassociated themselves from US policy and the Saudis intervened with Washington to dampen the crisis. Soviet support for Syria in the crisis raised the prestige of Syrian communists and Syria's Arab nationalists, feeling caught between Western and communist pressures, turned to union with Egypt for protection from both. Hailed as a Pan-Arab achievement across the region, the United Arab Republic (UAR) strengthened Nasser and threatened remaining Western influence. Thus, Western intervention amidst bi-polarity had proved counter-productive, actually strengthening unfriendly nationalist forces and weakening pro-western elites. Abd al-illah, Regent of Iraq, warned that Arab nationalism was so strong it would sweep the pro-Western states away if no counter-measures were taken. Dulles feared the UAR would expand and take in Jordan, Lebanon, Saudi Arabia and Iraq, creating a single Arab state ultimately under Soviet influence; if the supply of oil fell under the control of such a nationalist state, the threat to Western interests would be acute (Gerges 1994: 79–96; Mufti 1996: 82–89, 100–102; Walt 1987: 67–71).

The first test of the UAR's potential as the nucleus of a Pan-Arab concert came in the 1958 Lebanon crisis in which President Chamoun accepted the Eisenhower Doctrine in the hope of embroiling the US on his side in an intra-elite struggle in which his rivals got Egyptian support. Then, in a major turnabout, the 1958 Iraqi revolution, sparked by the Hashemite regime's close identification with the West, brought down the pillar of the pro-Western order in the region. Rather than protecting the Hashemite regime, its adherence to the Baghdad Pact, combined with the Iraqi government's failure to challenge (British owned) Iraq Petroleum Company concessions, inflamed domestic opinion against it and Iraqi army units dispatched to prop up the Jordanian monarchy turned on their own government. The new revolutionary regime's first acts included withdrawal from the Baghdad Pact and a demand for changes in the oil concession (Barnett 1998: 133–136; Gerges 1994: 38–39, 101–135). The US considered military intervention but the new leaders assured the West its oil interests would be secure (Alnasrawi 1991: 74). At Nasser's request, the Soviets conducted manoeuvres in the Caucasus to deter US intervention; Washington could see no credible alternative leadership which could be readily ensconced against an aroused public and the attempt to do so could bring a risky showdown with the Soviet Union (Gerges 1994: 116; Walt 1987: 75). However, convinced that all pro-Western regimes were endangered, the US landed troops in Lebanon while British paratroopers reinforced King Hussein's regime. Bi-polarity had only partially constrained the capacity of the West to project military power: if the Iraqi revolution indicated that restoring client regimes was deemed too risky and costly – at least when vital interests were not threatened – propping up client states was still possible and cost-effective.

The West's declining control over events in the Middle East nevertheless left it temporarily chastened. Dulles observed that you could not stand in front of the Arab nationalist tide, only contain its threat to US interests until such time as events deflated it (Mufti 1996: 180–193). In fact, this soon happened as the Iraqi revolutionary leader, Abd al-Karim Qasim, challenged Nasser's Arab leadership and the two strongest nationalist states turned into bitter rivals. The failure of Iraq to join the UAR dashed Pan-Arab expectations and, together with the stabilisation of pro-Western governments in Jordan and Lebanon, checked the Pan-Arab tide that had hitherto seemed so irresistible (Walt 1987: 75–79). Ironically, this check to Nasser's regional ambitions enhanced his ability to manipulate global bi-polarity. Soviet backing of Qasim precipitated a quarrel with Nasser who saw this as imperialist meddling in his sphere of influence. While Cairo and Moscow needed each other too much to let this proceed very far, it nevertheless revived American interest in Arab nationalism as a possible barrier to communism. Nasser exploited this to acquire US aid, especially food aid vital to Egypt's burgeoning population. Altogether, between 1954 and 1965, Egypt exploited superpower rivalry to extract over $1 billion in economic aid from the two sides. Their competition gave

Egypt a new freedom from overt dependence on or constraints from either superpower (Gerges 1994: 129–130; Walt 1987: 160).

The outcome of this decade of struggle for the Middle East was the emergence of a much more autonomous Arab states system than hitherto. The West failed to mobilise the area against communism because the Arabs, even conservative Arab states, saw the security threat to be less from the East than from Israel, regional rivals or the West itself. Nasser's Egypt managed not only to block the West's attempts to harness the region through an anti-communist alliance but was able to nationalise a strategic Western-controlled transit point, the Suez Canal, and precipitate a wave of Arab nationalism that forced a rollback of Western bases and treaties across the region.

It was bi-polarity that provided the conditions for this success. Without Soviet countervailing power, the Suez invasion would probably not have been aborted and Nasser would have been overthrown. His survival, seen as a successful challenge to Western imperialism in the Arab world, endowed him with legitimacy at home, thereby consolidating the Arab world's strongest state at a time when the other Arab regimes remained weak and dependent. This enabled Nasser to use Arab nationalism to mobilise the Arab masses against their own rulers, making it very risky for the West's regional allies to overtly stand against him or for the West to again intervene militarily against Egypt. The West and its allies were, thus, forced to compete with Nasser on the plane of ideological struggle where they were no match for him; indeed, overt identification with the West became a grave political liability for the West's clients. Nasser's unique trans-state appeal forced the relative unification of the formerly fragmented Arab world against external influence. Then, in a sort of virtuous circle, his Pan-Arab stature, making Egypt the pivotal Arab state, boosted Cairo's ability to exploit superpower rivalries to win aid and influence in world capitals (Gerges 1994: 35–40). This combination of regional unity and core rivalry maximised the Arab world's autonomy and stature in the international system.

Bi-polarity similarly provided the shelter in which a new crop of Arab nationalist regimes subsequently arose in Iraq, Syria, Yemen and later Algeria, Sudan and Libya. The Cold War enabled these states to extract the resources from the superpowers, especially the USSR, needed to entrench themselves politically and to dilute their economic dependency on the West. The end result was a pattern of superpower alliances with ideologically compatible Middle East regimes that replicated Cold War divisions. The region was polarised into pro-Western states (Israel, Turkey, Iran, conservative Arab states) and pro-Soviet ones (radical Arab nationalist states). Given Cold War competition, even in unequal patron–client relations between a global superpower and a regional power, the tail frequently wagged the dog, the smaller state exercising influence over the larger which needed it as part of global rivalries, especially if the client could threaten to switch sides (Evron 1973: 129–139, 159–161, 173–191; Gerges 1994: 21–40, 245–151; Walt 1987: 162–163, 171).

In this new era, aid, trade and diplomacy eclipsed military intervention as the means by which competing powers tried to maintain their influence in the region. Although intervention did not entirely cease – there were 11 cases from 1956 to 1973 – the checks each of the two superpowers placed on the freedom of action of the other made intervention the instrument of last resort. Given the importance of arms for security in a high-conflict region, arms transfers increasingly became the superpowers' favoured substitute instrument of influence. The West initially tried to condition delivery of arms on Arab acceptance of a Western alliance and Israel. Once the Soviets broke the Western arms monopoly, the relation between arms suppliers and recipients became less asymmetric. Thereafter, the Soviet Union's willingness to provide arms to client states became its single most important instrument of influence. However, although Egypt and Syria were relatively dependent on the USSR for arms and support against Israel, this translated into no durable Soviet domestic influence: Sadat's 1972 expulsion of the Soviet advisors showed how much Egypt merely sought to use the USSR for its own agenda (Rubinstein 1977). Much the same pattern characterised American deliveries to Israel.

The West, for its part, increasingly relied on alliances with states of the non-Arab periphery to counter Arab radicalism in the core of the region. In the 1950s Turkey played this role, pressurising radical Syria, while in the 1970s, the Shah of Iran acted as Western gendarme in the Gulf, notably intervening in Oman to suppress a Marxist rebellion. But it was Israel that proved to be the most durable, albeit ambiguous, surrogate for Western power in the region. The exceptional network of support – virtually strategic depth –

that Israel enjoyed for its assertive regional role repeatedly inflamed anti-Western sentiment in the region. Nevertheless, Israel came to be regarded by the US as a 'strategic asset'. US policy was to keep Israel militarily superior to any combination of Arab states and, in return, Israeli power was used to deter challenges to Western interests, such as the Arab nationalist threats to Jordan. Israel came to serve American interests in more subtle ways, too: after its 1967 conquest of Arab lands, the inability of the Arab states to recover their territories with Soviet arms made them increasingly dependent on US diplomacy to do so; this gave the US its opening, through Sadat's Egypt, to the Arab heartland, enabling it, after a long period of declining influence, to restore much of its contested power in the region.

The 1967 war and the revival of Western influence

The 1967 Arab–Israel war was the initial precipitant of a chain of events that brought a revival of Western power in the Middle East. The war had its own regional causes but was facilitated by American reaction to Nasser's growing success. Nasser's ability to use bi-polarity to shield his ambitions declined as he pushed his challenge to Western interests further without securing sufficient Soviet protection. First, Egypt had long propagated the principle that Arab oil was for all the Arabs, not the patrimony of the client sheikhs and Western oil companies (Cremeans 1963: ch. 8); the 1963 Egyptian intervention in Yemen to support the republican revolution and Egypt's support for radical nationalism in British Aden and the Gulf region seemingly gave practical teeth to this doctrine. It was seen as a threat to Saudi Arabia and to Western control of Gulf oil and ended a brief period of amicable Egyptian–US relations in the early 1960s. In the period when Arabism seemed irreversible and communism the greater threat, Washington had been willing to experiment with a tilt toward Arab nationalists but ultimately, as the aims of Arab nationalism proved incompatible with Western interests, particularly control of oil, the US turned against it. President Johnson cut off US food aid and Nasser, perceiving an imperialist counter-offensive, responded by stirring up anti-US radicalism in the Middle East and Africa and seeking a closer Soviet alignment (Evron 1973: 58). This prepared the way for Washington's complicity in Israel's 1967 strike at Egypt (see chapter 7). Once the scale of the Israeli victory became apparent, the US saw it as an opportunity to destroy or gravely weaken Nasser, strengthen conservative states, force Arab acceptance of Israel and resurrect US influence in the region. Israel's emergence from the war as a regional great power suggested a strategic alliance with it might be a viable basis on which to rest American Middle East policy (Gerges 1994: 230–231; Parker 1993: 3–35).

As Israel's strategic value in US eyes soared, Washington deferred to Israeli insistence on making withdrawal from the territories it occupied in the war conditional on Arab acceptance of Israel and of territorial adjustments in its favour; as such, the great powers did not, as in 1956, impose an Israeli withdrawal from conquered Arab territories. While Israel was now in a much stronger position to resist any such superpower pressures, the 'loosening' of the bi-polar system and muting of superpower competition in the Third World had also made the US less sensitive about offending the Arabs (Evron 1973:175–176). Indeed, the US began to supply Israel with increasingly sophisticated weapons that would allow it to keep control of the territories (Walt 1987: 105–108). As the US overtly took sides with Israel, the Arab nationalist states were pushed into greater dependency on Moscow. The Arabs' need for the Soviets allowed Moscow to acquire a strong regional presence by the early 1970s, including advisors, bases, treaties and naval power projection. Thus, the 1967 war opened the door to an increased military dependency of regional states and growing superpower penetration.

After 1967, Nasser was keen to manipulate bi-polarity to extricate himself from the humiliation of Israeli occupation of the Sinai. As Heikal wrote, with the regional balance tilted so much toward the Israelis, Egypt had to raise the conflict to the international level where the (Soviet–American) power balance was more equal by more deeply committing the Soviets on Egypt's side. Nasser hoped to derive leverage from Moscow's stake in the region and the fact of, as Heikal (1978a: 30) put it, the Soviets 'obsession with America'. But, although the Soviets rearmed Egypt, they procrastinated in supplying the offensive weapons needed to match Israel's and enable the military recovery of the occupied territories and instead urged a political settlement. They had little confidence in Arab fighting capabilities and feared Egypt would entrap them in the conflict and in a possible superpower showdown; moreover, the Soviets did not want to jeopardise their detente relationship with the United States (Riad 1982: 95–97, 144–146). The Arabs' greater dependency on the Soviets and the latter's investment in detente seemed to dilute Arab leverage over Moscow. Egypt showed, however, that it could upset the seeming satisfaction of the superpowers with the post-1967 status quo.

The first episode in this effort, Nasser's 1969 War of Attrition against Israeli forces occupying Egypt's Sinai peninsula, aimed to force the superpowers to intervene. Nasser hoped the USSR could be brought to provide greater support by the tacit threat that Egypt would otherwise be defeated in the confrontation with Israel, thus destroying the Soviet's credibility as an ally. He also sought to demonstrate to the Americans the dangers of increased Soviet penetration and even superpower confrontation that could result from allowing the Sinai occupation crisis to fester. When Israel responded to Egyptian artillery attacks on its forces on the east bank of the Suez Canal by bombing Egyptian cities, Nasser flew to Moscow, threatening resignation if the Soviets did not provide the air defence and support troops needed to stop the Israeli escalation. In fact, the Soviets provided SAM-3s and Soviet pilots and support troops; neither Soviet troops nor such sophisticated weapons had ever before been deployed outside the Soviet bloc. Israel, realising the magnitude of the Soviet involvement, stopped the deep penetration bombing. To defuse the situation, the US, in the Rogers Plan, proposed a ceasefire and a broader settlement of the Arab–Israeli conflict. Nasser's internationalisation of the conflict did not, however, break the occupation stalemate (Evron 1973: 96–101, 185–86; Riad 1982: 103–107; Smith 1996: 217–220; Walt 1987: 108–110).

Meanwhile, indeed, the US relationship with Israel grew ever closer despite certain conflicts of interest between them. To get even small Israeli concessions, such as acceptance of the Rogers Plan, the US had to pledge ever more support to Israel (Walt 1987: 108–110). Israel's arms dependency gave the US little leverage over it owing to the Israelis' penetration of US domestic politics and a tacit threat to escalate the conflict or even to 'go nuclear' if the US abandoned them (Evron 1973: 178–180). President Nixon and his Secretary of State, Henry Kissinger, developed a strategy that would make a virtue of Washington's weak leverage over Israel: by keeping Israel too strong to be defeated with Soviet arms, they aimed to force the Arabs to accept a settlement close to Israel's terms; at the same time, they positioned the US as the only power which could theoretically influence Israel to accept a settlement, thereby seeking to marginalise the Soviets from Middle East diplomacy (Brown 1984: 183; Walt 1987: 119). While the increased Soviet military presence in the region was crucial to the Arabs' attempt to balance Israel's post-1967 regional supremacy, the stalemate gravely undermined Moscow's prestige as a reliable ally and unleashed in Egypt the anti-Soviet sentiment that Anwar al-Sadat would exploit to switch superpower patrons after Nasser's death.

Sadat, on assuming power, came to believe that the Soviets preferred the status quo, which kept Egypt dependent, and that detente had reduced their willingness to make commitments comparable to the Americans' support of Israel. He tried to get a closer Soviet commitment through a Treaty of Friendship but his purge of Ali Sabri and other Egyptian allies of the Soviets was seen in Moscow as a bid for US support and reduced their incentive to assist him. Sadat's 1972 expelling of Soviet advisors was meant as a signal to Kissinger and to get the superpowers competing again for Egypt. This failed to shift Washington, which was satisfied with the pro-Israeli status quo, but it did get the increased Soviet arms deliveries that made possible the crossing of the canal in the 1973 war. That war, in turn, forced the US to adjust its policy to take account of Egyptian interests (Riad 1982: 211–243; Sela 1998: 136–138; Smith 1996: 226–228).

The 1973 war led to a major alteration of superpower relations with the region as the US successfully used the outcome to restore the influence the West had lost with the rise of Arab nationalism. On the face of it, the war and the associated oil embargo threatened US interests. It vastly increased Arab financial power and generated an unprecedented Arab solidarity behind a Cairo–Damascus–Riyadh axis that seemed well-positioned to extract major changes in America's pro-Israeli policy. But Kissinger's intervention in the conflict masterfully neutralised this threat. Kissinger's immediate objectives were to get the oil embargo lifted and to end the possibility of a renewed war that could intensify the threat to American interests. Believing a comprehensive settlement to be impractical, he aimed to use partial settlements to achieve these aims. In the longer term, he aimed to marginalise the Soviet Union in the region by detaching Egypt from its Soviet alliance.

Kissinger was not displeased that the 1973 war had produced a more even Egyptian–Israeli power balance more conducive to compromise on both sides and he sought to drag Israel into the partial concessions, principally to Egypt, that would relieve pressure on it for a comprehensive settlement. This would also start the process of detaching Egypt from its Soviet alliance and from the Arab–Israeli power balance; without Egypt the Arabs could not wage war and an Egypt lacking Soviet support and dependent on the US was no threat to Israel and could become a powerful force for regional de-radicalisation. The return of the occupied Sinai to Egypt as a part of this process would demonstrate to the Arabs that the US alone could get Israel to make territorial compromises but only if they in return were prepared to abandon radical Arab nationalism and their Soviet alignments. Sadat's strategy coincided with Kissinger's since he chose to use the leverage the war gave him to make his own gains at the expense of his Arab partners. Believing that the Soviets could provide neither the economic nor the diplomatic help Egypt needed and that the US 'had the cards' to force Israel to make concessions, Sadat started a dramatic shift in Egypt's global alignments toward Washington. His strategy was to compete with Israel for US favour by showing Egypt to be a more effective US surrogate in the Middle East. His first service to Washington was getting Saudi Arabia to lift the oil embargo after the first disengagement in the Sinai. Once Sadat became convinced that his realignment with the US was not enough to overcome the power of the Zionist lobby in Washington and get enough pressure on Israel to fully evacuate the Sinai, he sought to appease Israel and its American supporters through his dramatic trip to Jerusalem and, finally, by reaching a separate peace with Israel at the expense of Syria and the Palestinians. After the fall of the Shah, he made a bid to replace Iran as US regional surrogate, claiming that the USSR had become the main threat to the region. In return for Sadat's service in ending the Arab threat to Israel and marginalising the Soviet Union from regional diplomacy, the US mediated the return of the Sinai and provided Egypt with a substantial yearly subsidy (Brown 1984: 184–190; Sela 1998: 158–170; Sheehan 1976; Smith 1996: 230–233; Telhami 1990: 62–71; Walt 1987: 177–178).

Egypt's saga provides key evidence on the dynamics of international–regional power relations in an age of bi-polarity. Despite Egypt's dependence on external power, its strategic importance endowed it with considerable capacity to manipulate and extract benefits from the superpowers. Nasser, even when highly

dependent on Soviet protection, took his own decisions: the War
of Attrition, accepting the Rogers Plan; when Sadat ordered Soviet
advisors out of Egypt, they not only meekly departed but Moscow
later provided him with the extra weapons needed to cross the
Suez Canal (Rubinstein 1977: 334). Sadat's crossing of the canal
showed how a local power could upset a damaging status quo
that suited the superpowers, forcing Washington to intervene and
satisfy Egypt's non-negotiable demands (Brown 1984: 242). Once
Sadat had the US engaged, he did whatever was necessary to keep
the US on Egypt's side. There can be few more classic examples of
bandwagoning than Sadat's policy: if you cannot effectively balance a threatening power, you appease it (Walt 1987: 177–178).
Sadat's acceptance of an American-sponsored separate peace with
Israel successfully exploited superpower rivalry to extract tangible
gains or at least to cut Egypt's losses in the regional power struggle.
The cost, however, was that, by abdicating Egypt's Arab leadership
and fragmenting the Arab world, and by marginalising the Soviet
Union's competitive position in the region, Sadat did major damage
to the very conditions which allow regional actors such leverage
with core powers, namely, a conjunction of unity in the 'periphery'
and rivalry at the 'core'. It would be Sadat's successors and peers,
however, who would pay the price.

The political economy of dependency: is oil different?

According to dependency theory and other versions of Marxist
structuralism, underlying great power political penetration of the
Middle East is a network of economic dependency that keeps the
region underdeveloped and subordinate to the advanced capitalist
'core'. The Middle East economies do exhibit many of the classic
features of dependency. They are mainly primary product producers, often dependent on a single export such as cotton or oil. To the
significant extent that they fail to process their raw materials into
finished high-value products, their human capital remains underdeveloped and their economies dependent on the 'core' countries for
technology and manufactured goods. Dependency links the interests of their economically dominant classes – whether large agricultural exporters or partners of trans-national corporations – to those
in the core, while detaching them from the stake local populations
have in a 'national' form of development. Dependency creates a

'feudal' pattern of trade and investment linking individual states to the core economies rather than to each other, thereby constraining regional economic investment and trade.

According to dependency theory, economic dependence not only keeps states underdeveloped, it also keeps them politically weak. Dependent states cannot, except at considerable cost and risk, pursue autonomous foreign policies if these displease their patrons. The feudal pattern of economic dependency destroys the economic base of regional political solidarity that would be needed to restructure the power balance with the core. The overlap of the interests of dominant classes with the core powerfully works to align the foreign policies of dependent states with those of the Western core, despite widespread resentment of the West among local populations. To be sure, in states such as Nasser's Egypt or Islamic Iran, where plebeian elites came to power from outside the economically dominant classes, regimes challenged Western interests. Moreover, convinced that they could not sustain nationalist foreign policies without economic independence, they also undertook state-led industrialisation aimed at reducing dependence on primary product exports, and tried to diversify dependency among a number of rival outside economic powers. Thus, Egypt was able to pursue a nationalist foreign policy that advanced the autonomy of the whole Arab world, but only as long as it had a strong domestic economic base, supported by accumulated World War II surpluses and Soviet aid. However, once Egypt became dependent on American aid and fell into increasing Western debt, its foreign policy did a somersault: from being the main state resisting Western influence, it became under Sadat, the bridge by which Western influence came back into the region, seemingly vindicating dependency theory.

Arguably, however, OPEC, a striking case of sustained regional co-operation against the core by once seemingly dependent states, might be said to refute dependency theory. OPEC's ability to engineer massive increases in oil prices, the Arab producers' ability to use oil as a political weapon without suffering military intervention and the accumulation of seemingly enormous 'financial power' in the hands of the Gulf Co-operation Council (GCC) states seemed to show that the age of imperialism was dead and that dependency had been superseded by interdependence between the core and the oil-producing Middle East. Indeed, the period of OPEC success was arguably a window of opportunity situated between

the decline of Arab nationalism and the subsequent era of restored
Western hegemony when the dependency relationship could have
been radically restructured. Why this did not happen takes some
explanation.

From 'seven sisters' to OPEC

The main legacy of colonialism and the underlying problem of
the Middle East, according to Dilip Hiro, is that 'six families put
in place by British imperialism and propped up by the West control 34% of the world's oil reserves' (Frankel 1991; Hiro 1991b).
Through them two Western powers, the US and the UK, controlled
the oil of the Middle East and the changing balance in their relative
control reflected the transition in global hegemony between them:
thus before World War II, the US controlled 15% of Middle East
oil and Britain 70%; by the early 1950s, the US controlled 60% and
Britain 30% (Tibi 1998: 93). Under this order, the function of the
Middle East was to provide cheap fuel for the core's industrialisation and military power: oil was the key to British naval supremacy
and to Axis defeat in World War II while post-war Western Europe
was re-built on cheap Middle Eastern oil. Oil is the world's biggest
business and is central to other industries such as chemicals, plas-
tics and automobiles; those who control it are the richest of global
capitalists (Yergin 1991: 21–26), and nowhere are these more concentrated than in the United States.

The centrality of oil to the Middle East has, therefore, meant
its dependence on the most powerful of Western Transnational
Corporations (TNCs). For most of the twentieth century, the
trans-national producer cartel – the 'seven-sisters' oligopoly of
Anglo-American oil companies – controlled almost all the world's
oil production. The companies obtained control of Middle East oil
on extremely favourable terms (Spero 1990: 261–262): their power
came from their monopoly of production technology and mar-
keting infrastructure, and from long-duration concessions, usually
extracted under political pressure, which fixed low prices and prevented competitors from entering production. In addition, their collusion and their joint ownership of the operating companies in the
individual countries – ARAMCO was controlled by Texaco, Socol,
Exxon and Mobil – meant the divided Middle East states separately
confronted a unified cartel. The ability of the companies to increase
output in one country and decrease it in another gave them great

leverage over governments dependent on them for revenues and the stability of their economies. Thus, they were able to unilaterally set output and prices. For example, their ability to drive down the price of Arabian light from $2.18/barrel in 1948 to $1.80 in 1960 while increasing the price in the US from $2.68 to $3.28 allowed them to reap enormous profits (Alnasrawi 1991: 72–76).

The backing given the oil companies by their home governments made the system seem unassailable. This was dramatically demonstrated in the failure of the first challenge to it, Prime Minister Mohammed Mossadeq's nationalisation of Iranian oil: the companies' boycott of Iranian oil – replaced by their increased pumping in the Arab Gulf – caused an Iranian economic crisis that prepared the way for the CIA-engineered overthrow of his nationalist government (Cottam 1979). Despite this, the struggle for control of oil was on-going and while it ensured continual Western interference in the area, Western control was never wholly secure. The Suez invasion was in good part over control of the jugular artery of oil supply from the Gulf to Europe (Kubursi and Mansur 1993: 8). The West was poised to risk war over Iraq after the 1958 coup had the Iraqis not pledged to 'respect Western oil interests' (Sifry 1991: 27–33). The 1967 Arab–Israeli war generated immense popular sentiment for the nationalisation of oil; indeed, a brief oil embargo was rapidly abandoned because excess US capacity made it immune to such pressures; but a precedent had been set (Alnasrawi 1991: 76–77). The vulnerability of oil supply routes was demonstrated by the closing of the Suez Canal after the war and by the simultaneous sabotage of the Saudi pipeline across Syria to which the radical Ba'thist government refused to permit repairs (Dorraj 1993: 20).

As Middle East states acquired marginally greater autonomy owing to de-colonisation and the bi-polarity that gave them some protection from overt Western intervention, they were able to adjust the extremely unfavourable terms of agreements reached under imperial rule. Thus, in the 1950s concession agreements were amended, splitting profits 50–50; this tripled state revenues, but since oil prices were stable and the prices of manufactured imports steadily rose, the producers' terms of trade deteriorated over time. In 1959–60, price reductions by the companies, amidst an oil glut, sparked the founding of OPEC in an effort to check the companies' right to unilaterally set prices, but it had little immediate impact. In 1961, when Iraq expropriated non-utilised areas of the

Iraq Petroleum Company's concessions, the company froze Iraq's export of crude oil (Alnasrawi 1991: 72–73; Korany and Akbik 1986: 147; Spero 1990: 264–265).

By the beginning of the 1970s, increased demand, especially as the US became an oil importer, unmatched by expansion in capacity, put upward pressure on prices, creating favourable conditions for producers. But it took the rise of a new radical nationalist regime, catapulted to power by the 1967 war, with the political will to take advantage of these conditions, which precipitated a shift in the balance of power toward the producing states. The new Libyan revolutionary regime negotiated a much more favourable deal on prices and revenues by inviting in smaller independent oil firms, thereby bypassing the cartel, while unilaterally imposing production cuts; in 1972 Ba'thist Iraq followed by nationalising the IPC. This encouraged greater political will in the OPEC states and prompted the oil companies to allow them to buy shares in local subsidiaries; in 1972 Saudi Arabia started buying into ARAMCO and soon achieved majority control (Vassiliev 1998: 390). Middle East states were finally acquiring stakes in their own natural resources; their newly found co-operation was starting to balance the power of the Western companies and rising demand for oil was shifting market conditions in their favour (Spero 1990: 265–267; Terzian 1985).

From oil embargo to oil bust

It was the Arab political solidarity and nationalist arousal unleashed by the October 1973 war, however, that pushed an unlikely actor, Saudi Arabia, to take the next steps, using cartel power to raise prices and putting oil in the service of foreign policy. The US failure to temper its support for Israel despite Egyptian peace initiatives threatened Saudi Arabia as Arab opinion was radicalised after 1967. After the October war broke out and the US sent massive military aid to Israel, ignoring Saudi pleas for a more even-handed approach, the Saudis had to make a difficult choice: while they were loath to jeopardise their strategic relation with the US, they could not afford, in the climate of euphoria from initial Arab war successes, to be stigmatised as a reactionary regime less concerned with the Arab cause than the defence of American interests (Alnasrawi 1991: 83–93).

In this climate, Arab OPEC states unilaterally raised the price of oil by 70% from $3 to $5/barrel while cutting output and embargoing shipments to the US; the resulting oil shortage allowed them to raise the price of a barrel of oil to $11.65 in December 1973. This was a turning point in which price and supply decisions were transferred from the companies to the OPEC producing countries. In the 1970s, OPEC would attain a dominant share of world oil production (50–65%), exports (90%) and oil reserves (65–75%). At first it seemed that there had been a restructuring of power between Third World states and Western multinationals that could be a precedent for a new deal between core and periphery (Alnasrawi 1991: 76–84, 100, 186–187; Korany and Akbik 1986, 138–165; Spero 1990: 267–269, 279). Simultaneously, the Arabs' ability to challenge Israel militarily was a psychological shock to it and its backers which, combined with the oil embargo, potentially lent the Arab states the leverage to get a land-for-peace settlement with Israel. The oil embargo was, the Arab oil states announced, to remain in place until Israel's US backer forced it to withdrew from the occupied territories and satisfy Palestinian rights.

In the event, however, the oil weapon proved less than decisive in changing Washington's pro-Israeli policy. The US, a large oil producer itself, was not directly threatened or damaged enough to force it into such an abrupt policy turnabout; only about 15% of its energy consumption was from Arab imports at the time of the embargo (Spero 1990: 265). To be sure, the oil price hikes and the oil weapon initially appeared to be a serious indirect threat to the US since they weakened Western Europe in the face of the perceived Soviet threat and challenged American control of Middle East oil. In reality, US policy-makers distinguished between the increased price of oil, which was a matter of bargaining and oil's unacceptable political use. In fact, the embargo was quickly lifted. After the first disengagement on the Egyptian front, Sadat insisted that US policy had changed and that Washington should be rewarded; this was enough to relieve popular pressure on the producer states to keep the embargo in place, given that there had still been no movement on the Syrian front and Palestinian rights were not even on the agenda (Alnasrawi 1991: 93–98). The Nixon administration may have actually welcomed the price rises in the hope it could manage the new situation to encourage oil exploration outside the Middle East, undermine European and Japanese competition, precipitate a re-cycling of petrodollars through US banks, thereby restoring declining American control of world financial resources, and stimulate American exports to the oil producers. Western consumers and workers certainly did suffer from the oil price increases but the most powerful US corporations – the oil companies, banks and arms exporters – made huge profits from them or from the re-cycling of petrodollars. And US oil producers were the largest funders of the Republican Party and the Nixon, Reagan and two Bush campaigns (Kubursi and Mansur 1993: 10–13; Spiro 1999). Meanwhile, blame for the resulting economic dislocation could be put on OPEC.

Many Arabs continued to expect that the West's need for oil, the tacit threat of a new embargo, and the Saudis' special relationship with the US could still deliver the US pressure on Israel needed to achieve a peace settlement. In the end, however, the Saudis were neutralised by their American relationship. Even while the oil embargo was in place, the Saudis opted to deepen their special relationship with the US and a deal was formalised in the mid-1970s when it became less politically dangerous. Saudi Arabia would use its role as 'swing producer' to moderate oil prices, deploy the new influence its immense wealth gave it to de-radicalise Arab politics, and re-cycle its petrodollars through US financial institutions. The US, in return, would provide military protection and the technology to develop and diversify the Saudi economy; certainly the Saudis were led to expect the US would seriously attempt to resolve the Arab–Israeli conflict (Alnasrawi 1991: 109–113, 120–121, 127; Kubursi and Mansur 1993: 13; Spero 1990: 270). The American strategy was, in Bromley's (1994: 112) words, to integrate the Gulf oil states as 'relays in a metropolitan circle of capital' under which they would invest their surpluses in the core and thereby acquire a stake in its economic stability. Washington's strategy proved remarkably successful.

First, the oil boom accelerated the Western penetration of Saudi Arabia and the Gulf region, generating powerful domestic interests with a stake in relations with the West. Thus, the ruling families in the oil monarchies, with their major assets held abroad, arguably became junior partners of a 'global bourgeoisie'. Eighty-four per cent of Arab oil earnings was channelled into Western banks and investments. Saudi Arabia and Kuwait between them held $210 billion outside the region in the late 1970s. Saudi Arabia became the largest investor in US banks, treasury bonds and real estate, with $133 billion invested, yielding an income of $10 billion/year. Investment by the Arab Gulf states in the US alone may have eventually reached $1 trillion (Aarts 1994: 3; Vassiliev 1998: 398–404). Such investment in the core, in giving the Gulf elites a direct, often personal, stake in the health of the Western economy, created an incentive to moderate oil prices, thus limiting the revenues potentially usable to develop the Arab world. Moreover, the sharp increase in governmental spending on foreign imports and contracts fostered classes of middlemen – bankers, lawyers, subcontractors for oil companies, import-exporters, agents for Western firms – who made up rent-seeking bourgeoisies enriching themselves on relations with the West (Alnasrawi 1991: 21; Paul 1986: 18–22). At the same time, oil also allowed local populations to be politically de-mobilised: thus, in Saudi Arabia the formerly radical middle-class nationalist movement and the militant trade unions were peripheralised by the patronage and welfare spending oil revenues made possible (Vassiliev 1998: 474–482).

Second, oil much increased the security dependency of the Gulf oil producers on the West. The combination of super-riches, weakness and contested nationalist credentials, especially after the Iranian revolution, turned these states to the West for protection in a more overt and intensified way than hitherto. As part of the re-cycling deal, the Arab oil producers spent a large part of their surpluses – 32% of their oil revenues from 1974 to 1998 – on purchases of expensive and sophisticated Western arms. While in 1974 Saudi arms purchases absorbed only 7.5% of the value of its oil exports, in 1985 they absorbed 88%; Saudi Arabia alone accounted for 36% of total American foreign arms sales in 1977–82 (Alnasrawi 1991: 35, 114; Gause 1997; Vassiliev 1998: 398–399). These purchases deepened Saudi dependency on the US for spare parts, upgrading and contractors to run sophisticated equipment. They were accompanied by a massive and intimate American penetration of the Saudi military: sophisticated weapons systems required extensive Saudi-American military planning and a large (30–100,000-man) US training mission provided one US military advisor for every six Saudi soldiers. American contractors became involved in a vast array of imported development projects from hospitals to water supplies, petrochemical complexes to military bases (Cordesman 1984: 202, 205, 243, 349, 371, 380; Vassiliev 1998: 441–444).

Expensive Western arms purchases were a Saudi way of buying protection: they made Saudi control of oil acceptable in the West and deepened the West's stake in Saudi security. Thus, despite having to conduct a fierce lobbying struggle against Zionist influence in the US Congress to get delivery of F-15s, the Saudis preferred them over the readily obtainable French equivalent because of the decade of US political commitment to Saudi Arabia that the deal would institutionalise (Cordesman 1984: 206; Dawisha 1979: 28). The Saudis did not actually acquire autonomous control of many of the new weapons systems. To get sophisticated aircraft they had to agree to restrictions imposed to appease Israel; the AWACS intelligence gathering aircraft were operated by Americans and arguably gave the US a Saudi-financed flying base in the region which could be used for intervention against Middle East states (Alnasrawi 1991: 111–117). Western arms suppliers were candid that these arms deliveries contributed little to the kingdom's defence (Vitalis 1997); indeed, in 1990 Saudi Arabia still could not, apparently, hope to deter an Iraqi invasion and was forced to finance direct US intervention. After the second Gulf war, Saudi Arabia and the Gulf states signed new agreements expanding bases for American forces used against Iraq. With the return of foreign bases and protectorates, the pre-nationalist era appeared to have been restored in the region.

Arguably, Saudi oil policy was a key feature of this new relationship. This policy reflected the al-Saud's view of their responsibility to reconcile the interests of oil producers and consumers, ensure the stability of oil markets and even protect the global economy against the threats of inflation and recession from high energy prices. The al-Saud came to see Western and Saudi interests as nearly indistinguishable: oil price rises that damaged the Western economy would damage Saudi investments, reduce demand for oil and stimulate oil exploration in non-OPEC countries. The Saudis 'swing position', that is, their unique ability, based on their huge production capacity, large financial reserves and small population, to manipulate prices by contracting or expanding production, gave them powerful leverage to impose their will on other OPEC members. They repeatedly used this to ensure stable oil supplies at 'reasonable prices' for the West. This meant confronting the OPEC price hawks who, with large populations and ambitious development plans, wanted to raise prices to maintain their real purchasing power as inflation drove up the price of imports (Alnasrawi 1991: 129; Spero 1990: 270). Thus, in 1975, the Saudis blocked the desire of most OPEC members to increase oil prices to maintain income amidst inflation and the declining value of the dollar. While the real value of OPEC income declined perhaps 30%, Saudi threats of or actual over-production froze oil prices in the second half of the 1970s (Dawisha 1979: 28–30). A second oil shock was set off in 1978–80 owing to the Iranian revolution and the Iran–Iraq war, which took some 3.5 million barrels per day (bpd) off of the world market at a time of rising demand. Yet by 1980, the Saudis had swamped the oil market with a 2.5 million bpd oil surplus (Alnasrawi 1991: 215).

By the early 1980s, an oil glut had set in and market prices began to fall as a result of high Saudi and new non-OPEC production combined with reduced demand from earlier high prices, which had sparked improved energy efficiency and recession in consumer countries. Once prices started downward and maintaining them meant cuts in production and revenues, the conflicting interests of the OPEC states undermined their co-ordination (Alnasrawi 1991: 187–188). Countries started cheating on their quotas and, partly to protect its market position, Saudi Arabia increased its production. As OPEC production increased from 18.5 to 22.5 million bpd, the price fell in 1988 to $13/barrel – in real terms below the pre-1974 level (Spero 1990: 284). The Iraqi invasion of Kuwait caused oil prices to briefly rise to $40/barrel as Iraqi and Kuwaiti production stopped but the Saudis filled the gap and prices again fell (Alnasrawi 1991: 198, Aarts 1994: 6), dropping to a rock bottom $11 per barrel in 1998 at a time when break-even costs averaged $15 per barrel (*The Middle East,* March 1998, p. 35; May 1998, pp. 16–17). Seemingly, OPEC power had been broken with the complicity of the main OPEC producer. The al-Saud's oil policy was pursued not only at the immediate expense of other Middle East oil producers but also at a cost to the country itself. Thus, oil minister Zaki Yamani admitted that Saudi Arabia was pumping more than was rational since oil in the ground was more valuable than assets in Western banks (Alnasrawi 1991: 133). By 1985 the kingdom's revenues had plunged from $120 to $43 billion/year (Alnasrawi 1991: 208–212). State budget revenues fell 32% from 1981 to 1985 (Vassiliev 1998: 453). As a result of the Kuwait war and post-war arms purchases, Saudi

Arabia actually went into debt and had to begin liquidating assets (Sadowski 1991). In 1998, the Saudi government, suffering from a $12 billion budget deficit, was forced to reschedule debt repayments and cut domestic spending. Arab financial power had evaporated. Oil prices increased again in the 2000s, but by then the window of opportunity to re-structure relations with the core had passed.

Not surprisingly, therefore, in the end oil and OPEC did little to alter the power imbalance shaped by the dependency system or to challenge the dominance of core interests over the region. Saudi Arabia had failed to use its leverage to achieve the agreed objective of the Arab states, an equitable settlement of the Arab–Israeli conflict. Indeed, the oil embargo's main 'achievement' was to empower Sadat to engineer a separate Israeli–Egyptian peace that weakened the Arab world to the advantage of Israel and the US. Subsequent Arab impotence during the 1982 Israeli invasion of Lebanon showed that the Arab oil states had squandered whatever leverage they had once had from the oil weapon.

Oil, dependency and the failure of regional development

It is a major irony that the effect of oil has been to deepen rather than relieve the dependency of the region, with a host of negative developmental consequences (Kubursi 1999). To be sure, oil potentially offered the opportunity to overcome economic dependency and stimulate Pan-Arab economic development. According to Heikal (1975: 261–262), the oil boom ushered in the triumph of *tharwa* – resources, wealth – over *thawra* – revolutionary ideology; where oil-less nationalist regimes failed economically, could not their Western-friendly oil-rich rivals succeed in generating a regional economy which would, better than nationalist ideology, lead to regional strength? After all, oil revenues meant that the Middle East, or at least its oil states, enjoyed capital surpluses, potentially sparing them the haemorrhages of capital from interest on loans or the repatriated profits of foreign investment from which other LDCs suffered. While the Arab states individually lacked the ingredients of development, on a regional basis they were much better endowed. The oil states lacked skilled labour and arable land, but they had surplus capital, while capital poor states such as Egypt and Morocco possessed cheap semi-skilled labour and some states, notably Sudan, had vast agricultural land. They had only to put these factors of production together on a regional market and through joint investment ventures.

Indeed, during the oil boom, the Arab world became the only Third World region characterised by substantial intra-regional flows of capital and labour, generating new interdependencies (Shafiq 1999). The oil states transferred about 15% of their capital surpluses to the non-oil Arab states in the form of development and defence aid while *infitah* policies opened the latter's state-dominated economies to external Arab investment. By 1989, there were 252 joint companies or projects with $17.9 billion in capital (another $12.3 billion if firms with non-Arab partners are counted). There were also Pan-Arab development funds with an additional $24.2 billion in assets. The World Bank calculated that in the period of 1976–89 Arab development assistance to needy Arab countries was around $5.1 billion/year, totalling $70.8 billion (Sayigh 1999: 243). This was accompanied by a rhetorical commitment to enhanced regional planning and co-operation through several Pan-Arab economic institutions.

In addition, massive labour migration took place from poor to rich states, which acquired human resources for their ambitious oil-financed development while worker remittances flowed back to stimulate the economies of the labour-exporting states. From 1970 to 1980 the number of Arabs working in other Arab countries had swelled from 648,000 to nearly 4 million. In 1984 as many as 3 million Egyptians were working in Iraq, Saudi Arabia and the Gulf. As many as a million Yemenis were working in the oil countries as well as large numbers of Jordanians, Palestinians and Syrians. In 1980 two-thirds of the Kuwaiti labour force was made up of non-Kuwaiti Arabs and half of the teachers in Saudi schools were non-Saudi Arabs (Gause 1992: 462–464). About 70% of the Arab Gulf labour force was made up of migrants, about 55% of whom were Arabs. Due to migration, cross-regional income inequalities from the oil boom were arguably significantly less than they otherwise would have been (Shafiq 1999: 288–291, 296).

Yet, despite the apparent advantage of oil reserves, the region failed, non-oil Turkey and Israel aside, to produce a single credible candidate for newly industrialised country (NIC) status for several reasons. The oil industry remained an enclave in most local economies with few backward or forward linkages to stimulate development and, using relatively small amounts of largely

expatriate labour, did little to upgrade human capital. Oil deepened technological dependency, encouraging the wholesale import
of material technology packaged by foreign consultants and
contractors without actual transmission of the technology itself
(Sayigh 1999). In an Arab version of the Dutch disease, industry
and agriculture suffered from rising labour costs and scarcities
while excessive revenues were funnelled into construction and services. The raised exchange values of currencies deterred industrial
and agricultural exports and flooded domestic markets with cheap
imports (Chatelus 1993: 152–154; Chaudhry 1997: 186; Kubursi
1999: 310) Although oil permitted large investments in health and
education it reduced the incentive to capitalise on these (Kubursi
1999: 311). The secure rent derived from Western investments fostered a rentier mentality – satisfaction with easy short-term profits
that deterred risk-taking entrepreneurship in the region (Padoan
1997: 184). And the oil money was seemingly squandered: Arab
gross fixed capital formation of $2000 billion over the 1980–2000
decades produced only $380 billion in combined gross national
product (GNP).

What the oil boom did generate was a massive expansion in
vulnerability to the world market. As measured by foreign trade/
gross domestic product (GDP), vulnerability to the world market
rose from 50% to 84% in the 1970–82 period; the geographic
concentration of the foreign trade of the Arab states with the West
also increased: the West took 66% of exports and provided 75%
of imports in 1983. At the same time, oil generated a boom in
consumption demand, well beyond the productive capability of
local economies to meet, which translated into a massive import
dependency. In non-oil states the ratio of consumption to GDP for
1976–86 ranged between 80% and 96%, in good part funded by
oil transfers, but inevitably leading to trade deficits and debt. Food
self-sufficiency fell: with 4% of the world population, the Arab
world imported 29% of the world's cereal imports (Alnasrawi 1991:
177). Regional states' dependence on oil revenues – instead of taxes
and domestic investment – also made them extremely vulnerable
to big fluctuations in oil prices and declines in oil revenues. In the
1980s, the terms of trade for manufacturing imports turned against
the region as oil prices softened while the cost of imports never
similarly declined. In fact, if the $355 billion accumulated between
1972 and 1981 in the hands of the oil producers is adjusted by the

import price index, it amounted to only $160 billion (Alnasrawi 1991: 102–107, 164–166, 177).

When oil revenues fell sharply after 1986 and imports could not be cut without risking political stability, a wave of borrowing was unleashed. The ratio of external debt to GNP of the region increased from 10% in 1975 to 46% in 1988 (Alnasrawi 1991: 165–166). Debt as a proportion of GNP was among the highest in the world in five countries – Morocco, Egypt, Sudan, Tunisia and Jordan. Debt became a mechanism of capital drain to the core as debt service of $38.7 billion exceeded new loans of $22.3 billion in 1983–88 while the proportion of new loans devoted to interest payments increased. Increased debt, combined with the export of capital, gave outside donors and investors greater leverage over the terms of new loans to the region (Alnasrawi 1991: 175; Chatelus 1993: 148, 154–157). The austerity that this dependency enabled the IMF to impose on regional countries for the sake of debt repayment first hit investment levels, and then state spending on health and education, food subsidies and state employment. This, attacking the very basis of the 'social contract' in Middle Eastern states, sparked 'food riots' across the region. Capital, previously exported on a massive scale, was now being re-imported at the cost of debt, concessions to foreign investment and the same dependency typical elsewhere in the periphery.

At the same time, the positive potential of oil to foster Pan-Arab integration was never realised. Pan-Arab investment and joint ventures remained limited and no Arab investment market or Pan-Arab bourgeoisie emerged since most Arab capital surpluses were re-cycled to the West. According to Riad Ajami (*Christian Science Monitor*, 27 August 1990), of the oil producers' $125 billion in direct foreign investment, only 3% was invested in the Arab world. Of total private Arab foreign investment, said by Ayubi (1995: 161) to be $400 billion in 1989, 80% went to the West and only 10% to the Arab world (Alnasrawi 1991: 163). By the 1990s, 98% of private Arab foreign investment was outside the region.

There are various reasons for this. The huge oil revenues earned exceeded the immediate absorptive capacity of the region although the capital transferred to the non-oil Arab countries nevertheless filled only a third of these countries' long-term needs. The state-centric economies of the non-oil states were not entirely investor friendly, although all of them were economically liberalising and actively courting investors. The inescapable fact is that the oil producers perceived their economic interest to lie in the West where their deposits enabled them to live easily on rents rather than in the region where risks and bureaucratic obstacles were high and entrepreneurship was needed to turn a profit. On top of that, the oil boom generated an Arab banking system outside the Arab world, which, integrating Arab finances to the world economy, acted as a conduit for capital flight. The region has the world's highest rate of capital flight to GDP – 100% (Padoan 1997: 186).

In other ways, too, oil failed to generate an inter-Arab economy. Labour migration declined as a motor of regional interdependence as oil prices fell. The proportion of regional trade barely increased from the pre-oil era. The low proportional volume of intra-regional trade to total trade is, of course, partly a function of the high proportion of oil exports, but oil also fuelled the tendency of the oil states to import from outside the region. Regional planning needed to produce trade complementarity failed; thus, there was little co-ordination of the oil era's major regional investments in the petrochemical industry, even though much of it was in the similar GCC states which ended up duplicating each other's facilities (Sayigh 1999). By the 1990s Arab trade was being polarised between two poles, with the Maghreb increasingly trading with the EU and the Gulf with East Asia.

While oil did not propel enough economic integration to generate an objective Pan-Arab interest that could override the stake of regimes and dominant classes in the dependency relation, the geographical maldistribution of oil reserves actually differentiated the interests of the Arab states into oil and non-oil, rich and poor. Until the 1970s, this had not been the case: in 1962, the oil states' GNPs/capita averaged $270 and the non-oil states $164; the oil producers accounted for only 36% of Arab GNP and Egypt's GNP was double Saudi Arabia's (Alnasrawi 1991: 17). Non-oil producers had larger more diversified and advanced economies. But from 1972 to 1974 Saudi income increased from 74% of Egypt's to 234% and by 1981 the share of the oil states in Arab GNP had increased to 75% (Alnasrawi 1991: 19), with 90% of Arab oil revenues accruing to states whose combined populations made up less than 10% of the Arab world. By 1985, the 9.4% of the Arab population in the GCC states got 45% of the Arab GNP (Alnasrawi 1991: 156). Kuwait's $24,000 GNP/capita was 20 times Egypt's.

While oil states had $220 billion in external assets, the rest of the Arab countries were $112 billion in debt (Brown 1984: 256; Khalidi 1991a; *Christian Science Monitor*, 19 February 1991). As a result, the Arab world faced its own version of the north–south conflict, but, being based purely on fortuitous factors rather than development or strength, was more unnatural and probably even less legitimate. It is ironic that, generally, the most developed and populous Arab states with the human resources and potential for diversified economies lacked capital; while oil wealth was concentrated in the small tribal societies lacking the human and natural diversity for development (Alnasrawi 1991: 191).

The rich–poor cleavage enervated the notion of a common Arab interest. The rich had an objective interest in solidifying the separate sovereignties that protected their accidental super privilege while the poor Arab states still had a stake in an Arabism that might entitle them to a share of the oil wealth. It is not accidental that Egypt and Syria long promoted the notion of oil as the common Arab patrimony which should be used to promote Pan-Arab power and prosperity and on which they had a claim as the main Arab military powers that had incurred the costs of defending the Arab world against Israel. In their subsidisation of the front line states, the Gulf states did seem to acknowledge a certain Pan-Arab obligation but it was for them self-evident that oil was the property of the producing states and transfers would be at their discretion and entail a political quid pro quo. The rich Gulf states not only had no interest in a major wealth redistribution, but the wealth gap is what gave them counter-leverage over the advanced Arab states, without which they would become mere peripheries of the region.

The conflict over the distribution of oil wealth had profoundly damaging consequences for Arab security as well as Arab development. In their dealings with their main ally, Egypt, in the mid-1970s, Saudi Arabia and Kuwait concluded that their aid allowed Egyptians to live a subsidised life and they therefore forced Egypt to agree to IMF cuts in subsidies. This caused Egypt's 1977 food riots and was a major factor in Sadat's decision to shift his economic dependence to the US in return for the separate peace with Israel, thus rupturing the Arab world's political solidarity. Moreover, the reversal in the flow of oil resources to the non-oil states once oil prices fell caused economic stagnation and austerity in the poor states, producing social unrest and resentment of the oil sheikhs who people believed were squandering 'Arab' oil money or siphoning it into foreign banks. This sentiment was effectively articulated by Saddam Hussein and may have led him to believe the Arab world would tolerate his absorption of Kuwait (Khalidi 1991a: 168–169; Farsoun 1991; Edward Said in *Christian Science Monitor*, 13 August 1990). The Gulf war crisis – particularly the expulsion of Palestinian, Jordanian and Yemeni workers from Kuwait and Saudi Arabia – showed that the rich states manipulated access to capital and jobs by other Arabs for their own political ends. They were seen to deliberately replace Arab workers, who they feared might have hidden political demands and some claim to a stake in the countries where they worked, with Asian workers who were sure to return home at the end of their short-term contracts.

The massive inter-Arab inequalities generated by oil make extremely salient the function of the regional states system in maintaining unequal – and external – control over the region's main natural resource, oil (Bromley 1994: 106–118). To many people in the region, the state system is seen, not as an expression of natural national differences, but as a system of Western-constructed borders designed to protect small privileged populations in the Gulf against demands for a wider distribution of oil revenues to the Arab population. That militarily powerful poorer states are contiguous to these extremely wealthy states with low military capability makes for an anomalous and unstable situation wherein such insecure regimes were inevitably dependent on protection from the world hegemon, first Britain now the US, for their very survival. This structure embodies the classic dependency alliance between the 'core of the core' (Western MNCs and governments) and the 'core of the periphery' (Gulf sheikhs and citizens) at the expense of the periphery (the Arab masses, the non-citizens in the Gulf).

Renewed military penetration

The decline of Arab oil power was paralleled by restoration of the Western political-military penetration in the Gulf, which had heretofore been much diluted. Indeed, after the 1970s withdrawal of the British from the Gulf, this prize region threatened, from the Western point of view, to become a power vacuum in which radicalism could thrive. Under the Nixon Doctrine, Washington tried to fill it by building up such regional surrogates as Iran under the Shah. However, the fall of the Shah seemed to destroy the main pillar of US policy in the Gulf. Washington's inability to save him or force the release of the American hostages taken in Iran and Lebanon showed the limits of superpower influence in the Middle East.

The US was, however, able to use local conflicts to restore its position in the Gulf. The Iran–Iraq war neutralised the two main anti-imperialist powers that had the potential to assert Gulf hegemony in place of Western influence. The US aimed to contain the war's spread, prevent victory by either side, and allow the two warring states to wear each other down. When Iraq had the upper hand, Washington traded arms for hostages with Iran, but when Iran took the offensive, it tilted toward Iraq. Iraq's dependence on the Gulf oil states to prosecute its war with Iran and its accompanying detente with Washington neutralised what had once been an Arab nationalist obstacle to American penetration; Baghdad's new tilt toward Washington, in turn, enabled the pro-American Gulf states to become much more overt in their American alignment without incurring Arab nationalist disapprobation. Washington also successfully used the Arab Gulf states' fear of Iran to strengthen its Gulf alliances and presence. Airborne Warning and Control System (AWACS) aircraft were introduced into Saudi Arabia and bases established in Oman; as the 'tanker war' escalated in 1986, Kuwait asked for international protection (re-flagging) of its tankers, facilitating the injection of increased US naval forces into the Gulf (Stork and Wenger 1991). After the second Gulf war, the vulnerability of the Gulf's oil-rich but militarily weak states made them so dependent on the West for security against Iraq that it was inconceivable the oil weapon could again be used in the foreseeable future.

Conclusion

Neither Arab nationalism nor Arab oil were able to overcome the legacy of fragmentation and dependency inflicted on the region by the West and neither proved able to restore the Arab world or the Islamic Middle East as a major world power. During the period when Cold War splits in the core restrained Western intervention while Pan-Arabism and later OPEC and the oil weapon relatively united the region, the Middle East enjoyed considerable autonomy and carried some weight in the international system. However, as the region again fragmented, with the decline of Arabism, the drive to autonomy was reversed. The US was able to use the region's economic failures and conflicts, particularly the threat to the Arab states from the non-Arab periphery, to contain the two main attempts – from Arab nationalist Egypt and Islamic Iran – to challenge its hegemony. The failure of nationalist economic development undermined the economic base of independent foreign policies, most crucially in Egypt. This facilitated Washington's ability to exploit Israeli power and diplomatic and economic aid to turn Egypt from a regional buffer against American influence into a conduit for it. Similarly, the US used Saudi Arabia's need for protection from states such as Iran and Iraq to enlist it in the moderation of oil prices and the neutralisation of the oil weapon. The core's penetration of the region was, in the end, actually reinforced by the oil boom, which gave the Gulf's ruling families a much greater stake in the core while dividing Arab states between rich and poor. Washington needed only the withdrawal and collapse of Soviet countervailing power to sweep all before it; with the core relatively united behind the sole American hegemon and the region fragmented, many of the features of the imperialist age started to be restored. This outcome could not be attributed to the sagacity of American policy-makers; with few exceptions, such as Kissinger's Machiavellian manipulations, America came out on top in spite of its own policy and, as Quandt (2001: 72) put it, 'sometimes at extraordinary cost to the peoples of the Middle East'.

The continuing impact of the international system on the region in the post-Cold War era is analysed in chapter 8, but the argument can be prefigured here. Basically, the post-Cold War transformation in the world system, specifically Soviet collapse and unchecked American hegemony, further narrowed the autonomy of many regional states. Two wars against Iraq gave the US an unparalleled military presence in the region from the 1990s. Most MENA states became embedded in the patron–client networks the US established to co-opt the local allies it needed to control the region (Hinnebusch 2011). In parallel, the globalisation of capitalism subordinated most local states to the demands of international finance capital exercised through the IMF. The exception was the handful of super-rich, small-population oil states which, via their 'sovereign wealth funds', further invested in the global economy, albeit now in East Asia, and to a greater degree than hitherto, in the Middle East. While globalisation met more resistance in the Middle East than elsewhere, notably in the region's evasion of full economic liberalisation, increasingly regimes and the crony capitalists around them saw it as an opportunity for increased investment, markets and profits. But, to the extent external penetration tended to generate popular local resistance – in the rise of political Islam and in the Arab Uprising – elites found themselves caught between external demands and those of their populations. Finally, the cautious entry into the region of other great powers, notably China into the Gulf in the 2000s and Russian involvement in the 'new struggle for Syria' after 2011, combined with US retrenchment after its withdrawal from Iraq in 2010 and the increasing difficulty of external management of such a turbulent region, gave local powers marginally more room to manoeuvre in dealing with the US and may presage a return to multi-polarity in the region.

In summation, the impact of the region's position in the world system on the regional states and state system is by no means straightforward. Where the interests of local regimes overlap with those of global patrons MENA states tend to 'omni-balance' with their patron to contain local threats, opening the region to great power penetration. On the other hand, global penetration of the region regularly generated resistance and where nationalist movements came to power, they sought to organise a regional coalition to balance against external powers. However, this was only possible when the great powers were divided (as in the Cold War) and hegemonic intervention thus deterred – and the region simultaneously relatively united (the Nasserite 1950s and 1960s) against the outside. The end of the Cold War reunited the core and, especially after the outbreak of the Arab Uprising, a new magnet drawing great power attention to the region, regional unity was nowhere in evidence.

3

Identity and sovereignty in the regional system

The divergence of identity and territory: arrested nation-building?

In the Westphalian model that European expansion ostensibly globalised, a relative congruence between identity and sovereignty, nation and state, endows states and the states system with legitimacy. Social mobilisation creates, in modernising societies, receptivity to identification with larger communities – nations – potentially coterminous with a state; in an age of nationalism, such identity communities seek a state and state leaders seek to forge a common national identity among their populations. Where the drive to bring state and nation into correspondence is obstructed, states suffer legitimacy deficits and irredentist conflicts foster inter-state conflict. Nowhere is the divergence of identity and state sharper than in the Middle East. There popular identification with many individual states has been contested by strong sub- and supra-state identities, diluting and limiting the mass loyalty to the state typical where it corresponds to a felt nation (Ayoob 1995: 47–70; Hudson 1977: 33–55).

Historically, identification with the territorial state in MENA has been weak, with popular identity tending to focus on the sub-state unit – the city, the tribe, the religious sect – or on the larger Islamic *umma* (Weulersse 1946: 79–83). This is because states, the product of outside conquerors – imported slave-soldiers without local roots, or religio-tribal movements – typically disintegrated after a few generations and when a new wave of state-building came along the states' boundaries were often radically different. Moreover, in an arid environment of trading cities and nomadic tribes, peoples, notably the Arabs, lacked the defined sense of territorial identity and attachment to the land associated with peasant societies. The important exceptions, those societies with substantial peasantries – Turkey, Iran and Egypt – are those where contemporary states most closely approximate national states.

Aggravating the situation was the way the contemporary states system was imposed at the expense of a pre-existing cultural unity deriving from centuries of domination by extensive empires ruling in the name of the Islamic *umma*. Where, historically, a common supra-state identity had embraced local communities and a mosaic of identity groups around an imperial centre, Western imperialism's creation of artificially bounded states divided the region into a multitude of competing state units. Instead of the natural processes of sorting out boundaries through war and dynastic marriage which took place in the northern world, the boundaries of the modern Middle East state system were arbitrarily imposed and frozen by the Western powers according to their own needs, not indigenous wishes (Ayoob 1995: 33; Lustik 1997). This process disrupted a multiplicity of regional ties while reorienting many economic and communications links to the Western 'core'. In reaction, new supra-state ideologies, expressive of the lost cultural unity, were increasingly embraced in Arab lands: Pan-Arabism by the Arabic speaking middle class and political Islam among the lower middle classes. Both, at various times, challenged the legitimacy of the individual states and spawned movements promoting the unification of states as a cure for the fragmentation of the felt community. The result has been that the Arab world constitutes, in Kienle's argument, a system of territorial states, but not, so far, nation-states (Hudson 1977: 33–55; Kienle 1990: 1–30; Korany 1988: 164–178).

At the same time, all the states of the region suffered competition from the mosaic of sub-state identities on which the state boundaries were haphazardly imposed. There are ethnic minorities in all Middle East countries, notably the Kurds, spread between Iraq, Iran, Turkey and Syria, and the Berbers, who spill across North African boundaries. Iran is the premier multi-ethnic society, its Persian core flanked by Azerbaijanis, Kurds, Turkomans, Arabs and Baluchis. Religious pluralism is even more striking: Sunni Muslims are the majority community in the Arab world, although not in certain states, while Shia Muslims, the majority in Iran, spill across the Arab region where they are pivotal minorities or deprived majorities in Bahrain, Kuwait, Iraq and Lebanon. Several

Shia offshoots, notably the Druze, Ismailis and Alawis, are histor-ically important in Syria and Lebanon, while the Zaydis dominate Yemen. Offshoots of the purist Kharijites are to be found in Oman (Ibadies). A multitude of Christian minorities, divided by the lan-guages of their liturgies or allegiances to Eastern Orthodoxy or Rome, are scattered across the region.

Where, as is frequent, such identity groups spill across borders – becoming 'trans-state' – the lack of correspondence between borders and identity may foster irredentism. This, in turn, may generate inter-state conflicts as states contest each other's borders or 'interfere' in each other's 'domestic' affairs by supporting irre-dentist groups, a practice which may escalate into actual military confrontation between states. The best example of this is the case of the Kurds who have been regularly used by their host states in their rivalries with each other and who have attempted to exploit these state rivalries in their struggle for national rights; this has reg-ularly led to inter-state conflict, notably between Syria and Turkey and between Iran and Iraq. In Lebanon where a multitude of sects, never effectively subsumed by a common Lebanese identity, led to civil war, each warring sect sought outside patrons, thereby making Lebanon a battlefield between other states, notably Israel and Syria (Gause 1992: 444–467 Ayoob 1995: 7, 47–70).

Against this reality must be set a century of on-going state for-mation. The consolidation of regimes in individual states created vested interests in the new fragmentation. State-builders struggled to contain the penetration of their territory by trans-state forces and tenaciously defended their sovereignty against either a re-drawing of boundaries or the sub-state autonomy that might satisfy minority demands. The individual Arab states have outlasted the Pan-Arab movements that sought a solution to the 'one nation – many states' dilemma by merging them in Arab unionist projects such as the abortive UAR between Egypt and Syria. States effectively balanced against efforts to export Pan-Arab or Pan-Islamic revolution. The insecurity of the states system spurred state formation and a greater acceptance at elite levels of mutual respect for sovereignty. Moreover, the international system, in guaranteeing state borders, obstructed Bismarckian attempts at forceful absorption of neighbouring states, such as Saddam Hussein's attempt to absorb Kuwait. Thus, the bor-ders imposed at the birth of the state system remain largely intact. The durability of the states system does not necessarily imply the stability or legitimacy of the individual states, which have suffered from chronic legitimacy deficits ultimately rooted in the shallowness of popular identifications with them. If, however, the states are here to stay, as seems likely, the challenge of state-builders is to reconcile such individual statehood with popular identity.

This may, indeed, be happening, for identities are plastic and that which triumphs in a state is the 'constructed' product of contestation by rival leaders and movements. State-builders who command the instruments of socialisation – mass media, mass education – enjoy a decisive advantage in promoting a certain identity among the rising generation. However, it is by no means the case that all identities have equal chances of success; rather, the pre-existence of linguistic unity, facilitating social communication between elites and masses of a particular group (while obstructing it across groups), and historic memories of a common community give decisive advantage to some identities over others that may appear 'artificial', such as a 'Babylonian' identity for Iraq or the Ottomanism that ultimately proved impotent against Slavic, Arab and Turkish nationalisms having linguistic roots. Given the greater popular credibility of Arab–Islamic identity over most alternatives, rulers in the contemporary Arab states vacillate between legitimising themselves as Arab–Islamic leaders and relying on state identities; they cannot fully rely on Arabism or Islam since their borders are not congruent with the Arab or Islamic communities, and adherence to Arabism may sacrifice state interests; yet they cannot fully rely on state identities which lack sufficient credibility (Anderson 1991: 72). They may try to overcome this dilemma by 'statising' a supra-state identity as the official state ideology, as when Ba'thist Syria claims to be the special champion of Arabism or Saudi Arabia of Islam. The problem rulers face is that to benefit from supra-state identities, their foreign policies must be seen to promote the interests of the larger community, but external material constraints (Israeli power, dependence on the US) increasingly have prevented this. As late as 2006, more respondents (Telhami and Zogby International 2007) still thought elites should act in the Arab or Muslim interest (46%) than in the state interest (42%); by 2009 this had dropped to 43% and in 2011 to 30%, with 58% believing state interest should come first, possibly indicative of the attrition of the Pan-Arab generation (Telhami, Annual Arab Opinion Survey, 2011a).

While the multitude of identities from which Arab citizens can choose seems compatible with a post-modern world, the considerable extent to which this means states cannot depend on being the object of their citizens' primary political loyalty has pushed state-builders into authoritarian strategies. The more stable Arab states have, with few exceptions, advanced through a process of primitive power accumulation, in which authoritarian state-builders established tightly knit ruling cores through extensive use of sub-state loyalties (kin, tribe, sect) while exploiting supra-state identities – Arabism and Islam – as official ideologies. But this is a vicious circle: such reliance on top-down state-building has limited the mass mobilisation that was a crucial ingredient in the West's prototype nation-building and comes at the expense of the democratic inclusion and minority rights which could, in principle, generate a sense of common territorial citizenship from which new state-centric identities might develop. As such, most Middle Eastern states still face competition for the loyalty of their citizens from both sub- and supra-state identities and these remain powerful tools for the mobilisation of opposition against state establishments. Significantly, nation-building has proceeded with most success in Turkey, Israel and Iran where indigenous state-builders were able to determine borders and ensure a rough correspondence between them and the dominant identity.

Alternative identities and foreign policy

Pan-Arab nationalism and its rivals

There was every reason why an Arab identity would be uniquely compelling for the citizens of most of the Arab states. These states, mostly successors of the Islamic Ottoman Empire, retained a cultural similarity. Most important, they shared a common Arabic language – the critical ingredient of nationhood. The 'awakening' of Arab identity was a product of the spread of mass education and literacy, especially in the 1950s and often by the Egyptian teachers recruited across the Arab world who helped shape the educated middle class. The spread of a standard newspaper and radio Arabic made the language more homogeneous, stunting the evolution of national dialects as the linguistic basis of separate nations. The advent of Arab satellite TV reinforced cross-border participation in a common discourse. All this makes the Arab world, in Noble's

(1991: 56) words, a 'vast sound chamber' in which ideas and information circulate widely. In addition, similar food, marriage and child-rearing practices, music and art are recognisable region-wide. Extended family ties frequently crossed borders and cross-border immigration has been constant: in the 1950s there were major flows of Palestinian refugees; since the 1970s labour migration to the Gulf oil-producing states has been substantial. Niblock (1990) argues that the interests of the separate states are too intertwined – by labour supply, investment funds, security, water, communications routes and the Palestine issue – for them to develop self-sufficient coherence. Long after the creation of the Arab states system, Noble (1991: 57) could credibly argue that the Arab world was less well represented by realism's impenetrable 'billiard balls' in which governments insulated domestic society from foreign influence than by a set of interconnected organisms separated only by porous membranes.

As a result, supra-state identities – Arabism and Islam – are, for many people, more emotionally compelling than identification with the state. There is a widespread feeling of belonging to a distinct Arab World (*al-'alam al-arabi*). According to a 1978 survey of respondents throughout the Arab world, 78% believed the Arabs constituted a nation, 53% believed the state boundaries were artificial and the vast majority supported doing away with them in favour of a larger, perhaps decentralised state (Korany 1987: 54–55). Arabism is enshrined in state constitutions: Jabbour found 13 Arab constitutions that defined the nation as the Arab nation, with only Lebanon and Tunisia referring to a Lebanese and Tunisian nationhood (Ayubi 1995: 146). Uniquely in the Arab world, not this or that border, but state boundaries in general, have been seen by many Arabs to be arbitrarily and externally imposed at the expense of Arabism, and hence lack the legitimacy and sanctity they enjoy elsewhere. At the level of formal ideology, this sentiment was manifest in the doctrines of Pan-Arab nationalism which viewed all Arabic speakers as forming a nation, the states of which ought to act in concert or be confederated, or, in its most ambitious form (as in Ba'thism), be merged in a single state embracing this nation.

It is not that most Arabs adamantly rejected contemporary state boundaries and even Arab nationalists have not necessarily insisted on a single Arab state. But the extreme fragmentation of the region is viewed as a divide and rule strategy by imperialism and a cause of Arab weakness. Historical memories of greatness under unity and the experience that the Arabs are successful when they act together (e.g. the 1973 war and use of the oil weapon), and are readily dominated when divided, keep Arabism alive. So does the sense of common victimisation: the Crusades are part of every school boy or girl's historical worldview; the loss of Palestine is seen as a common Arab disaster; and the 1967 war shamed all Arabs, not just the defeated front-line states. In the 1990s, the suffering imposed on Iraqis by the Western economic sanctions was not seen as the affliction of another nation which, however regrettable, was not the business of Syrians or Tunisians, but as humiliation and pain inflicted on members of the same community. On the other hand, the relative success of Arab armies in the 1973 war inspired solidarity across the region and all Arabs shared Lebanon's euphoria at Israel's evacuation of southern Lebanon under Hizbollah pressure in June 2000.

As against these Pan-state sentiments, there have always been territorial fault lines in the region that could potentially underlie identities supportive of territorial-based (as opposed to linguistically or ethnically based) separate nations. Harik (1987: 19–46) argued that a viable basis of statehood (or even nationhood) exists in a multitude of geographical entities with distinct historical experiences: where minority sects established autonomous regimes (Yemen, Oman, Lebanon); where tribal or tribal-religious movements founded regimes (Saudi Arabia); where Mamluk elites achieved autonomy as Ottoman power declined (Tunisia, Algeria). The Western imposition of the contemporary state system on these 'proto-nations', defining permanent boundaries that protected them from absorption and endowing them with ruling elites and state apparatuses, crystallised their individuality.

The result is that multiple levels of identity co-exist in varying ways, from those where identification with the separate states overshadows without wholly displacing Arabism to those where state identities remain subordinate to the sense of being an Arab. At the first end of the continuum is an oil city-state such as Kuwait where Farah and Salam's study (1980: 141–142) found state identification came first (24.3%), then religious affiliation (14.4%) and Arabism last. If Kuwait were acknowledged to be a mere part of the Arab nation, then Kuwaiti oil would be an Arab patrimony to be equitably shared with other parts of the Arab nation, not least the legions of Arab expatriates working in Kuwait. The geographically separate Maghreb has always identified less with Arab nationalism than local statehood. Some Tunisian writers defend the idea of a distinct Tunisian nation and Morocco has a long history under an independent dynasty (Ayubi 1995: 144). Yet in the 1973 Arab–Israeli war Morocco's pro-Western ruler thought it to his domestic advantage to send a contingent of troops to the far-off Syrian front; and the strong reaction in the Maghreb to the 1991 Western attack on Iraq showed that Arab–Islamic identities remain powerful, if usually latent.

In Egypt where a strong sense of territorial identity is based on the Nile valley and a history of statehood predating the Arabs, theorists such as Louis Awad contrast the 'reality' of an Egyptian nation with the 'myth' of an Arab nation (Ayubi 1995: 144). Yet Egyptian identity is Arab–Islamic in content, and attempts to construct alternative definitions of Egyptianness – 'Pharaonic' or 'Mediterranean' – have failed. Thus, even in the late 1970s when Egypt was withdrawing from Pan-Arab commitments and engaged in bitter disputes with other Arab states, a survey of high-status Egyptians (normally less receptive to Arabism) indicated that, although 71.3% identified with Egypt first, 71.1% said Egypt was a part of the Arab nation, indeed the natural leader of the Arabs (Hinnebusch 1982: 535–561). This strong sense of kinship with the Arab world meant that decisions taken purely on grounds of state interest – Egypt's separate peace with Israel, membership in the Gulf war coalition – which would be perfectly natural were Egypt a consolidated nation-state, were extremely controversial and probably damaging to regime legitimacy.

In many Mashreq cases, where externally imposed borders corresponded to no history of independent statehood, much less nationhood, Arabism was the dominant identity. It is no accident that the main Pan-Arab nationalist movement, Ba'thism, was born in Syria, and was most successful there and in Iraq and Jordan. If the natural geo-historical unit, *bilad ash-sham* (historic and geographical Syria), might have supported a viable nationhood, its artificial fragmentation into four mini-states prevented the truncated rump from becoming a strong uncontested focus of identity; the attempt to generate a non-Arab Syrian national identity by the Syrian Social Nationalist Party came to nothing, although when a Pan-Syrian identity is defined as Arab in content, it carries resonance. In Iraq, the opposite case of an artificial state constructed by throwing rival communal groups together, Arabism was embraced by some as the only satisfying solution.

Inter-Arab politics amidst supra-state identity: the contest of Pan-Arabism and state sovereignty

The power of supra-state identity and the absence of national states arguably makes for a different, even unique, kind of regional system in the Arab core of the Middle East. Rather than an international system of self-contained national communities whose borders distinguish between 'us' and 'them', the Arab world might better be seen as an 'overarching Arab polity' within which the individual states constitute a set of semi-permeable autonomous units (Kienle 1990: 9, 27; Sela 1998: 9–10). Yet these units are sovereign and the supra-state community, lacking a common centralised authority, is 'anarchic'. Combining sovereignty with shared identity and norms, this system is closer to Bull's (1995) 'international society', than to an 'international system' defined merely by mutual vulnerability and insecurity; but supra-state identity in the Arab world is arguably stronger than in Bull's Western-inspired model. In such a system, where sovereign states are embedded in a supra-state community, state actors arguably must respond *both* to the competitive dynamics of the state system and to the norms deriving from shared identity (Barnett 1998: 10–11, 25–27).

In this system, as constructivist Michael Barnett (1998) argues, shared Arab identity infuses the content of the foreign policy roles which states assume and generates norms that constrain state sovereignty. The core issues that define Arabism are rejection of Western domination, defence of the Palestine cause, the desirability of Arab unity, and the expectation that the Arab states should act in concert in world politics in defence of all-Arab interests. Because the actions of one state regarding common Arab issues affects them all, all have an interest in participating in the definition of all-Arab interests and norms through Arab collective institutions such as the Arab League and the Arab summit system (Barnett 1998: 2, 7; Sela 1998: 12; Thompson 1970).

Yet just because the Arab world has made up a single political arena, conflict has been endemic and competition region-wide. Because boundaries lacked the impenetrability or sanctity of the Westphalian system, with ideological influences and trans-state movements readily crossing state lines, each state was highly sensitive to and vulnerable to the actions of others. In this context, aspirations for Pan-Arab leadership were realistic and rivals had an incentive to manipulate trans-state ideological appeals in ways that would be ineffective and viewed as a violation of sovereignty in a conventional nation-states system. The game was played by ideological or symbolic competition in which leaders ambitious for Pan-Arab leadership, trumpeting their own Arab credentials and impugning those of rivals, sought to sway public opinion and to mobilise the Arab 'street' to pressure (even overthrow) rival governments from below. The effectiveness of such cross-border appeals to the populations of other states was itself testimony to the existence of common identities and norms transcending borders.

Such a unique context should make the conduct of *inter-Arab* politics qualitatively different from *international* politics, but how far this is so is a matter of controversy between constructivists and realists like Stephen Walt who, in his classic realist study, *The Origin of Alliances* (1987), insists that the region demonstrates the universality of realist rules. For him, Arabism was not a constraint on sovereignty but an instrument of power used, much like an army, by stronger states pursuing their 'national interests' against weaker ones. The reality is, however, far more complex than this and there is evidence that inter-Arab state behaviour has departed in key ways from that typical in a conventional states system.

Inter-Arab competition has been intense, but it was quite different from a conventional 'realist' power struggle. It was not chiefly over territory or other tangibles but over the desired normative order of the Arab system. Crucially, the typical currency in this struggle – in stark contrast to that between the Arab and non-Arab Middle East – was not military power but ideological appeal: it was legitimacy, derived from being perceived to observe the norms and play roles grounded in Arabism, which gave the power to affect outcomes (Barnett 1998: 2, 6, 16; Noble 1991: 61). The struggle over the Baghdad Pact was not resolved by the distribution of military power but by Nasser's winning the normative debate over the desired regional order (Barnett 1998: 16). Nasser's blessing was sought and his censure feared not because of his army but because he was seen as the guardian of Arab nationalist norms and could bolster or subvert the domestic legitimacy of other leaders. Before Nasser, Egypt had enjoyed no such advantage over its Arab rivals and after he died, Egypt's trans-state power dissipated overnight; for while its material power had barely changed, his successor had none of the moral authority that had enabled Nasser to make Egypt a pole of attraction for the populations of other states (Hudson 1999: 86).

To speak of a supra-state community assumes that common norms, inter-state 'regimes', or collective institutions, to some extent substitute for the absent common government in constraining the use of violence in political competition. To be sure, low-level violence was part of the inter-Arab game: Arab nationalist activists who tried to subvert or overthrow governments in other states were sometimes recruited and supported by revisionist states, chiefly Nasser's Egypt; but this was a struggle over the balance of political opinion, not a contest of military forces, and arguably, such conduct was borderline between what would be expected in a states system and what would be acceptable within a single political community.

Walt rightly argues that, even at the height of Pan-Arabism, balancing against the Egyptian hegemon was pervasive within the Arab world, at the expense of co-operation for common interests. This was practised not just by the conservative monarchies but even by ostensibly Pan-Arab regimes in Syria and Iraq when Nasser posed a threat to their sovereignty. However, what he neglects is that the threat from Nasser was not military and that the balancing took the form of propaganda and, in the long run, the state-building needed to immunise regimes from Pan-Arab ideological penetration. Moreover, Pan-Arab norms did put far greater restraints on state actors than the rules of sovereignty in a Westphalian state system, excluding certain non-Arab alliance partners which might have made sense from a power-balancing perspective, notably alliances of the weaker Arab monarchies with Israel against stronger radical republics. Pan-Arabism was initially constructed in the successful struggle to require the Arab states to adhere to a Pan-Arab collective security pact rather than a Western-dominated one (the Baghdad Pact), establishing the norm of an 'Arab national interest'.

Finally, Pan-Arabism was never merely a state instrument, not even of Nasserite Egypt, which most successfully exploited it. Pan-Arab movements, trans-state in organisation and 'multi-state' in composition, were autonomous of Cairo; they used Nasser as much as he used them and they constantly pressured him into increasing his commitment to the common cause against his own better judgement. Even if Arabism was manipulated to serve the interests of states in their competition more than to advance all-Arab interests, this competition tended, Barnett argues, to establish norms of behaviour that constrained all Arab states.

The bottom line is that the embedding of a states system in a supra-state community built an enduring tension into the Arab system between the logic of sovereignty, in which each separate state, insecure amidst the anarchy of a states system, pursues its own interests and security, often against its Arab neighbours, and the counter-norm which expects states sharing an Arab identity to act together for common interests. Given this enduring rivalry between the norms of sovereignty and Pan-Arabism, what weight should be given to each was inevitably a product of contestation. Moreover, because Pan-Arab norms were themselves never fixed and had to be adapted to changing conditions, they were always open to considerable interpretation: what kinds of foreign policies were compatible with Arabism – that is, how far ties to the West were permitted, the conditions of a settlement with Israel, etc. – was never self-evident. As such, Pan-Arabism itself developed over time through what Barnett (1998: 6, 28, 40) calls inter-Arab 'dialogues'. And, as a result of this process, the balance between Pan-Arabism and sovereignty altered, swinging first against sovereignty and then back in its favour.

While the ingredients of Arab identity long existed, it was, ironically, inter-Arab leadership competition that played a central role in the overt 'construction' of Arab identity and the institutionalisation of its norms. In the 1950s and 1960s, a process of 'outbidding' took place in which rival state leaders sought to mobilise mass support by escalating the standards and radicalising the goals of Arabism. This led to demands first for more militancy toward imperialism and greater integral unity between Arab states (as embodied in the UAR and subsequent unity projects) and later for greater militancy on behalf of the Palestine cause. Once begun, this was a game that all parties had to play in order to win or retain popular support. Even pro-Western status quo elites were forced to protect their domestic support against external subversion by asserting or defending their own Arab nationalist credentials (Barnett 1998: 47–52; Kienle 1990: 1–30). This provided conditions for a Pan-Arab hegemon to emerge as Nasser, having attained the status of a Pan-Arab hero, sought to institutionalise Pan-Arabism in an informal 'international regime' which laid down a foreign policy consensus on core Arab issues largely enforced by Egypt but which outlived the decline of the Egyptian hegemon by at least a decade (Jourjati 1998; Telhami 1990: 84–106).

This contest between Arabism and sovereignty was not exclusively played out at the inter-state level and a state's adoption of Pan-Arabism (or not) was in good part a result of internal power struggles. The most successful political movements inside many Arab states in the 1950s and 1960s mobilised their constituents under the banner of Arabism: radical versions of Arabism were normally the ideological weapon of rising social forces with an interest in change, specifically the new middle class challenging the oligarchy in the 1950s. Ex-plebeian elites newly arrived in power, especially in states insecure in their separate identity or those with the potential for Pan-Arab leadership, used Pan-Arabism to legitimise their often-precarious rule. Sovereignty, on the other hand, was the ideology of satisfied social forces, normally traditional elites, monarchs on the defensive and without the potential for Pan-Arab leadership.

At a certain point, however, Pan-Arabism began an apparent decline or at least underwent a reinterpretation to the advantage of sovereignty. This 'de-construction' was, in the first instance, Barnett argues, a result of the interaction of state leaders. Over time the competition and insecurity natural in a states system, particularly where regimes were vulnerable to trans-state subversion, reinforced the territorial differentiation between the individual states; moreover, from the beginning, those states whose sovereignty was threatened by Nasser's attempt to impose Pan-Arab uniformity formed anti-hegemonic alliances against Cairo. Also, inter-Arab rivalry, forcing competitors to act on their Pan-Arab rhetoric, 'entrapped' Arab leaders in unrealistic or risky commitments potentially costly or damaging to the interests of the individual states. This tendency climaxed in the provocative rhetoric by which Syria and Egypt blundered into the 1967 war with Israel. Once the costs of outbidding had become prohibitive and were incurred by many individual states, the scene was set for a mutual de-escalation of ideological competition. Especially after 1967, formerly radical elites, now fighting for their very survival at home, agreed with conservative counterparts to make the Arab summits system the arena for a mutual deflation of the standards of Arabism. The most portentous outcome of this was the collective legitimisation of a political settlement with Israel in return for its evacuation of the territories occupied in 1967. The normative balance started to shift from Arabism toward sovereignty, notably in the growing acceptance of the view that Pan-Arab norms had to be defined by an inter-elite consensus in which the interests of the individual states would inevitably be prioritised. The Arab summits became a system through which attempts were made to reconcile agreement on common Arab interests with state sovereignty (Barnett 1998: 40–52; Sela 1998: 3–8).

However, the much increased insecurity issuing from Israel's overwhelming post-1967 superiority and the growing militarisation of the conflict increasingly encouraged a resort to 'self-help' among the front-line states. While this insecurity could, in principle, have issued in the strengthening of Arab collective solidarity against the common Israeli threat, and, indeed, did so for most of the 1970s, the relative ineffectiveness of collective institutions soon stimulated, instead, the build-up of individual state capabilities and the individual search for diplomatic exit from war and occupation. Although this did not rule out such alliances as that between Syria and Egypt in the 1973 Arab–Israeli war, thereafter the same Egypt that had once enforced Pan-Arab standards now pioneered their sacrifice to individual state interests in its acceptance of a separate peace with Israel. This, in dramatically increasing the insecurity of other Arab states, notably Syria, encouraged them to similarly look to self-help through militarisation. The Iran–Iraq war had a similar effect in the Gulf. The increase in threats and in state capabilities from the arms race unleashed by these wars between Arab and non-Arab states, moreover, started to militarise inter-Arab disputes as well, and these were now more often over territory than Arab legitimacy: there were only 10 such conflicts between 1949 and 1967 but 19 between 1967 and 1989 (Barnett 1998: 203). Iraq's invasion of Kuwait marked a new order of magnitude in this tendency. In this new environment where survival depended more on raw military power than success in ideological competition, the world of constructivism was giving way to that of realism.

Finally, the 1970s oil boom had an ambivalent but mostly deleterious effect on Arabism. On the one hand, it generated trans-state movements of labour and capital that, to an extent, integrated the

Arab world; oil aid was used to heal inter-Arab conflicts, making the summit system more effective. On the other hand, oil differentiated the interests of the Arabs into rich and poor, detached the oil producers' interests from the Pan-Arab interest, and funded arms races that increased security dilemmas between Arab states. At the domestic level, oil financed a decade of state-building which made states' populations less susceptible to trans-state ideological mobilisation and allowed the formerly Pan-Arab middle classes to be co-opted by the individual states. As the Pan-Arab mobilisation of the public declined, elites were freer to put state interests over Pan-Arab interests in their foreign policies. Ironically, Pan-Arab movements were transformed into state parties and Arabism became an official ideology used to legitimise the sometimes state-centric policies of individual states.

Arabism, despite credible claims that Arabs had most of the conventional ingredients of nationhood, was seemingly defeated by the resilience of the states system, and suffered continual reverses that were bound to erode faith in its precepts: the failure of the UAR and other unionist initiatives; the defeat of the main Arab nationalist states by Israel in the 1967 war, which made Arab collective security appear unrealistic; the vacuum left after the 1970 death of Nasser, the Pan-Arab hero and the failure of would-be successors such as Muammar al-Qadhafi or Saddam Hussein to fill Nasser's shoes; Arabism's inability to constrain states' sacrifice of all-Arab to state interests (notably, Sadat's separate peace with Israel); and inter-Arab wars, such as the Iraqi invasion of Kuwait and the conflicts between the Yemens (Ajami 1977–78; Faksh 1993).

Political Islam and the international relations of the Middle East
Whether political Islam – which rose parallel with the decline of Arabism from the late 1970s – constitutes a functional substitute for Arabism as a supra-state ideology is a matter of debate. It is far from clear that Islam similarly detracts from the legitimacy of the individual states. Vatikiotis (1987: 42–44) argues that Islam withholds legitimacy from nationally separate states in the name of a Pan-Islamic *umma* and that its call for the rule of God deters the sense of national citizenship that could solidify identifications with a territorial state. Others, however, argue that Islam takes distinctive 'national' forms compatible with individual statehood as well as secularisation and democratisation (Eickelman 1998; Ibrahim

1997). Middle Eastern rulers have routinely used Islam to legitimise their regimes. To be sure, political Islam has become the main ideology of protest and Islamic movements constitute the main political opposition in most Middle East states. In some ways, just as Pan-Arabism was the ideology of the rising middle class before it acquired a stake in individual states, so political Islam is that of the marginalised petty bourgeoisie and the masses who have been left out of state patronage networks, have carried the heaviest costs of the post-oil-boom structural adjustments in the region and who therefore remain susceptible to a supra-state ideology. But Islamic movements typically seek to Islamise the state, not to abolish it and arguably their objection is to the secularity of the individual states, not to their existence. Where regimes permit it, Islamists join the political process to work toward the Islamisation of public life while the states, in responding to this by Islamising their rhetoric, as well as their education, law and media, have arguably satisfied some Muslim discontent with the secular state; even when Islamists are excluded from politics, they often seek to create their own civil society – schools, welfare societies, businesses – in order to Islamise the state from the bottom up. This partial Islamisation of the state may be bringing it into greater congruence with society. In other cases, such as Syria or Algeria, regimes, battle hardened by facing down Islamic movements, came to present more obdurate obstacles to Islamic revolution than heretofore. Facing stronger states than their Pan-Arab analogues ever did in the 1950–60 period, Islamic movements were forced to concentrate on creating Islamic societies within individual states rather than seeking a Pan-Islamic order.

The impact of Islam on the international behaviour of states is even more ambiguous. Although secular Arabism and political Islam have ideologically incompatible visions of domestic order, and although the boundaries of the Arab and Islamic worlds are not coterminous, the foreign policy preferences of political Islamists and Arab nationalists largely reinforce each other. Islam and Arabism both prioritise Arab or Islamic unity over individual reason of state, both insist on economic and cultural autonomy from the Western-dominated world system and both reject the legitimacy of Israel. Nationalist and Islamic identities overlap. Thus, radical Islamic movements such as Hamas and Hizbollah are as much manifestations of Arab national resistance to Israel as they are of Islamic resurgence; Islam has become the ideology of trans-state terrorist networks that are animated by grievances almost indistinguishable from those of Arab nationalism: the Western presence in the Gulf, the victimisation of Iraq, the Palestine cause.

To be sure, Islamic movements have generally not had the capacity, even where Islamists managed to gain access to the levers of power (as in Turkey in 1997) or amassed influence in the legislature (as in Jordan, Kuwait, Morocco, Yemen), to be able to force a significant Islamisation of the foreign policy of states. Yet, given the continued legitimacy deficits of the individual states and their inability to find a credible legitimising substitute for Arabism or Islam, state elites have still needed to be seen to defend Arab–Islamic norms in the face of a public now aroused by Islamic rather than Pan-Arab movements. Even if regimes could now more easily weather dissent in the streets than hitherto, there was still a legitimacy cost to be paid for openly violating such norms, and in certain circumstances Islamic activists were able to call leaders to account for that; arguably the assassination of Sadat was in part a response to his separate peace with Israel, while the 1980s Islamic rebellion against Asad's Syria was in part a result of the legitimacy loss suffered by the regime for its 1976 intervention in Lebanon against the Palestine Liberation Organisation (PLO), keeper of the Palestine cause (Noble 1991: 53–54). Particularly in time of crisis with Israel or the West, the older generation of Arab nationalists and younger Islamic militants came together to put pressure on regimes from below and it was chiefly the fear of de-legitimisation at home which forced states to justify, disguise or refrain from policies that affronted the Arab–Islamic identity of their populations.

Islamic movements have in a few cases seized state power and in the most significant case, that of Iran, the Islamic regime explicitly sought to export a Pan-Islamic revolution. Iran aimed to create similar Islamic states that would have been expected to pursue similar policies, namely challenging 'world arrogance' – the United States and its regional client regimes – in the name of the oppressed (*mustaza'fin*) of the Muslim and Third Worlds (George 1996: 82). Iran's example and encouragement did much to spread Islamic movements and opposition across the region. But early post-Cold War fears of an all-powerful supra-national Islamic threat sweeping away status quo regimes proved unfounded. Iran's export of Islamic revolution was contained, not least by the alignment of the mildly Islamic Gulf states with secular Iraq in the Iran–Iraq war. No secular regime was overthrown; rather, it was Iran's Islamic ideologues who were displaced from power after Khomeini by pragmatists such as Rafsanjani. Although there are now more overtly Islamic states than hitherto, these regimes – in Afghanistan, Iran, Pakistan, Saudi Arabia and Sudan – are too different from each other to constitute a Pan-Islamic axis: they profess different versions of Islamic ideology and are more often than not in open conflict with each other.

At the supra-state level, there is no evidence of a Pan-Islamic 'regime' comparable to Nasserist Arabism, which could enforce agreed norms regarding what constituted an 'Islamic' foreign policy (George 1996: 79–80). There is a Pan-Islamic institution, the Organisation of the Islamic Conference (OIC), but, significantly, its charter acknowledges state sovereignty, it has no power to co-ordinate common action and it has been paralysed by rivalries, such as that between Iran and Saudi Arabia. Many Muslim countries, encouraged by the OIC, have provided aid to Muslims in conflict with non-Muslims (as in Bosnia and Palestine); but few Muslim states were prepared to take economic or military risks for such causes. The OIC did have some success in articulating a Muslim consensus on international issues that affected the Muslim world. Thus, after the 11 September events, the OIC condemned terrorism but rejected 'any linkage between terrorism and rights of Islamic and Arab peoples, including the Palestinian and Lebanese ... to self-determination ... [and] resistance to foreign occupation [which are] legitimate rights enshrined in the United Nations charter' (OIC Qatar communiqué, 10 October 2001 in Murden 2002: 204). Ironically, at the international level, the OIC was a defender of state sovereignty and international law – embracing the principles of the states system as defensive barriers against Western hegemony (Murden 2002: 197–204). But the OIC could hardly be said to constitute an effective Muslim bloc in world politics. In Murden's judgement, it is in the battle for culture in the homes and streets of the Islamic world that Islam is most potent: 'In a world rapidly being swallowed by an all-pervasive global system, Islam [is] a diffuse grassroots counter-hegemony' (Murden 2002: 204).

In summary, while decision-makers cannot wholly ignore political Islam in foreign policy-making, no Islamisation of foreign policy has resulted. It is, however, probably premature to conclude that political Islam has been tamed by the states system in a way similar to the fate of Pan-Arabism. Indeed, in the period after 2000, quite different varieties of Islamism appeared re-empowered, from the Turkish AKP's bid for regional leadership under the banner of a shared Ottoman-Islamic civilisation to Al-Qaida proliferation in post-Arab Uprising failed states.

From New Arab Cold War to the New Sectarianism

The death of Arabism was repeatedly announced in parallel with its failure to deliver on its aims and the decline in the permeability of the Arab states to trans-state discourse as they were consolidated in the 1970s and 1980s. However, some argued that Arabism persisted, albeit diluted and adapted to state sovereignty and mixed with Islamism, as a still-powerful force at the societal level (Abu Khalil 1992; Sirriyeh 2000). From the 1990s, the supra-state public arena was reinvigorated by Arab satellite TV and later by the Internet. As Marc Lynch argued, the new media created a more robust Arab public sphere; Al-Jazeera, for example, brought the Palestine conflict and the US invasion of Iraq into the living rooms of Arabs across the region. In the 'New Arab Cold War' of the late 2000s, Israeli wars on Lebanon (2006) and Gaza (2009–10) and the failure of US-aligned regimes in Cairo and Riyadh to stand up for the Arab side, were played out in a battle for public opinion, which the anti-Western 'Resistance axis' seemed, even though led by non-Arab Iran, to be winning. Its leaders – Ahmadinejad, Asad, Hizbollah's Nasrallah – were far more popular in regional polls than their counterparts in US-aligned regimes (Valbjørn and Bank 2007; Telhami 2011a).

In the 2000s, surveys suggested that Arab, Islamic and state identities remained roughly equal in power, with identifications averaging 24% as citizen of an individual state, 28.5% as an Arab and 32% as Muslim. However, at the level of foreign policy Arab and Islamic identities appeared to have partly merged in that they were associated with very similar anti-imperialist and anti-Zionist foreign policy preferences, as symbolised by posters across the region depicting 'Nasser 1956' alongside 'Nasrallah 2006' during the Lebanon war (Telhami and Zogby International 2007; Valbjørn and Bank 2007). Arab publics still evaluated foreign states on their attitude toward all-Arab issues such as Palestine and Iraq, not on their behaviour toward their own state (Furia and Lucas 2006) and, regardless of their regimes' alliances with the US, large Arab majorities saw America (72%) as a threat – exactly because of Palestine and Iraq. By contrast, despite pro-Western Sunni regimes' attempt to construct a Shia/Iranian threat in this period only 11%, even in the Arab Gulf, feared Islamic Iran. Thus, it appeared that while Arabism was increasingly excluded from the calculations of state policy-makers such as Mubarak and King Abdullah, it had retreated to the level of civil society and the Arab 'street', where it was re-united with Islam.

The Arab Spring or Uprising of 2011 again manifested the powerful role of identity in regional politics. The de-legitimisation of regimes like Mubarak's was in significant part a result of his close alignments with the US and Israel in violation of both Arab and Islamic identities of Egyptians. Indicative of a shared Arab public space was the contagion effect by which uprisings in one Arab state inspired imitations in another (but not beyond the Arab world) and a resultant perception by all Arab governments that they were vulnerable; this was amplified by Pan-Arab satellite TV and other forms of trans-state media technology by which opposition movements shared tactics (Phillips 2011). However, the Uprising also re-opened contests over identity, between sub-state, state (*watani*) and supra-state loyalties, in which Arabism soon faced fierce competition. The content of the demands and grievances of the anti-regime youth movements that led the uprisings were state-centric, marginalising traditional Pan-Arab agendas and discourses, whether anti-imperialist, anti-Zionist or Pan/unionist (Rahim 2011). The uprisings were against the republican regimes created by the earlier Arab nationalist revolutions, and however much these might be seen to have betrayed their own ideologies, Arabism suffered from association with repressive regimes, notably in Syria, Arabism's traditional heartland. Powerfully competing with state identities, however, was trans-national Islam. It was given a new impetus by the post-revolutionary electoral empowerment of Islamic movements, notably the variants of the Muslim Brotherhood beginning in Tunisia and Egypt, which had a close affinity with the ruling party in Turkey as well as the governing or rising parties in Morocco, Yemen and Syria. While these movements sought mostly to Islamise the individual states they were nevertheless linked by trans-state networks and their simultaneous rise toward the levers of power initially seemed likely to strengthen a certain Pan-Islamic identity; however, their rise was checked by resistance from secularists, minorities and state establishments notably in Egypt and Syria. Rival salafi networks were, in parallel, being funded and inspired by Saudi Wahhabism which was associated with a deepening sectarian character of Islamic identity, mobilised by Riyadh against Iran, as part of their wider geopolitical contests. The deepening of the Sunni (Saudi)–Shia (Iran) cleavage had local manifestations in Lebanon, Syria, Bahrain, Yemen and Iraq, with the consequent insecurity intensifying sub/trans-state sectarian identities. In parallel, Al-Qaida's revolutionary and anti-imperialist version of Pan-Islamism, which had seen the Western 'far enemy' as the target of resistance, was initially deflated by the success of Islamic movements in achieving power through the ballot box; but it was re-empowered by the anti-Morsi coup in Egypt and new opportunities to establish an armed presence in failed states, notably Yemen, Libya, and, especially in Syria and Iraq, where their vision of a trans-state 'caliphate' challenged the territorial boundaries put in place by the post World War I Sykes–Picot agreement. Equally significant, Al-Qaida's various avatars were at one with salafis in demonising Shias, Alawis and to a lesser degree other minorities. As Dergham (2012) put it, 'The smell of sectarian wars is becoming ever more redolent across the whole region.'

Territorial identity and foreign policy in the non-Arab periphery
Political identity is, of course, constructed and need not necessarily be rooted in either Arab ethno-nationalism or political Islam. The territorial state based on habitation of a common territory – especially where boundaries correspond to some historical memory – and equal citizenship rights under a common government could become an alternative or reinforcing basis of identity and legitimacy in the Middle East. In the Arab states, this potential has been arrested by the very limited extent to which citizens have acquired the rights needed to feel the state is 'theirs'.

It is in the non-Arab states where territory has more closely coincided with ethnic-linguistic identity and/or a history of separate statehood that entities approximating territorial nation-states have been consolidated. Turkey and Iran have long histories as separate imperial centres and have constructed modern nations around their dominant ethnic-linguistic cores with considerable success despite the unfinished task of integrating a multitude of minorities, above all the Kurds. Israel's very identity as a state is inseparable from its role as a homeland for Jews, despite its Arab minority and diverse ethnic origins. This more established identity, in turn, has made democratisation less risky, consolidating identification with these states.

These relatively secure identities may be more compatible with state-centric reason of state than are supra-state identities such as Pan-Arabism, but they are not necessarily less revisionist, nor are the policies they inspire less conflictual. Trans-national ideologies, such as Pan-Turkism, Zionism and Islam, have still played important roles in each of the non-Arab states; each has been engaged in irredentist-inflamed border conflicts with Arab neighbours; and each has, in significant ways, constructed its identity in opposition to that of the Arab core: Israel sees itself besieged by the Arab world and Turkey's modern secularity was long aimed to differentiate it from its Arab–Islamic hinterland. In addition, Turkey and Israel faced sub-state identity groups – Palestinians, Kurds – which they could not assimilate and would not allow to separate.

Moreover, territorial nationalism has not ruled out the use of Pan-Islam to assert a role in the Arab world. The 2002 rise of the Islamist AKP to power in Turkey marked a major change in Turkish identity, which was now defined in Islamic civilisational and 'neo-Ottoman' terms that bridged the ethnic identity difference with the Arabs, positioned Turkey to bid for leadership in the Arab world and enabled greater accommodation with the Kurds. Iran's position was more ambivalent. The Persian–Arab cleavage had been exacerbated by Pahlavi Iran's aspirations to act as the regional guardian against Arab nationalism. This was superseded after the revolution by an Islamic identity shared with the Arab world that made Iran seek a leadership role there. But Iran's Shiism still differentiated it from the Sunni Islam predominant in the Arab world and Iran's leadership claims, based on Islamic paramountcy, were not recognised by the Arab states, except as a threat; against Iran's pretensions to universal Islamic leadership, its Arab rivals played the sectarian card.

Conclusion

The incongruity of identity and territory continues to destabilise the politics of the Middle East and to significantly qualify the

Westphalian model. While Arab states had seemed to consolidate their sovereignty in the face of supra-state ideology, in the making of foreign policy, legitimacy still required that their leaders balance between the two. Inter-Arab politics arguably remained qualitatively different from 'international' politics. The Arab Uprising re-empowered trans-state identity movements, weakened states and again called territorial boundaries, never fully legitimised, into question. Irredentist conflicts continued to bedevil two near-nation-states, Turkey and Israel. Meanwhile, Iran embraced its communal mosaic and projected its foreign policy under the banner of Pan-Islamic identity.

4

State formation and international behaviour

State-building

State-building is the effort of rulers to institutionalise state structures capable of absorbing expanding political mobilisation and controlling territory corresponding to an identity community. In the Middle East, the flaws built into the process from its origins have afflicted the states with enduring legitimacy deficits (Hudson 1977). Because imperialism drew boundaries that haphazardly corresponded to identity, installed client elites in them and created the power machineries of the new states, state elites, long after independence, continued to depend on external protection and on resources provided by external powers or markets rather than raised domestically through consent; as such, most Middle East states were and remain relatively less accountable to domestic society than where they are indigenous products.

State-building was accompanied by class conflict because imperialism had fostered dominant classes that privately appropriated the means of wealth production, notably land at the expense of peasantries or natural resources (oil), stimulating plebeian revolts and political mobilisation which fragile state structures could not initially contain. As such, state-building meant the expansion and indigenising of imported instruments of rule used in 'primitive power accumulation', a typically violent process entailing the co-optation of some social forces and the exclusion of others. Only gradually after 1970 did many individual states come to enjoy increased stability as rentier monarchies and authoritarian republics were relatively consolidated as the two dominant forms of state in the Arab world. Neither type of regime, however, effectively resolved the legitimacy deficit for both tended to centre on exclusivist tribal, personalistic or ethnic ruling cores, generated new privileged state-dependent classes, and either brought the mass of citizens to trade political rights for socio-economic entitlements or repressed their demands for political participation. Such patterns of state formation have profound consequences for foreign policy: if the state itself is contested, foreign policy may entail its defence as much against internal as external threat, with external support; if few welfare or political rights are delivered, precarious legitimacy is exceptionally dependent on the nationalist or Islamic credibility of foreign policy (Dawisha 1990).

Aspects of state formation and foreign policy

This study will argue that several aspects of state formation are pivotal in determining the international behaviour of states and specifically to explaining variations in their foreign policies.

(1) The circumstances of a state's *initial composition* tend to set it on a particular foreign policy tangent, either status quo or revisionist. (a) Because state formation is coterminous with a contested process of identity construction, whether a state's boundaries satisfy or frustrate identity shapes its foreign policy role. During the initial formation of the states system, imperialist boundary-drawing literally built irredentism into many states; however, where indigenous state-builders were able to achieve some correspondence between the dominant political identity and the state's boundaries, as for example in Turkey and Saudi Arabia, foreign policy has been relatively free of irredentist revisionism. (b) Because primitive state formation always involves some degree of inclusion and exclusion, whether the specific social forces incorporated at the founding of regimes were largely satisfied (privileged) or dissatisfied (plebeian) also tends to set states on opposing status quo or revisionist tangents. Specifically, those, often monarchies, forged around traditional satisfied classes or groups implanted or created, penetrated and supported by the Western 'core', were biased toward status quo policies, while the wave of revolt against this, in which states were captured from below by dissatisfied plebeian forces and turned into radical republics, infused revisionist ideology into many states' foreign policies, at least until radical elites, becoming new classes, acquired stakes in the status quo.

(2) The *level* of state formation (or consolidation) shaped the rationality and effectiveness of states' foreign policies. Rationality in foreign policy denotes reason of state, that is, the choice of ends through a cost–benefit calculation and the matching of ends with means: scaling down ambitions to match capabilities and/or building up capabilities to sustain ambitions. Effectiveness denotes the capacity to implement policies. Arguably, state consolidation depends on some balance between the institutionalisation of state structures and the incorporation of mobilised social forces into them (Huntington 1968). A balance endows elites with both sufficient autonomy to make rational choices and sufficient legitimacy and structural capacity to mobilise the support and extract the resources to sustain and effectively implement these choices.

Traditional states (landed oligarchies, tribal monarchies) with both low levels of political mobilisation and institutionalisation may face limited opposition to their foreign policies at home but lack the ability to mobilise domestic support and resources to project power abroad. *Consolidated* states, with high levels of mobilisation incorporated into strong institutions, enjoy both domestic support and the military capabilities to be formidable foreign policy actors (e.g. Israel with its citizen army). For a long time, most Middle Eastern states have suffered from one or another type of structural imbalance. Where there is insufficient institutionalisation to organise mobilisation (*praetorian* regimes), the main threat to states may be domestic and the 'domestic vulnerability model' of foreign policy may hold in which policy is chiefly designed to contain internal instability by exaggerating an external enemy or indulging in anti-imperialist rhetoric (Calvert 1986; David 1991). Where, in reaction to this, *neo-patrimonial* strategies, combining modern and traditional power techniques, were used to 'over-develop' state control structures at the expense of political participation, elites were buffered from accountability; this may be compatible with the 'leadership-dominant model' which assumes leaders face few institutional constraints at home and can translate their personal values, styles – and pathologies – into foreign policy (Clapham 1977). In either case, foreign policy is arguably more likely to lack rationality and effectiveness than where institutionalisation and participation are in balance.

The traditional, praetorian, neo-patrimonial and consolidated models may best be seen as four ideal types reflective of extreme cases. Actual regimes may more or less approximate one or a combination of these models. Most important, a number of scholars argue that, after several decades of state-building in the region, *partly consolidated* regimes (combining aspects of the consolidated with one or more of the other models) became typical (Dawisha and Zartman 1988; Mufti 1996: 9–16) for several decades – until some collapsed in the Arab Uprising. Arguably, these regimes were sufficiently institutionalised that foreign policies were less directly shaped by the unconstrained biases of the top leader or by internal instability and more by the external challenges that had become so salient.

(3) Finally, the affect of the *structural type* of the state – specifically its authoritarian or democratic/pluralist character – on foreign policy behaviour needs to be tested in the Middle East. Democratic states, if consolidated, are likely to be strong foreign policy actors. But those claiming that democracies are more pacific are disputed by the argument that transitional democracies may actually be *more* susceptible to war (Mansfield and Snyder 1995) and by Middle East evidence that 'irredentist democracies' are particularly belligerent while authoritarian regimes may be *either* status quo or revisionist.

The phases of state-building and foreign policy

State-building in the Middle East has varied considerably over time.[1] Five identifiable stages in Arab state formation are adumbrated below, with comparisons to the non-Arab states made where appropriate. At each stage, the formation of the individual states is a product of interaction between internal political forces and the simultaneously developing systemic (international and regional) structures in which the states were embedded. State formation, in turn, is a major determinant of the foreign policy behaviour of the individual states, for, as will be argued, at each stage in state formation different kinds of foreign policies are typical.

Stage 1: pre-consolidated traditional states (1920s–1948)
The pre-consolidation traditional era in the Arab world was one of weak states governed by semi-independent narrowly based oligarchic republics, monarchies or dictatorships ruling over small albeit mobilising middle classes and relatively unmobilised masses. The colonial powers had, in many countries, imposed borders, bureaucracies and

formally liberal institutions (parliaments, elections) and fostered or co-opted the landed-commercial notability (*ayan*) out of which the first-generation nationalist elites arose. These elites represented a thin upper stratum linked to society mostly through urban patronage networks and control of landed estates; reluctant or unable to mobilise sustained mass resistance to the imperialist powers, they could not avoid compromises with them (e.g. permitting bases, treaties) in return for formal independence (gradually acquired from the 1930s onward), which, together with irredentist dissatisfaction with borders, invariably tarnished their legitimacy.

For the Arab states, the continued presence of imperial powers in the region, extreme economic dependence and limited military capabilities meant the international system sharply constrained state options. As long as societies were unmobilised, domestic constraints were weaker, yet owing to intra-elite fragmentation and low institutionalisation many regimes were too unstable and narrow-based to conduct rational or effective foreign policies. Policy tended to take one of two paths: either rhetoric meant to appease domestic opposition or efforts to secure outside security guarantees against it. By contrast, Turkey, Israel and Iran, more the products of indigenous state-builders than foreign imperiums, enjoyed the greater legitimacy that made possible more (although by no means wholly) inclusive states. In Turkey and Israel, the combination of democratic legitimacy and institutionalisation gave leaders the autonomy in foreign policy-making needed to pursue policies resembling classic reason of state and directed chiefly at perceived external threats. This unevenness of state formation, issuing from the earlier independence of Turkey and the transplant of a mobilised Zionism into the region, meant the Arab states confronted much stronger non-Arab opponents.

Stage 2: pre-consolidation praetorianism and divergent paths: revolutionary republics, traditional survival (1949–70)

The Palestine war, the struggle to throw off imperialism and the Arab–Israeli conflict rapidly accelerated political mobilisation in the Arab region, ushering in the next, praetorian stage. Nationalist politicisation dovetailed with middle-class demands for a share of power and labour and peasant ferment over the region's highly unequal forms of capitalist development. Presidents and kings sought to concentrate power but, given the weakness and fragmentation of parties and parliaments and the manipulation of elections, their weakly institutionalised regimes could not achieve the incorporation of the rising middle class needed to stabilise the state. Political mobilisation came instead through radical ideological parties that turned the newly mobilised against the semi-liberal oligarchic political order. The recruitment of the radicalised middle class into the army led to widespread military intervention in politics which destroyed the rule of the notables in several of the more settled and developed societies and opened the door to praetorianism – an era of factional struggle for power marked by coups and counter-coups which lasted until the 1970s. In a few settled societies (Jordan, Morocco), external support or exceptional leadership allowed the old order to survive while in the less developed Arabian Peninsula, persistent tribalism, the smallness of the educated class and/or continuing British tutelage delayed these tendencies.

By the 1960s (earlier in Egypt) and peaking in the 1970s, state-building was underway across the region. It was initially driven by the need to master domestic instability and trans-state penetration and/or to dilute international dependency. However, state-building put states on quite different (status quo or revisionist leaning) foreign policy tangents. The main root of this differentiation was the impact of imperialism. Where the length and intensity of the independence struggle radicalised social forces (as in Egypt or Aden) or where the imposition of the regional state system thwarted indigenous interests and identity (whether creating 'artificial' states in Syria and Iraq or leaving irredentist ambitions unsatisfied), the dominant status quo social forces were weakened and more radical, middle-class or even plebeian forces were mobilised in the struggle for power. Where this issued in revolutionary coups, the new radical republics harnessed foreign policy to the revisionist sentiments of the social forces they incorporated. Conversely, the more the new states relatively satisfied indigenous interests and identity, as in Turkey or Saudi Arabia, or where independence was achieved without political mobilisation (the Arab Gulf), the more status quo elites survived and newly independent states followed policies accommodating themselves to the West.

Although there were exceptions, the resultant regimes, differentially incorporating satisfied or dissatisfied social forces, tended to pursue one of two quite different archetypal state-building strategies. *Traditional monarchies* tended to survive in small-population unmobilised (or communally divided) societies, mostly in the Arabian Peninsula. Tribal chiefs-turned-state-elites sought legitimacy through traditional versions of Islam and the manipulation of tribal and kinship links now reinforced by the creation of new bureaucracies and Western or oil-financed patronage. The main threat from the mid-1950s was from Egyptian-sponsored Pan-Arabism, which found resonance among the small but dissatisfied middle and working classes (typically in the petroleum sectors). These geopolitically weak states required Western protection from regional threats, but, in the Pan-Arab era of relative Western roll-back from the region, they needed also to appease trans-state and domestic Arab nationalist opinion; this resulted in policies which wavered between close Western alignment and a distancing from Western patrons in times of crisis or which used symbolic politics – such as Saudi Arabia's use of the banner of Islamic solidarity – to disguise Western dependence and counter Pan-Arabism. The exception was Iran's larger more mobilised society where the Shah had to construct a more elaborate technology of control, heavily dependent on clientelism, repression and external backing.

In the *authoritarian-nationalist republics,* where regimes originated in middle-class overthrow of Western client elites by nationalist officers, state formation meant the wholesale reconstruction of states against the opposition of the displaced upper classes and amidst Western hostility, requiring, therefore, a measure of mobilised popular support. Charismatic presidents rose to power through the army but directly appealed to the mass public. Especially in those republics lacking oil, popular support and autonomy of the dominant classes were sought through wealth redistribution (e.g. land reform) and statist development based on nationalisations and a public sector. Economic dependency was eased or diversified as state control of economic links to the world market displaced client classes while aid and markets were accessed in the Eastern bloc. These regimes attempted, with some success, to incorporate the new middle classes, the organised working class and land reform peasants. But because the military remained the main vehicle of factional politics, because these regimes lacked a secure social base in a dominant class, and because opposition persisted among the traditional landed, tribal and commercial elites and their often-Islamist followers, the republics remained unstable. Possessing neither traditional nor democratic legitimacy, they sought legitimisation in radical nationalism: hence foreign policy took the form of anti-imperialist and anti-Zionist rhetoric while bi-polarity provided the necessary conditions for these policies: protection from Western intervention.

Because military power projection capabilities remained limited, while the Arab states, Egypt aside, were vulnerable to trans-state ideological penetration, the main threat elites faced was domestic opposition exacerbated by external subversion (Maddy-Weitzmann 1993). Foreign policy was chiefly shaped by its expected domestic consequences in the legitimacy contest between the radical Pan-Arab and conservative camps. The divergent strategies of the rival camps had their own risks and costs. The monarchies' search for external protection against domestic opposition only exacerbated nationalist rejection of them, most evident in Iraq where the regime's identification with the Baghdad Pact was its undoing; but appeasing Pan-Arabism also held its dangers, as when King Hussein was swept into the 1967 war. In the republics, playing the nationalist card risked Western-backed intervention, subversion and/or Israeli attack, most notable against Syria during the 1950s. Finally, the nationalist outbidding of regimes over the Palestine issue that the 'Arab Cold War' encouraged (Kerr 1971) prepared the way for the 1967 war, which opened an era of 'hot wars' that would have a profound effect on state formation.

Stage 3: semi-consolidation and convergence (1970s–80s)
A third stage was apparent by the 1970s, namely the increased, albeit incomplete, consolidation of both monarchies and republics. The incentive for state consolidation against domestic threats was now reinforced in key cases by high external military threat (particularly for the front-line Arab states in the conflict with Israel and later with Iran). In making war, states 'constructed' a regional system fraught with insecurity, which, in turn, precipitated a reconstruction of the states in ways that allowed their survival in this dangerous environment. Military threat spurred advances in defensive state formation and a preoccupation with the accumulation of power needed to balance against threats. War also precipitated the oil price explosions that gave states the means to consolidate themselves and expand their military capabilities, which, however, only increased the security dilemma for each individual state. Against this threatening regional background, state-builders deployed dual

'modern' and 'traditional' strategies (Tripp 1996) that blurred the difference between republics and monarchies. The resultant regimes moved away from both the 'traditional' and 'radical praetorian' scenarios toward semi-consolidated mixtures of the 'neo-patrimonial' and 'consolidated' models in the following key ways:

(1) The character of leadership shifted within regimes from radical demagogues and populist leaders challenging the status quo to national security specialists – pragmatic generals, technocrats and intelligence operatives – obsessed with stability. Executive centres were institutionalised and ruling elites became more cohesive. While oil patronage reinforced the solidarity of large extended ruling families in the monarchies, in the republics years of intra-elite factional conflict was overcome by the emergence of dominant leaders ensconced in virtual 'presidential monarchies' endowed with cults of personality. Crucial to this was the use of traditional sectarian, tribal and family *assabiya* to create cores of trusted followers around the leader similar to royal families in the monarchies.

(2) In their search for legitimisation, state elites made use of sub- and supra-state identities to make up for thin popular identifications with the state itself. In the monarchies patriarchal loyalties and Islam were the favoured formula; in the republics Pan-Arabism, the official ideology, was buttressed by the exploitation of sub-state loyalties, whether it was Tikriti solidarity in Iraq or that of the Alawis in Syria.

(3) There was a widespread expansion of bureaucratic structures and the modern means of coercion and communications. In the republics, presidents commanded expanding bureaucratic pillars of power – army, bureaucracy, party and *mukhabarat*. In these regimes, which had emerged from military coups, the military remained the core pillar of power, but its disciplining and relative de-politicisation, achieved through a combination of purges, controlled recruitment, intelligence surveillance, privileges and professionalisation (driven by the need to counter external military threats), turned armies from sources of coups into reliable chains of command. Ruling parties developed from small cliques into Leninist-like single or dominant party apparatuses, loosely modelled on those in the East bloc, of impressive size, complexity and functions, which now penetrated the rural peripheries of society and were better able to incorporate large cross-class bases of support. Corporatist structures such as professional associations afforded

control over the upper-middle and middle classes. Where political parties did not exist, as in the oil monarchies, enormous extended ruling families acted as surrogate single-party systems while their use of tribal networks to funnel patronage downwards was analogous to the corporatist structures of the republics. Intelligence and security apparatuses, commanding greater technology and human resources, proliferated in both kinds of state: the '*mukhabarat* state' had arrived. Thus, in both types of state, inherited patrimonial strategies of control were grafted onto modern technology and political organisation.

(4) Increased state penetration of society was reflected in heightened government control of resources. As measured by government expenditure as a percentage of GDP, Egypt pioneered the process with a rise from 37% in 1952 to 70% in 1968 and 81% in 1974 – a function of statism and war – thereafter declining to 40–50%. Syria, Iraq and Saudi Arabia only reached such levels in the 1970s and 1980s (Gause 1992: 460). While this reflected, to a degree, the ability to collect oil rent and disguised a limited ability to extract taxes from society, it nevertheless gave regimes autonomy from society and made good parts of the population dependent on the state. State-sponsored education, aiming to inculcate political loyalties as well as skills, increased dramatically in all states: from 1955 to 1980 the percentage of primary and secondary school age children in the school system increased from 24% to 89% in Iraq, from 51% to 91% in Jordan and from 4% to 48% in Saudi Arabia (Gause, 1991: 16). There was an enormous rise in state employment. Civil bureaucracies expanded regardless of regime type. In Egypt from 1962–63 to 1970 the bureaucracy increased by 70%. In Kuwait, the bureaucracy employed 34% of the labour force in 1975, and the figure for Syria was 20% in 1979. In Saudi Arabia, the civil service grew from a few hundreds in the 1950s to 245,000 in 1979–80 (Ayubi 1988: 15–19). The more effective control that this structural proliferation afforded over the territories of states made them less permeable and susceptible to trans-state ideological penetration.

(5) Movement toward state consolidation was associated with the creation of new state-dependent classes, attaching to state structures the strategic class interests needed to anchor them against the winds of trans-state popular sentiment. The expanding bureaucratic strata's command of public resources gave them stakes in the particular interests of their individual states. In the republics,

the old landed-commercial bourgeoisie was eclipsed by new state bourgeoisies with a stake in the status quo and by the subsequent transformation of part of the surviving middle-sized business sectors into dependent clienteles thriving on state monopolies, commissions, contracts and inputs. In the monarchies, commercial and tribal elites were similarly transformed via state patronage into new bourgeoisies.

(6) Long-term stability also depended on the incorporation of a sufficient segment of the middle and lower strata, which, in turn, depended on sufficient economic resources to give them a stake in the status quo. In monarchies and republics alike regimes forged a sort of populist social contract: in return for support or acquiescence, the state provided jobs, free education, subsidised foodstuffs and labour rights. In the republics, this initially relied on the 'socialist' redistribution of upper-class assets but with the oil price boom it could be funded more generously. In the monarchies, the one-time threat from the growing new middle class was contained by co-opting it into state jobs but excluding it from the military.

Advances in state consolidation had foreign policy consequences. Top elites, their power relatively consolidated and able to balance conflicting social forces, generally attained hitherto lacking autonomy from society in the making of foreign policy. How far this resulted from a better balance between institutionalisation and participation or from the neo-patrimonial de-mobilisation of civil society is an empirical question that varies by case. Generally, however, this elite autonomy, combined with increased regime stability, declining vulnerability to trans-state ideology and rising threats from neighbouring states, issued in increased weight being given to geopolitical reason of state over identity issues in foreign policy-making. This meant more prudent and effective policies, but also a certain sacrifice of longer-term Pan-Arab interests to more immediate individual state interests. Power capabilities generally increased as oil rent enabled states to make exceptional arms purchases, stimulating arms races. Additionally, the increased oil resources and military capabilities of regional states made them more autonomous of external great powers. As the threat from neighbouring states increased, more remote international powers were seen less as threats and more as sources of protection and resources in the regional struggle.

These tendencies spelled a significant convergence in the policies of monarchies and republics. In the republics, radical elites, either displaced or chastened by defeat in war, moderated their ideological radicalism. Egypt and Syria were forced, by the need to recover the occupied territories from Israel, to bury the ideological Cold War with the monarchies, to moderate anti-Western policies and to seek a negotiated peace with Israel while, at the same time, the monarchies used oil resources to subsidise the nationalist states and briefly attempted to win nationalist legitimacy by using the 'oil weapon'. Later, the Gulf monarchies would be driven by fear of Iran to seek detente with republics such as Iraq. As such, the systemic level, specifically regional threats, tended to recast states, originally very different, into similar 'realist' moulds following similar pragmatic foreign policies.

There were, however, important exceptions and counter-trends to the regional tendency toward realism and moderation. Even as Arab nationalism declined as a threat to regimes, it was replaced by a new supra-state revisionist ideology, political Islam. The 1967 war, in discrediting secular Arab nationalism, had left an ideological vacuum while the negative side effects of state-building – the corruption and inequality that oil money encouraged – turned those who felt excluded to political Islam as an ideology of protest. These factors precipitated revolution in Iran and the attempt of the Islamic republic to export its revolution, leading to war in the Gulf. This was paralleled by the rise of the revisionist Likud party in Israel that similarly led to war in Lebanon.

These developments in turn arrested the tendency toward convergence, as key republics, locked into intractable conflicts on the non-Arab periphery, became major 'war states'. Iraq's regime was consolidated in the crucible of the war with Iran and Syria's buttressed by the war with Israel in Lebanon. War drove an upward trajectory in the size of armies; Syria and Iraq, where wars and threat levels were the highest, achieved exceptional levels of military mobilisation – increasing from 6.4 and 6.7/1,000 population in 1955 to 36.2 and 62.4/1,000 of population in 1987. In good part this was a necessary reaction to high levels of such mobilisation in Israel (which reached 145/1,000 in 1987) and in revolutionary Iran (Gause 1992: 457–458).

As state construction matured, the once fragile republics showed an ability to survive the worst crises, including defeat in war. In

1967 Egypt and Syria survived a greater defeat than the one that brought down the *ancien regimes* and mobilised the power to challenge Israel in 1973; in the early 1980s, Syria survived back-to-back Islamic rebellion and conflict with an Israeli-American *combinazione* in Lebanon. Iraq survived the enormous pressures of the war with Iran and did not split along communal lines as might have been expected; Saddam Hussein's regime also survived the much more intense pressures applied by the US in the Gulf war and its aftermath, including military defeat, economic blockade and loss of full territorial control. By contrast, the monarchies, unable to trust the middle class, kept their armies small and recruited from extended royal families and loyal tribes. This forced them to rely for their security on high-tech oil-for-arms purchases from the West and an increasing US naval presence in the Gulf.

The main consequence of the period was the considerable extent to which the generalisation of external insecurity, state consolidation and reason of state brought the regional system into closer approximation to the Westphalian model. It was, however, Iraq's invasion of Kuwait, injecting military insecurity into inter-Arab politics, where competition had hitherto largely remained at the political-ideological level, which crowned this process.

Stage 4: state vulnerability and global penetration (1990–2010)
A fourth stage, whose origins can be traced back to the 1970s but which only fully emerged in the 1990s, was marked by growing economic crisis and loss of Soviet patronage in the republics and military shock (the Iranian threat, Iraq's invasion of Kuwait) in the monarchies, exposing the fragility of state-building in both. This coincidence of domestic vulnerability with major changes in the international system – the end of bi-polarity, the globalisation of capitalism – opened the door to a reconstruction of dependencies that, in the previous period, had seemed to be minimised.

The root of the new vulnerability in the republics lay in domestic economic weaknesses. Inefficient public sectors, the exploitation of economies for military ends and populist distribution policies had enervated capital accumulation and led to the exhaustion of statist import-substitute industrialisation, driving moves to open economies to private and foreign capital: the so-called *infitah*. The boom/bust cycle of the international oil economy also impacted on state formation. Oil rent financed a burst of state-building that ended in overdeveloped states exceeding the capacity that their own economic bases could sustain. Enormous resources were expended on arms races. Oil rent and *infitah* also encouraged import booms rather than investment at home. This, combined with the 1980s oil bust, left the republics saddled with balance-of-payments crises and debt that greatly increased their vulnerability to external pressures from Western donors and to IMF demands for structural adjustment.

At the same time, a transformation in the social base of the republics was taking place, with the old populist coalition being replaced by new '*infitah* (internationalist) coalitions'. The roots of this goes back well before the 1990s. The authoritarian-populist state, which initially had balanced 'above' classes, in time generated a new dominant class from within. It was made up of an alliance of the 'state bourgeoisie' (formerly plebeian but 'embourgeoised' military officers, highly paid state managers and senior bureaucrats) with a revived private bourgeoisie of contractors and middlemen doing business with the state. As the public sector was exhausted as a source of wealth and careers, the state bourgeoisie looked to economic liberalisation to diversify the state's economic base as well as provide opportunities for it to invest its accumulated wealth in private business and thereby transform itself into a property-owning class; the private bourgeoisie saw new opportunities in *infitah* for foreign partners and to acquire public-sector assets. The revival of private capitalism, first initiated by Sadat in Egypt, spread across the region. Many states were increasingly entangled in a web of economic relations with core states, whether they were forced into export strategies to repay accumulated debt or perceived potential opportunities to secure capital inflows. This required that investors be favoured over the mass public, hence *infitah* was typically accompanied by a rollback in subsidies and welfare measures and the beginnings of privatisation of public sectors.

Authoritarian power structures largely persisted but whereas previously such power was used to attack privileged groups and to broaden equality, it was now deployed to protect the new economic inequalities that followed on *infitah*. This post-populist period is associated with uneven political liberalisation: while the interest groups of the bourgeoisie were given greater corporatist and parliamentary access to power and safety-valve opposition parties for the middle class were tolerated within strict limits, mass organisations and trade unions were brought under stricter control and excluded from the access to decision-makers they often formerly enjoyed in the populist era.

Parallel alterations in the global power balance, also evident before the 1990s, reinforced domestic change to drive a nearly uniform Westward re-alignment in foreign policies. The declining Soviet ability to provide the Arab states with the military capability to match that given to Israel by Washington, hence the perceived indispensability of American power to ending the Israeli occupation of Arab lands, was a major factor reinforcing Egypt's repositioning in the world order; where Egypt led, others followed. The decline of the Soviet Union as an alternative market and source of technology and aid also meant, once buffering oil rent also declined, that there was no alternative to reintegration into the world capitalist market. Crucially, the collapse of the Soviet Union left the radical republics exposed, without the political protection or military patronage they needed to pursue autonomous policies that challenged Western interests.

The result was a further moderation in the foreign policies of formerly radical republics. Even as some of them had previously harnessed their economies to foreign policy, so economic troubles now drove many to harness foreign policy to the economy – that is, into the practice of 'trading' Western-friendly foreign policy for economic aid and investment. This tendency was reinforced by economic globalisation which seemed to provide new opportunities for inward investment: an attractive investment climate and re-integration into the international economy required moves toward settlement of the Arab–Israeli conflict and a Western foreign policy alignment in place of balancing between the superpowers.

A different kind of vulnerability was exposed in the oil monarchies. There, family states with tiny, pampered, citizen populations dependent on expatriate labour combined great wealth with low military capability. Their chief liability was their location contiguous to much larger, poorer and militarily stronger states – Iran and Iraq. The Iran–Iraq war spared the monarchies their immediate attentions throughout the 1980s, but the Iraqi invasion of Kuwait administered a shock to these regimes that paralleled the economic crisis in the republics. It showed they could not survive in a world of powerful predatory neighbours without much-enhanced Western protection. The resultant foreign policy change took the form of a much more overt Western presence (bases, treaties). Their key security interest was to maintain the flow of oil revenues needed to appease constituencies at home while enlisting Western protection against threats from their stronger neighbours.

If the state-building of the 1970s and 1980s was driven in good part by external security threats, this started to decline in the 1990s as enhanced Western penetration left far less scope for the ambitions of potential regional hegemons, especially after the Iraq and Afghan conflicts demonstrated a renewed ability of the American hegemon to project power into the region. Rather, the most salient determinant of policy became the effort of regimes to balance between the increased international demands on them and domestic resistance to these demands. Regional states were becoming transmission belts for the enforcement of West-centric globalisation at the possible expense of indigenous interests and identity: this could involve the imposition of structural adjustment, unpopular and inequitable peace treaties with Israel and co-operation with US campaigns against terrorism and so-called 'rogue states'. This, however, spelled increased domestic risks. While the Middle East region still proved more resistant than others have to the neo-liberal rules of the international economy, even its incremental integration into this order threatened to undermine the very foundations of states. Regimes that built their legitimacy on a distributive social contract were being pushed toward a policy of trickle-down capitalism. At least in the short term, this was bound to leave a more or less large segment of the public marginalised. Marginalised strata were the most likely to be attracted to sub- and supra-state identities and available for anti-system mobilisation by counter-elites: indeed, the victims of economic liberalisation were among the main constituents of Islamic opposition movements. If the stronger states in place contained and localised the political threat of such movements, the gradual Islamisation of society at the grassroots potentially spelled longer-term indigenous resistance to the globalisation on regime agendas. Especially to the extent that economic integration into the world system facilitated Western penetration of their societies, while conflict between the US hegemon and a variety of Muslim states continued to assume a high profile, regimes risked whatever Arab or Islamic legitimacy they might still enjoy without yet having found a credible substitute for these supra-state identities.

Whether democratisation could serve as an alternative basis of legitimacy was not really tested. It was obstructed or limited by ruling elites' dependence on trusted in-groups or privileged classes and the consequent stunting of political institutions. Limited political liberalisation left ultimate power in the hands of the executive, while tending to disproportionately empower the educated and wealthy classes at the expense of the masses. However, where democratisation proceeded further, it empowered domestic reaction against the tilt toward the West and Israel, which Islamic movements exploited, prompting regimes to halt or reverse these experiments. The case of Jordan showed dramatically how a regime's responsiveness to outside demands – for peace with an Israel unwilling to concede Palestinian rights, the price of restored American aid after the second Gulf war – was necessarily paralleled by a contraction of domestic democratisation and responsiveness to domestic opinion. It also illustrated how the dependence of many states' revenue bases on aid from the West, rather than taxes from their own population, made their foreign policies more responsive to the former than to the latter. The increased penetration of Middle East states by the core, combined with the failure of democratisation, meant that increasingly local states were pursuing foreign policies in the face of broad if apparently shallow opposition from their own publics.

Stage 5: the Arab Uprising (2011–)

The Arab Uprising was a reaction to the authoritarian, West-centric and in-egalitarian rule of the post-populist era, a revolt manifest in the overthrow of presidential monarchies and initial empowerment of the outsider Islamic movements. It was encouraged by diffusion from the West of Internet technology and the parallel spread of Western discourses of democratisation and human rights that de-legitimised local political practices.

In the short term, the result of the Uprising was further state weakening. Where the central power survived in the more cohesive societies of Tunisia and Egypt, state weakening resulted because political mobilisation exceeded the capacity of institutions to absorb; in particular, because publics became sharply divided along sectarian and Islamist vs. secular lines, and between remnants of the old state establishment and radicals wanting more thorough revolution, producing a three-sided struggle over the very rules of political order. Contesting elites still dominated but the masses were now a key resource in intra-elite power struggles. This renewed 'praeto-rianism', in which politics was played via street protests, riots and military intervention, as well as elections, without agreed rules of the game. State capacity to deliver services and sustain order was widely damaged, even in Tunisia, where the transition was most peaceful. Elsewhere, notably in Egypt, hybrid regimes combined persisting authoritarian practices with elections in which rivals used identity politics to mobilise constituencies.

Where, in more fragmented societies, the regime collapsed, fully or partially, as in Libya, Yemen and Syria, civil war generated armed social movements; the domestic security dilemma (from anarchy) pushed people into self-defence militias; insecurity and economic need gave rise to warlords profiteering via protection rackets; and armed trans-state movements, various Al-Qaida ava-tars, filled the vacuum where the state lost control over parts of its territory (as well as oil wells and arms depots).

The Uprising rendered the republics too fragmented to pro-duce coherent foreign policies. Rather, the weakening of the state combined with the omni-balancing of rival elites seeking external resources and support in their internal power struggles made the post-Uprising states battlegrounds of 'competitive interference' by the non-Arab states, Iran, Israel and Turkey, by the Arab monar-chies that had escaped the Uprising, and by global powers. The republics' immunity to trans-state penetration plummeted, with the use of the Internet by dissident youth, and the Gulf monarchies' manipulation of satellite TV and financing to governments and Islamist movements. State weakening re-empowered trans-state forces and ignited highly divisive Shia–Sunni discourse wars. In parallel, dependence on the IMF and core powers actually deepened as economies were destabilised.

Conclusion: state formation and the system level

At each stage, the system level has been decisive in driving MENA state formation, the changing features of which, in turn, have shaped the changing character of the system. First, imperialism literally constructed the system and its state components which were too weak to threaten each other but whose precarious legiti-macy could not withstand powerful trans-state identities, Arabism and Islam, inherited from Ottoman collapse, with regional politics largely taking the form of trans-state discourse wars. These, in turn, stimulated state formation, based, in the authoritarian republics, on populist social contracts and statism; somewhat later regional war both motivated and legitimised further state formation advances and precipitated the trans-state oil flows that provided resources needed for state consolidation in both the monarchies and republics, and, in parallel, for the militarisation that created a classic realist security dilemma. Yet by the 1990s, globalisation, combined with state economic weakening, had turned regional states from buffers against external intrusion into transmission belts of it, producing a peculiar version of authoritarian crony capitalism that deconstructed the republican social contract and paved the way for the Arab Uprising against these post-populist republics. As the Arab states reached and passed the peak of state formation, their ability to resist global and trans-state penetration again declined and with it, not only their capacity to pursue hegemonic ambitions, but even to defend their sovereignty.

While these region-wide forces have shaped similar patterns of state formation, the behaviour of any individual state can only be explained by the interaction between its unique geopolitical location in the regional system, its specific state formation path and its particular policy process, as chapters 5 and 6 will show.

Note

1 The following account of state formation benefits from a number of classic accounts including Hudson (1977); Dawisha and Zartman (1988); Ayubi (1995), especially chapters 6–10; Bromley (1994: 119–154); Mufti (1996); Owen (1992); Chaudhry (1997); Anderson (1986, 1987); Beblawi and Luciani (1987); Crystal (1991); Dawisha and Zartman (1982); Luciani (1990); Richards and Waterbury (1996), chapters 7–9, 11–13; Trimberger (1978); Berberoglu (1989); and Tachau (1975); as well as numerous single-country studies.

5

Foreign policy-making in the Middle East

It is frequently claimed that foreign policy-making in Middle East states is either the idiosyncratic product of personalistic dictators or the irrational outcome of domestic instability. In fact, it can only be adequately understood by analysis of the multiple factors common to all states, namely: (1) foreign policy *determinants* (interests, challenges) to which decision-makers respond when they shape policies and (2) foreign policy *structures and processes* which factor the 'inputs' made by various actors into policies addressing these determinants.

Foreign policy determinants

In any states system state elites seek to defend the *autonomy* and *security* of the regime and state in the three separate arenas or levels in which they must operate, although which level dominates attention in a given time and country may vary considerably.

The regional level: geopolitics

In a states system like the Middle East, where regional militarisation greatly increased external threats, these have been salient on states' foreign policy agendas; just as often, however, the perceived threat is one of trans-state subversion. While, generally speaking, threat tends to precipitate a search for countervailing power or protective alliances, it is a state's *geopolitical position* that specifically defines the threats and opportunities it faces. It constitutes a state's neighbourhood where border conflicts and irredentism are concentrated and buffer zones or spheres of influence sought. Position determines natural rivals: thus, Egypt and Iraq, stronger river valley civilisations, were historical competitors for influence in the weaker, fragmented Mashreq; Iran and Iraq were long natural rivals for influence in the Gulf. A state's power position in the regional system, shaped by its resources, size of territory and population and the strategic importance or vulnerability of its location, shapes its ambitions: hence small states (Jordan, Gulf states) are more likely to seek the protection of greater powers and larger ones to establish spheres of regional influence (e.g. Syria in the Levant, Saudi Arabia in the GCC).

The international level: dependency

The impact of the core great powers and the international political economy constitutes a dilemma for regional states. The global core is both the indispensable source of many crucial resources and of constraints on the autonomy of regional states. The constraining impact of the core ranges from the threat of active military intervention or economic sanctions to the leverage derived from the dependency of regional states, maximised where the client state has a high need and a lack of alternatives. In extreme cases, foreign policy may be chiefly designed to access economic resources by appeasing donors and investors. Vulnerability to core demands, such as for structural adjustment, can inflame domestic opposition. However, shared security and economic interests between the core powers and status quo regional elites may make such costs seem worth incurring.

The domestic level: identity

In most Middle Eastern states identity is complex, with sub- and supra-state identities contesting loyalty to the state. Where sub-state identities are strong, they may produce irredentist pressures on decision-makers. Where supra-state Arab and/or Islamic identities are strong, regime legitimacy may be contingent on adherence to Arab–Islamic norms in foreign policy. This may mean contesting the penetration of the region by the core powers and it may de-legitimise relations with certain states: thus, while some Arab states have been pushed by economic dependency or security considerations to establish relations with Israel, these remain largely illegitimate at the societal level.

The impact of identity is not, of course, uniform. Where there are high levels of public mobilisation and low levels of state consolidation, elites are more vulnerable to Pan-Arab or Pan-Islamic opinion in foreign policy-making. Because supra-state identity is often an instrument of opposition forces or of subversion by rival states, status quo elites have an incentive to create state-centric identities compatible with sovereignty and to pursue the higher levels of state formation that enhance their autonomy from such pressures. However, where revisionist social forces dominate states, they may foster and use supra-state identities in the service of their foreign policy.

Decision-making

Foreign policy-making elites are 'Janus-faced', looking both inward and outward, attempting to reconcile demands from domestic actors with threats or constraints from external powers. Coping with a threat at one level normally requires accessing resources at another and maximising one value (autonomy, security, wealth, identity) may require sacrificing some of another. Thus, for example, to counter a regional threat may require protection by a core state, increasing dependency at the international level at a possible cost in domestic legitimacy. Conversely, mobilising the support of revisionist domestic forces in order to increase autonomy from core pressures may increase the risk of regional war or of economic sanctions from core states. The trade-off is well illustrated by the way the Salman Rushdie affair (1989) caught Iranian elites between the need to preserve the domestic legitimacy derived from the Khomeini heritage and the need, for economic reasons, to repair relations with Western Europe which this affair strained. According to David (1991), elites' rational assessment of where the threat is greatest at a particular time shapes their choices. The highest rationality may be the ability to 'omni-balance' between threats at various levels.

However, because policy-making is seldom simply a matter of a rational actor weighing costs and benefits to identify the one obviously best course of action and because, as constructivists insist, interests and threats, far from being self-evident, are a 'constructed' function of identity, a state's choices are 'filtered' by its historic *foreign policy role* (Holsti 1970). A role is a durable tradition rooted in identity that defines orientations toward neighbours (friend or enemy), great powers (threat or patron) and the state system (revisionist or status quo), and which incorporates a country's experience in balancing and reconciling conflicting imperatives. State/regime formation is one decisive factor in shaping role; thus,

Israel's conception of itself as a besieged refuge for world Jewry is rooted in its formation as a product of the Zionist movement. Geopolitical position is another: thus, Egypt's regional centrality led its decision-makers to seek influence in the Arab East, North Africa and the Nile Valley. Although manipulated by elites, once a role is established and shapes the socialisation of the next generation of policy-makers, it sets standards of legitimacy and performance, which, to a degree, constrain elites, imparting a certain consistency to foreign policy despite changes in leadership and environment.

Yet roles seldom provide ready-made answers to particular policy dilemmas, particularly since how they apply in particular situations requires interpretation; as such, the personalities, perceptions and misperceptions of leaders are inevitably pivotal in determining choices. Where elites are themselves competing in a process of 'bureaucratic politics' to promote rival policies, outcomes will be determined by the power distribution among them as shaped by the state's governing institutions. The interests and differential weight carried by different actors – public opinion, business, the military, diplomats – seeking to influence the ultimate decision-maker will bias the direction of choices; whether the internal power advantage is held by a nationalist/populist coalition or an *infitah* (internationalist) coalition may be decisive.

Finally, outcomes depend on policy implementation, in part a function of the instruments of influence available to state elites such as economic rewards and punishments, propaganda machinery and military capabilities. But outcomes cannot be adequately explained merely by the balance of such tangible resources among states: the diplomatic skills and bargaining strategies of leaders, including intangibles, such as credibility and 'will', also count.

The foreign policy process

The following survey of the policy process examines the typical actors, with the least influential treated first and the most decisive last, while paying special attention to the consequence of the distribution of power among the latter.

'Outside' actors: inputs into the foreign policy process
Public opinion   In the Middle East, public opinion normally plays little *direct* role in foreign policy formulation, which is normally

the special business of top elites. The majority of the population is often inattentive, uninformed and divided by class or ethnicity, hence easily manipulated by elites on foreign policy issues. This is, in good part, because political opposition is typically repressed, divided or co-opted and the press, to varying extents, controlled. The public itself may be dependent on the patronage of a distributory state (especially in the low-population oil-rich GCC states) that trades economic benefits for political acquiescence. Accountability mechanisms are largely lacking in the Middle East and in most states the public has not had the opportunity to choose between different foreign policies or to hold leaders accountable for them in elections.

When leaders have enjoyed external support or a consolidated base, they have routinely ignored public opinion and although they have paid a price, it has seldom been unacceptable. Thus, external support allowed King Hussein of Jordan to escape unscathed from his repeated defiance of public opinion, including his dismissal of an elected pro-Nasser government in 1957, his repression of the Palestinians in Black September 1970 and his 1990s peace treaty and normalisation of relations with Israel. Asad of Syria, atop a consolidated regime at home, also defied public opposition to his 1976 intervention in Lebanon against the PLO, his alignment with Iraq in the Iran–Iraq war and his joining of the Western coalition against Iraq in the Kuwait crisis. Sadat defied the public and part of elite opinion in pursuing a separate peace with Israel; while this inflamed Islamic opinion, weakened the regime's legitimacy and played a part in his assassination and the subsequent Islamic insurgency Egypt faced, public opposition did not force a change in Egyptian foreign policy.

Leaders can also reshape public opinion. Nasser was the prime example of a charismatic leader who altered public opinion, bringing Egyptians to see themselves as Arabs and raising Arab nationalist consciousness across the region (Dekmejian 1971: 39–40, 76–80, 101–108). By contrast, since the 1990s, Arab leaders have attempted to educate their publics as to the constraints they face in pursuing Arab nationalist ambitions and the benefits to be derived from abandoning them. Thus, from the time he took power, Asad attempted to lower the Syrian public's expectations from the aim of liberating Palestine to that of recovering the occupied territories. Sadat's Egypt and Jordan's King Hussein campaigned for their peace treaties with Israel, promising that they would bring prosperity to ordinary people.

One would expect public opinion to play a greater role in the foreign policy process where regimes have party competition, a free press and electoral accountability mechanisms. In the Arab world, increased susceptibility to public opinion from even limited democratisation put pressure on elites to distance themselves from the West: it was those Arab states which were experimenting with democratisation – Tunisia, Jordan, Yemen and Algeria – that proved most vulnerable to pro-Iraqi public sentiment during the Gulf war. As the cases of Turkey and Israel suggest, if elites can win public support through nationalist rhetoric, the effect of elections may be less to restrain than to encourage elite foreign policy activism. But elections do give the public the ability to punish these elites when things go awry, as several Israeli prime ministers have found out (see chapter 6, pp. 168–169, and 7, pp. 208–209). And populations may, at key junctures, restrain involvement in foreign adventures, as democratic peace theorists expect: thus, it was wide public opposition to the 2003 invasion of Iraq that led Turkey's wavering political class to reject US requests for the use of Turkish bases to attack Iraq.

Even in personalistic and authoritarian regimes the public can sometimes play an *indirect* role in affecting foreign policy. Especially when the state is weak or state elites are in a power struggle or when they fear the opposition can effectively use foreign policy issues against them, informal mechanisms of accountability may operate. The 'food riots' that were a region-wide response to 'structural adjustments' deterred regional responsiveness to pressures from international institutions and arguably slowed the region's integration into the world capitalist economy. When the public is aroused and unified by a crisis with Israel or the West, it may even play a role in forcing decisions that elites would not otherwise take. Thus, Sadat faced intense public despair at the 'no war – no peace' situation in the early 1970s, making even a risky war preferable to doing nothing; in Jordan when the public was intensely aroused by the 1967 and Kuwait crises, the same king who at other junctures defied the public was pushed by public pressures into policies at odds with the interests of his regime (Salloukh 1996). The case of Iran where the Shah's pursuit of policies in defiance of nationalist and Islamic opinion helped stimulate a revolution which turned those policies upside down is quite exceptional, but a precedent of which other leaders have not been unmindful.

Whether the impact of public opinion on foreign policy will increase as a result of the Arab Uprising and democratisation attempts in the Arab republics remains to be seen but it is bound to be constrained by both internal forces – the preferences of the 'deep state', particularly the security services – and external ones – the leverage given to Western states and IFIs from the dependencies generated by previous regimes. Thus, while the Egyptian public had high expectations that Egypt would recover its lost foreign policy sovereignty as a result of Mubarak's overthrow, little in fact changed.

Economics, business and foreign policy-making   The extent to which the business bourgeoisies of the Middle East act as a foreign policy pressure group is debatable. The Syrian bourgeoisie's opposition to Nasser's statist policies helped to engineer the break-up of the UAR and at the time Nasser reputedly perceived a comparable threat from its Egyptian counterpart (Dawisha 1976: 106), but this appears an exceptional case. Business is relatively weak, especially in the Arab world: the top 20 Middle East companies are in Israel, Turkey or are Gulf based oil-linked or banking firms. Rent and indirect taxation such as import duties relieve most states of dependency on the bourgeoisie for tax revenues, which might give the latter the leverage to demand a share of power, and business is often quite dependent on the state (for contracts, licences, etc.). Business lacks the institutionalised access and clout it enjoys in developed capitalist states: in the authoritarian republics, the military and bureaucracy and in the monarchies, royal families dominate foreign policy-making. Even in liberal states such as Israel and Turkey, business has still normally taken second place to the national security establishment in foreign policy matters, at least in times of crisis and on issues of high policy.

Nevertheless, the foreign policy choices that states make are intimately connected to their internal socio-economic structure, specifically the social composition of the ruling coalition, the resulting relation between the state and business and the logic of the development strategies these coalitions imply. Thus, in Marxist thinking, the trajectory of Third World states has been intimately shaped by the relative power of the internationalised 'comprador' bourgeoisie – bankers, import-exporters, agents for foreign firms – which is seen as a vehicle of Western influence versus that of the 'national bourgeoisie' – local industrialists – whose interests are compatible with an independent national economy (Hussein 1973). Where alliances of a radicalised military and a national bourgeoisie were ascendant, in the authoritarian republics in the 1960s, the latter's demands for protection from foreign competition overlapped with the former's desire to construct a base of national power. The nationalist foreign policy such an alliance asserted required easing or diversifying Western economic dependence – in the Cold War era by relying on the Soviet Union for aid, technology and markets.

By contrast, the oil monarchies incorporate alliances with tribal-commercial bourgeoisies which, living on petroleum rent, Western investments and middleman operations with the Western market, have a clear interest in pro-Western foreign policies. In states such as Egypt and Tunisia, the *infitah* bourgeoisie that arose from the time of the 1970s was likely to advocate the liberal foreign economic policies needed to establish an attractive investment climate and attract foreign partners; such bourgeoisies, integrated into globalised money markets, enjoyed leverage over governments from their ability to damage the local economy through capital flight. Where the top political elite are themselves major business operators and investors – the ruling families in the Gulf states, the Turkish military, the presidential clan in Tunisia – the personal ties and interlocking interests among overlapping political and business elites may be decisive.

A major issue is whether globalisation has increased the power of internationalised (*infitah*) bourgeoisies to advance the integration of the Middle East into the world economy and whether this was likely to spread the 'zone of peace' to the region since such economic integration arguably requires the resolution of regional conflicts and an end to nationalist challenges to the West. In fact, even where business has influence, it does not necessarily speak with one voice. While it might be expected that business would lobby for the enforcement of internationally accepted legal standards and for co-operation with the neo-liberal prescriptions of international economic institutions, it is by no means a monolithic champion of unrestrained global integration. On the contrary, it is likely to be divided between merchants and bankers with a stake in international trade and finance and local industrialists who flourish on state protection, subsidies and contracts. Crony capitalists will lack an interest in universalistic standards of law and regulation and favour a partial opening to the world market that still allows the politically connected to enjoy rent-yielding monopolies.

It is normally assumed that the economic interests of capitalists affect their stances on foreign policy issues but, just as their economic interests are competitive, not uniform, so they are not monolithic on many foreign policy issues. Most business elites are probably more pro-Western than other parts of the population because their interests tie them to Western markets and partners. They may be more dovish on war/peace issues than other parts of the population because peace, in reducing the role of the military, would increase their influence, and would provide a better investment climate and opportunity for foreign joint ventures. Leaders pursuing dovish policies usually attempt to co-opt business with promises of the new business opportunities improved external relations would encourage. Sadat pursued this policy, but initially Egyptian business was by no means an enthusiastic advocate of a separate peace with Israel, which threatened to isolate Egypt from the Gulf investors and Arab markets it needed. On the other hand, the Egyptian-American Business Association subsequently emerged as a powerful block with a stake in joint ventures with American firms and in the flow of American aid to Egypt that rewarded Sadat's separate peace. The emergence of crony capitalist post-populist regimes certainly increased the weight of such well-connected business interests; thus in the 2000s, the Egyptian-American Business Association acquired increasing clout in the ruling NDP and the neo-liberal government sponsored by Gamal Mubarak, which it used to deepen trans-state economic links to the US and Israel.

On the other hand, Syrian businessmen were often as nationalistic as other citizens and feared peace with Israel could bring Israeli economic competition, not just investment opportunities. Palestinian businessmen, insecure in the Diaspora and convinced that security for their wealth required a state of their own, funded the PLO (Smith 1986). Many Jordanian businessmen boycotted an Israeli trade fair to protest Israel's reversion to hard-line policies after Oslo. In fact, to the degree they are seeking Arab markets, Arab businessmen may be Pan-Arab nationalists and fear Israeli economic competition under peace.

In more liberal states such as Israel and in Turkey, where a more developed bourgeoisie is well organised in business associations such as the Turkish Association of Industrialists and Businessmen, the bourgeoisie appears better equipped to lobby for its interests as a class. The Turkish bourgeoisie, perhaps the most developed in the region apart from Israel, has an internationalist wing in partnership with MNCs and is a strong advocate of entry into the EU and a provincial Islamic wing. The latter, more oriented to the domestic market, provided support for the Islamic parties which called for Turkey's reorientation to regional Islamic markets; indeed, the rise of the AKP in Turkey increased its influence as the voice of the 'Anatolian Tigers' whose interests were reflected in Turkey's 2005–10 drive for economic integration with its Arab neighbours.

On the whole, Middle East business cannot yet be seen as an engine of 'internationalist coalitions' able to redefine states' foreign policy agendas.

The national security bureaucracies: the pivotal role of the military
The role of the military in the policy process carries greater weight in most Middle Eastern states than elsewhere. The military literally founded most of the authoritarian republics and remained the central pillar of these regimes; in 1999, presidents were officers or ex-officers in Egypt, Syria, Libya, Tunisia, Algeria, Yemen and Sudan. In most Middle Eastern states the military was, for a long time, the most developed, modernised and weighty institution in the political system.

The political role of Middle East militaries has, however, changed significantly over time. In earlier periods when traditional landed-commercial elites ruled, the military, recruited to a great extent from the rising middle classes, expressed their desire for the reform or overthrow of the old order, and the narrow-based old regimes offered little obstacle to military intervention in politics (Ayubi 1995: 258–260; Halpern 1963: 251–280; Trimberger 1978). However, as the military became politicised, it often fragmented along sectarian, regional, ideological or personal lines. Factions vying for political power destabilised Syria in the 1950s and 1960s and Iraq for a decade after the revolution of 1958. The military might be colonised by particularistic interests, as in Syria where the Alawi sect came, as a result of intra-military political struggles, to dominate the officer corps. Intra-military struggles often damaged the military as a fighting force, discrediting military involvement in politics; thus, the 1967 defeat discredited military politicians in both Egypt and Syria and enabled political leaders, themselves from the military, to appoint professional commanders who rebuilt military discipline. But it often took a power struggle for rulers to establish their authority over the military. In Egypt, for example, Sadat had to defeat challenges from several politicised officers. Saddam Hussein, a civilian, relied on the party and security forces to defeat or deter challenges from the military, often pre-empting them by purges and executions.

As state-building strengthened civilian institutions and authority of office, the vacuum that had originally encouraged military intervention was filled. The military relinquished overt political leadership in many states and became more professionalised, de-politicised and therefore more subordinated to quasi-civilian political control. Policy-makers were freed from the factional instability that had hitherto frustrated coherence in foreign policy-making. Nevertheless, the role of the military in policy-making remained central. Political leaders could not dispense with military support to acquire office and the propensity of the military to intervene in politics, though declining, required that rulers attend to its concerns or risk instability. The Minister of Defence, normally an officer, represented the military in the government as much, or more, than he ensured government control of the military. The high salience of national-security concerns and hence the influence of national security elites ensured that the de-militarisation of the polity remained within limits – even in Turkey and Israel. As the case of Turkey shows, even a professionalised military may reserve the prerogative to intervene in politics when the politicians are perceived to put national stability and security at risk. Militaries have usually considered themselves entitled to a decisive voice in matters of war and peace, and are self-appointed defenders of the borders and integrity of the state, whether from internal or external threats. Professionalised militaries routinely operate as pressure groups on behalf of arms purchases, and for better pay and conditions for soldiers, and their weight is enhanced by a continuing perception of high external or internal threat. Periodic cycles of modernisation needed to keep up with the new generation of weaponry mean the military's voracious appetite for scarce resources can never be sated, locking it into zero-sum conflicts with civilian groups over national budgets. In the 1980s when arms purchases were at their height, Iraq, Syria and Israel – all of which experienced wars – devoted 23%, 18% and 15% respectively of their GNPs to the military and

Saudi Arabia and Jordan 17% (Korany, Noble and Brynen 1993: 305). Egypt, Syria, Iran and Turkey had around a half million men under arms and Iraq a million. Moreover, the military everywhere extended its reach into the economy, becoming, to an extent, a state within a state, founding not only armaments industries but others aiming at self-sufficiency in everything from food to housing (Ayubi 1995: 270–273; Sayigh 1993; Zartman 1993: 249–254).

Perhaps most dramatic was the gradual transformation in the ideological outlook of militaries. In the 1950s and 1960s, young Arab officers were radical, modernising and nationalist in orientation; the Egyptian officer corps saw itself as 'defender of the revolution'. However, as the military became a pillar of ruling establishments, as it accumulated privileges and, especially, where it went into business 'on the side', the military elite became a main component of the state bourgeoisie with a stake in the status quo. Everywhere, as a result of this process, officer corps were de-radicalised, becoming less nationalist, less populist and more supportive of capitalism (Ayubi 1995: 273–276; Picard 1988). Moreover, because the military is typically secular and because mass opposition to regimes came to be expressed in Islamic terms, the military became the bastion of secularism against Islamic radicalism. This was apparent in Algeria, Egypt and Syria where the military repressed Islamist movements; the Egyptian military's overthrow of Muslim Brotherhood President Morsi is only the latest manifestation of this. Only in Iran was the military itself Islamised, although the top brass have had to fight off Islamic penetration of the lower ranks of the military elsewhere (Ayubi 1995: 264–265). However, the armies that once challenged imperialism or championed Pan-Arabism have for the most part become shields of state autonomy from societal challenges, often enforcing re-integration into the world capitalist market.

Nevertheless, there remained certain variations in the political orientation of Middle East armies and in their effect on the state's foreign policy, in good part owing to differences in their historic roles and bases of recruitment; this can be illustrated through a comparison of the Syrian and Turkish armies.

The military in Syria: persistence of a 'praetorian' army Syria is a case where a radicalised military led a revolution from above and where its special social composition – rural and plebeian – imparted a radical nationalist, populist thrust to the state, the residues of which long continued to make a difference for Syria's foreign policy orientation.

The radicalisation of the Syrian army was partly a function of its predominantly lower middle class and ex-peasant social composition. Recruitment under the French from the Alawi and Druze peasant minorities into the local military forces established a tradition of military service as a route out of poverty for them that continued after independence. The sons of the Sunni upper class, on the other hand, eschewed a military career (Van Dusen 1975: 124) and the small contingent of urban upper-class officers was decimated as a result of the purges following Western conspiracies against the nationalist government in the late 1950s (Seale 1965: 37, 48, 119).

The politicisation of the officer corps was a function of its formation in a time of nationalist ferment. The loss of Palestine, blamed on the corruption and incompetence of the traditional civilian elites, was the direct catalyst of army intervention in politics. In the face of the Israeli threat, the army was rapidly expanded and the military academy provided scholarships to bright underprivileged applicants; as a result, Sunnis from the provincial lower middle class and the peasantry were also increasingly recruited into the army. Indeed, by 1952, a majority of graduates were rurals. Particularly under the influence of the radical politician Akram al-Hawrani, youth entered the military academy with political motives: an army career began to be seen as a vehicle of political activism. The sons of impoverished Alawi small-holders or sharecroppers under Sunni landlords imbued with agrarian radicalism flocked to radical parties, notably the Ba'th, before entering the army. Subsequent developments, such as Israeli attacks on army positions at the front and the Suez war, reinforced and accelerated the radical politicisation of the officer corps. But political intervention split the army into factions in the 1950s and 1960s, making Syria the symbol of military praetorianism. It was from this crucible that a small group of Ba'thist officers carried out the 1963 coup that brought the Ba'th party to power (Devlin 1976: 204; Perlmutter 1969: 835).

From the moment Ba'thi officers brought the party to power, they were the senior partner in the new military-party state. In the first years after the power seizure, the Ba'thi 'military committee', a secret organisation of Ba'thist officers dominated by Alawis and Druze, acted as a unified body to extend its control over the army through massive purges and wholesale recruitment of politically loyal new elements, frequently Ba'thist teacher/reserve officers. This Ba'thisation of the army turned it into a rural and, increasingly, a minority stronghold. These officers also worked to achieve dominant roles in party and government institutions. The army's Ba'thisation infected it with all the Ba'th's internal conflicts while the militarisation of the Ba'th meant that such conflicts were decided as much by the command of tanks as by votes in party assemblies. The resultant recruitment, dismissal and promotion of officers on the basis of political loyalty displaced professional standards and as sectarian solidarity became a shorthand for loyalty, intra-Ba'th power struggles led to the decimation of non-Alawi groups in the army. Initially, Alawi officers appeared the most militantly radical force within the Ba'th, the most intense carriers of peasant grievances against the urban establishment. Their strong solidarity, as opposed to the more regionally and class-divided Sunni officers, accounts for their political ascendancy (Drysdale 1979; Rabinovich 1972; Van Dam 1981).

After a 1966 radical coup within the Ba'th regime, the victors tried to transform the military into an 'ideological army' committed to Ba'thism whose coercive power would give the regime the autonomy from the dominant classes necessary to launch the Ba'th revolution from above: indeed, in the following years the army repressed no less than seven major anti-regime urban disturbances by some combination of merchants aggrieved at state socialism and Islamists alienated by minority dominance. However, once the radical Ba'thists' politicisation of the army was discredited by its miserable performance in the 1967 war, they rapidly lost support among the officer corps. The moderate Ba'thist defence minister, General Hafiz al-Asad, asserted control over appointments and transfers in the name of rebuilding the army's professional standards and this allowed him to eliminate his rivals and seize power in 1970: when party authority and Asad's military command clashed, the latter triumphed easily (Van Dam 1981: 83–97).

Under Asad, the military, apparently triumphant, was gradually turned from a vehicle of regime change into one of several pillars of state subordinate to the presidency. As Drysdale (1979) points out, Asad pursued a dual policy in seeking to reconcile Ba'thist political control and military professionalism. On the one hand, praetorian guard units primarily charged with regime defence and certain coup-making armoured units were recruited on the basis of political loyalty and (Alawi) sectarian and kin affiliation. On the other hand, equally preoccupied with the conflict with Israel, Asad put a new stress on professional competence and discipline in the wider army and purged non-political officers were reinstated. Steadily expanding in size and benefiting from a 'cornucopia of sophisticated modern weapons', the reformed Syrian army acquitted itself respectably in subsequent conflicts with Israel (Drysdale 1979: 372; Picard 1988).

This strategy, together with the social and political congruence between the top political and military leadership, elaborate police surveillance of the army and its increasingly privileged position in society, helped Asad to end the long era of coups, an achievement crucial to his stabilisation of the Syrian state. Moreover, the steady expansion in the size and firepower of the military made violent opposition to the regime very costly, if not futile: the Alawi military showed the extremes to which it would go to protect the regime in its 1982 bombardment of an Islamic uprising in Hama. By the 1970s, the once radical officer corps had become an integral part of a new political establishment with a stake in the status quo. It was a powerful interest group advocating increased defence spending and especially influential on security issues and matters of war and peace with Israel. Senior politicised officers still manoeuvred to insert allies and clients into top party and government posts and ambitious politicians sought their backing. Ex-officers headed ministries and officers ran military-owned companies, were involved in smuggling rings or acted as brokers allocating state contracts and goods to clients (Picard 1988: 139–144). Seemingly immune from accountability, they became major obstacles to attempted reforms of the corruption and power abuses in the regime. Moreover, in alliance with the revived Damascene Sunni bourgeoisie, they came to constitute a 'military-mercantile complex' bridging the 'new' state and 'old' private bourgeoisies. Nevertheless, continued recruitment of the military from Alawi villages and sectarian barriers to intermarriage between Alawis and the Sunni bourgeoisie were major obstacles to amalgamation of these elites into a new unified upper class. Because the Sunni bourgeoisie was still better situated to benefit from manipulation of the market and the Alawis from exploitation of the public sector, the Alawi military remained a brake on the economic liberalisation which was integrating other Middle Eastern countries into Western-dominated markets. The military also retained a residual commitment to Arab nationalism and militancy toward Israel that was reflected in the country's foreign policy. The contrast between the Syrian military's continued loyalty to Bashar al-Asad amidst the Syrian uprising and the Egyptian military's unwillingness to repress mass protest against Mubarak reflected the lesser institutional autonomy and continued politicisation and selective communal recruitment of the Syrian compared to the Egyptian army.

The Turkish military: above and against society? In Turkey the military historically has had a strong sense of institutional identity. Its view of itself as the guardian of the interest of the state against particular societal concerns was manifested in three coups carried out against elected governments. But the social composition of the officer corps inevitably shaped its conception of this interest, which evolved over a century from a radical modernising to a conservative one.

The military became a key actor in defensive modernisation from the beginning of Ottoman reform when the defence of the empire became inseparable from its rapid modernisation against the resistance of 'traditional forces'. The military was a key support for modernising ministers and, when reform failed to ward off external threats, it became a vehicle for a more radical revolution from above under Ataturk that preserved while reshaping the state (Ahmad 1993: 3–4).

This does not mean that the army was isolated from and unreflective of society. Liberal versus radical cleavages among officers under the Young Turks and under Ataturk tended to reflect the social strata from which such factions were recruited. However, Ataturk used his prestige to insulate the military from politics, turning it into a reliable and professionalised instrument of his regime. Then, in the post-Ataturk period, the military assumed the role of defender of the Kemalist heritage, although its interpretation of Kemalism altered as its social composition changed (Ahmad 1993: 6–9).

The 1960 coup, launched in the name of defending the Kemalist revolution, was the last gasp of military radicalism. It was engineered by junior officers of provincial lower middle-class background resentful of the Democrat Party government – and of the co-opted top brass – which impugned the army's prestige and allowed inflation to so erode military salaries that officers experienced downward mobility even as the new business class was enriched (Ahmad 1993: 9–10, 121–125). The coup opened the door to a further democratisation of the political system and an opening to the left, which included allowing workers the right to strike and the formation of a socialist party.

This experience taught the military high command and the state establishment that the army had to be given a vested interest in the system if future revolts against senior officers were to be prevented. After the coup, centrist senior officers under General Gursel got the upper hand, radical officers were purged and the high command began the systematic policing of the political attitudes of the officer corps. The army's role as guardian of the state was institutionalised in the National Security Council in which the high command acquired the right to regular consultations with the cabinet. At the same time, the officer corps was turned into a privileged elite, enjoying high salaries, pensions and perks. Retried officers were recruited into state-run businesses and a military industrial complex emerged. The Army Mutual Assistance Association began investing officers' pension funds in private business, becoming the full or joint owner of auto, insurance and petrochemical companies, including a partnership with Renault of France. The officer corps thus became an extension of the bourgeoisie with a stake in stability and order. It became increasingly sympathetic to the conservative parties that advocated market capitalism and alienated from Ataturk's old Republican Peoples Party (RPP) as the latter reinvented itself as a social democratic party appealing to the middle and lower classes and took a stand for a more independent, less pro-NATO foreign policy. The 1971 coup, while made in the name of order, targeted the left while tacitly encouraging the forces of the right (Ahmad 1993: 130–132).

This tendency reached its full dimensions in the next 1981 coup under General Kenan Evren. The coup, according to Ahmad (1993: 174–80), in part reflected the growing responsiveness of the top military to US government perceptions and interests at a time when the Iranian revolution and the Soviet invasion of Afghanistan heightened the American need for a reliable ally in the region. The centre-right Demirel government was resisting US requests to situate its (anti-Iranian) rapid deployment force in Turkey, would not make the concessions to Greece needed to protect the cohesion of NATO's south-eastern flank, and was dependent on the anti-American Islamic Salvation Party. The military, bypassing the government, made concessions to Greece and forced the signing of a defence agreement with Washington, which restored military aid suspended over Cyprus. At the same time, Demirel began to implement an IMF austerity plan which removed subsidies, reduced protection for industry and started a shift from import-substitute industrialisation to the export strategy required to pay Turkey's debts; but massive worker strikes resisted this and the RPP and Islamic Salvation Party came together to oppose closer links to the West. This precipitated the coup that put an end to the 'disorder' that made Turkey seem a dubious ally for Washington. The military regime embraced the economic liberalisation and structural adjustment measures of Turgut Özal's new government and provided the repression of labour needed to enforce it. Foreign policy was reoriented to a close US alliance. A new constitution invested the military-dominated National Security Council with responsibility for protecting the integrity of the country and gave it the sole right to interpret its own mandate: in short, elected politicians became accountable to the military, not the reverse.

The military was not, however, a complete monolith. In the mid-1980s, as civilian rule was restored and Özal emerged as the dominant political leader, a new test of the political power of the military developed. An ambitious general and leader of the 1980 coup, Chief of Staff Necdet Urug, was positioning himself to succeed to the presidency after General Evren; contemptuous of civilians and little Westernised, he had antagonised Washington by objecting to some of its co-operation proposals. With US support – and that of President Evren – Özal passed over Urug's candidate to succeed him as chief of staff in favour of a Westernised general, and then – in a 'civilian coup' – had himself elected president instead of the expected military candidate. Similarly, when in 1992 the chief of staff resigned in protest at Özal's close alignment with the US against Iraq, the military was too divided to act. While it is usually the military that is united and the politicians divided, when the opposite is the case, the military can be restrained (Ahmad 1993: 213–218; Mufti 1998).

By the mid-1990s, however, the more usual situation had been restored: weak civilian governments faced a more politicised military seemingly united against perceived threats from the Kurdish insurgency and the rise of political Islam. The military not only carried out a virtual coup against the Islamist prime minister, Necmettin Erbakan, but bypassed the politicians in striking a close military alliance with Israel supposedly needed to win US support for the counter-insurgency against the Kurds. Links with Israel were also seen as crucial to the military's massive modernisation programme. The military appeared increasingly determined to impose its own conception of Turkey's national security needs on the political system.

However, in the 2000s, when the moderate Islamist Justice and Development Party (AKP) acquired unprecedented majorities in parliament in three successive general elections, the civilian prime minister Recep Tayyip Erdoğan was able to turn the tables on the military; he used trials of retired officers accused of plotting a coup to secure control over the military and neuter its political role and influence. A leader enjoying such a popular mandate was clearly in a better position to assert his authority than prime ministers presiding over weak coalition governments and fragmented parliaments, which had been typical from the 1970s. This appeared to radically reduce the role of the military in Turkey's foreign policy, opening the door for Prime Minister Erdoğan and his foreign minister to pursue an un-Kemalist like bid for leadership in the Arab world. This necessitated the jettisoning of the high-profile security alliance with Israel that the military brass had promoted; Erdoğan, with broad public support, was able to marginalise a relation that his Islamist predecessor, Erbakan, had been powerless to oppose.

Decision-making structures: variations in the concentration of power

The state structure – the features and coherence of institutions and the way they distribute power and channels of influence in the policy process – most immediately affects actual foreign policy choices.

In the Arab republics, often thought to approximate the leader-dominant model, the chief executive has enjoyed wide discretion and autonomy in foreign policy-making. Presidential dominance is typically enshrined in constitutional distributions of powers: the president has the main, if not the exclusive, right to conduct foreign policy and is commander-in-chief of the armed forces. He is little constrained by standard operating procedures or formal checks and balances.

Yet the president's actual ability to exercise his formal powers of office cannot be taken for granted. Even in Egypt, which has the most institutionalised presidency, presidential dominance within the top political elite was the product of power struggles in which the leader had to acquire enhanced personal stature or build sufficient coalitions in order to prevail. Nasser initially made policy in consultation with his Free Officer colleagues and it was only the growth of his personal charismatic stature, combined with the 1956 establishment of a constitution endowing the presidency with enormous powers, that elevated him above the rest of his colleagues; even then he continued to meet opposition from other Free Officers and had to rule by exploiting divisions among them (Cremeans 1963: 32–33; Dawisha: 1976: 104–105, 115, 117). Sadat, on assuming the office, immediately asserted Nasser's presidential prerogative. A major issue in the power struggle with left-wing Free Officers in the ruling party after Nasser's death was Sadat's insistence on his unilateral presidential right to make foreign policy decisions such as his offer to open the Suez Canal in return for a partial Israeli withdrawal from its banks and his decision to join the Federation of Arab Republics with Libya and Syria. In the showdown over presidential power, Sadat benefited from the respect of professional officers for the chain of command which the presidency headed, but he had also to build a supportive coalition of more conservative officers, bureaucrats and elements of the Westernised bourgeoisie and he only prevailed because his rivals lacked effective links to their potential constituents among the Nasserite masses. Although Sadat's purge of these rivals gave him a freer hand, before the October 1973 war he still lacked the legitimacy to take the biggest decisions alone; as such, the planning and decision to launch this war was made in close consultation with the military and political elite (Korany 1986: 96–99). Even after the war consolidated his stature, Sadat was only able to pursue his intensely personal course toward a separate peace with Israel by a wily step-by-step policy. Had he revealed at the outset that he sought such an end – if indeed he did – much of the Egyptian political elite might well have combined against him; however, his first steps along this path – the decisions to seek a diplomatic settlement and a US opening to balance the Soviet alliance – were acceptable to all but hard-line Nasserites. Further steps along the road – expulsion of the Soviet advisors, the decision to launch a merely limited war in the Sinai – had the support of a majority of the elite. The final steps, however – the first disengagement and second disengagements with Israeli forces in the Sinai, the final break with the Soviets, and Camp David – were presented by Sadat to the elite as *fait accompli*, each of which further enmeshed Egypt in a web of commitments while narrowing alternative options (Hinnebusch 1985: 65–69). Sadat's successor, Mubarak, faced no similar challenge within elite ranks, but nevertheless moved, in his first decade, toward the centre of elite opinion, paying lip-service, at least, to Nasser's heritage, before moving, in the 1990s and thereafter, further along the Western-dependent path initiated by Sadat; however his neo-liberal course and the grooming of his son, Gamal, to succeed him, opened up rifts with the military leadership which help explain its failure to defend him against the popular uprising of 2011. President Morsi never consolidated his authority against the military-led 'deep state' and hence made little headway in altering Mubarak's tangent. In Syria, Bashar al-Asad was constrained for the first half-decade after his 2000 succession by power sharing between the presidency and the Ba'th party collegial leadership where the 'old guard', the elder generation brought to power by his father, were concentrated. However, he was able to use presidential powers of dismissal and appointment to consolidate his control over the army and security services before moving to engineer the retirement of the party old guard at a 2005 national party conference.

Where the president's authority is consolidated, he does normally dominate decision-making. However, in some cases a more collegial or factionalised 'bureaucratic politics' (Allison and Halpern 1972) may give other elites, speaking for rival branches of the bureaucracy – army, ruling party, foreign ministry, national security council, intelligence services, etc. – opportunities to influence decision-making. Normally, these rival branches of the state seek to advance their own particular role, budgets and solutions, with the chief executive choosing between them. Episodes of conflict between ideological parties and the army were salient in late Nasserite Egypt (the so-called centres of power), in pre-1970 Ba'thist Syria and in post-independence Algeria. Even where bureaucratic politics is more muted, presidents may wish to consult within the elite in order to generate a maximum consensus behind controversial or risky policies, and a national security council may regularise such consultation. The president's national security advisors, who

may be part of his *shilla* – his network of long-time close personal supporters – may exploit their personal relations with him
in the battle over policy. While the council of ministers (cabinet)
normally discusses a decision after the leader has taken it and is
basically a policy implementing body, bureaucratic politics plays a
role in shaping the 'normal' day-to-day administration of foreign
relations in which the leader's commands may be variously interpreted or distorted by his subordinates. That being said, the scope
for bureaucratic politics in the authoritarian republics is normally
strictly limited: other elites, typically being the 'president's men',
are less likely than in more pluralistic states to identify with the
interests of their organisations or to enjoy the support to make
them power bases from which to stand up to the president; this, in
turn, reflects the lesser institutionalisation of the state in the Middle
East (Ayubi 1994: 35; Korany 1986: 52–56).

This is even more true of parliaments and the committees of ruling
parties, which, subservient to the president, are seldom able to do
more than approve executive initiatives. For example, although the
Egyptian parliament acquired more power under Sadat's limited
political liberalisation, he brushed aside numerous attempts by a
near parliamentary consensus, remarkable in a body dominated
by the government party, to restrain his march toward a separate
peace. These included resolutions to give the Arab Defence Pact
priority over the peace treaty with Israel, to make normalisation
of relations contingent on a comprehensive settlement, and to link
it to the West Bank autonomy provided for in the Camp David
accords. Eventually, a fed-up Sadat dissolved this parliament and
made sure elections to its successor eliminated all leading critics
(Hinnebusch 1985: 175).

In some of the Arab monarchies and in the more pluralist
regimes, foreign policy-making is likely to be more collegial than in
the authoritarian republics. In the monarchies, the extended ruling
families often constitute an informal consultative group to which
the monarch is expected to listen and senior royal princes simultaneously head the various national security bureaucracies. In more
democratic states, such as Israel and Turkey, power is more diffused among senior cabinet ministers and military officers, the foreign policy professionals have more influence, and parliaments have
more power to hold the executive accountable. In Israel, where
the cabinet, in which each minister has one vote, must approve

strategic decisions, prime ministers, notably Ben Gurion and Begin, were on several occasions restrained by fellow ministers (Brecher 1972: 211, 228, 280). In semi-pluralist Iran, power is diffused between the spiritual leader, the president and parliament. Aspects of bureaucratic politics have more scope to operate in pluralist regimes, especially when the top elite is factionalised, and although the chief executive normally has the last word, he or she may have to arbitrate between opposing factions or make concessions to other elites to maintain their support.

Variations in the concentration of power, in the extent of bureaucratic politics, and in the range and character of actors included in the policy process inevitably shape the character of policy outcomes. The typically limited access to the policy process in most Middle East states may narrow the alternatives considered and bias the policies adopted. Foreign ministries in principle provide much of the information and diplomatic skills needed for the conduct of foreign policy but in the Middle East they are, by world standards, weak in professionalism, resources and influence over foreign policy. This means a lack of institutional support (policy analysis and planning) for decision-makers and limited institutional memory to ensure policy continuity. Especially in the authoritarian republics, the foreign minister is likely to be a client of the leader without an independent power base, who can be dismissed with ease, and thus cannot present an independent institutional view. Even in Egypt, the Arab state with the most professional diplomatic corps, the extent to which the president is guided by the foreign minister is, according to Boutrus Boutrus Ghali (1963: 320), who served under Nasser, a matter of his personal choice; the ministry as an institution chiefly deals with day-to-day transactions (Ayubi 1994: 8–9, 14). If the diplomats are undervalued, the role of the security and intelligence services is everywhere central to foreign policy-making because intelligence bosses are sometimes major political actors and because they are pivotal in the monitoring of both external and internal threats. The exceptions to this picture are only partial. In Turkey the foreign ministry enjoys high prestige and in Israel it is highly professional; yet in both states the military, ex-military politicians and the intelligence services nevertheless frequently overshadow the diplomats. The limited influence of professional foreign policy establishments, together with the dominance of the policy process by military and intelligence bureaucrats, may give special weight to the advocates of the use of force over negotiation in achieving ends and to 'national security' considerations over other issues, such as economic interests or identity, in the policy process.

The over-concentration and personalisation of power so typical of Middle Eastern states is widely thought to threaten the rationality of decision-making. It may mean a lack of checks on the ability of leaders to translate their idiosyncratic choices into policy. It may obstruct the channelling of sufficient information and policy alternatives to the top decision-makers, making them more prone to miscalculation. Yet the ideal of a rational actor implies a unified leadership and, where the elite is fragmented by competing factions not effectively reconciled by the top decision-maker, foreign policy issues may become weapons in the domestic political struggle. The outcome may therefore represent less a rational plan to achieve some geopolitically defined national interest than a reflection of the intra-elite power balance at a given moment. Rationality would seem to be enhanced by a process that combines enough pluralism in the policy process to secure sufficient input into it with a reasonably unified leadership enjoying the legitimacy to make decisions free of constant worries about the domestic power struggle; but this balance appears to be the exception rather than the rule.

There do not, however, seem to be hard and fast rules. The personalisation of power in Iraq under Saddam led to disastrous miscalculations. In Syria, by contrast, the fragmentation of the pre-Asad Ba'th regime encouraged the factionalist outbidding which led to the cataclysmic 1967 war, while, after Asad's personalisation of power, foreign policy was widely seen to approximate the rational actor model. Sadat's personalisation of foreign policy allowed him to pursue a high-risk policy, which, overriding the caution of his bureaucrats and advisors, permitted key breakthroughs in reaching peace with Israel. But as a result, mistakes, such as the total break with the Soviet Union and the excessive reliance on the US, were not corrected. Three successive foreign ministers resigned in protest over Sadat's tactics in the negotiations with Israel in which he made seemingly impulsive concessions on matters he considered trivial but which they regarded as crucial. In the Camp David negotiations, Sadat's lack of accountability to other elites or the public meant he could not claim to be constrained by them from making concessions. By contrast, Begin's bargaining hand was strengthened by his claim to be more constrained by his slim parliamentary majority and his hard-line party in Israel's more accountable political system (Telhami 1990: 157–195). Nevertheless, the personality of the leader and whether it is appropriate to the 'needs' of the period may be as important a variable in determining the rationality of decisions as is the character of the policy process.

The idiosyncratic variables: how much difference does the leader make?

While an uncritical concentration by foreign policy analysts on the leader has been rightly criticised (Korany and Dessouki 1991: 8–9), where domestic political systems are in transition, as in the Middle East, institutions and standard operating procedures which might constrain the leader are not well established and, indeed, may be the recent creations of the leader himself. Where society lacks strong interest groups or classes, where the tradition of patrimonial rule prescribes loyalty to the person of the ruler and where legitimacy depends on his role as a hero, especially in foreign policy, the leader is more likely to shape public opinion than to be constrained by it (Ayubi 1994: 6–7). The relative absence of institutionalised checks on leaders in the Middle East does not mean there are no informal domestic constraints or pressures on them; the leader inherits the foreign policy role conception of his country which affects his perceptions and preferences and the preservation of regime legitimacy may depend on foreign policy performance in the service of this role (Dawisha 1990). But rather than being sharply constrained by such roles, leaders, to a considerable extent, construct or re-construct them or implement them in idiosyncratically distinct ways.

To the extent that foreign policy-making is exceptionally personalised in the Middle East, a state's foreign policy performance is more dependent on the leader's personal style, capabilities, values, goals, strategies, perceptions – and misperceptions – than in more institutionalised states. Choices, particularly in a crisis or a critical bargaining situation wherein policy-making tends to be especially centralised, are inevitably to some extent idiosyncratic. The relative weight of and role of the idiosyncratic variable can be assessed by comparing different leaders in the same state facing similar situations (Nasser vs. Sadat) and different leaders in similar states in the same time frame (Asad vs. Saddam).

From Nasser to Sadat To what extent did the change in Egypt's leadership from Nasser to Sadat explain the radical change in Egypt's foreign policy after 1970 – specifically the turn from the USSR to the US and from Pan-Arabism to a separate peace with Israel? Nasser had, it is often argued, started the changes, in his acceptance of the Rogers Plan for a peaceful settlement with Israel under American auspices, which Sadat would take to their logical conclusions. Nevertheless, this decision would not necessarily lead to a separate peace and, indeed, such an outcome would arguably have been incongruent with Nasser's personality.

Nasser was, from his youth, a rebel against a world where unjust force was perceived to govern (Ayubi 1994: 92–93). According to Wynn, the humiliation Nasser experienced from being looked down on for his *baladi* (plebeian) background sparked a psychological drive to make himself and his people proud, not ashamed, to be Egyptians (Dawisha 1976: 108). As a *saidi*, a product of upper Egypt's stress on honour and manhood, Nasser was, Dawisha argues, 'almost obsessed' with personal dignity and extremely sensitive to slights. He believed Egypt and the Arabs needed a hero who would battle against superior malevolent powers and he sought this role. It should not be imagined that Nasser's policy simply grew out of irrational or emotional flaws. At a time when most of his Free Officer colleagues were Egypt-firsters, Nasser was the Free Officer with a strategic regional vision, convinced that only together could the Arab states ward off the imperialist and Israeli threats (Seale 1965: 193, 225). His experience in power convinced him, after a period in which he sought accommodation with the West, that the West's interests in the reinforcement of Israel and control of Middle East oil were fundamentally at odds with those of the Arabs (Dawisha 1976: 125). But his personality traits lent a particular intensity and tenacity to his anti-imperialist orientation. This orientation was, moreover, powerfully reinforced when Nasser's defiance of the West sparked enormous enthusiasm from the Pan-Arab public; Nasser's charisma grew out of the correspondence between his own experience and that of the man in the street, between his personal values and the dominant mass value system of the time (Dawisha 1976: 129). Once he became a charismatic hero, his personal dignity and Egypt's became, to him, inseparable. Nasser's deepest instinct when challenged was to go on the offensive, to seize the psychological initiative needed to recapture the imagination and enthusiasm of his followers (Kerr 1971: 27, 29). He would not give in to superior power under threat and sought, instead, to mobilise new resources to reconfigure the power balance. He was ready to take risks rather than accept humiliation: the Suez Canal nationalisation, the Yemen intervention, the events leading up to the 1967 war and the War of Attrition were all partly calculated risks, partly emotional reactions to challenges (Dawisha 1976: 92–93, 95–107).

The stunning defeat of 1967 was Nasser's greatest reversal; but his immediate response was a defiant call for the Arabs not to relinquish the fight against imperialism (Dawisha 1976: 50). Nasser could not abandon his role as Arab hero or give up dignity by submitting to American or Israeli power. He was prepared for a just political settlement but was deeply sceptical of American intentions; US arms deliveries were maintaining Israeli superiority while Israel rejected any return to the 1967 lines. Believing that, in a world where force was respected, one could not negotiate from a position of weakness, he launched a major overhaul and expansion of the armed forces and, in the War of Attrition, contested Israel's hold on the Sinai peninsula (Dawisha 1976: 56–57); only when he had thereby partly righted the power imbalance did he accept the Rogers Plan and a ceasefire.

Had Nasser lived, he would have faced similar constraints to those faced by Sadat and, as an experienced strategist, was pragmatic enough to have similarly mixed diplomacy and concession with military force in seeking to roll back the Israeli occupation (Kerr 1971: 156). But his intense anti-imperialism and the psychological difficulty of reversing the principles on which his heroic Pan-Arab role rested limited his flexibility in pursuing partial diplomatic solutions while his history of conflict with Israel and the US made them little interested in accommodating him. To the end, he rejected a separate solution (Dekmejian 1971: 99–101; Vatikiotis 1978: 266–309). Had Nasser not died young, Egyptian policy in the post-1973 peace process would arguably have more closely resembled that of Syria under Asad and have been pursued in co-ordination with Syria. Whether this would have resulted in a comprehensive settlement is debatable but it might have preserved the Arab leverage that was dissipated by Israel's ability to divide its opponents.

However much Egypt's deteriorating economic and military situation may have made Anwar al-Sadat a man appropriate to his

time, his policies were by no means inevitable for, far from express-
ing an intra-elite consensus, he repeatedly made decisions in defiance of elite opinion and these were quite distinct from those of
his predecessor: if, when facing superior power, Nasser's instinct
was to 'balance' against it, Sadat's was to 'bandwagon' with it.
Arguably also Sadat's personality traits and personal style made
a decisive difference in Egypt's negotiating stances and the sub-
optimal separate peace reached with Israel. As Ajami suggests, his
desire to be accepted by the West led him into wishful thinking.
According to his Foreign Minister, Ismail Fahmy, he was 'con-
sumed by his desire to become an international hero' in Western
eyes and Kissinger is said to have admitted that Sadat squandered
the leverage from the 1973 war and the oil embargo out of a weakness to be acclaimed as a 'hero of peace'. He personalised relations
between states, naively convinced that his embrace of American
leaders, including his 'friend Henry' [Kissinger], would be enough to
change America's pro-Israeli policy. His eagerness to jettison Soviet
support and rely totally on American diplomacy was an eccentri-
cally personal choice that appalled his professional foreign policy
advisors. To Sadat, the Russians were 'crude and tasteless people'
while Egypt's alienation from the US was unnatural, not the result
of a conflict of national interests but a matter of misunderstanding
(which he would put straight) or a product of Egypt's Soviet alliance
(which he would abandon) or of Israel's influence (which could be
overcome by embracing a US alliance). This craving for acceptance
by the West was, paradoxically, paralleled by over-confidence. A
big picture thinker, uninterested in details, Sadat completely lacked
Nasser's voracious appetite for information and did not like reading
the reports of his foreign policy advisors. Seeing himself as a 'master
of decision' whose 'electric shock diplomacy' would upset the Arab–
Israeli status quo, he was unwilling to heed the advice of the foreign
policy professionals and enjoyed surprising them by his personal
initiatives. In negotiations over Sinai I and Sinai II, the disengagement agreements with Israel after the 1973 war, he excluded his
top advisers from key sessions with United States Secretary of State
Henry Kissinger and overrode their objections to many details of the
agreements, disregarding the warning of his senior general that these
agreements would forfeit the military option. He made his momentous decision to go to Jerusalem without even bothering to create
an elite consensus behind him and allowed his top generals little

say at Camp David (Ajami 1981: 102, 109–116; Dessouki 1991: 168–171; Fahmy 1983: 14, 72–74, 136–137, 173–175, 283–290; Heikal, 1978a: 75–79, 113–116; Heikal 1983: 71; Karawan 1994: 250, 257; Sadat 1978: 93–95, 107–119).

Telhami's analysis (1990) of the bargaining at Camp David gives sharper focus to the impact of the idiosyncratic factor. While Telhami accepts that the power asymmetry with Israel was decisive in forcing Egypt to seek a negotiated solution, he argues that the role of leadership in the bargaining process decided the exact terms of the settlement in Israel's favour. At Camp David and thereafter, Israel got all that it wanted – a peace treaty which took Egypt out of the Arab–Israeli conflict and left it free to incorporate the West Bank/Gaza area – while Egypt failed to get recognition of the principle of Palestinian rights, failed to link normalisation of relations with Israel to progress on the Palestinian front, and failed even to get a freeze on Israeli settlements during the negotiations over Palestine. Had Egypt been more successful in its diplomacy, it might not have had to sacrifice its Arab leadership to attain peace.

Bargaining theory advises keeping the opponent uncertain of your bottom line position. But Sadat had a history of making concessions in advance. At his first meeting with Kissinger, he reputedly declared that he was finished with the Soviets and that Egypt had fought its last war with Israel (Heikal 1983: 75); in 1978 he told Israeli Defence Minister Ezer Weizman that he would make peace whether or not Israel conceded a Palestinian state (Fahmy 1983: 289). At Camp David, he told President Carter he would be flexible on Egypt's official demands for a comprehensive peace; predictably, once the Israelis learned this, they became more unyielding. Theory also advises that the top man should not negotiate alone or settle the details and should allow subordinates who have limited authority to prepare the way, but Sadat personally negotiated everything. Sadat's wishful thinking, his unwillingness to engage in a sustained power struggle with Prime Minister Begin and his overconfidence led him to rely on Carter to secure him an acceptable outcome.

By contrast, Begin was a strategic thinker who never lost sight of his strategic dream of a Greater Israel incorporating the West Bank. Yet he kept his eye on the details and never let his bottom line be known. He bargained stubbornly, starting from an extreme position, i.e. making such a fuss over retaining Israel's Sinai settlements that he diverted attention from other issues and was able to give the impression that he had made a big concession when he gave way on the issue. So stubborn was Begin that when Carter faced dead-lock, he went to Sadat for concessions – and got them. According to Telhami, Sadat failed to understand that Begin also needed and wanted a deal and hence gave in too readily to what would be a separate peace. After Camp David, Sadat's yearning to be the hero of peace made him so impatient with diplomatic bargaining over the Egyptian–Israeli peace treaty that he undermined the efforts of Egyptian negotiators to establish a firm linkage between the treaty and the actualisation of the accompanying autonomy agreement for the Palestinians: Sadat destroyed their hand when he let it be known he would proceed with the former without the latter (Heikal 1983: 74–75; Telhami 1990: 157–195).

It is not that Sadat's personality wholly explains the course Egypt took; much of the foreign policy establishment – even Nasser for that matter – constrained by Egypt's limited resources, would have adopted similar strategies of trying to manipulate the superpowers to obtain a negotiated settlement with Israel; where Sadat made the difference was the poor hand he played in this game and the sub-optimal outcome he achieved.

Asad vs. Saddam Syria and Iraq in the 1970s and 1980s were ruled by branches of the same party and had similar leader-army-party authoritarian regimes that professed the same ideology of Arab nationalism. Both Hafiz al-Asad and Saddam Hussein rose to power from the lower strata of society and the socialisation of both took place in the heady days of Nasserism. Both were men of pride and self-confidence, intolerant of opposition. Both enjoyed near-absolute power over foreign policy-making. But there the similarity ends. Their foreign policy decisions could hardly have led to more contrasting outcomes. Asad turned Syria from a victim of stronger neighbours into a formidable player that was generally thought to punch above its weight in foreign affairs. Iraq, on the other hand, enjoyed the most balanced combination of power resources in the Arab world, but, Saddam Hussein, in the course of two devastating wars, dissipated these resources and turned Iraq into a victim-ised pariah state. Do the personalities and attitudes of the leaders explain a significant part of this different outcome?

According to Seale (1988: 492–495), Asad was 'a man of 1967': his harrowing experience when, as defence minister, he saw his unprepared forces mauled in a war brought on by the recklessness of ideological-minded colleagues decisively shaped his outlook. He learned 'realism' which he compared with the 'ideology' of the pre-1970 Ba'th radicals who, fatally neglecting the balance of power, gave Israel an excuse to attack Syria. With a strong sense of Syria's limited resources, aware that he could not afford to make a mistake, that, in Seale's words, at every stage he risked being knocked out of the game, Asad developed qualities necessary for battle in a tough environment. According to Ma'oz (1988: 32, 34, 41–42), Asad demonstrated a 'winning' combination of traits: consistency, patience, caution, coolness and shrewdness. Aided by his huge capacity for work and excellent memory, he never succumbed to wishful thinking or moved without a thorough analysis of the balance of forces. He was ruthless but used violence with economy, while reserving the carefully calibrated use of military force for the right time and place.

Saddam Hussein was almost the opposite kind of personality: a man of 'pent-up violence' with little sense of limits. Having begun his career as a street fighter, his courage and fearlessness gave him a reputation as a *shaqawah* – a tough man to be feared. He rose to power through a combination of conspiracy, organisation and violence, including the Stalinist-like terror and purge of all who stood in his way. Saddam admitted to an admiration for Stalin and his favourite movie was said to be *The Godfather*. It may not be an exaggeration to say that he epitomised a political culture where personal strength and ruthlessness enjoyed high respect, arguably reflective of the Iraqi yearning for order amidst the chronic instability that followed the 1958 revolution. In foreign affairs, Saddam proved to be a high risk taker with grandiose ambitions sought through resort to violence. Arguably, Saddam externalised in the international realm the violent political methods that had served him so well at home. But he overestimated the international permissiveness for such methods and repeatedly miscalculated the will and capacity of his opponents – Ayatollah Khomeini, President Bush – to oppose his plans. For example, expecting Iran to quickly submit, he had no fall-back strategy once his initial attack failed to unseat Khomeini (Devlin 1992: 1052; Khalil 1989: 118–120; Marr 1985: 218–220; Miller and Mylroie 1990: 24–41).

It is hard to escape the conclusion that leadership does indeed make a big difference. Outcomes therefore depend on whether the leaders' qualities match the requirements of the external situations in which they operate. Sadat was a wishful thinker who under-played his hand and was victimised by the stronger personalities of his rivals, Asad and Begin were rational actors best able to combine limited goals with flexible means, while Saddam's risk-taking led to gross miscalculation that squandered Iraq's power. The differential results of their policies validate the realist maxim that success in international politics depends on the prudent and effective use of power. But the differences in their uses of power appear so largely idiosyncratic that the concern with leadership psychology and perceptions in foreign policy analysis seems vindicated.

6

Comparative foreign policies: historical sociology explanations for foreign policy variation

What explains the similarities and differences in the foreign policy behaviour of Middle East states? The relative explanatory weight carried by domestic politics versus that of the systemic arenas in which states operate is a matter of some dispute between pluralists, liberals and Foreign Policy Analysis, on the one hand, and realists and structuralists on the other. On the face of it, if the domestic level is determinant, different kinds of states should follow different foreign policies and similar ones similar policies. If the systemic level is determinant, a state's domestic features should make little difference, at least over the long run; similar systemic situations – power position, economic dependency – of initially domestically dissimilar regimes should drive a convergence in their foreign policies while differing systemic situations should pull initially similar regimes in divergent directions. Moreover, as, over time, to the extent the regional system moves toward a Westphalian system of consolidated states wherein internal threats are muted and external ones enhanced, the system's capacity to drive a convergence of its 'parts' toward 'realist' behaviour should increase.

Neither view is wholly supported by the empirical evidence from the Middle East. Rather, as historical sociology would anticipate, neither state features or systemic forces alone but the *interrelation* between a state's specific position in systemic structures and its particular internal features determines its foreign policy behaviour. More broadly, MENA states' formation was initially the product of the interaction of systemic forces, above all the initial flawed formation of the regional system under Western imperialism, and at the regional level *either* nationalist resistance or elite collaboration. Then, in a second moment, each state's specific initial formation, shaping its ruling coalition, structure (regime type) and identity, tended to put it on a particular (status quo or revisionist) foreign policy tangent. Subsequently, systemic forces – the balance of power, economic dependency, trans-state ideological tides – might deflect it from this course. However, its level of consolidation – a domestic variable – determined whether it remained a victim of its systemic environment or became an effective actor in it; at the same time, a state's consolidation might well be shaped by the resources it could access from the international system. Finally, decision-makers, by virtue of their location at the intersection of the systemic and the domestic, can make choices that set states on new tangents; in particular, if the ruling coalition is transformed, identity, hence the perception of threats may radically alter. This argument about the interaction of system and state levels will be illustrated by comparative case studies of divergence and convergence in foreign policy.

Regime origins and the limits of convergence: Saudi Arabia and Syria

Comparison of a conservative rentier monarchy, Saudi Arabia, with Syria, a radical republic, highlights both the enduring effects of contrasting state formation paths in differentiating foreign policy tangents and the extent to which systemic forces make for convergence in behaviour.

Origins of the state

Saudi Arabia was founded by the al-Saud clan's dual mobilisation of tribal military power and the Wahhabi Islamic movement. Unlike most Middle Eastern countries, the state was, thus, founded by indigenous forces, never experienced an imperialist occupation or protectorate and was therefore spared the accompanying collaboration with imperialism that often discredited traditional elites. This does not mean that Saudi state-building was a wholly indigenous product, for the impoverished Arabian peninsula lacked the economic surplus to sustain more than ephemeral states and formation of a stable state depended on assistance from Western powers (Gause 1994: 22, 30, 42). The British provided state founder, Abd al-Aziz Ibn Saud, with subsidies and the military means to discipline the militant Ikhwan wing of his Wahhabi coalition which wanted to carry on jihad against British client states in the region. The

American oil companies provided him with the financial resources to incorporate unruly tribes into state-centred patronage networks. Thus, external powers endowed the al-Saud regime with the hallmarks of statehood – territorial demarcation and internal security – in return for eschewing Wahhabism's universalistic Islamic mission. To minimise his consequent dependency, Ibn Saud sought to play off his British and American benefactors. But the Saudi state was, from the outset, secure enough in its Islamic identity and autonomy to pursue close mutually beneficial relations with the West (Bromley 1994: 142–147; Salame 1989).

Saudi Arabia's main vulnerability was a function of its large, sparsely settled territory, with long, difficult-to-defend borders, in a dangerous region where the balance of power favoured the more settled developed states. Once its oil reserves made it a potential target of stronger states, insecurity became a constant in Saudi policy. In addition to seeking external protection, the Saudis played the regional balancing game, initially aligning with Syria and Egypt against the Hashemite states to ward off their schemes for Arab unity or revenge for the Saudis' conquest of the Hijaz at their expense. Then, much as today, the main threat to the al-Saud was from regional, not Western, powers. The combination of satisfaction with its statehood, beneficial relations with the West and a sense of threat from the region made Saudi Arabia a naturally status quo power.

Syria, by contrast, was born frustrated and revisionist. In the wake of the 1917 Arab revolt, Syrians expected the creation of an independent Arab state in historic and geographical Syria (*bilad al-sham*) linked to a wider Arab federation. Instead, betraying their promises to the Arabs, the Western powers subjugated the Arab East and dismembered historic Syria into four mini-states, Syria, Jordan, Lebanon and Palestine. Imperialism also sponsored the establishment of the state of Israel in Palestine. Thereafter, a powerful revisionism was rooted in the impulse to merge the Syrian state, seen as an artificial creation of imperialism, in a wider Arab nation and in the utter rejection of the legitimacy of Israel.

The newly independent Syrian state was, however, weak, insecure and the victim of acute domestic instability. It was fragmented, with a multitude of ethnic and sectarian groups. It was governed by a narrow-based traditional oligarchy that suffered a mortal blow to the precarious legitimacy won in the independence struggle when the government failed to defend Palestine against the 1948 establishment of Israel. This weak state was exposed on all sides to countries which, at one time or another, constituted threats. The threat from Israel was particularly keenly felt as Syrian–Israeli animosity escalated from 1948 onward, feeding on border skirmishes over the de-militarised zones left over from the war. Syria was also the object of Hashemite ambitions to absorb it via the Greater Syria or Fertile Crescent unity schemes. Stronger Arab states financed and backed rival Syrian elites and the coups that changed governments while all Syrian players looked for patronage and protection abroad. It was a combination of this vulnerability and its Arab identity that led Syria to sacrifice its sovereignty to Egypt by joining the United Arab Republic in 1958 (Seale 1965: 5–15: Mufti 1996: 43–59).

Political mobilisation

The era of political mobilisation impacted differentially on the two states, propelling them further in contrasting directions, with Saudi Arabia containing threats to its status quo orientation and Syrian revisionism reaching a peak.

Saudi Arabia faced the 'King's Dilemma' which proved fatal for several Middle East monarchies: how to modernise, yet prevent the new social forces created by modernisation from destroying the traditional order (Huntington 1968: 177–191). In the 1950s and 1960s, the regime was vulnerable to Pan-Arab ideology manipulated from Cairo as the small, educated, new middle class and the working class in the oil fields, attracted by Nasser, embraced Arabism and reform. The al-Saud had, however, enough traditional legitimacy and enough resources from oil revenues to combine limited modernisation in the economic and technical spheres with the preservation of the traditional culture and political order.

Crucially, the regime incorporated conservative social forces, enjoying the support of the tribal elite, which controlled the tribal masses, and the *ulama* that legitimised the regime among the people (Gause 1994: 158). A capitalist class emerged but rather than a 'national bourgeoisie' with an interest in industrialisation and reform, it was satisfied with the status quo, including Saudi connections to the West. Its dominant firms started as trading companies enriched as importers and agents for foreign firms: the Alirezas were agents for Ford or Westinghouse, the Juffaili were guarantors for foreign contractors while Adnan Khashoggi made his fortune brokering Western arms contracts. The bourgeoisie invested much of its surplus in Western banks and real estate. The requirement that Western companies have local partners widened this parasitic bourgeoisie during the oil boom of the 1970s (Vassiliev 1998: 404–412, 461).

Also crucial to the survival of the Saudi regime was its ability to bring under control the two groups that were the potential vehicles of opposition, the military and organised labour. There was a string of coup attempts by Arab nationalist middle-class officers in the 1950s and 1960s. The air force, which was most exposed by its higher education to politicisation, was particularly vulnerable: thus, Saudi pilots sent to support Yemeni royalists defected to Egypt in the 1960s and, as late as 1977, an Islamic/Libyan inspired plot was crushed. Such periodic threats only fuelled the regime's distrust of its own military, the most common vehicle of regime change in the Middle East. The al-Saud sought to control the military by keeping it small and balancing it with a tribally recruited National Guard. Pakistani mercenary units were imported and royal princes trained in the West packed the air force officer corps (Gause 1994: 123–126; Vassiliev 1998: 368–372). Organised labour, concentrated in the oil fields, which became a crucible of Arab nationalist and leftist opposition in the 1950s and 1960s, was controlled by repression. Strikes of oil workers in 1953 and 1956, which challenged the regime's pro-Western foreign policy, were brutally suppressed – including the flogging to death of two pro-Nasserite labour leaders.

At first, the al-Saud tried to use foreign policy to appease Nasser and the nationalist middle class by diluting its overt Western alignment. As Nasser became more threatening, however, Saudi policy moved from bandwagoning with Cairo to balancing, together with the Hashemite monarchies and the West, against Cairo. When Nasser's ideological threat became a more concrete military one after the Egyptian army was sent to protect the republican revolution in Yemen, King Feisal responded with closer military links to the US (Dawisha 1979: 1–5; Vassiliev 1998: 350–353).

In *Syria*, by contrast, radical forces successfully challenged and swept away the old order. Oligarchic-dominated political institutions failed to absorb the political mobilisation of the middle class and to address the growing agrarian unrest from the country's extremely unequal land tenure structure. The military, expanding to meet the Israeli threat and recruited from middle-class and peasant youth, was a hotbed of populist dissent, radicalised by the conflict with Israel and Nasser's anti-imperialism. The West's backing of Israel inflamed the people against it and de-legitimised pro-Western politicians and the Western economic ties of the commercial oligarchy. This fuelled the rise of radical parties – notably the Ba'th party – and the military coups and counter-coups that destabilised the state and gradually pushed the oligarchic elite from power (Seale 1965; Torrey 1964).

The coup that brought the Ba'th party to power in 1963 ushered in a new era of unstable radicalism (1963–70). The Ba'th regime had a narrow support base, owing to conflict with mass Nasserism (over the failure of a 1963 Arab unity project) and from the opposition of the old oligarchs and Islamic rivals. On top of that, the regime was split into 'radical' and 'moderate' wings which used foreign policy as tools in their power struggle – each trying to win support by advocating greater militancy against Israel. The radical faction led by Salah Jadid seized power in a 1966 coup, ousting the more moderate party founders, Michel Aflaq and Salah ad-Din Bitar (Rabinovich 1972). The radical Ba'th attempted to carry out a revolution from above through land reform, nationalisations and government control over the market, and to contain the fierce urban resistance this provoked by mobilising peasants on its side. The Ba'thi radicals, driven by ideological militancy and seeking the legitimacy to entrench their precarious rule, also aimed to make Damascus the bastion of a war of Palestine liberation by supporting Palestinian fedayeen raids into Israel. They also sought to push the Arab states into confronting Israel and to stimulate the revolution in the pro-Western monarchies needed to enlist Arab oil in the battle. This, however, ignored the balance of power – Israeli military superiority – and brought on the 1967 defeat and the Israeli occupation of the Syrian Golan Heights (Hinnebusch 2001: 52–57; Yaniv, 1986).

Watershed wars and convergence

Two watershed wars propelled the Saudi and Syrian regimes on a path of convergence in both structure and policy. The 1967 war, a disastrous defeat for Syria, split the regime, discredited the radical Ba'thists and precipitated their ousting by the Defence Minister, Hafiz al-Asad, who set Syria on a new 'realist' course. Asad put revolution on hold to concentrate on the recovery of Syria's occupied territory and containment of the Israeli threat through a military build-up. Since this required Saudi financing, Asad, as well as Nasser, was ready to bury the ideological Cold War with the traditional monarchies (Kerr 1975). For Saudi Arabia's King Feisal this was an opportunity to end the Arab nationalist threat and gain nationalist legitimacy for his regime while moderating the radical regimes. This convergence between republics and monarchy was consolidated in the 1973 war when the Saudis' use of the oil weapon won them enormous nationalist prestige and precipitated the oil price explosion which enabled them to consolidate their regime at home (Vassiliev 1998: 383–392). Transfers of rent to Syria allowed a similar consolidation there. Although relations between the two states subsequently had their ups and downs, their mutual ability to damage the other and their shared interest in an equitable resolution of the Arab–Israeli conflict made them interdependent.

Oil and state consolidation

Oil gave impetus to the consolidation of both states. Oil revenues radically increased the *Saudi* regime's autonomy from society, whose taxes it no longer needed. At the same time, the centralisation and bureaucratisation of the state enabled the al-Saud to subordinate autonomous social forces. The once autonomous Hijazi merchants were absorbed into corporatist relations with the bureaucracy; the *ulama* lost their independent financial base and the regime fostered a loyal Nejdi business class entirely dependent on state patronage. Bureaucratic expansion absorbed at least a half of nationals into the state-employed middle class and once-radical workers were transformed into welfare recipients or white-collar employees. In a tacit social contract, the mass public eschewed political rights in return for vastly increased material and welfare benefits. The division of the country into privileged citizens, many of whom did little work, and non-citizens, who worked but were not entitled to benefits, arguably gave citizens a stake in the status quo. At the centre, the Saudi clan, with its more than 5,000 princes, presided over the levers of government power and operated like a single party system, an enormous solidary network stretched throughout society. As a lion's share of the new wealth accrued to the Saudi clan, its position and cohesion was consolidated: 'reformist' liberal or Arab nationalist princes disappeared as enormous wealth gave the clan an overriding stake in the status quo (Gause 1994: 11, 15, 42–77; Vassiliev 1998: 435–439, 474–482; Chaudhry 1997: 43–76, 100–147; Cordesman 1984: 373).

The limits of Saudi state-building were, however, underlined by the regime's inability to mount a credible defence against external threat. While its population was comparable to that of Syria and Israel, they had armed forces about four times as large as its 111,500 troops (Gause 1994: 125; Cordesman 1984: 200). The regime's low capacity to mobilise defence manpower resulted, in good part, from fear that a conscripted population would demand political rights or that a large army would inevitably recruit from more plebeian ranks of society whose loyalty to the monarchy could be suspect (Gause 1994: 123–124). Instead, the al-Saud opted for a small, high-tech military, especially an air force that could be realistically dominated by Saudi princes; but this strategy intensified dependence on the US for equipment, operations and training (Vassiliev 1998: 441–444).

In *Syria*, the state was also consolidated in the 1970s under Hafiz al-Asad. Previously, Syrian regimes, unstable and unconsolidated at home, were unable to pursue effective foreign policies, making Syria the prize over which stronger states fought. Indeed, Asad's power concentration was accepted as necessary to confront the gravest threat the country and regime had ever faced, a defeat and occupation of Syrian land by Israel brought on by the recklessness of a factionalised regime. It was only as Syria attained relative internal cohesion and regime autonomy that foreign policy-makers were able to act effectively in Syria's external environment.

Under the radical Ba'thists, the regime had already achieved autonomy from the dominant classes by breaking their control over the means of production and mobilising workers and peasants through the Ba'th party. Within this regime, Asad increasingly concentrated power in a 'presidential monarchy' through a policy of balancing the elements of his political base. Thus, he used the army to free himself from Ba'th party ideological constraints; then, he built up his *jama'a* – a core of largely Alawi personal followers in the security apparatus – to enhance his autonomy from both army and party. At the same time, he appeased the remaining private bourgeoisie through limited liberalisation and fostered a state-dependent new bourgeoisie as a fourth leg of support to minimise dependence on the others (Batatu 1981; Dawisha 1978a; Perthes

1995: 146–154). While elements of the Damascene Sunni bourgeoisie entered into tacit business alliances with Alawi military elites at the top, the party and its auxiliaries incorporated a significant mass base, particularly in the villages, Sunni as well as non-Sunni. New state-dependent constituencies were widened as education and state employment expanded the salaried middle class, while agrarian reform transformed a large part of the landless proletariat into a smallholding co-operatised peasantry dependent on regime support. Thus, Asad built a cross-sectarian coalition which held together even in the face of the major Islamic fundamentalist uprising of 1977–82 (Batatu 1982; Hinnebusch 2001: 93–103, 115–125; Seale 1988: 317–320, 455–460).

A sign of the autonomy of the regime was its ability to harness the economy to its foreign policy and military strengthening. Syria's turn to statist 'socialism' from the late 1950s was, in good part, driven by the belief that a nationalist foreign policy could only be pursued by diluting economic dependency on the West and the world market. The 1967 defeat stimulated a massive military build-up aimed at recovery of the lost Golan Heights while Egypt's separate peace and Israel's 1982 invasion of Lebanon set off similar build-ups, all of which had to be financed. A high degree of state control over the economy allowed Asad to devote 15–17% of GNP and 20% of manpower to the armed forces at its height in the 1980s. Aid from the Arab oil states was crucial to Syria's military enhancement, but Asad escaped the constraints such dependence could have put on his options by balancing between rival Soviet/ East European, West European, Arab Gulf and Iranian sources of aid (Clawson 1989; Diab 1994: 87; Waldner 1995). By 1986, Syria had enormous armed forces for a state of its size: 5,000 tanks, 500,000 men under arms and some 400 ballistic missiles. According to Evron (1987), the result was a mutual deterrence that relatively stabilised the Syrian–Israeli military confrontation.

Decision-making

In *Saudi Arabia*, foreign policy decisions are taken consensually by the king and senior princes of the royal family, producing caution and continuity in policy, deeply reflective of Saudi Arabia's character as a status quo power. The muted competition that exists within the royal family also encourages a risk-averse attempt to appease – 'bandwagon' between – conflicting pressures from the West and the Arab world. Thus, in the 1980s, the preferences of the 'Suderi Seven' – notably then King Fahd, Defence Minister Prince Sultan and Interior Minister Prince Nayef – for a Western alliance and Western-backed modernisation were balanced by Crown Prince Abdullah's more Arab nationalist and socially conservative sympathies (Cordesman 1984: 182–183, 226, 376–378; Gause 1994: 120: Vassiliev 1998: 354–360).

The Saudi inner circle is not formally accountable for its decisions but the *ulama*, given the obligation of an Islamic ruler to consult them, and because they head the institutions which can most credibly claim to represent wider public opinion, may represent a veto group able to restrain regime policy; the 1990 Gulf war precipitated an unprecedented attempt by a part of the *ulama* to exercise their right of consultation (Gause 1994: 158). The threat of domestic dissent also tends to keep the regime on a cautious centrist path. The 1979 attack on the Grand Mosque by hundreds of radical Islamists led by a self-proclaimed 'Mahdi' and recruited from traditionally supportive tribes and shari'a students antagonised by the growth in corruption and Westernisation awakened the regime to the dangers for a conservative Islamic regime of perceived departures from Islamic probity. The subsequent growth of radical Islamic dissent – of which Osama bin Laden was a product – tends to counter pressures on the regime from Washington.

Syria, faced with a more threatening environment, developed a more centralised command structure. Power was concentrated in the hands of the president, enabling Asad to make decisions free of overt constraints by hawkish or dovish factions. To be sure, at least initially, he tried to govern by intra-elite consensus, taking account of the ideologues of the Ba'th party, but he was also prepared to be out in front of elite opinion and to subordinate ideology to realpolitik if external constraints demanded it. Thus, in the disengagement negotiations after the 1973 war, Asad took pains to consult the political elite (in contrast to Sadat's unilateral decisions), but, in the end, accepted Kissinger's final proposal and dragged his reluctant lieutenants along with him (Dawisha 1978b; Jourjati 1998: 51). Thereafter, Asad took several unpopular foreign policy decisions, notably the 1976 intervention against the PLO in Lebanon, the alignment with Iran in the Iran–Iraq war, and that against Iraq after its invasion of Kuwait. As long as he could justify these decisions as necessary to the long-term struggle with Israel, he calculated that opposition could be contained. They, nevertheless, had domestic costs; arguably the 1976 conflict with the PLO so damaged the regime's legitimacy that it was much more vulnerable to the Islamic rebellion of 1977–82. The link between the external and internal arenas was not that foreign policy was designed to deal with domestic threats, but that decision-makers could not ignore the impact of policies designed to cope with external threats on their precarious domestic legitimacy (Hinnebusch 2001: 147–149 Sheehan 1976).

Foreign policy behaviour: the persistence of divergence

Regional threats most immediately shape *Saudi* foreign policy. As a weak, rich, pro-Western state nearly surrounded by stronger, more populous, but poorer nationalist regimes, Saudi Arabia inevitably faced significant security threats. The Saudis long feared encirclement from various combinations of the republican and Marxist Yemens in the south, Islamic Iran and Ba'thist Iraq. External threats all had a trans-state dimension: the Saudis perceive the Middle East as a cauldron of instability that could spill across their borders, a product of their experience with Nasserism in the 1960s. In the 1980s the Soviet invasion of Afghanistan generated a perception of Soviet penetration of the region while revolutionary Iran, contesting the validity of the Saudis' 'American Islam', represented both a military and ideological threat (Dawisha 1979: 20–25; Vassiliev 1998: 469–473). These threats have made Saudi Arabia highly dependent on Western, particularly American, protection.

Yet this, far from being a solution to the regime's insecurity, itself created a major dilemma. On the one hand, the identity of the Saudi state, astride the birthplace of Islam, the product of the Wahhabi Islamic revivalist movement and the guardian of Islam's holy places, was virtually indistinguishable from Islam; on the other hand, the al-Saud had become a part of the international financial oligarchy, utterly dependent for their continued wealth and security on the US, a state widely perceived to be a main enemy of Islam and backer of Israel. This dual character of the regime generated contradictory pressures on its foreign policy: the first drove it to distance itself from and even oppose aspects of US policy connected with Israel, the second dictated close partnership with Washington (Vassiliev 1998: 475–476).

The regime historically tried to reconcile this contradiction by insisting that the main threat to Islam came, not from the West, but from atheist communism, of which Zionism was claimed to be an offshoot. The US alignment was therefore justified on the basis of common anti-communism and the claim that good US relations could bring Washington to pressure Israel into concessions to the Arabs. The regime also historically sought to keep the US connection as unobtrusive as possible: 'over-the horizon' and pre-positioned US capabilities rather than overt US bases. However, the Iraqi invasion of Kuwait sharply exposed its dependency on the US, while the subsequent US failure to resolve the Arab–Israeli conflict de-legitimised this dependence, stimulating dissent among the strongly Islamic elements that were the regime's putative constituency (Dawisha 1979: 23–34; Gause 1994: 121–122).

The regime's built-in contradictions shaped certain characteristic features of its foreign policy, above all a propensity to bandwagon between (appease or bend before) the contrary pressures from the region and the West. In the region, the Saudis' style was to avoid confrontation unless it was forced on them. In periods of greater weakness or intense regional pressures, the Saudis bandwagoned, seeking to appease radical Arab states: in the 1950s King Saud attempted to appease Nasser and Pan-Arab opinion until they became too hostile to the monarchy. King Faisal re-established the regime's anti-Zionist credentials by the use of the oil weapon in 1973 and by financing the Arab front-line states. As the Saudis' economic resources increased with the oil boom, they deployed 'riyal' diplomacy to pre-empt threats and to 'moderate' radical Syria and the PLO, mediating inter-Arab conflicts which could widen regional instability and financing anti-communist Islamic movements, such as the Afghan mujahadin. That the last was driven less by Islamic zeal than by a pragmatic desire to strengthen what they identified as conservative forces is evident from the Saudis' curbing of aid to Islamic groups which sided with Iraq in the Gulf war and their increasing support for governments fighting Islamic movements (Dawisha 1979: 26; Gause 1994: 121, 172).

Equally characteristic of Saudi Arabia's policy has been its failure, the brief oil embargo aside, to decisively deploy its seemingly incomparable 'oil power' to achieve an end to the Arab–Israeli conflict, arguably the single most important source of the regional instability and domestic dissidence which threatens it (*Middle East,*

January, 1999, p. 23). In 1980 Saudi Arabia had some $111 billion in financial reserves, 35–40% of that of all the IMF countries (Dawisha 1979: 17), entitling it to a seat on the IMF. Yet although it used its petro-power to serve American interests – re-cycling petrodollars, moderating oil prices, and rejecting renewed use of the oil weapon – Washington failed to deliver the even-handed policy needed to achieve a settlement of the conflict. The Saudis' continued deference to Washington in spite of this partly reflects their economic interests in the West, partly their heavy dependence on the US for their security. Yet far from trying to diversify this dependence, the Saudis deliberately intensified it (Dawisha 1979: 28; Gause 1994: 179–183; Vassiliev 1998: 398–404). This was, in great part, an artefact of state formation: the domestic dangers of a popularly recruited defence force had to be avoided even if this meant deepening dependence on the US. The al-Saud's external insecurity and dependency are, thus, intimately connected to their domestic vulnerability.

The contradiction embedded in the *Syrian* state was that between the revisionism rooted in its Pan-Arab identity – which stood for the unification of the Arab states and the liberation of Palestine – and geopolitical realities: the durability of the status quo state system and the reality of permanent Israeli military superiority (Ma'oz 1972). The immediate challenge Asad faced was to elim-inate the consequences of Syria's failed revisionism, Israel's 1967 occupation of Arab lands, amidst an unfavourable power bal-ance and without sacrificing nationalist legitimacy. It was only the autonomy and stability with which Asad endowed the state that enabled him to manage these dilemmas in a way approximating a rational actor.

First, he replaced Syria's impotent irredentism – the messianic goal of liberating Palestine – with the limited but still very ambi-tious goals of recovering the Golan and achieving a Palestinian state in the West Bank/Gaza. In pursuit of these goals he demonstrated great consistency and tenacity: in a quarter century of diplomatic bargaining, he refused to settle for less than a full Israeli with-drawal from the Golan and eschewed a separate settlement with Israel at the expense of the Palestinians. When these vital interests were at stake, he was prepared to take high risks, as illustrated by his obstruction of the 1983 Lebanese–Israeli accord at a time when Israeli and American power were being projected right on his 'Lebanese doorstep' (Hinnebusch 2001: 151–153; Ma'oz 1988; Seale 1988: 494).

Second, Asad was a rational actor in his development of the increased capabilities needed to match his goals. He proved himself a master of adapting a mix of foreign policy instruments – alliance formation, limited war, negotiations – to the changing and usually unfavourable balance of power he faced. In simultaneously sustaining alliances with the conservative Arab oil states, radical Libya, Islamic Iran and the Soviet Union, he got the necessary economic resources, arms and protection needed for the struggle. He built up the military forces needed for the 1973 war to recover the Golan and, when this failed, he entered the Kissinger-sponsored disengagement negotiations. Although Asad was extremely wary of the pitfalls of negotiating with Israel, he was prepared to do so when it could be done from a position of sufficient strength and when he judged he could exploit US fears of Middle East instability to get pressure on Israel to withdraw from conquered Arab territory. When Egypt's separate peace destroyed his bargaining position, rather than concede principle, Asad preferred to work for a favourable change in the power balance, while seeking to obstruct any further separate settlements with Israel by Jordan or the PLO. As the Golan front stagnated, and the conflict was diverted into a low-intensity proxy war in Lebanon, paralleled in the 1990s by a diplomatic struggle over the conditions of a peace settlement, Asad invested in the relative military parity with Israel which allowed him to avoid bargaining from weakness, and even enabled him to apply military pressure on Israel in southern Lebanon at reasonable risk. After his Soviet patron declined, Asad seized the opportunity of Iraq's invasion of Kuwait to join the Gulf war coalition as a way of building credit with the remaining American superpower and re-enlisting its diplomacy on behalf of a land-for-peace settlement with Israel. Thus, Asad parleyed limited resources into greater influence than would be expected from Syria's base of national power and turned Syria from a recurrent victim of its neighbours into a powerful regional player (Cobban 1991: 112–138; Hinnebusch 2001: 147–163; Seale 1988: 226–266, 267–315, 344–349, 366–420).

The foreign policies of Syria and Saudi Arabia converged as both states were consolidated enough to become rational actors pursuing limited goals. However, the Israeli occupation kept Syria a dissatisfied power pursuing redress through the maximisation of power while Saudi Arabia's satisfaction and inherent weakness made bandwagoning its natural strategy. Differences in decision-making structures reflected these different priorities: one building in caution, the other designed to enable the maximum in geopolitical manoeuvring. So did the differential development of capabilities: Syria sacrificed its economy to mobilise the power needed to reach its foreign policy priorities just as Saudi Arabia sacrificed an independent foreign policy and military strength for economic interests and domestic stability.

Similar regimes, divergent policies: Egypt and Syria seek exit from war

The very different paths followed by *similar* regimes in Egypt and Syria in dealing with their common Israeli enemy seem to demonstrate the inadequacy of state formation patterns, in themselves, to explain foreign policy. Egypt and Syria were, by the mid-1960s, ostensibly similar authoritarian nationalist regimes that had originated in similar plebeian revolts against imperialism and oligarchy and initially promoted radical ideologies reflective of these origins. Thereafter, commonly experienced systemic forces seemed to divert them on to the same road toward moderation. They shared the defeat of 1967 and the rise to power, in reaction, of newly 'pragmatic' leaders – Sadat and Asad – in 1970. Both initiated limited liberalisation at home and inter-Arab detente abroad. Together they launched the October 1973 war and together they started on the path of post-war negotiations with Israel. Together – and only together – they might have reached a comprehensive Middle East peace for, as Henry Kissinger remarked, the Arabs could not wage war without Egypt or make peace without Syria.

Yet this break with the radical past was much sharper in Egypt under Sadat than in Asad's Syria and by 1980 they had become bitter rivals, as Egypt abandoned Nasser's Arab nationalism, pursued a separate peace with Israel which ignored the touchstone of Arabism, the Palestine cause, and embraced alliance with America. Syria became the main standard bearer of Arab nationalism, was branded a rejectionist state in the West and remained locked in bitter conflict with Israel. What explains this spectacular divergence? That such similar states should pursue such different policies suggests that, as realism holds, their *different positions in the regional power balance* or, as structuralists might suggest, their *differential economic dependency*, were ultimately decisive. Yet, as will be seen, subtle differences in *state formation* and *identity* shaped different conceptions of state interest which, given the right systemic factors, drew the two states in opposing directions.

State formation

Identity and legitimacy For *Egypt*, a homogeneous society with a long history of separate statehood and confidence in its own particular identity, pursuit of Egyptian 'national' interest was a viable alternative to Arab nationalism and the sacrifice of Arab nationalist principles much less damaging to regime legitimacy than it would be in Syria. Even under Nasser, Arab nationalism was, to a considerable extent, regarded instrumentally, and while there was considerable recognition that Egyptian and Arab interests coincided, once the costs of Arab involvement exceeded the benefits, a more overtly Egypt-first attitude appeared in the ruling establishment. After 1967, Israel's now dominant military position left few opportunities to pursue Pan-Arab ambitions and after Nasser's death Egypt could no longer readily manipulate Arabism against other Arab states. Egyptian elites had been 'socialised' by the costs of Arabism into embracing the rules of a conventional state system in which sovereignty was valued above supra-state ideology. This change in elite values did not include a consensus on a separate peace with Israel but such a peace could be justified as putting Egyptian interests first and the elevation of sovereignty over Pan-Arabism meant that, once the Sinai was returned, irredentist grievances against Israel would be satisfied. In addition, Egyptian elites resented their new dependency on the Arab oil states and Sadat hoped to use alignment with the US to assert another sort of regional leadership based on mediating between the West and the Arab world (Dawisha 1976: 78; Dekmejian 1971: 105–108; Telhami 1990: 12–17, 90–106).

By contrast, in *Syria*, a mosaic society lacking a history of statehood, the main alternative identities were initially either sub-state sectarianism or Arabism, the main unifying ideology through which a cross-sectarian coalition needed to consolidate the state could be forged. In fact, the Ba'th regime's Arab nationalist mission, as the most steadfast defender of the Arab cause in the battle with Israel, became the basis of its domestic legitimacy and the regional stature that entitled it to the financial backing of other Arab states. This is not to say that hostility to Israel was a mere function of the regime's need for an external enemy. Asad neither invented nor sought to wilfully prolong the Arab–Israeli conflict; indeed, he scaled down Syria's definition of its Pan-Arab mission to liberation of the occupied territories (Hinnebusch 2001: 139–142). What it does mean is that the regime's need to protect its Arab nationalist legitimacy and regional stature put certain outside boundaries on policies that could be safely pursued toward Israel, and a separate peace which abandoned the Palestinians was long seen as a dishonourable offence against Arabism. Israel might have been prepared to concede the Golan had it believed such a settlement would be legitimised and turn Syria inward to its own state-centric affairs; but Israeli leaders were convinced that, unlike in Egypt, Arab nationalism was too strong in Syria for this to happen, at least without a contemporaneous settlement of the Palestinian issue (Jourjati 1998; Sheehan 1976).

Political structures and process   Despite outward appearances of similarity, differences in the structures of the Syrian and Egyptian states also help explain their differential paths. In Egypt under Nasser a strong state was early consolidated around Nasser's charismatic authority and command of a reliable bureaucratic apparatus ruling a hydraulic society conditioned to submit to the state. Nasser made the presidency a powerful office, endowed with his personal legitimacy and immense legal prerogatives; Sadat inherited and was able to similarly exercise this presidential power but, ironically, on behalf of a reversal of Nasser's Arab nationalist policy (Hinnebusch 1985: 78–91).

Sadat's course cannot be detached from his needs and strategy in consolidating his power. He inherited Nasser's office but not his popular support and he lacked Nasser's capacity to use Pan-Arab leadership to bolster his position at home. As such, he chose to root his rule in the support of the bourgeoisie – the social force that was both most strategic and most prepared to support a leader promising a reversal of Nasserism. The bourgeoisie wanted an end to war, economic liberalisation and an opening to the West (Hinnebusch, 1985: 89–90).

While Sadat had to find some solution to the crisis of Israel's occupation of the Sinai if he was to survive, once he won legitimacy in the 1973 war, he acquired a remarkably free hand in post-war diplomacy. There were no domestic interests threatened enough and strong enough to constrain his incremental movement toward Western alignment and a separate peace. The military elite was resentful of the USSR and attracted by promises of US weapons, owed much to Sadat's rehabilitation of them in the 1973 war, and had no desire to risk the honour won in that war in another round with Israel; the minority of officers who challenged this consensus were easily purged by the dominant presidency (Hinnebusch 1985: 125–131; Telhami 1990 141–143). Because the ease of Nasser's power consolidation had not required him to create a strong ideological political party, there was no corps of ideological militants with a stake in Arab nationalism and socialism that could balance the bourgeoisie's growing interest in a Western alignment and economic liberalisation. Once Nasser was gone, there was little obstacle to transformation of the state's social base through purges of the nationalist left and new bourgeois recruitment under Sadat. The public was more concerned with economic troubles than foreign policy and the official media stirred up their resentment of the rich Arabs who refused to share their wealth with Egypt while promising that an economic bonanza would follow from peace with Israel. Those opposed were prevented from mobilising by the authoritarian state.

State formation proceeded differently in Syria. In Syria's more intractable society, the 1960s Ba'th regime, facing powerful urban upper-class and Islamic opposition, relied on a dual strategy to survive. Before 1970 a strong ideological party rooted in plebeian strata had institutionalised Ba'thist Arab nationalism. Secondly, especially under Asad, recruitment of the core military elite was from property-less minorities, especially Alawites who had embraced secular Arab nationalism as an ideology that gave them equal citizenship; yet because their Arabism was suspect to the Sunni majority, they had to prove it by being more militant than their Sunni opponents. Party and Alawi recruitment from plebeian strata deterred solidification of a new bourgeoisie that might have had an interest in a Westward tilt as happened in Egypt under Sadat (Hinnebusch 2001: 67–88).

In Syria, the president also dominated foreign policy, but Asad was, at least until the 1980s, more dependent on a politicised military and an ideological party that were less deferential than their

Egyptian counterparts and which still took ideology and anti-Israeli militancy seriously. More concerned to sustain an elite consensus on the extremely risky matter of dealing with Israel, Asad was less willing to take diplomatic risks to get a breakthrough than was Sadat, particularly since rivals could more readily mobilise public opinion against policies seen to be a betrayal of Arabism (Sheehan 1976). Moreover Asad, having played a role in the loss of the Golan for the sake of Palestine, had to recover it without abandoning Palestine. He built and legitimised his regime for the struggle to do so and to settle for less would mean his whole career was a failure and the sacrifices he had imposed on Syrians for many years wasted.

These differences in the political needs and power of the two presidents shaped differences in their approaches to the post-1973 negotiations: Sadat's willingness to make concessions to Israel and Asad's stubborn refusal to do so.

Systemic forces

Geopolitics While state formation explains why Egypt, unlike Syria, *could* readily make a separate peace, it was their comparative geopolitical situations after the 1973 war that best explains why the leaderships actually did follow such divergent strategies. Since Egypt and Syria failed in the 1973 war to militarily recover their occupied territories, a political settlement would have to be reached which satisfied Israel and Israel sought a partial deal, not a comprehensive peace that could satisfy both Egypt and Syria. These states' quite different geopolitical power positions vis-à-vis Israel determined which of the two would be satisfied. Egypt was tactically weak but strategically strong. Tactically, Israeli leverage over Egypt was higher since at the end of the war Israeli forces had penetrated the West Bank of the Suez Canal and encircled the Egyptian Third Army, putting intense pressure on Sadat to accept an unconditional disengagement of forces. On the other hand, as the most powerful Arab state, Egypt's strategic bargaining hand was strong since Israel had a strong interest in reaching a separate peace, which would take Egypt out of the Arab–Israeli military balance and effectively end the Arab military threat. Similarly the US, its interests threatened by the 1973 war outcome, was prepared to extract the limited territorial concessions from Israel needed to appease and win over Sadat in order to relieve pressures for a comprehensive settlement at Israel's expense and to exclude Soviet influence from Egypt. Tactical weakness set Egypt on the road to a separate peace and strategic strength got it to the end of that road (Fahmy 1983: 69–81; Riad 1982: 317–339; Sela 1998: 165–170; Sheehan 1976; Telhami 1990: 6–9).

Syria, by contrast, was tactically stronger than Egypt. Because the ceasefire on the Syrian front left Asad in a less vulnerable position, he had less immediate need to make concessions and was even able to start a war of attrition to strengthen his hand in the disengagement negotiations. But strategically, Syria's leverage over Israel was weaker since Israel had little interest in a settlement with it, especially once Sadat showed his willingness to settle separately. The US also had much less interest in satisfying Syria than Egypt. Syria was not the key to the Arab world and it could not start another war once Egypt was removed from the Arab–Israeli power balance; there was, therefore, no need to antagonise Israel by pushing it into concessions on a second front. Asad's search for military parity after Egypt's withdrawal from the Arab–Israeli power balance reflected the geopolitical reality that until the balance was restored he could not effectively bargain with Israel. Lacking Egypt's incentive to be flexible, Damascus remained adamant for a total comprehensive settlement. Tactical strength and strategic weakness prevented Syria from even getting on the road to a separate peace (Ma'oz 1988: 113–134; Seale 1988; 226–315, 344–49; Sela 1998: 153–154; Sheehan 1976).

Geo-economics and dependency Economic factors did not determine the difference in regime paths but reinforced decisions probably taken chiefly on other grounds and locked the two states into their separate courses. Egypt's economic crisis was much deeper than Syria's. It suffered from the worst population/resource imbalance in the region. Egypt's war-associated economic costs from the loss of the Suez Canal, Sinai oil fields and tourism income were $350 million annually and Arab assistance only $250 million into the early 1970s, while defence expenditures were enormous; after the war, Arab aid to Egypt declined from $1,264 million in 1974 to $625 million in 1976. The 1977 food riots shook the Egyptian regime and increased the urgency of access to new sources of aid from the US (Brecher 1972: 115; Telhami 1990: 96–99)

None of this necessarily had to lead to Sadat's separate peace: Egypt could have expected to continue receiving both US and Arab aid by simply staying in the peace process and the riots could have been resolved by less risky, potentially de-legitimising means; moreover, the separate peace cost Egypt its Arab aid and peace did not substantially lift its military spending burden. To be sure, *infitah* spawned a business class wanting foreign investment and therefore a peace settlement but much of this class saw the Arab oil states as their main market and capital source and these were jeopardised by the separate peace (Telhami 1990: 6–9). However, it is true that, as Sadat's step-by-step moves toward a separate peace were rewarded with increased American economic aid, a reversal of course would have been very costly as Egypt became increasingly entrapped by dependency on its yearly American aid 'fix'. The *infitah* bourgeoisie was enabled to enrich itself on the American aid and Western joint ventures that in good part replaced the lost Arab aid.

Syrian foreign policy was free of comparable economic pressures. Syria's economic crisis was less severe and the Golan had much less economic value than the Sinai; on the other hand, Arab aid given to Syria in its role as front-line state against Israel made a bigger difference to its smaller economy than the impact of such aid in Egypt. While Syria's economy did fall into crisis in the 1980s, Asad had diversified his economic dependencies sufficiently that they could not be used to leverage his foreign policy. While Sadat's bandwagoning led Egypt into a total economic dependency on the US, which locked the country into his separate peace, Asad's balancing between a multitude of powers allowed him to avoid such a separate peace.

Leadership

It is not uncommon to explain these different outcomes as functions of the personalities and values of Sadat and Asad. Given the power of the other variables analysed, it might, however, be thought that the leadership variable is not needed to explain them. Where leadership may have made a difference was in its effect on these deeper seated factors: while Nasser would probably have worked against pressures for a separate peace, Sadat's power needs led him to push them forward. Moreover, as was seen in chapter 5, Sadat's wishful thinking, craving for Western approval and impulsive propensity to make concessions led him to play his cards poorly in the extended peace negotiations. By contrast, Asad's 'realist' view of international politics, which put no faith in the good intentions of either

Israel or the US, his extreme wariness of being tricked by them and his tenacious bargaining may have better corresponded to reality than Sadat's worldview. However, it may also conceivably have led Asad to let later deals with Israeli leaders Yitzhak Rabin and Ehud Barak slip through his fingers. However, these differences were not simply idiosyncratic but reflected divergent situations and interests: Sadat's separate peace, after all, conceded Palestinian and Syrian interests for Egyptian gains and that, in turn, put Asad in a weaker position in which he could not afford to readily give up any of his few remaining bargaining chips.

Pluralist regimes and foreign policy

Does democratisation or even merely pluralisation of the political system produce a generically different kind of foreign policy outcome? Democratic peace theory suggests that Middle East wars are, in part, a function of the region's democratic deficits which prevent publics from holding leaders accountable or constraining their foreign adventures. Realists, however, argue that elites in all states, regardless of internal features, act to maximise security and power and that the public largely defers to or is readily manipulated by such elites. Mansfield and Snyder (1995) suggest that in unconsolidated democracies, where electoral success may depend on playing the nationalist card, competitive politics may actually introduce higher levels of bellicosity into the policy-making process. The test cases in the Middle East, which arguably best approximate the democratic-pluralist model, are Israel and Turkey by virtue of their higher levels of institutionalisation, tolerance of opposition and regular use of competitive elections in elite recruitment. These cases give quite mixed signals on the issue of the democratic peace thesis.

The determinants of Turkish foreign policy: the primacy of state formation

Turkey is, as pluralists would expect, essentially a status quo state whose foreign policy has normally been cautious and defensive. However, the *primary* determinant of Turkey's policy has been its initial state formation and subsequent alterations in policy were more the products of geopolitical struggles or shifts in economic dependencies than democratic politics. Indeed, the structural type of the Turkish state, which varied from Ataturk's authoritarian regime to the fragmented parliamentary system of the 1970–2000 period, explained little variation in its foreign policy. However, in the decade of the 2000s, the more thorough democratisation of the Turkish state did seem to have significant consequences for foreign policy; it propelled an alteration in identity, hence perceptions of threats; this, however, was at least partially congruent with objective shifts in regional geopolitics.

Turkey's state formation experience set it on a status quo, West-centric tangent. Ataturk's successful war of independence against Western designs on Anatolia imposed by the Treaty of Sevres spared Turkey colonial subjugation and enabled the establishment of a territorial state within boundaries that satisfied Turkish national identity. The consequent eclipse of former alternative identities, Ottomanism and Pan-Turkism, meant the eschewing of revisionist ambitions in the Middle East and Turkic central Asia. The satisfaction of identity also allowed independent Turkey to re-establish relations with the West on an amicable basis. This was reinforced by Ataturk's investment of the nationalist legitimacy, with which the independence war endowed him, in a Westernising brand of modernisation, which created a large secular-educated middle class and wove a Western orientation into the fabric of the state establishment. Thus, Turkey's dominant social forces have, from the state's founding, been largely satisfied, not irredentist and their identity durably West-centric (Ahmad 1993: 47–51).

Until Turkey felt fully secure in its independence, it followed a foreign policy of balancing between the rival European powers and a statist import-substitute industrialisation policy to secure an independent economic base. Once, however, Turkey opted for capitalist export strategies, jump-started by US aid after World War II, economics helped lock in a pro-Western foreign policy (Ahmad 1993: 67–68). Turkey's historic sense of geopolitical threat from its powerful northern neighbour, Russia, revived by post-war Soviet pressures, superseded post-Sevres fears of the West and pushed the country into NATO, consolidating its Western identity. Turkey's desire for admittance to the EU was advanced by its subsequent capitalist development and this same political economy imperative – the need for aid and markets – led the Özal government to consolidate close ties with the United States.

Foreign policy-making in Turkey: realism in command

Turkey's military and diplomatic establishment long made foreign policy relatively insulated from popular pressure. Foreign policy was the reserved sphere of elites, notably the military and the foreign ministry bureaucrats, responding to external exigencies, filtered via their view of the national interest, rather than to public opinion or domestic interest groups. This elite pursued a policy of caution, eschewing irredentist ambitions or entanglements in foreign conflicts, whether under democratic or non-democratic regimes. The predominantly defensive geopolitical considerations which governed the elite's calculations enabled Turkey to stay out of costly wars, remarkable given its fraught location. The Middle East was seen as a region of turmoil from which Turkey's Western identity separated it and against which its borders were securitised.

In the limited cases where electoral politics or public opinion significantly impacted on foreign policy, they tended to produce a more nationalistic, less pacific outcome. Elected politicians were more likely than the unelected state establishment to advocate adventurous regional policies such as Adnan Menderes' enlistment of Turkey against Arab nationalism in the 1950s and Turgut Özal's involvement of Turkey, against the caution of the establishment, in the 1990 Gulf war (Robins 1991: 65–73). Rivalry with Greece was the one foreign policy issue which had major domestic resonance: outcomes in this conflict could make or break politicians and party competition discouraged diplomatic initiatives which could make leaders vulnerable to the claim that they were soft on Greece. Turkish Cypriots acted as a domestic pressure group of some potency, obstructing a diplomatic settlement of the Cyprus conflict (Ahmad 1993: 174–180; Fuller 1997: 53–57; Mufti 1998: 42–45; Robins, 1991: 3–16, 27–45).

Turkey's foreign policy behaviour: the effect of systemic pressures

Systemic pressures largely reinforced Turkey's initial foreign policy tangent. While Ankara remained neutral in World War II, its subsequent 'bandwagoning' with the triumphant Western allies corresponded to an influx of Western aid and capital, the Soviet threat and NATO membership, and democratisation, all of which consolidated Turkey's West-centric orientation. Turkey joined the Western powers and Iran in the Baghdad Pact/CENTO and made moves under the Eisenhower doctrine to 'quarantine' Syria's Arab nationalism, briefly assuming guardianship of the Middle East status quo on behalf of the West (Ahmad 1993: 118–120, 224–225; Fuller 1997: 43–48).

Turkey was partly and temporarily diverted from its essentially Western and status quo orientations by several systemic level factors encouraging it to 'balance' between the West and other alignments. First, geopolitical rivalry with Greece and the conflict over Cyprus drove a wedge between Turkey and the West, especially when the US imposed an arms embargo after the Turkish invasion of northern Cyprus. Turkish elites, no longer seeing Turkey's national interest as always compatible with that of the West, undertook to diversify its ties to the Middle East and Third World (Ahmad 1993: 139–142, 225–226). This departure was reinforced by temporary economic anomalies. Thus, in the 1970s, an economic crisis brought on by the rise in oil prices forced the government to seek oil at concessionary prices from Saudi Arabia while Turkish business was attracted by export markets in the newly oil-rich Middle East. These developments were paralleled by a more pro-Arab–Islamic foreign policy which included the refusal to allow US use of Turkish bases in the re-supply of Israel in the 1973 war, support for the Palestinian cause, condemnation of Israel's annexation of Jerusalem, refusal to impose sanctions on Iran over the American hostage crisis and Turkey's adhesion to the Organisation of the Islamic Conference (Robins 1991: 74–86; Yavuz and Khan 1992). In periods when Turkey's international economic dependencies were diversified in this way, its predominantly Western foreign policy alignment was similarly diluted (Robins 1991: 100–113). However, Turgut Özal's sacrifice of Turkey's Iraqi market for American ones in the second Gulf war expressed Ankara's return to its deeper-rooted political-economy tangent.

This reversion was initially reinforced by the end of the Cold War. The felt threat from Russia declined while an opportunity for a sphere of influence was perceived in Turkic central Asia, but Turkey's main preoccupation was fear that its value to the West would suffer from the end of the Cold War. The rebuff of Turkey's bid for EU membership led, not to a Turkish revival of its Islamic identity, but to a compensatory tightening of relations with the sole American hegemon.

However, it was still unresolved aspects of nation-building, re-opened in the post-Cold War era, namely the Kurdish conflict, which most immediately drove Turkey's foreign policy, drawing it into conflict with Syria, involvement in Iraq, alliance with Israel, and closer to Washington. The Southeastern Anatolia GAP Dam project was seen as a way of economically integrating the Kurdish regions into the state and neutralising Kurdish disaffection through economic development; however, the conflict which the diversion of Euphrates water sparked with Syria and Turkey's insistence that it would unilaterally determine Syria's share of Euphrates water led Damascus to support the Kurdish insurgency (Fuller 1997: 47–54; Robins 1991: 28–37, 87–99).

The Turkish establishment's view of the Kurdish threat to national security led it into a policy watershed – alliance with Israel – which sharply underlined the supremacy of geopolitics over domestic politics in the policy process. This axis was by no means an ideologically inspired alliance of democracies: it had no popular constituencies in either country, was unpopular among Turkey's Islamist forces, and was largely imposed by the military. Its roots were geopolitical: Turkey and Israel perceived a common threat from the Syro-Iranian axis: while Turkey felt threatened by Syrian support for the Kurdish Workers Party (PKK) guerrillas (who had training bases in the Lebanese Bekaa valley), Israel felt aggrieved by Syrian and Iranian support for the Lebanese Hizbollah. Their co-operation in anti-terrorist measures and their alliance was meant to encircle and pressure Syria. In addition, Turkey used the alliance to enlist the Israeli lobby in the US congress against the supporters of Greece. The alliance manifests the classic checkerboard pattern of realpolitik power balancing wherein 'the enemy of my enemy is my friend'. But it was also compatible with Ankara's swing back to its pro-Western tangent and the initial post-Cold War weakening of its links to the Middle East and the Third World (Ahmad 1993: 226–227; Mufti 1996: 47–48).

The transformation of Turkey's foreign policy: between identity and geopolitics

The gradual deepening of democratisation opened the policy process to a wider spectrum of influence from below, but the foreign policy establishment long retained the last word. The increased political mobilisation and Islamisation of the mass public incrementally increased the impact of Turkey's long-suppressed Islamic identity on foreign policy; thus, in the 1970s the Islamic Salvation

Party was instrumental in forcing the government to abandon its friendly ties with Israel. The rise of Islamic electoral power, however, had little initial impact on the pro-Western foreign policy establishment's conviction that Turkey was essentially European. Although the Islamist leader Necmettin Erbakan tried, during his brief tenure as prime minister in the 1990s, to strengthen ties with the Islamic world, he was constrained by establishment vetoes and ultimately removed by military ultimatum. Similarly, various ethnic pressure groups sought to push Turkey into post-Cold War involvement in the Caucasus and Central Asia but this was also rebuffed by the foreign policy establishment. Still, as the centrality of Turkey to NATO declined, and as its bid for EU membership was rebuffed, Turkey began to reconsider its exclusively Western identity and alignment and to re-orient itself to its former Ottoman space.

However, it took the rise of the Islamist Justice and Development Party (AKP) to transform Turkish politics and foreign policy; its capacity to win secure repeated majorities in several elections allowed it to push the West-centric Kemalist establishment aside. This meant a virtual revolution in the social forces in the ruling coalition, displacing the military, the secular middle class and the Western oriented bourgeoisie. In place of the latter, the AKP's constituency encompassed the Islamic-oriented entrepreneurial class, the 'Anatolian tigers', and a more religiously pious provincial public. In parallel, Turkey's Islamist leaders constructed a new neo-Ottoman and Islamic identity that blurred the former antagonisms between Turkish and Arab nationalisms. Moreover, by the mid-2000s, Turkey's economic growth drove a booming export capacity, which made new markets in the Middle East increasingly important. Inspired by its geopolitical strategist, Ahmet Davitoglu, the AKP government perceived the Middle East as its natural sphere of influence where it had a historical responsibility to fill the on-going unstable power vacuum left by the fall of the Ottoman empire. Soft power would replace Turkey's former reliance on hard power in dealing with the region; a so called 'zero-problem' approach to its neighbours was pursued through an active diplomacy of resolving disputes (e.g., mediating between Syria and Israel), projection of Turkey as a model of an economically successful Islamic democracy, and economic integration meant to construct liberal interdependencies. Emblematic of the de-securitisation of Turkey's relations with the Middle East was the abolition of visas on the

Turkey–Syria border in the late 2000s. Such de-securitisation had the advantage for the AKP of diminishing the influence of its main domestic rival, the Kemalist military, while the positive response in the region to Turkey's new stance and the government's neo-Ottoman discourse put opposition parties on the defensive.

The first sign of change was Turkey's unexpected refusal to grant the US permission to attack Iraq from Turkish bases in the 2003 Iraq war, by contrast to Turkey's stance in the 1990–91 war on Iraq. A certain convergence of geopolitics and democratisation explains this break with precedent. Turkey's policy partly reflected a changed perception of the utility of the US alliance, especially for countering its most pressing national security threat – that of Kurdish separatism and particularly the insurgency of the Kurdistan Workers Party (PKK). In the 1990–91 war, Turkey had suffered severe economic losses and had seen US policy empower the Iraqi Kurds at the expense of the Baghdad government; a further war on Iraq risked a break-up of the country to the advantage of the Kurds and the encouragement of Kurdish separatism in Turkey. Still, on the eve of the 2003 war, Turkish–US negotiations had seemingly arrived at an agreement in which Turkey would receive significant economic aid needed to recover from an economic crisis, and Turkish forces would enter Iraq with the Americans and be in a position to counter threats from the PKK or the fragmentation of Iraq. That this deal fell apart in the end, failing to win parliamentary approval by a handful of votes, resulted from domestic politics – namely, widespread public opposition to the impending US invasion of Iraq, which seeped up into the ruling party and governing elite. Not only did AKP parliamentarians oppose a war entailing 'bombing Muslims' but the main opposition Kemalist party argued against participation in a war of aggression and the generals refrained from pushing for it, in spite of their intimate relations with the US military and dependence on US military aid. Thereafter, anti-American sentiment spread in Turkish public opinion, which suspected Washington was using the PKK as a tool to penalise Turkey for its defiance and was covertly promoting the creation of a Kurdish state in Northern Iraq.

The next indicator of a major change in Turkey's policy was a reversal of its regional alliances. While in the 1990s, Turkey had aligned with Israel to balance against Syria and Iran, in the 2000s, Turkey realigned from Israel toward Syria and Iran. In one respect this was owing to a decline in enmity with Syria and Iran, as these ceased to support the PKK, while, in parallel, both Israel and the US began to support the Kurds in Iraq: the change in the location of threat led to a change in alignments, as realists would expect. Yet the end to the alliance with Israel was also driven by Israel's wars in 2006 against Lebanon and in 2009 on Gaza, both of which inflamed Turkish public opinion. Reflecting the views of his constituents and encouraged by the positive acclaim in the Arab world, Turkey's Prime Minister Erdoğan condemned Israel for the atrocities committed in Lebanon and for waging what he called an 'unjust war'. Turkey also found common interest with Syria and Iran in an informal 'Tri-lateral Front' that grouped the three to deal, collectively, with the threat from Iraq's instability, buffer the region from further US intervention and deal with the turmoil left by the foundering of America's post-invasion policy in Iraq. Emblematic of this was Turkey's mid-2000s defiance of the US/EU drive to isolate Syria over its roles in Iraq and Lebanon. Security co-operation spilled over into growing Turkish economic and energy links with Iran and with Syria, which was seen as Turkey's gateway to the Arab world, with a free trade zone projected also to embrace Lebanon and Jordan. At the same time, Ankara's attempt to mediate between Iran and the West over the former's nuclear programme – with a compromise proposal mounted in tandem with Brazil – betrayed an ambition to use regional leadership to propel an enhanced global role. When this initiative was rejected in Washington, Turkey voted against a Western-inspired further round of UN sanctions on Iran, arousing fears of Turkey's alignment with the anti-Western axis. At the same time, however, the AKP projected Turkey to the US/West as a partner able to mediate with MENA countries on behalf of Western interests and after Obama replaced Bush in the US presidency, this claim was in part acknowledged.

However, Turkey's zero-problems policy starting unravelling as early as 2010 when, forced to choose between NATO and Iran, it succumbed to pressure to allow the stationing on its territory of Western anti-missile defences aimed at Iran. Then its relationship with the Asad regime, the showcase of the zero-problems policy, collapsed over the Syrian uprising. Once Turkish leaders failed to convince Asad to moderate repression of anti-regime protestors, Turkey sponsored several conferences which organised the opposition to Asad and supported its turn to armed insurgency, leading to the remilitarisation of the Syria–Turkey border and a return to enmity between the two states. As Turkey and Iran backed opposing sides in the Syrian uprising, they drifted apart. As Turkey proved impotent to resolve the stalemate in the war, which spilled over in the form of massive refugee flows, cut Turkey's trans-Syrian economic links and risked empowering the PKK, Ankara reverted to dependence on its US/NATO connection to deal with the fallout. The idea of a Turkish-led axis to buffer the region from ill-advised Western intervention was shelved and instead Turkey joined the pro-Western Middle East Sunni axis and called for NATO intervention in the Syrian crisis. Turkey's response to the Syrian uprising was evidently driven by its identity as a democratic power, at cost to its geopolitical interests and its bid for regional leadership. It is arguable (Hinnebusch and Tur 2013) that Turkey had overreached its capabilities in its bid for regional leadership and independence from its US patron, a reality exposed by the Syrian crisis; as realism would expect, the system level – the relative power balance – rebounded on Turkey to curb the AKP's ambitious foreign policy. There was – it seemed, something in realism's claim that identity and domestic politics may shape what a state *wishes* to do, but the external power balance determines what it actually *can* accomplish.

The limits of liberal explanations

It seems clear that state formation, geopolitics and economics have most directly shaped Turkish foreign policy. Public opinion and democratic politics have had some impact on it, particularly in forcing Westernised elites to take more account of the Islamic side of Turkey's identity. But where public opinion has forced a policy alteration, it has been working in tandem with geopolitical or political economic forces and issues (the Cyprus issue and the need for Arab oil) and when these have pulled the other way, the elite has ignored public opinion – as in the alliance with Israel. It is also far from clear that democratic politics produces a uniformly more dovish kind of foreign policy: it exacerbated the conflict with Greece while it constrained decision-makers from involvement in the 2003 war on Iraq. If the impact of the Turkish public on foreign policy has not generally been bellicose, this is in good part because Turkey's identity is largely satisfied by its boundaries; hence the public harbours no deep-seated irredentism and, as such, elite and public attitudes are largely congruent in support of a basically status quo foreign policy.

In Israel, covered in more detail in chapter 7, the purported pacific impact of pluralism is negated, shaped by and subordinate to irredentism and security fears. In Israel, the belief that secure borders required incorporating parts, at least, of the territories conquered in 1967, which a significant portion of the Israeli public (the Likud-settler bloc) also consider properly to belong to Israel, has rendered the territorial conflict with Arab neighbours intractable and fuelled the security dilemma between them and Israel. This shapes the domestic environment. Thus, neither elections nor deepening party pluralism in Israel altered the disproportionate recruitment of the policy-making elite from a security establishment which sees military force as the main instrument for dealing with Israel's neighbours (Jones 2001). Moreover, given the much more powerful irredentist sentiment in Israel, as compared to Turkey, electoral politics has much more systematically rewarded politicians who professed hawkish and irredentist rather than dovish sentiments. Indeed, the deepening of Israel's political mobilisation over time strengthened the revisionist 'right' at the expense of the more status quo centre-left: Labour party dominance gave way after 1977 to alterations in government in which the right-wing Likud usually held the edge. According to Brecher (1972: 122), 'elections are profoundly influenced by the degree of chauvinism in relation to the Arabs', with each party claiming to be more resolute against the Arab threat than the others. While Brecher (1972: 125) insisted that this did not necessarily affect the strategic content of elite decisions, Roberts (1990: 43) argued that 'the dominant fact of political life confronting any peace initiative or "peace policy" was a strongly hawkish climate of opinion in Israel' which the leadership had helped create but which thereafter constrained any leader who might have thought a peace settlement in Israel's interest. Not surprisingly, therefore, Israel, the most pluralistic state in the region, has been in more wars than any other and has attacked its neighbours, including semi-democratic Lebanon, more times than any other state.

The contrast between Turkey and Israel reinforces the evidence that the *form* of government is of secondary importance in determining the pacific or revisionist direction of foreign policy, compared to whether the dominant social forces are satisfied or not.

Democracy's main effect is in strengthening identification with the state to facilitate the mobilisation of the population for national ambitions. As such, in democracies with contested borders or unrealised territorial ambitions, and above all, in those founded as settler states – what might be called 'irredentist democracies' – the putative pacific effect of widened political participation is seemingly reversed.

Explaining foreign policies: the state formation-systemic dynamic

Distinctive types of foreign policy orientation do appear to be associated with variations in state formation in two important respects: (1) whether identity needs and the dominant social forces in a regime are satisfied or unsatisfied; (2) whether the level of consolidation of the state is higher or lower. These variables come together in four ideal-typical scenarios associated with variations in foreign policy behaviour, as indicated in Table 1.

Table 1: State formation and foreign policy behaviour

		State consolidation	
		lower	higher
Ruling social forces	unsatisfied	(1a) radical rhetoric	(2a) revisionist power
	satisfied	(1b) external protection	(2b) status quo power

In less consolidated states, policy-making elites, buffeted by or reflecting the views of powerful dissatisfied domestic/trans-state forces, are likely to either (a) appease these forces through radical nationalist rhetoric or (b) seek external protection against them. This choice tends to be determined by whether the ruling elites issue from and/or seek support from plebeian forces rebelling against the dominant regional order (1a) or have their power bases in satisfied dominant classes (1b). Pre-Asad Syria corresponds to the first case and pre-oil boom Saudi Arabia and Jordan to the latter.

By contrast, only reasonably consolidated states can effectively act to enhance the state's external interests, but the differentiation in their ruling social forces will distinguish those

(2a) which use enhanced capabilities to mount revisionist challenge to the dominant regional order (Nasser's Egypt, Saddam's Iraq) or pursue territorial expansion (Israel) from those which (2b) seek to defend the status quo (post-boom Saudi Arabia and Turkey).

The importance of differential state formation experiences for a state's foreign policy orientation is evident in the comparison of Saudi Arabia and Syria: satisfied identities and social forces produced a status quo orientation in the first while frustrated identities and plebeian social forces produced revisionism in the second. It can be seen even more dramatically in the contrast between Jordan and Syria, which, although once part of the same country, *bilad ash-sham*, have been taken by their differing regimes in entirely different foreign policy directions. While the Hashemite monarchy is a beneficiary of Western imperialism's dismemberment of historic Syria, the Damascus regime arose from nationalist rebellion against this victimisation of the country. Consequent differences in the domestic constituencies of the regimes hardened their contrary orientations: Jordan relied on conservative tribal forces to exclude the Arab nationalist middle class and the innately irredentist Palestinians, who make up at least half of the population, from politics. In Syria, the regime arose from the Arab nationalist middle class and was dominated by a formerly deprived minority peasant community seeking acceptance through the championing of Arab nationalism. This case also underlines how differential state formation paths differentially position regimes in the global political economy which, in turn, reinforces the original tangent: thus both Syria and Jordan depend on external rent, but Jordan got much of its support from the West to sustain its role as a buffer state which obstructed the mobilisation of its Palestinian majority against Israel and kept the armies of radical Arab states from its front line with Israel; Syria, by contrast, received Arab rent to sustain its resistance to Israel. Differential state formation translated into opposing foreign policy alignments and strategies: while Syria relied on the Soviets to balance American support for Israel and to achieve the military capability to balance Israeli power, Jordan bandwagoned, appeasing Israel through a long history of secret relations, while relying on a US security umbrella against other regional threats. These differences usually put them on opposing sides of most regional issues and relations were more often bad than good (Brand 1995; Harknett and VanDenBerg 1997; Salloukh 1996).

Similarly, Saudi Arabia and Islamic Iran, while both ostensibly Islamic oil states, are the products of quite different state formation histories that have shaped opposing policies. In Saudi Arabia the militant Ikhwan was early pushed out of the regime coalition in favour of conservative *ulama* and a tribal elite subsequently turned into a petro-bourgeoisie; in Iran the revolution's catapulting to power of un-Westernised elites transformed Iran from the main surrogate of the US in the Gulf to its main challenger. Iran's revolutionary Islam, cast by Khomeini into an expression of revolt against monarchy and Western dominance, was the opposite of the Saudis' conservative establishment Islam. Arguably, these diametrically opposed versions of Islam were expressive of the two countries' opposing experiences of the West: while Saudi Arabia never experienced colonialism and actually achieved independence with Western support, Iranians perceived the West to have overthrown their nationalist leader, Muhammad Mossadeq, in favour of the last Shah. The oil/population ratio in Saudi Arabia allowed a massive export of capital giving Saudi elites a big economic stake in the West; in revolutionary Iran, oil revenues were needed at home to sustain the welfare of its much larger population and to conduct a war brought on by the effort to export Islamic revolution.

Nevertheless, it also seems clear that 'external' systemic forces can powerfully *reinforce or divert* regimes from their original tangents. Thus, Arab nationalist Egypt was only able to pursue its Pan-Arab challenge to the status quo because bi-polarity lifted the main systemic constraint, Western dependency and/or intervention, while the region-wide spread of Arab identity constituted an indispensable system-level resource. However, changes in the balance of systemic forces from the late 1960s, including the unfavourable Arab–Israeli power balance and the oil-boom-induced flow of influence to conservative states, pushed revisionist regimes toward more moderate policies not too different from those of the status quo states. This began when, in the 1967 war, the costs of putting ideology over realism shifted power in Syria and Egypt from revisionist elements toward national security pragmatists. Islamic Iran, similarly 'socialised' into the realist rules of the game by its war with Iraq, also adopted more moderate policies. Mutually reinforcing system-wide forces – the decline of trans-state ideology, the rise of military threats, and the consequent consolidation of the individual states – drove a convergence in the foreign policies of initially very different regimes toward 'realist'-type behaviour (see chapter 4).

Nevertheless, such convergence never ends in uniform behaviour for several reasons. The very different roads taken by Syria and Egypt, operating under the same systemic pressures, in their attempts to recover their lost territories from Israel, make the point that *there is never only one possible response to system pressures,* even among similar regimes. If at first these pressures drove the two states along similar paths, ultimately they responded differently. In Syria, the result was the state-building and realpolitik through which Asad was enabled to pursue more limited goals more effectively. The more intense pressures on Egypt so shifted Sadat's ruling coalition toward embourgeoised class fractions that republican Egypt's initially nationalist foreign policy was turned on its head. Such an outcome can only adequately be understood by analysis of the interaction between the unique features of each state's formation and the unique systemic positions each occupied. It was chiefly the difference in their geopolitical power position that determined why Egypt had the option of a separate peace and Syria probably did not. But domestic features decided how the two states responded to their environments: differences in identity and levels of presidential dominance explain why the Egyptian regime *could* make a separate peace at reasonable cost and the Syrian one *could not*; differences in the bases of the leaders' support explain why Sadat had an incentive and Asad a disincentive to take such a path.

Additionally, as realism itself acknowledges, the 'realist' behaviour supposedly imposed by the states system can take two diametrically opposite forms, the balancing that stronger (and autonomous) states tend to pursue and the bandwagoning typical of weaker (and dependent) ones. It is differential state formation, locating states in varying power or dependency positions in the system, that makes the difference in state conduct. Thus, in spite of a substantial convergence toward realism by the Saudi and Syrian regimes, driven by the shared Israeli threat and facilitated by the similar effects of oil on state formation, differences persisted. These were initially rooted in the contrasting impacts of imperialism on identity, but were, in certain ways, reinforced by subsequent differences in their systemic positions. Syria, locked by the consequences of its earlier revisionism into a drive to recover the occupied territories from a militarily superior Israel, restructured itself to match Israeli power and, despite a certain post-Cold War bandwagoning toward the US forced by the collapse of Soviet power, largely continued to balance against Israel. Saudi Arabia, a status quo power enjoying Western protection, had no comparable incentive for military strengthening and domestic reasons to eschew it. Its weakness wedded it to a policy of bandwagoning – temporarily bending before the most intense pressure of the moment. Thus, in 1973 the threat from trans-state ideological penetration initially bent the kingdom's policies in an uncharacteristically radical direction – the oil embargo against its US patron – at odds with the interests of its conservative ruling social forces; however, once released from Pan-Arab pressures, it quickly reverted to its traditional deference to Washington. More important, Saudi Arabia's sheikhs, thereafter transformed into wealthy partners with the Western oil companies, acquired such a stake in the Western economy that Arab nationalism and Islam could be no more than thin veneers of limited relevance to foreign policy.

Finally, even where systemic forces divert states off their original tangents they have seldom been strong or sustained enough to wholly overcome the biases built in by state formation. Thus, while systemic pressures – the Iranian threat – drove a convergence in the policies of Jordan and Iraq, making them close allies in the 1980s, this did not persist. Iraq's need for Western and Gulf support against Iran temporarily moderated Saddam Hussein's nationalism, but when the Iranian threat was turned back, Iraq reverted to its original revisionist tangent. Although the trans-state ideological arousal of its population could temporarily force Jordan's weak status quo monarchy into policies incompatible with its interests, such as joining Nasser in 1967 and Saddam Hussein in 1991, once such pressures passed, the regime quickly reverted to its 'natural' pro-Western posture.

Globalisation is expected by some liberals to transform states through democratisation and, in consequence, to put an end to realist dynamics at the system level by spreading the 'zone of peace' to the region. So far, however, the record suggests no such straightforward association between regime type and foreign policy behaviour. Authoritarian regimes can be status quo or revisionist: Nasser's Egypt fought three wars with Israel in the name of Arab nationalism and Sadat's Egypt made peace with it at the expense of Arab nationalism. Absolutism was associated with foreign policy caution in the Gulf monarchies and foreign policy recklessness in Saddam's Iraq. Nor do Turkey and Israel show there to be any necessary relation in the Middle East between democratisation and foreign policy behaviour. Pluralistic political institutions have incorporated significant levels of mass participation in each country but its effect on policy-making has been neither as important nor as 'pacific' as the democratic peace thesis expects. In both, foreign policy is primarily shaped by elite conceptions of security and geopolitical interest. Moreover, when non-elite influences impact on policy, they tend to express irredentism, not pacifism, but much more so in Israel where dissatisfaction with status quo (pre-1967) borders runs deep. Because such democratic states enjoy greater popular support, hence mobilisable capabilities, they may well be more dangerous than their ultimately weaker authoritarian counterparts. The region's most pluralist states stand out for their irredentist activism in neighbouring territory: Morocco's annexation of Western Sahara, Israel's settlement of the occupied territories and Turkey's role in northern Cyprus. Although democratic peace theorists will argue that peace mostly obtains between democratic states and only kicks in when they dominate a regional system, the Middle East evidence suggests that the democratic peace may be chiefly an artefact of regions where satisfied states enjoy secure identities. As long as irredentism and insecurity remain basic features of the Middle East regional system, the foreign policy impact of the form of government will, as realism expects, be relatively limited (Goldgeier and McFaul 1992).

7

War and order in the regional system

The roots of war

War has profoundly shaped the Middle East regional system. The Middle East has two of the world's most enduring conflict centres, each originating in the impact of the West on the region. The establishment of Israel at the expense of the indigenous Palestinians led to a chain of wars, each of which added new grievances and issues complicating the possibility of a resolution. In the Gulf, the struggle over oil and oil routes has been expressed in another chain of wars, which can be traced back to the Western overthrow of Muhammad Mossadeq, who had attempted to nationalise Iran's oil; this was a major factor in the Iranian revolution, which set the stage for the first and second Gulf wars. Conflicts over Israel and oil have tended to feed on each other, as in the 1973 oil embargo triggered by the Arab–Israeli war of that year.

War has originated in domestic-level dissatisfaction shaped by these struggles which, when institutionalised in rival states, is expressed in conflict at the states system level, frequently over territory. Everywhere, in a region afflicted with irredentism, domestic politics encourages nationalist outbidding. Revolution in states such as Egypt and Iran brought leaders to power who sought to export their ideology; revolution, in mobilising new social forces, tended to strengthen certain states and upset power balances. Demographic, ideological or political expansionist impulses have been built into the very fabric of some states, as is arguably so of Israel (a settler state) and Iraq (an artificial state), which, between them, have launched five wars against their neighbours. Weak or authoritarian regimes have made repeated miscalculations, plunging their states into unplanned wars, as in 1967, or mis-planned ones, such as Iraq's misadventures. While the anarchic logic of a states system need not, in itself, reproduce a struggle for power, each war has been a watershed in the 'construction' of such a Hobbesian system in the Middle East. The security dilemma has been played out to the full, with states' fear-driven accumulation of power only increasing insecurity for their neighbours and generating periodic power imbalances that provided occasions of war. The failure of order-building efforts to address these war-inducing factors has made the Middle East immune to the spread of the 'zone of peace'.

The emergence of a Middle East system

Built-in irredentism, origins of the Arab–Israeli conflict
In observing that the Middle East states system was 'born fighting', Buzan and Waever (2003) point to how the simultaneity of formal Arab independence and the outbreak of the first Arab–Israeli war established the major line of identity cleavage, threat and alliance formation around which the regional system was rapidly organised. The irredentism built into the flawed states system imposed on the region after World War I was epitomised by the conflict over Palestine.

This conflict originated in the rise of the Zionist movement whose profoundly irredentist project was to literally recreate an 'old nation' on the ruins of a newly awakening – Arab Palestinian – one. The Zionist movement believed the Jews made up a nation and were entitled to a state, logically on the territory of biblical Israel. They convinced the British government, which calculated that a Jewish presence in Palestine would support its control over the area, to sponsor a homeland for Jews in Palestine (the Balfour Declaration), although contemporaneously Britain was (in the MacMahon–Hussein correspondence) also making a largely incompatible commitment to Arab self-determination in historic Syria (Gerner 1991: 29–30, 34–35; Knightly 1991: 11; Schulze 1999; Smith 1996; 45–46). After Britain acquired the post-World War I mandate over Palestine, Zionist settlement began in earnest. Although the Balfour Declaration specified that the Jewish homeland should not 'prejudice the rights of the existing population', the Zionist project meant two peoples claiming the same land and conflict between incoming settlers and the Palestinian community was inevitable. In 1890, Jews made up 3% of the population of Palestine and 11% in 1922 but by 1948 they constituted around one-third. They were initially concentrated in urban enclaves but by 1948 they were able to acquire 8–10% of the land, largely through purchase from absentee landlords (Gerner 1991: 11, 17–18; Smith 1996: 24, 107).

Zionist emigration provoked the political arousal of the Palestinian community and engendered a distinct Palestinian identity. Palestinian resistance took the form of protests and non-co-operation with the British authorities and in 1936–39 a major uprising. This rebellion failed due to Palestinian divisions and British imperial might, but, to appease Arab opinion, Zionist emigration was limited until World War II when the Jewish exodus from Europe began. When the British withdrew from Palestine in 1948 and the Palestinians rejected a UN resolution partitioning Palestine at their expense, the Zionists declared the founding of the state of Israel. The armies of Arab states intervened, ostensibly to rescue the Palestinians.

The first Arab–Israeli war is often depicted as an unequal contest in which the infant Israeli state fought off Arab attempts to strangle it in its crib. In fact, the virtual destruction of the Palestinian national movement in the British repression of the 1936 rebellion left the Palestinians nearly defenceless while the British had allowed their Zionist counterpart to arm itself during World War II – thereby sowing the seeds of the Israeli army (Gerner 1991: 44–46; Smith 1996: 115–117, 140). The well-organised and mobilised Zionist movement entered the conflict as a state-in-formation while the fragile Arab monarchies and oligarchies were too dependent on the West and too paralysed by rivalries to adopt an effective position against it. Far from being zealous for war, it was only their fear that Arab public opinion would hold them responsible for the loss of Palestine that led to their half-hearted intervention. Egypt's Prime Minister Nuqrashi told the Egyptian commander that intervention would be a mere political demonstration for public consumption. Saudi Arabia was completely unwilling to endanger its US relations by adopting the anti-Western economic sanctions called for in Arab League resolutions (Maddy-Weitzman 1993: 61–67). Jordan's King Abdullah reached an understanding with the Zionists to occupy the Arab areas in the partition plan and thereafter maintained a tacit ceasefire that permitted them to make gains at the expanse of the Egyptian army in the south and in Galilee during the second round of the war. In large part because of Abdullah's ambitions and the concern of the other Arab states to thwart them as much as to counter Israel, the Zionists were able to wage successful offensives against each Arab army consecutively (Sela 1998: 40). Similarly, in the truce negotiations with Israel, Egypt and Jordan eschewed the common stand that might have improved their leverage. Subsequently King Abdullah not only annexed the Palestinian territory that his army controlled (the 'West Bank') to his kingdom in defiance of the Arab League and Palestinian claims, but was even prepared to enter a separate peace with Israel.

The first Arab–Israeli war created the conditions for further wars since the fighting was ended by a mere armistice that left the main issues unresolved. Israel had acquired much more territory than the UN partition plan allowed, indeed over three-quarters of Palestine, leaving the so-called 'West Bank' rump in the hands of Jordan and the Gaza strip under Egyptian control. Fears of being caught in the fighting, aggravated by Zionist terror, led to a massive flight of Palestinian refugees who were not allowed by a triumphant Israel to return to their homes when the fighting ended in spite of UN resolutions to that effect. This Palestinian exodus left large concentrations of them on the West Bank, significant numbers in refugee camps in Lebanon and Syria, and smaller numbers in Egypt and the Gulf. The loss of Palestine threatened Palestinians, now a stateless people, with the loss of their identity. However, the Palestinian Diaspora throughout the Middle East produced a stratum of politically active intellectuals who helped radicalise the rising middle-class nationalist movements in the various Arab countries and kept the Palestinian cause at the top of political agendas. The refugee camps became the crucible of the Palestinian resistance; they were reservoirs of disaffected youth, who, increasingly educated under UN administration, but without normal economic opportunities, had little to lose by joining the national liberation movement that would eventually become the Palestine Liberation Organisation (PLO). A minority of Palestinian villagers who remained in Israel received a second-class form of citizenship, which did not prevent continual creeping confiscations of their land by the Israeli state. On the other hand, Jews from the Arab countries immigrated to Israel, fleeing Arab animosity, sometimes deliberately stirred up by Zionist agents. This allowed the construction of an undiluted Jewish identity for Israel (Gerner 1991: 50–56, 59, 62–63; Peri 1988: 44; Sela 1998: 40–41; Smith 1996: 142).

The sub-state communal conflict of Palestinian and Jew had now been transformed into an inter-state conflict between Israel and its Arab neighbours (Gerner 1991: 49). The Arab states rejected peace with Israel. In Arab eyes, Israel was no ordinary state but an extension of the West, a bridgehead of world Jewry rejecting assimilation into the area, and which, seeking to incorporate Jews from around the world and with access to global resources, had a limitless appetite for expansion. To head off popular pressures for a second round – at least until there might be a decline in Israel's external support – the Arab League states refused to establish normal relations with Israel and imposed an economic boycott against it. The Arab League consensus was enforced against King Abdullah of Jordan who had negotiated a non-belligerency agreement which even his own political elite rejected (Sela 1998: 51) and which led to his assassination. Before long, championship of the Palestinian cause would become an indispensable nationalist credential for aspiring Arab political leaders.

For Israel, the war left unfinished business that shaped its subsequent foreign policy. It lacked secure readily defensible borders, especially with Jordan, while a portion of biblical Israel (the West Bank) remained in Arab hands. Security was foremost on the agenda of the new state because, although the military capabilities of the Arab states were modest, Israel's small geographic space, lack of strategic depth and encirclement by a hostile Arab world with ten times its population led to a sense of permanent siege. David Ben Gurion, Israel's founding leader who shaped much elite thinking, expressed Israel's perception of the Arabs: Israel, he asserted, had been inhabited by Arab invaders for 1,300 years but once the homeless persecuted Jews had finally achieved a small notch of territory, the Arabs sought to reduce her territory, flood her with refugees, seize Jerusalem and ghettoise her by blockade (Brecher 1972: 552; Gerner 1991: 44).

Israel responded to Arab hostility, as Brown (1988: 134) put it, with 'both bristling aggressiveness and poignantly stated yearning for peace with its neighbours'. On the one hand, Israel sought to negotiate a peace settlement that would relieve it of Arab hostility; on the other hand, the Ben Gurionists urged the permanent application of force to extract recognition and normalisation of relations on Israel's terms: Arab acceptance of its control of most of Palestine without Israeli concessions over borders or the Palestinian refugees. Ben Gurion insisted the Arabs would only accept Israel once it was shown to be invincible; they had, moreover, to be taught the costs of challenging it through disproportionate punishment. Incursions by displaced Palestinians, armed or not, across Israel's new borders with Jordan and Egypt were met by massive retaliation against these countries, including the targeting of civilian populations suspected of harbouring guerrillas. Continual disputes between Israel and the Arab states over poorly demarcated borders, de-militarised zones and water rights also regularly escalated into military clashes, particularly on the Syrian–Israeli frontier. The periodic clashes with neighbouring Arab countries which Israeli policy promoted had, however, the effect of inflaming and spreading Pan-Arab nationalism which preached the idea of a common Arab nation united against Israel and its Western backers. They contributed to the rise of more radical governments, more motivated and better equipped to confront Israel, and made trusteeship of the Palestine cause a prize sought by states vying for Pan-Arab leadership (Brecher 1972: 251–290; Roberts 1990: 17–21; Smith 1996: 157–159; Walt 1987: 57).

From oligarchic multi-polarity (1945–55) to the Egypt-centric Pan-Arab system (1956–70)

In the aftermath of World War II, a rudimentary Middle East order emerged amidst pervasive irredentism. The periphery states, Turkey, Iran and Israel, more advanced in nation-building, militarily stronger and aligned with the West, flanked a weak, fragmented Arab core just emerging from colonial control. The Arab regimes were narrow-based oligarchies or dynasties, highly penetrated by the great powers, above all by Britain, which retained bases and treaty relations with regimes headed by its clients, and moderated regional conflicts.

Dissatisfaction with artificial boundaries was an immediate issue. The initial source of revisionism within the Arab world was unfulfilled Hashemite ambitions: Iraq's dreams of becoming an Arab Prussia unifying the Fertile Crescent and Jordan's Greater Syria scheme. The counter-alliance of Egypt and Saudi Arabia with Syria, which was most directly threatened by the Hashemite states, the restraint put on the Hashemites by their British patron, and limited military capabilities on all sides helped preserve the systemic status quo. In addition, the shared elitist (dynastic or oligarchic) ideology of the regimes brought them to accept the rules of a multi-polar system – that no state should endanger the vital interests of its neighbours (Maddy-Weitzman 1993; Mufti 1996: 21–59; Seale 1965: 5–99). The Arab League attempted to both institutionalise respect for the sovereignty of individual states while acknowledging shared Arab identities and facilitating a collective response to the common threat from Zionism. Its legitimacy was, however, tarnished by its failure to co-ordinate the defence of Palestine and the most it achieved was a consensus against relations with Israel.

The main underlying threat to this early order was the instability within the individual states: the weak popular loyalty to newly imposed regimes within arbitrary boundaries, gross maldistribution of wealth, still incomplete de-colonisation, and the loss of Palestine all soon more or less de-legitimised the regimes. Their weakness meant the system could be rapidly transformed by the intersection of two forces: the political mobilisation of the Pan-Arab middle class and the rise of Egypt's Nasser who sought, with considerable success, to replace Western hegemony with an Egypt-centric Pan-Arab order.

Nasser successfully upset the oligarchic power balance on which the existing order rested but not through military superiority. Part of Egypt's pre-eminence derived from its stature as the most stable and coherent of the Arab states, with a developed bureaucracy and, unusually, a coincidence between state borders and a relatively distinctive identity. Egypt was also the most populous Arab state, having 30% of the Arab population. It had, as well, the largest GNP, which gave it a limited ability to provide economic aid, and supported the largest army through defence expenditures double those of any other Arab state (Walt 1987: 53; Noble 1991: 61–65, 74–75). But Egypt normally could not use its army to project power, being cut off from the Arab East by Israel and constrained by international norms. What gave Egypt hegemony was Nasser's asymmetrical ability to project trans-state ideological influence, that is, to mobilise domestic pressure on other Arab leaders by appealing to their own populations in the name of Pan-Arabism while his own regime was relatively immune to similar penetration.

Behind this asymmetry was the coincidence of several developments: Nasser's successful incorporation of popular support at home, giving his regime much greater stability than the Western-dependent oligarchies and monarchies; the emergence of middle-class nationalist movements across the region, radicalised by the Arab–Israeli conflict, the struggle with imperialism and the traditional elites' unwillingness to share power; the advent of the transistor radio which allowed Radio Cairo to reach this audience; and Nasser's foreign policy victories against the West – notably the Czech arms deal, his successful stand against the Baghdad Pact and the Western failure at Suez – which transformed him into a Pan-Arab hero. Nasser was enabled to unleash an Arab nationalist revolutionary wave which precipitated coups and movements against pro-Western regimes across the region, culminating in the fall of Hashemite Iraq, the pillar of the pro-Western order and the formation of the UAR which briefly united Egypt with the most intensely Pan-Arab state, Syria. In time, this wave was consolidated in a series of kindred Arab nationalist regimes in Syria, Iraq, Algeria, the Yemens, and later in Sudan and Libya. This outcome was a function of an imbalance in state formation and ideological legitimacy, not in military power (Barnett 1998: 100–103, 128; Cremeans 1963; Dawisha 1976: 174–175).

Egypt's ideological hegemony positioned Nasser to lay down standards of Pan-Arab conduct that forced even the remaining Western-dependent regimes to observe common Arab nationalist norms. Indeed, Nasser arguably created an informal 'Pan-Arab regime' which, in enforcing values already pervasive in Arab political culture, constrained the unfettered exercise of state sovereignty in foreign policy. The power of one core norm, independence from imperialism, was established by the defeat of Hashemite Iraq, which had insisted on its sovereign right to protect its security through the Baghdad Pact, against Egypt's claim that all Arab states had obligations toward a Pan-Arab community whose independence could only be consolidated by shouldering its own collective defence. Egypt's victory was reflected in the widespread cancelling of Western base rights and treaties and the reluctance of conservative states to overtly align with their Western protectors as they sought to appease – bandwagon with – Egypt. The second norm, the rejection of the legitimacy of Israel and support of the Palestine cause (ideally the liberation of Palestine), did not translate into effective common action against Israel but it did enforce Israel's isolation; thus, Jordan, even when most threatened by its Arab nationalist neighbours, refrained from alliance with Israel, although covertly the kingdom benefited from an understanding that Israel would intervene if Jordan appeared in danger of absorption. Finally, lip service, at least, was given to the view that inter-Arab conflict should be settled peacefully in arenas such as the Arab League or through mediation and, in fact, such conflict was largely confined to low-intensity ideological subversion. The 'Pan-Arab regime' was facilitated by the shared identity of Arab elites and enforced by their fear of the internal opposition Nasser could mobilise against its violation. Nasser did not become the Bismarck of the Arab world but his Pan-Arab hegemony imposed some foreign policy coherence on it and made it much more impervious to Western influence and intervention than heretofore (Barnett 1998: 8–18; Brown 1984: 88, 162–117; Gerges, 1994: 245–251; Kerr 1971; Walt 1987: 206–212). This combination allowed the establishment of a relatively autonomous regional system.

Nevertheless, the Pan-Arab 'regime' was always precarious. Disagreements over Pan-Arab norms – the extent of permissible relations with the West, the degree of militancy toward Israel – and Cairo's attempt to impose its interpretation, especially when this spilled over into a revolutionary challenge to the very legitimacy of rival states, provoked an anti-hegemonic backlash. When the 1958 revolution toppled the Hashemites in Iraq and it looked as if the conservative side would be overwhelmed, Western intervention in Lebanon and Jordan checked the domino effect and helped stabilise conservative regimes. After this, Nasser's conservative rivals were less reluctant to defy him. The consequent 'Arab Cold War' (Kerr 1971) interlocked with the competition of the two superpowers whose aid and protection to the opposing camps reinforced a regional polarisation, loosely mirroring bi-polarity. However, Nasser's unwillingness to share power even with ideological allies, manifest in the failure of the UAR, stimulated an anti-Cairo reaction among kindred Pan-Arab leaders as well. Thus, the revolutionary camp split when Abd al-Karim Qasim, Iraq's revolutionary leader, rejected Egyptian tutelage and Nasser, in response, joined Jordan and Saudi Arabia in sending troops to protect Kuwait from Qasim's 1961 challenge to its independence. The 1963 Ba'thist coups in Iraq and Syria raised the potential of a powerful new Pan-Arab bloc, but the Ba'thists' fear of Nasser's domination caused the fail-ure of the unity talks with Egypt: instead the weaker Syrian and Iraqi regimes balanced against ideologically kindred Egypt and chal-lenged Nasser's leadership of the radical camp which again pushed Nasser into detente with the conservative regimes. The ideological bi-polarity that had put pro-Western regimes on the defensive was thus cross-cut by phases of 'revolutionary polycentrism' in which Nasser tacitly aligned with conservative regimes against Pan-Arab rivals, relieving the pressure on the former. Moreover, in a classic act of realist balancing, the periphery states, Israel, Iran and Turkey, aligned, albeit tacitly and intermittently, in the so-called 'periphery pact' to contain the putative radical nationalist threat from the Arab core (Barnett 1998: 129–145; Kerr 1971; Walt, 1987: 67–79, 204).

As such, from the mid-1950s through the mid-1960s the regional order combined features of the balance of power with those of a supra-state community. On the one hand, the sovereignty of the individual states and the status quo state system were preserved by anti-hegemonic balancing and, in a crisis, outside intervention. On the other hand, trans-state Pan-Arabism (amidst global bi-polarity) reduced the historic permeability of the system to outside penetration and confined inter-Arab competition to the ideological level. As a security regime, this order was, however, fundamentally unstable: in institutionalising the cleavage with the non-Arab periphery, it provided no instrument, other than a pre-carious power balance, for addressing the security dilemma on these fault-lines; and its ideological heterogeneity provoked the nationalist competition and, ultimately, the crisis with Israel in May 1967, in which this balance was destabilised.

Two Arab–Israeli wars and the reshaping of the Middle East system

The June 1967 war

Wars are catalysts for change in states systems and the 1967 war, no exception, signalled the decline of Egyptian hegemony and the Egypt-centric 'Arab regime'. The 1973 war precipitated a second watershed, the beginning of the Arab–Israeli peace process. These two wars initiated a transition period from the Pan-Arab era toward a more multi-polar state-centric system in which sovereignty started to eclipse Arabism.

The roots of war: Israeli geopolitical needs   Israel launched the 1967 war and its motives constitute its immediate cause. There was a certain expansionist impulse literally built into the fabric of Israel's identity. Israel considers itself not an ordinary state or a Middle Eastern society but the territorial base of world Jewry, the Diaspora – a trans-national sense of kinship which has no exact parallel in world politics (Brecher 1972: 38). Although only about 17% of Jews lived in Israel in 1966 (2.3 million out of 13.4 million), it was, in principle, committed to their 'ingathering': according to the Law of Return, Diaspora Jews have an automatic right of citizenship (Gerner 1991: 59; Peri 1988: 44) and Israeli policy actively promoted Jewish immigration, often settled on land from which Palestinians were dispossessed. Absorbing a growing population in an arid land led Israel to seek greater control over regional water resources, initiating projects to divert the waters of the Jordan River in the 1960s that the Arabs took as a provocation and a bid to further emigration. The parallel pressure for more land was reinforced by dissatisfaction among many Israelis with the incomplete Judaisation of the territory of ancient Eretz Yisrael and the consequent belief among militant nationalists that the completion of the Zionist project required the incorporation of 'Judea/Samaria' – before 1967 the Jordanian-controlled 'West Bank' of the Jordan River. This ambition was explicit and institutionalised in the Herut party but latent throughout Israeli society (Smith 1996: 193).

It was, however, security needs that most immediately motivated Israeli decision-makers. Even though Israel had twice defeated its divided Arab neighbours, the loss of even one war could spell national extinction. Israel's frontiers were uniquely vulnerable; in particular, the Jordanian-controlled West Bank was a salient protruding into Israel from which an Arab thrust to the sea could cut Israel in two. Moreover, the potential of Arab demographic and resource superiority shaped Israeli security doctrine and military practice in a way that was likely to provoke war. Given the vulnerability of its borders, Israel could not afford to fight a war on its territory and had to take one into the enemy's territory before it could threaten the homeland. Because Israel's superiority was problematic if the Arab forces effectively combined and forced a multi-front war on it, preventing such a combination was a constant of Israeli policy and this required a pro-active military stance. Additionally, because Israel, being reliant on the mobilisation of reserves, could not sustain a prolonged war without great damage to its economy, wars had to be won quickly through overwhelming force. These vulnerabilities resulted in a doctrine favouring a 'pre-emptive' (first strike) strategy that aimed at quickly smashing the enemy and, in a multi-front war, would allow one opponent to be neutralised in order to cope with the other/s. Since collective Arab action had normally been a function of Egyptian success in uniting the Arabs and, particularly, co-ordinating with Syria and Jordan, Israel considered a whole range of Egyptian-initiated actions to be a casus belli justifying a first strike, notably the concentration of Egyptian forces in the Sinai and the ascendancy of Egyptian influence over Jordan: the Israeli 1967 first strike responded to such an emerging scenario (Brecher 1972: 51, 67).

Later wars are often the continuation of earlier rounds and 1967, no exception, was a product of dissatisfaction at the outcome of the 1956 Suez war, which was, itself, a continuation of the unfinished business left over from the 1948 first Arab–Israeli war. Regarding the Suez war, Egypt's arming of displaced Palestinians in Gaza who launched incursions into Israel in the early 1950s had precipitated disproportionate Israeli retaliation against Egyptian positions and sparked an arms race between Egypt and Israel, with France becoming Israel's main supplier and the Soviet Union Egypt's. In the years before 1956, there had been some dispute within the Israeli elite over whether to escalate or de-escalate this rising conflict through diplomatic conciliation. Moshe Sharett, foreign minister and briefly prime minister, urged the latter and Ben Gurion the former; it took Sharett's ousting from power by the Ben Gurionists to prepare the way for war while Nasser's nationalisation of the Suez Canal, facilitating Israeli collusion with Britain and France, made the international environment permissive for a first strike on Egypt (Brecher 1972: 389–392). Israel's 1956 attack, in which it occupied Egypt's Sinai peninsula, aimed to destroy Egypt's new military capabilities, force it to reopen the Straits of Tiran which it had closed to Israeli shipping after 1948, and either destabilise Nasser's Arab nationalist government or force it to concede a peace treaty in return for evacuation of the Sinai.

Israel achieved the opening of the straits and a UN force on the border that ended infiltration from Gaza, but US President Dwight Eisenhower forced its withdrawal from the Sinai without further political gains and, indeed, the Israeli use of force achieved the opposite of its aims. It accelerated the spread of Arab nationalism and consolidated Nasser's stature as a Pan-Arab leader carrying responsibility for the Palestinian cause, thereby locking Egypt into confrontation with Israel. Egypt was also dissatisfied by what it considered to be the rewards Israel had received for its aggression, notably the opening of the Straits of Tiran, and in the pre-war crisis of May 1967 Nasser again closed them. Israel's powerful Ben Gurionists, whose ambitions for defensible borders and/or more living space had been frustrated in 1956, found in this crisis another opportunity to realise them (Gerner 1991: 66–69; Smith 1996: 171–174; Walt 1987: 66).

Israeli elites were also initially divided in 1967, and the decision for war was, in some ways, a product of intra-elite power rivalries. An activist camp, dominant in the military and led by disciples of Ben Gurion such as Moshe Dayan, the hero of the Suez campaign, Yigal Allon and Shimon Peres, saw the Arabs as an implacable enemy and Nasser as the new Hitler. They were convinced that Israel enjoyed the decisive military superiority to take on the enemy (Brecher 1972: 552; Smith 1996: 196). At the same time, the irredentist Herut party of Menachem Begin was growing in influence as a pressure group for expansion and also had its advocates in the military (Brecher 1972: 247; Roberts 1990: 36; Smith 1996: 192). A pragmatic tendency in Israeli elite thinking, normally a minority view in the establishment but temporarily on the ascendancy in the mid-1960s, was more prepared to seek accommodation with the Arabs and argued against military actions that could alienate Israel's supporters in the West. The cautious and pragmatic Levi Eshkol, prime minister in 1967, was closer to the moderate camp.

The Ben Gurionist hawks, who had split from the ruling Mapai party, used their image as war heroes to paint the pragmatists as soft on the Arabs. Backed by the military establishment, they used the May 1967 crisis to demand key cabinet positions in a national unity government from which they would push Eshkol into a first strike. Dayan became defence minister while Begin also received a portfolio in this government. While Dayan and Allon were planning a war to enlarge Israel's borders, Eshkol, innocent of such strategic visions, wished to rely on American diplomacy to defuse the crisis and was averse to a pre-emptive strike. However, he succumbed to military pressure and the hawks, in charge of actual military decision-making, launched Israel's first strike (Kimsche and Bawly 1968: 45, 57, 62, 69; Peri 1983: 244–251).

Domestic-driven Arab regional dynamics   Israel's attack on its neighbours unleashed the war but it was the dynamics of Pan-Arabism which gave Israeli hawks the opportunity to realise their ambitions; specifically Nasser's need to protect his Arab leadership against challenges from both the left and the right led him into fatal brinkmanship in the spring of 1967 (Barnett 1998: 153–159; Stein, 1993: 62–67).

From the mid-1960s, Egypt, as Pan-Arab leader, was under growing pressure to act against Israel's diversion of the Jordan River. Also, the Palestinian refugees were increasingly impatient for Arab action to resolve their plight; indeed, newly founded groups such as al-Fatah launched a guerrilla struggle against Israel that they hoped would detonate a wider Arab–Israeli war. Nasser argued that the Arab world had to build up its forces, modernise and unify before it would be ready for confrontation with Israel and, with his best forces tied down in the Yemen civil war, he could hardly afford a war. But his Arab rivals, particularly Syria, used the issue to put him on the defensive (Sela 1998: 52–53, 78). The Syrian–Israeli conflict dated back to differences over the de-militarised zones established by the 1948 armistice. Israel's 'creeping annexation' of these zones (Gerner 1991: 70), Syrian shelling of the paramilitary settlements Israel implanted in them and the resulting massive Israeli retaliation generated a particularly radical version of Arab nationalism in Syria and was a factor in bringing the Ba'th party to power in 1963. The radical but narrow-based Ba'thist regime began championing the Palestine cause to win domestic legitimacy and outbid Nasser for Pan-Arab leadership. To contain revisionist Syria, Nasser initiated Arab summit meetings to spread responsibility for inaction among the Arab leaders. The summits agreed to counter Israel by diverting the Jordan River sources which, since these rose in Syria, would force Damascus to bear the consequences of its own militancy. However, the Syrian Ba'th used Israeli attacks on its diversion works to embarrass Nasser, criticising the UN buffer force in the Sinai (UNEF) which prevented him from deterring Israel. Saudi Arabia, at odds with Egypt over Yemen, taunted Nasser for having troops in Yemen when they were needed against Israel. Syria took advantage of this to entice Nasser into a radical Cairo–Damascus axis. While Nasser hoped this would remove Syria's incentive for nationalist outbidding, Damascus viewed it as the essential backing for its sponsorship of Palestinian guerrilla warfare against Israel. This fedayeen action was the immediate precipitant of the escalation that would lead to war (Kerr, 1971: 96–128; Sela 1998: 75–90; Walt 1987: 86–87). It also prepared the ground for bringing Jordan into the Arab coalition encircling Israel. An Israeli raid on Jordan because of guerrilla attacks sponsored by Syria had convinced King Hussein that Israel did not reward moderation. He responded to the Cairo propaganda attacks that were stirring up his population by goading Nasser for his inaction, helping to bring about the inflamed crisis of May 1967 in which aroused public opinion forced him to stand against Israel. Even knowing it could cost him his territory and army, domestic pressure left Hussein no choice but to align with Egypt and Syria as war approached (Stein 1993: 65–66).

From unstable strategic environment to crisis A situation of strategic instability existed in the Middle East in 1967 because the decisive military advantage lay with offence: since weapons, particularly aircraft, were vulnerable while no country enjoyed much strategic depth, a first strike could give decisive advantage once one or more sides had acquired a significant offensive capability. Both the Soviet Union and the West (France and the US) stepped up arms deliveries in the 1960s. While Soviet deliveries to Egypt, Syria and Iraq were quantitatively greater they were mostly defensive in nature while Israel received weapons giving it an offensive capability (Smith 1996: 196). Although far from evident to the Arabs, an imbalance of power in Israel's favour had emerged and the Israeli generals' planning for a pre-emptive war was entirely rational. However, it took a crisis to translate this predisposition into actual war.

That crisis was provoked when in May 1967 Israeli retaliations for guerrilla incursions by Syrian-backed Palestinians climaxed in an Israeli threat to attack and overthrow the Syrian regime. The Soviet Union prodded Nasser to deter Israel and, as leader of the Arab world, he felt obliged to do so. Nasser realised the power balance, with his best forces tied down in Yemen, was unfavourable and did not, therefore, want a war but he could not remain passive. He therefore requested UN withdrawal from the Sinai and sent troops into the peninsula as a deterrent and with defensive instructions that assumed an Israeli first strike. Israel abandoned plans for an attack on Syria but began a counter-mobilisation, which put it in a position to launch a more general war (Gerges 1994: 213; Gerner 1991: 71; Sela 1998: 91–93; Stein 1993: 64).

Nasser could have de-escalated but he allowed himself to be pushed into further brinkmanship by the expectations raised by his own nationalist rhetoric. Seeing a chance to win another political victory and perhaps extract some concessions from Israel on the Palestinian issue, he re-closed the Straits of Tiran to Israeli shipping. Popular euphoria that the Arabs were finally confronting Israel swept the front-line states into a defence pact encircling Israel. In essence, the Arab-nationalist 'outbidding' in which the rival Arab states had engaged was leading them into a war none wanted. In Israel, the crisis raised the public's sense of threat to its maximum: Egyptian troop movements, the closing of the straits and the three-front Arab alliance gave the Israeli hawks their casus belli. Once Israel began to mobilise, at economic cost, it would not long wait for diplomacy to end the closure of the Straits. The actual military threat to Israel was moderate: Nasser had no intention of striking first and the Israeli generals were confident of victory. The real threat was political: a superpower-brokered resolution of the crisis that could strengthen Nasser and further embolden the Arabs (Gerner 1991: 71–72; Smith 1996: 199). For the Israeli hawks, the crisis was less a threat than an opportunity – to smash Nasserist Egypt and the Pan-Arab movement while Israel still had military superiority, to achieve secure borders, force the Arabs to accept Israel and, for some, such as Menachem Begin, to realise Eretz Yisrael. Pre-emption was Israel's historic strategy and the main restraint on it had always been fear of the international repercussions, but in June 1967 the international situation was unusually permissive (Barnett, 1998: 146–159; Peri 1983: 244–251; Sela 1998: 91–93; Smith 1996: 196–202).

International permissiveness   Even as expansionist pressures were peaking in Israel, the great power restraints that had long maintained relative stability on the Arab–Israeli front were breaking down. While the Tripartite Declaration had initially restrained the arms race, the French were now giving Israel sophisticated weaponry out of resentment at Nasser's backing for Algerian independence. Nasser's challenge to Western interests in the region, inescapable if he wished to retain his leadership of Arab nationalism, had earned him accumulated resentment in the West where he was increasingly perceived as a Soviet client who should be brought down (see chapter 2, pp. 39–40).

Nasser overplayed his hand in the crisis of spring 1967 in part because he had become complacent about his ability to manipulate bi-polarity. With the Suez precedent in mind, he miscalculated that the US would restrain Israel for fear a war would inflame Arab opinion against the West or bring confrontation with the USSR. Nasser's defence minister, General Shams ad-Din Badran, apparently misled him into believing the Soviets had promised intervention to deter Israel; but, in fact, it was Moscow that would be deterred when war broke out by fear of a confrontation with the US (Gerges 1994: 224–225). Moreover, Nasser had given the US a commitment that Egypt would not be the one to initiate war and was led to think that the US was trying to broker a negotiated settlement of the crisis that would give him a Suez-like political victory (Gerges 1994: 218–222). But unlike the Suez war in which Egypt, clearly the victim, benefited from world opinion, in 1967 Arab rhetoric allowed Israel to portray itself as the victim of aggression to world opinion, generating a permissive environment for an Israeli first strike.

Meanwhile, US President Lyndon Johnson, a Cold War ideologue and friend of Israel, initially counselled Israeli restraint. He expected Israel would win a war, but did not want to have to intervene on Israel's behalf if the outcome was less than decisive (Gerges 1994: 230). But because he was also not ready to use US forces to open the Straits of Tiran he became resigned to letting Israel do it. Once convinced that an Israeli attack on the Arab states would not draw Washington into the conflict, Johnson, according to Israeli elites such as Dayan and Peres, gave Israel a tacit green light (Kimsche and Bawly 1968: 57). Indeed, according to Israeli foreign minister Abba Eban, the US actually encouraged Israel to move against Syria once it had defeated Egypt (Gerges 1994: 222–224). When the Soviets warned the US that they would intervene to stop Israel's attack on Syria in defiance of a Security Council resolution for a ceasefire, Johnson sent a counter-warning by moving the US Sixth Fleet, although he did advise Israel to stop once it had taken the Golan Heights. The Soviets' failure to prevent the defeat of their allies was a first step in the restoration of American power in the region.

Explaining the 1967 war   The war was the product of a convergence of forces on several different levels. The root cause lay in a protracted conflict of sub-state ethno-nationalisms which had become institutionalised in a system of rival states: on the Israeli side, a settler state with built-in insecurity and expansionist impulses pursuing a strategy of force to impose acceptance by its neighbours and, in the process, only inflaming their resentment; on the other side a displaced Palestinian Diaspora well positioned to drag the Arab states into support for its cause. In these conditions war was always possible but it was the dynamics of the state system – a fluid imbalance of power in Israel's favour, an unstable strategic environment and international permissiveness – which allowed the war to happen at this particular time.

The war was not, of course, inevitable and, on the contrary, resulted from leadership choices; hence it can only be fully understood by factoring in leadership rivalries, ambitions, perceptions and miscalculations. Janice Stein (1993: 56–57) differentiates between 'wars of vulnerability' in which external and domestic threats combine in such a way to make war or at least brinkmanship seem the least costly course, and sought-after 'wars of opportunity' in which elites believe a power advantage will allow them to make gains through the use of force. The 1967 Arab–Israeli war is surely a mixed case. For Israeli elites, it was an *opportunity* to end Israel's strategic *vulnerability* by acquiring more defensible borders and forcing its acceptance in the region. For the Arab leaders, the actions they took which gave Israel an excuse to go to war issued from vulnerability rooted in the regional and domestic power struggles in which firmness against Israel was essential to legitimacy; this resulted from the rise of Pan-Arab nationalism and the inter-Arab rivalry played out through dangerous 'outbidding' and brinkmanship (Barnett 1998: 159). Far from being a mere accident, this was a war waiting to happen which could only have been prevented by international and regional statesmanship, both of which were utterly lacking.

The consequences of the 1967 war The war ushered in major alterations in the Arab–Israeli balance of power and re-drew the regional map to Israel's advantage. Israel not only decisively defeated the Arab armies but also seized the Sinai peninsula and Gaza Strip from Egypt, the Golan Heights from Syria and the Palestinian populated 'West Bank' from Jordan. In upsetting the status quo, the war might have led to an Arab–Israeli peace. UNSC resolution 242, jointly sponsored by the superpowers in the aftermath of the war, provided an internationally accepted framework for a settlement. It amounted in essence to a proposed trade of 'land for peace'; in linking the inadmissibility of the acquisition of land by conquest to a call for all states in the region to be recognised as having the right to live in peace, it affirmed that the Arab states would now have to finally accept the existence of Israel and Israel would have to withdraw from the just-occupied territories. Although Israel denied the resolution required it to withdraw from *all* the territories, all other states, including the US, interpreted the resolution to mean virtually complete withdrawal (Smith 1996: 211–213).

The 1967 war also unleashed a major transformation in Arab attitudes to Israel. To be sure, in the short term, the conquest of the 1967 territories further locked the Arab states into the conflict with it. The defeated Arab nationalist regimes could not yet overtly accept a directly negotiated peace settlement and wanted a UN-sponsored end to belligerency and Israeli withdrawal. But they were under no illusion that they could avoid a formal peace treaty if they were to recover their lost lands. Despite some short-term inflammation of radical public sentiment, the 1967 defeat, in giving a mortal blow to Pan-Arab dreams, started the process of Arab acceptance of the permanence, if not the legitimacy, of Israel. Egypt's defeat precipitated a realist pragmatism in the hegemonic Arab state as Nasser himself began looking to mend relations with the US and to find a diplomatic solution to the Israeli occupation (Gerges 1994: 228, 236); Asad's rise in Syria marked a similar moderation of nationalism there. Radical Arab states that had challenged Israel on behalf of the Palestine cause, in disregard of the power imbalance against them, were 'socialised' the hard way into the rules of realist prudence needed to survive in a dangerous states system. King Hussein's 1970 crushing of the Palestinian fedayeen's attempt to turn Jordan into a base of operations against Israel was another watershed that started the gradual moderation of the PLO leadership: it would soon reduce its goal to the establishment of a Palestinian state in the West Bank and Gaza. To be sure, as the chance of a diplomatic settlement faded in the years after 1967, the survival of the front-line regimes would require they re-vindicate themselves against Israel: they could not rest until the occupation of their territory, touching on vital state and regime interests more directly than the Palestine cause had ever done, was rolled back. However, as the notion of the liberation of Palestine gave way to the aim of recovering the occupied territories, an irreconcilable 'existential' conflict between the two sides was gradually transformed into a limited one over territory that was much more amenable to a compromise settlement (Sela, 1998: 27–30, 97–109; Smith 1996: 235–237).

Unfortunately, if 1967 marked the beginning of the end of Arab nationalist revisionism, it had the opposite effect on a triumphant Israel. Although the military hegemony Israel achieved in the war gave it cause to feel more secure, the success of a military solution to its insecurity not only reduced its motivation to reach a permanent settlement with the Arab states but actually whetted its irredentist appetites. Israel insisted that a peace settlement would require the Arab states to accept direct negotiations and that it was unprepared to return to the 1967 lines. It wanted to keep strategic parts of its conquests that it insisted were needed to give it 'secure borders' including the Golan Heights, control of the Jordan River Valley and parts of the Sinai (Roberts 1990: 25–30). Additionally, the simultaneous rise of an irredentist right-wing settler movement and of the Likud party, which, beginning in 1977, started to win elections, propelled attempts to colonise and incorporate the territories even though this meant permanent repressive rule over a large Palestinian population in violation of international law (Peleg 1988: 60; Peri 1988). The settlement drive decisively obstructed the potential to trade the occupied lands for peace. In essence, the 1967 war did not result in the compromise settlement outlined in UN Resolution 242 because the power asymmetry gave the Israelis no incentives to concede it and the Arab states no capacity to extract it. As a result, 1967 set the stage for three more wars in the space of about a decade, the Egyptian–Israeli War of Attrition (1969–70), the 1973 Arab–Israeli war and the 1982 Israeli invasion of Lebanon (Gerner 1991: 72–75; Smith 1996: 201, 208–211, 228–230).

The Arab states system from Arab triangle to separate peace (the 1970s)

The Arab Triangle   Another effect of the 1967 war was to transform the Arab system from the Egypt-centred Pan-Arab one to what Ajami (1977–78) called the 'Arab Triangle'. Nasser's death and replacement by Sadat overnight reduced Egypt from hegemon of the Pan-Arab order to the status of a 'normal' state. Egypt had never had the resources of a well-rounded hegemon. It never enjoyed much capacity to project military power in the Arab world and its one attempt to do so, in Yemen, ended in stalemate; Egypt's economic superiority was never enough to allow it to provide much in economic rewards and by the late 1960s, the costs of hegemony – first from Yemen, then from the 1967 defeat – were impoverishing the country while the growing oil revenues accruing to the oil monarchies was shifting the balance of economic power to them. Cairo's hegemony had been based largely on the ideological appeal of Arabism, but this was shattered by the 1967 defeat while growing state formation made other states less permeable to ideological penetration. Sadat, having neither the will nor Pan-Arab stature to continue Nasser's Pan-Arab role, subordinated all other concerns to the recovery of the occupied Sinai. The Pan-Arab regime had lost the hegemon that had enforced and held it together.

With the decline of the Egyptian hegemon, other Arab states acquired greater freedom to pursue state interests but those interests were now shaped by the much-increased threat from Israel. Before 1967, the expectation that the great powers would restrain Israel, the greater immediate threat Arab rivals posed to each other, and the little practical possibility of liberating Palestine had deterred effective alliance-building against Israel (Walt 1987: 265–266); afterwards, a militarily preponderant and expansive Israel had to be contained while the occupied territories were potentially recoverable. This was only possible through inter-Arab co-operation and the much-reduced threat of Cairo made this co-operation less risky for the other Arab states. Thus, Israel's military preponderance sparked an effort on the Arab side to balance it through alliance formation and military build-up (Walt 1987: 117, 120–121).

Egypt was still the pivotal Arab state and the natural leader of an Arab coalition against Israel, but it had now to lead by consensus. Gradually Egypt and Syria, under new pragmatic leaders, were thrown together by their common interest in a war for recovery of the occupied territories while Saudi Arabia took advantage of their need for financial backing to moderate their policies and achieve full partnership in core Arab affairs. If no one state had enough assets to play the Arab hegemon, an axis of the largest (Egypt), the richest (Saudi Arabia) and most Pan-Arab (Syria) states could pool complementary resources and forge an Arab consensus on war and peace. This 'Arab Triangle' would, for a period, replace Egyptian hegemony as a new basis of Arab cohesion, allowed by the greater equality, hence trust, between the main leaders, Sadat, Asad and Feisal (Ajami 1977–78; Sela 1998: 142–145, 148; Taylor 1982: 49–56).

The three leaders began exploring two tracks for the recovery of the occupied territories. Egypt and Syria continued re-building their armies with Soviet arms financed by Arab oil money, while Sadat and the Saudis tried to enlist American pressure on Israel for a diplomatic settlement. Nasser's acceptance of the Rogers Plan had laid the grounds for a settlement and Sadat made new efforts to enlist US help in reaching one. However, another Arab–Israeli war became inevitable when the US rebuffed Sadat's diplomatic initiatives: in October 1973, Egypt and Syria launched a co-ordinated attack on the Israeli-occupied territories while Saudi Arabia deployed the oil weapon to force the intervention of American diplomacy (Heikel 1975; Sheehan 1976; Smith 1996: 226–228; Walt 1987: 117–121).

The fourth Arab–Israeli War of 1973　The conduct and outcome of the 1973 war were both shaped by and reshaped the Arab–Israeli power balance. On the one hand, tactically, Egypt's fears about Israeli air superiority led it to adopt a flawed war plan aiming at the mere seizure of a strip of land on the east bank of the Suez Canal (in order to break the diplomatic stalemate); this allowed Israel to concentrate first on its northern and then its southern fronts, forfeiting the advantage of the two-front joint Egyptian–Syrian assault. When a ceasefire was called, while the Egyptian army was still clinging to its foothold in the Sinai, Israeli forces were entrenched on the west bank of the canal and the Egyptian Third Army surrounded and in bad need of American intervention to restrain Israeli violations of the ceasefire and bring about a disengagement of forces. On the other hand, overall, the war altered the strategic power imbalance that had deprived the Arabs of all leverage to negotiate an acceptable settlement with Israel. The Arab armies failed to liberate the occupied territories, but their ability to challenge Israel and inflict high costs on it, and the oil embargo, in threatening vital Western interests, sufficiently upset the status quo to force American intervention on behalf of a negotiated settlement. At the same time, the relative Arab success in the war (compared to 1967) endowed the front-line states with a legitimacy windfall that made it less politically risky for them to move toward a peace settlement. Arab summits following the war, led by the 'Arab Triangle' powers, legitimised a 'comprehensive peace' with Israel in return for its full withdrawal from the occupied territories and the creation of a Palestinian state in the West Bank and Gaza. They also designated the PLO as the sole representative of the Palestinians in peace negotiations. Arguably, the war gave the Arab states increased leverage to extract the settlement they wanted if they stuck together and played their cards right. Israel, for its part, still had the military upper hand at the end of the war and had an interest in a partial settlement, that is, one with Egypt, if that left it free to avoid settlements on its other fronts (Sela 1998: 211–213).

A new Arab order: stillborn The 1973 war seemed to revive the defunct Pan-Arab system, albeit in new form. The war caused a massive resurgence of Arab nationalism that drove all Arab states to close ranks behind Egypt and Syria: Iraqi and Jordanian forces played crucial roles in containing Israeli counter-offensives against Syria while Morocco and Saudi Arabia sent token contingents to the front lines and Algeria and the Gulf states provided finance for Soviet arms deliveries (Sela 1998: 145). Not just the shared threat but also a shared resource, the new oil wealth from the price boom unleashed by the oil embargo, generated interdependence between the Arab states. The expectation that the new wealth would be shared with the states that had fought and sacrificed for the common Arab cause was partly realised by significant transfers of wealth to the latter, the migration of excess labour to the labour-scarce oil producers and the transfer of remittances home. The 'Arab Cold War' was decisively buried as the conservative states used aid to moderate the radicalism of the nationalist republics and ideological subversion and media wars gave way to inter-state diplomacy (Barnett 1998: 153; Dessouki 1982: 319–347).

These developments seemed to lay the foundations for a new more state-centric version of Pan-Arab order organised around the Arab summit system. Summits had been initiated by Nasser in 1964 in an early acknowledgement that Egypt's hegemony could no longer be imposed and that an Arab order had to be negotiated among sovereign states. Aiming not to promote Pan-Arab action but to contain Syria's demands for it by spreading the responsibility for inaction, summits began and continued as a mechanism for reversing the radicalisation of Pan-Arab norms from inter-Arab 'outbidding' (Barnett 1998: 122; Kerr 1971; Sela 1998: 75–94). But it was only after Israel replaced Egyptian hegemony as the main threat to Arab elites that summits took on sustained momentum.

Summits reaffirmed the qualified sovereignty embodied in the Arab League, pledging participants to refrain from intervention in each other's internal affairs while co-ordinating the policies of the individual states to defend the common Arab interest. In the early 1970s summits legitimised and set the conditions for a peace settlement with Israel while marginalising radical regimes (Iraq) which sought to use outbidding to derail the peace process. In the late 1970s summits tried to contain Egypt's unilateralism in negotiations with Israel. In the 1980s they were called to mobilise all-Arab resources, above all financial aid, to counter threats on the non-Arab periphery – from Israel and Iran.

Summit agendas were pre-negotiated by the major states, their resolutions, normally reached by consensus, were reflective of the lowest common denominator and their implementation was dependent on leadership provided by a cohesive 'Arab triangle'. Reflective of the growing Arab fragmentation after Egypt's separate peace shattered the triangle was the decline in the effectiveness of summits in the 1980s when they were often boycotted by key feuding states. But Saudi Arabia filled the vacuum, using financial incentives agreed at summits to preserve some cohesion or to heal splits. Thus, the Arab summit of May 1989 healed the split over Egypt's separate peace with Israel. By 1996 there had been 19 summits and they arguably had made enough difference in inter-Arab politics to establish a system somewhere between Pan-Arab aspirations of collective action and a purely state-centric 'Westphalian' system (Sela 1998: 2–23, 341–346).

Yet, simultaneously, centrifugal forces were deepening. Consolidation of the individual states meant their increased ability to put state sovereignty over Arabism. If the 1973 war and associated oil boom fuelled inter-Arab interdependencies, at the same time relative wartime success restored some of the legitimacy of the individual states and the new oil money fostered state-building. The distribution of oil revenues across the system allowed states to build large armies and bureaucracies, generate new bourgeoisies with a stake in regimes, and co-opt the middle class, which, once the constituency of Arabism, now became or aspired to be part of the new state establishments. The very durability of the states as the customary framework of political life fostered their growing acceptance, if not strong affective support for them. States became far less vulnerable to Pan-Arab penetration as the Pan-Arab movements, once so readily manipulated by Nasser against his rivals, virtually disappeared or were 'statised': thus Ba'thism became the official ideology and the Ba'th party an instrument of state co-optation in Syria and Iraq. The Sadat regime, once it opted for a separate peace with Israel, fostered an Egypt-centric reaction against Arabism, exploiting Egyptians' resentment of the failure of the 'rich' Arabs and 'ungrateful' Palestinians to fund and appreciate Egypt's long sacrifice of its economic well-being to defence of the Arab cause. Indeed, the single most important event that unhinged the new Arab order was the defection of its very centre, Egypt (Barnett 1998: 183; Noble 1991: 65–70; Sela 1998: 148–150).

The shattering of the Arab Triangle: Egypt's separate peace Just as the conflict with Israel gave birth to the Arab Triangle, so disagreements over the conflict's resolution destroyed it as, after the 1973 war, Egypt's Sadat proceeded step-by-step down the road to a separate peace at the expense of his Arab partners.

Although Sadat was amenable to a separate solution from the start, it was Egypt's military vulnerability at the time of the cease-fire that actually started him down this road. Sadat embraced US mediation to reach a first disengagement agreement with Israel that rescued his position on the banks of the Suez Canal; but the price of this was the virtual abandonment of the war option as Egyptian offensive forces were rolled back from the Sinai front. Needing the US to deliver Israeli withdrawal from the Sinai and its financial aid to solve Egypt's economic crisis, Sadat gradually sacrificed all other options to appease Washington: he further weakened the Arabs' hand and undermined Syria by pushing for a lifting of the oil embargo before there was even a first disengagement on the Syrian front and well before any comprehensive peace was in the cards; he broke his pledge to Jordan that similar Israeli withdrawal on the West Bank would have to precede further disengagement on the Egyptian front and in 1975 agreed to Sinai II, a second disengagement that left Jordan and Syria sidelined. Sinai II, in accelerating Sadat's advance along a separate road to peace and in de-militarising Israel's southern front, sharply reduced Israel's incentive to reach a comprehensive settlement (Fahmy 1983: 170–187, 188–251; Heikel 1983: 72–81; Taylor 1982: 54–81). Knowing Israel was prepared to trade the rest of the Sinai for a peace that would remove Egypt, the strongest Arab state, from the Arab–Israeli power balance, and that if he stuck with Syria and the PLO in insisting on a comprehensive settlement and a Palestinian state he might get nothing, Sadat entered into negotiations at Camp David for what would be a separate peace (Sadat 1978: 302–304; Smith 1996: 256). For Israel's Begin, the Sinai was a price worth paying since, as it became apparent that Sadat would abandon the Palestinians, he saw the chance to keep the West Bank. While ostensibly the Camp David agreement provided for Palestinian 'autonomy', the subsequent failure of this to be realised did not deter Sadat from signing a separate peace with Israel in 1979. At the second Baghdad summit, Iraq and Syria jointly forced Saudi Arabia and other wavering states to ostracise Egypt. This, in forcing Egypt into greater dependence on the US, allowed the virtual neutralisation of the core Arab state by a superpower deeply biased toward Israel (Smith 1996: 256–258).

The failure to reach a comprehensive peace showed the centrality of the balance of power to order-building. The relative Arab–Israeli power balance resulting from the 1973 war meant neither side could hope to impose its will, hence each had an incentive to seek a diplomatic solution. This chance was, however, missed, in part because US arms deliveries to Israel and Egypt's separate peace restored Israel superiority. This not only reduced its incentive to reach a comprehensive peace but radically upset the regional power balance as well. Egypt's opting out of the Arab–Israel power balance amounted to a form of 'buck-passing', a practice that enervates the alliance stability needed to deter powerful states. In this case, the resulting power imbalance would lead directly to the fifth Arab–Israeli war of 1982.

Sadat's move toward a separate peace had, from at least the mid-1970s, profoundly damaging consequences for the Arab system. First, it generated deepened insecurity throughout the Arab world that intensified the retreat to state-centric self-help by the Arab states, notably Syria, while disillusioning the PLO that Palestinian interests could be peacefully attained. The first and most destructive symptom of these tendencies was the Lebanese civil war, unleashed by conflicts over the Palestinians in Lebanon. The Sinai II agreement sparked a showdown between a coalition of Palestinians and radical Lebanese Muslims who wanted to challenge Israel in southern Lebanon and Maronite Christians determined to eradicate this disruptive threat to Lebanese sovereignty. At the same time, Syria, left extremely vulnerable to Israeli power by the collapse of its Egyptian alliance and seeking to redress the imbalance, tried to use the Lebanese civil war to impose its leadership in the Levant, especially on Lebanon and the PLO. This precipitated a PLO–Syrian conflict that would never be wholly healed (Barnett 1998: 191–200; Sela 1998: 153–213; Smith 1996: 242–253).

Thus, if, in the 1973 war, co-operation between the Arab states benefited all, thereafter – caught in a classic prisoner's dilemma – none could trust the other not to seek individual gains unilaterally. While the Arabs as a bloc may have had the leverage to extract a comprehensive settlement if no one of them settled for less, Kissinger's step-by-step diplomacy had divided them and henceforth forced them to individually play weakened hands in negotiations with Israel. When such vital interests as recovery of territory, perhaps even political survival, were at stake, each actor fell back on the self-help typical of a states system. Even as Nasserite Egypt's hegemonic role had established Pan-Arab constraints on sovereignty, Egypt's promotion under Sadat of sovereignty over Arabism released many remaining such constraints. By the mid-1980s major Arab leaders were effectively insisting that Arabism had to take a back seat to sovereignty in foreign policy-making. King Hussein argued that to make Arabism the norm required collective institutions that were lacking. Sadat's successor, Husni Mubarak, told the Arabs that the only way to limit inter-Arab conflict was tolerance of a diversity of foreign policies since each state best knew its own interests. In this way, the individual states were 'deconstructing' the Arab system (Barnett 1998: 206–207; Seale 1988: 185–213; Sela 1998: 189–213).

The consequent popular disillusionment precipitated a parallel decline in Arabism at the mass level during the 1980s, but identifications did not necessarily attach to the states. Rather, the negative side effects of state-building – notably the explosion of corruption and inequality accompanying the oil bonanza – left states with legitimacy deficits and with no convincing substitute for Arabism or Islam as legitimating ideologies. Indeed, the vacuum left by the decline of Arabism was filled by heightened identification with either smaller sub-state identities or with the larger Islamic *umma*, especially after the 1979 Iranian Islamic revolution endowed political Islam, an alternative supra-state ideology, with enormous new credibility. Both tendencies were manifest in the Lebanese civil war in which, over time, nationalist movements fragmented into sectarian or regional factions or were displaced by the rise of Hizbollah, a trans-national Islamic movement.

While stronger states facing less mobilised, more fragmented publics were now better positioned to pursue reason of state to the neglect of Arab norms, they nevertheless still paid a legitimacy cost which opened the door to Islamic opposition. Islamic uprisings occurred in Egypt, Syria and Algeria in the 1980s and 1990s. Iraq was especially threatened by Iran's trans-state penetration of its large Shia population. Even Saudi Arabia and the Gulf states who sought legitimation through Islam were vulnerable to Islamic Iran's denunciation of their 'American Islam'. As Meridi Nahas (1985) argues, the decline of Pan-Arabism made regimes especially vulnerable to revolutionary Islam because the same ills and identities that had fuelled the rise of Pan-Arabism persisted but the disaffected now turned to Islam because many states had appropriated Arab nationalism as their legitimating ideology while blatantly violating its norms.

War and revolution on the peripheries (the 1980s)

Egypt's separate peace and Iran's revolution set the stage for two wars on the 'peripheries' of the Arab core that again reshaped the Middle East system. These events massively intensified insecurity, which states sought to address not through collective institutions but through self-help: state strengthening and arms races. Even as the Arab states were better enabled to manage trans-state pressures at home, each one, by thus strengthening itself and freeing itself of Pan-Arab constraints also started to become more of a potential threat to and less of a potential ally for its neighbours. This and the collapse of the Arab triangle, leaving the Arab world centre-less, spread the security dilemma from the fault-lines with the non-Arab peripheries into the heart of the Arab system. In these conditions of fragmentation, the classic realist balance of power increasingly became the main source of order. This balance, however, proved disastrously unstable in good part because Arab fragmentation radically weakened the Arab states in the face of the non-Arab peripheries. The coincidence of abrupt power imbalances and the rise of revisionist leaderships in Israel, Iran and Iraq led to two major wars which accelerated movement toward something more closely approximating a 'Westphalian' type multi-polar states system.

The emergence of Arab multi-polarity

Within the Arab core, a multi-polar struggle for power among several contending states, pursuing reason of state yet still ambitious to exercise Pan-Arab leadership, had emerged by the 1980s. This was a function both of Egypt's relative decline and the rise of other Arab powers. Military capabilities were now much more equally distributed: in 1970 Egypt's military expenditure was still much higher than that of other Arab states but by 1979 Syria and Iraq matched it and Saudi Arabia had soared ahead. In 1965 Egypt's GNP was still almost three times Saudi Arabia's; by 1978, Saudi wealth was triple that of Egypt. Egypt's share of Arab GNP declined from 23.4% in 1965 to 7.9% in 1977 (Noble 1991: 65; Telhami 1990: 96–97). Economic decline was paralleled by the eclipse of Cairo as the Arab world's political hub, registered in a drop in the percentage of inter-Arab official visits to Cairo from 52% of the total in 1958–63 to 23% in 1970–75 and completed by its isolation after the separate peace with Israel (Thompson 1981). Formerly Egyptian-dominated inter-Arab institutions were now funded by and under the increased influence of the oil monarchies. Other states also caught up with Egypt in their levels of state formation: the conservative states were now stabilised through the use of oil wealth to incorporate middle strata while Ba'thist Syria and Iraq grew organisational muscle to control their fractious societies.

But no new hegemon or concert emerged to regulate inter-Arab conflict or defend the Arab core from external threats. Iraq, in a peripheral location and long contained by hostile Turkey and Iran, was finally internally consolidated and, strengthened by oil and Soviet arms, made a bid for Arab leadership. It remained marginalised under the banner of rejectionism but when Sadat forfeited Egypt's Arab leadership and the Pahlavi gendarme of the Gulf collapsed, Saddam Hussein perceived power vacuums Iraq could fill; however, he soon dissipated Iraq's potential in his war with Iran. Asad's Syria internally stabilised and with diversified (Gulf and Soviet) resources took advantage of Egypt's isolation and Iraq's embroilment with Iran to assert Pan-Arab leadership against Israel; but it was handicapped by the decline of Pan-Arab sentiment and, in the 1980s, the preoccupation of Arab regimes with the Gulf conflict. Saudi Arabia hesitantly assumed inter-Arab leadership, building on the leverage it could potentially wield in the West on behalf of Arab interests as the swing producer in OPEC and by using its wealth to moderate inter-Arab conflicts: indicative of this, in the 1970s it became the focus of most inter-Arab official visits. However, its military weakness made it vulnerable and therefore extremely cautious and the decline of its oil revenues after the mid-1980s oil bust and its growing dependency on the US for protection from Iran checked its rise. Each Arab state was strong enough to prevent hegemony by the other, but all were too driven by particular interests to forge an axis of states able to engineer all-Arab cohesion and security (Mufti 1996: 197–252; Noble 1991: 65, 71–72; Walt 1987: 137).

Its fragmentation made the Arab world exceptionally vulnerable to the powerful revisionist impulses that were being unleashed on its peripheries. Initially, the Iranian revolution snapped the Tehran–Tel-Aviv axis against Arab nationalism and threatened to shift the power balance against Israel; but Iran's effort to export revolution to its neighbours, Iraq and the Gulf states, at a time when its own military capabilities had been decimated by revolution precipitated the Iraqi invasion of its territory and the eight-year-long Iran–Iraq war. This immediately reshuffled the deck to Israel's advantage: Iraq's marginalisation combined with Egypt's removal from the Arab–Israeli balance freed Israel, where a revisionist government took power in 1977, to project its power in the Arab world with little restraint: in the early 1980s, Israel attacked an Iraqi nuclear reactor, bombed PLO headquarters in Tunis and invaded Lebanon. At the same time, the feeling of vulnerability of the Arab Gulf monarchies was greatly heightened by a dual perceived threat: on the one hand, the Soviet invasion of Afghanistan, plus Soviet activity in the Horn of Africa and in Democratic Yemen; on the other hand, once Iran reversed the Iraqi invasion, its intense military pressure on Iraq, on Kuwait and on Gulf shipping (Sela 1998: 217–246).

The fifth Arab–Israeli war: the Israeli invasion of Lebanon

The roots of the Israeli invasion of Lebanon lay in the ascendancy of irredentism, always latent in Israel, at a time of regional power imbalance favouring it. Israeli irredentism grew out of the militarist Zionism of Vladimir Jabotinsky, of which the Irgun movement led by Menachem Begin was a leading element. This Israeli 'right' saw the world as a permanently hostile place for Jews and the Arab–Israeli cleavage as irreconcilable. As Israeli right-wingers saw it, in a world where the strong dominated, Israel had to use any means necessary to attain its goals, a worldview that, according to Peleg (1988: 62–64), expressed a 'monumental overcompensation' for the repression of Jews in the East European Diaspora. At a time when the mainstream of Israeli politics had considered the 1949 armistice lines as Israel's final borders, Begin had refused to accept their legitimacy. He rejected any return of the occupied territories, which he identified as ancient Judea and Samaria, part of 'Eretz Yisrael'. Historically, the Israeli right also laid claim to Jordan in contrast to the Labour party (Mapai), which valued good relations with the Hashemite dynasty.

The Labour party's relative failure in the 1973 war shattered its traditional dominance of Israeli politics and shifted the Israeli political spectrum toward the irredentist right. In 1974, Begin's Herut party joined with militant disciples of Ben Gurion, who had split from Labour, to form the Likud party. The National Religious Party, previously more centrist, joined the irredentist camp after 1967 while several rightist splinter parties later emerged holding even more radical views, such as the Tehiya party which regarded the return of the Sinai as a Begin sell-out; the Moledet faction which advocated expulsion of the Palestinian population to Jordan; and the militant settler movement, Gush Emunim, which promoted illegal settlements in the occupied West Bank. When the Likud party won the 1977 elections, a former 'terrorist' leader, Menachem Begin, became prime minister of Israel (Roberts 1990: 45–88).

The likelihood of a more militant foreign policy under Begin was initially checked by Sadat's trip to Jerusalem, which generated such public euphoria in Israel and such a strategic opportunity that Begin had to respond (Peretz 1988: 32). He pursued two tracks, a more accommodationist diplomacy toward Egypt and simultaneously a highly revisionist thrust in the occupied territories. Even while accepting the 'autonomy' for the West Bank prescribed by Camp David, Begin claimed Israeli sovereignty over the area, insisting that it was Israeli land temporarily and illegally occupied by Jordan in 1948. Settlements increased threefold and settlers tenfold while Israeli acquisition of land and control of water resources was greatly accelerated. Arab mayors were dismissed and expulsions of Palestinians, demolition of their houses and seizure of their property increased (Peretz 1988: 33–35). Begin decreed the annexation of Jerusalem in 1980 and of the Golan Heights in 1981. The 1981 elections brought an even more radically irredentist leadership to power including Begin, defence minister Ariel Sharon and foreign minister Yitzhak Shamir. While the previous Begin government had included moderates such as Ezer Weizman who had promoted peace with Egypt, the new government saw this peace as an opportunity to use military power to remake the map of the Middle East.

The 1980 Egyptian–Israeli peace treaty, far from ending the Arab–Israeli conflict, had merely displaced the battlelines toward the occupied West Bank/Gaza and to Lebanon. The PLO, expelled from Jordan in 1970, had in the following decade entrenched itself in Lebanon from which it sought to carry on a desultory guerrilla war against Israel. Israeli retaliation against Lebanon was a major factor in sparking the Lebanese civil war; the consequent collapse of the Lebanese government had left a no-man's land in southern Lebanon, eliminating remaining restraints on PLO activity there, and facilitated the 1976 Syrian intervention in Lebanon which had opened up a potential new front between Syria and Israel. The emergence of a PLO 'state-within-a-state' in southern Lebanon, followed by the removal of Egypt, via its separate peace, from the Arab–Israeli power balance, and the consolidation of a revisionist government in Israel, set the stage for Israel's 1981 invasion of Lebanon.

The Likud government's aim was to establish unchallenged regional hegemony by smashing the PLO and punishing Syria, the last obstacles to its incorporation of the West Bank and Golan into Greater Israel. It aimed to drive both out of Lebanon and impose a client regime in Beirut, thereby isolating and encircling Syria. Hitherto, such ambitions would have been restrained for fear of the unpredictable international consequences, but at this juncture the international system was again exceptionally permissive: specifically, the very pro-Israel Reagan administration in Washington, seeing Syria and the PLO as Soviet surrogates in a new Cold War it was waging against Moscow, gave Israel a virtual 'green light' for the invasion (Peleg 1988: 64; Schiff and Yaari 1984: 31–43, 71–77; Seale 1988: 373–376; Smith 1996: 267–270).

Because of the simultaneous Iran–Iraq war and Egypt's separate peace, Israel's invasion of Lebanon did not, as it would once have done, stimulate a Pan-Arab counter-coalition in defence of Syria and the Palestinians. Neither Egypt or the Gulf Arabs, who were preoccupied with the Iranian threat, could afford to antagonise Israel's US patron and were, in any case, not unhappy to see Syria pummelled because of its alignment with Iran in the Iran–Iraq war (Sela 1998: 256–257). Militarily, Syria took a beating at the hands of Israeli forces driving into Lebanon, and, although the Syrian army extracted a price from Israel and stubbornly refused, as Israel expected, to retreat from Lebanon, Israel pushed Syrian forces from strategic sectors of Lebanese terrain, including the nerve centre, Beirut. Moreover, it expelled the PLO from Lebanon and, in the wake of the war, an American-Israeli *combinazione* installed a Maronite client regime in Beirut, tried to impose a virtual peace treaty on Israeli terms and made Israeli withdrawal from Lebanon contingent on Syria's. The US and Israel believed a militarily weakened and isolated Syria had no choice but to accept the Lebanese–Israeli accord and withdraw or face continued Israeli occupation of Lebanon. Yet Syria chose to defy their overwhelming military power and in a short time brought about a remarkable turnabout in the balance of forces (Petran 1987: 295–334, 345–348; Rabinovich 1987; Schiff and Ya'ari: 1984: 286–300; Seale 1988: 366–393).

Unprecedented Soviet arms deliveries, including a sophisticated air defence network, cast a protective umbrella over Syria. Syria took advantage of Iranian backing and the growing resentment of Lebanese Muslims, especially the Shia, against Israeli and Maronite domination to strike an alliance with them. Buttressed by Syria, Muslim militias checked the Maronite Jumayyil government's consolidation of power over the country and the intervention of American guns and planes on its behalf could not deter them. Israel, wearied by the casualties of Lebanese occupation and aware of the risks of a renewed drive against a Soviet-backed Syrian army, chose to withdraw from most of Lebanon. The car-bombing of US Marine positions and the downing of American bombers flying against Syrian forces in Lebanon demonstrated to the US the costs of involvement and brought about its withdrawal, too. The weakened Maronite government was forced to annul the accord with Israel. Israel, under Syrian-backed guerrilla threat, withdrew southward, ending the immediate military threat to Syria, although an Israeli 'security zone' in the south of Lebanon was consolidated. Thus, through a shrewd use of proxies, steadfastness under threat and Soviet backing, Syria's Asad snatched victory from the jaws of defeat. Israel found that its environment had become far more intractable than in 1967 when military power had so successfully redrawn the regional map in its favour; in particular, Syria was far better armed, organised and determined while Lebanon proved to be an ungovernable swamp (Seale 1988: 394–420; Smith 1996: 272–275).

The Israeli leadership, in overreaching itself, had destroyed the domestic consensus it needed to carry on. Israeli society was polarised and Israel suffered international condemnation for its siege of Beirut and the subsequent massacres of Palestinian civilians, while thereafter the occupation of Lebanon meant mounting military casualties for no perceivable gain (Gerner 1991: 87–88). Lebanon exposed the limits put by Israel's pluralistic political system on the conduct of foreign policy: a hawkish leadership had little trouble stirring up an irredentist population, but when the costs to Israel seemed to exceed the attainable gains, the loss of public support sharply constrained leadership options and electoral politics permitted a change in leadership and policy. The public mood shifted under Begin's feet and in the 1984 elections neither major party won enough support to form a government and a national unity coalition had to be formed to extricate Israel from Lebanon. Israel's failure in Lebanon marked the beginning of a realisation that it, much like its Arab neighbours, could not attain its ends chiefly by military force. Thereafter under the Likudist Yitzhak Shamir, Israel pursued the more modest and negative ambition of evading pressures for peace long enough to irrevocably settle and incorporate the West Bank.

The Lebanon venture was to have enduring costs for Israel. It alienated Lebanon's Shia community and unwittingly helped give birth to Hizbollah, an Islamic resistance movement backed by Iran which contested Israel's continued hold on its southern Lebanon 'security zone', embroiling Israel in its own version of a Vietnam quagmire until it finally unilaterally withdrew in 2000. Moreover, the 1981 defeat of the PLO in Lebanon, rather than demoralising the Palestinians, stimulated the West Bank population to take its fate into its own hands, unleashing in Gaza and the West Bank the 'intifada' – a sustained civil uprising between 1987 and 1992 which made Israel's continued occupation more materially and morally costly than hitherto. Ironically, at the very time when its Egyptian peace treaty had virtually neutralised the external security threat to Israel from Arab armies, its irredentist drive to incorporate the occupied territories and impose its will in Lebanon resulted in new low-intensity but on-going security threats which were now 'internalised' within the bounds of territories Israel controlled. A final consequence of the war was Syria's drive for military parity with Israel that established a 'deterrence relationship' between the two states in which the level of armaments made a war too costly and probably unwinnable for both (Evron 1987; Schiff and Ya'ari 1984: 306–307; Smith 1996: 293–300).

The Islamic revolution and the first Gulf war

Revolutions, in bringing revisionist leaders to power and upsetting power balances, frequently lead to war which, in turn, re-shapes states (Halliday 1994: 124–46). The radical transformation in Iran's foreign policy – from a main supporter of the pro-Western Middle East status quo under the Shah to its main challenger after the revolution – seemingly demonstrates the power of domestic politics to shape international behaviour. On the other hand, the case also underlines the resilience of the state system: the limited success of Islamic Iran in exporting its revolution revealed the extent to which regional states had become more immune to trans-state ideology while power balancing against Iran imposed constraints and costs which, in time, tilted the balance of Iranian domestic forces against foreign policy revisionism.

The foreign policy roots of revolution The Iranian revolution had its roots in domestic inequality and political repression but the intimate connection between this and its position in the international system inevitably made the revolution a nationalist one with profound international repercussions. The origins of the revolution went back to the 1952 nationalisation of Iranian oil by the nationalist prime minister, Muhammad Mossadeq. Mossadeq acted in the belief that foreign control kept Iran's elites in the pockets of Britain and the Anglo-Iranian oil company. The consequent boycott of Iranian oil by Western oil companies ignited an economic crisis, which paved the way for the CIA-backed military coup that brought him down and restored the Pahlavi Shah to power (Cottam 1979). Thereafter, Iran had to agree to the virtual denationalisation of its oil industry in which the Americans now took a 40% share (Ramazani 1986: 202). For Iranian nationalists, the US was perceived to have eclipsed Britain and Russia as the main threats to Iranian independence.

The Pahlavi Shah's whole domestic strategy and regime were shaped by a profound legitimacy deficit rooted in his restoration by foreign powers at the expense of Iran's nationalist hero. Feeling intensely threatened at home by nationalist and leftist opposition, sometimes backed by the Soviets, the Shah naturally opted to rely on the Americans to consolidate his rule. Yet, a conservative nationalist and driven to prove himself to Iranians, he sought to make Iran a regional power and major player in the world political economy. This, ironically, led him to pursue policies that would undermine his own regime. His oil-fuelled development programme, in its spread of education, modern employment and the consequent growth of the middle class, and in its neglect of agriculture and consequent rapid urbanisation, greatly increased the potentially politically conscious and active population. The rapid expansion of higher education created a large student body and a much-enlarged intelligentsia susceptible to opposition ideologies. At the same time, however, lacking nationalist legitimacy, the Shah could not afford to establish effective and legitimate political institutions that could accommodate their aspirations for political participation. On the contrary, his power consolidation meant repression of both the nationalist centre – Mossadeq's National Front – and the Marxist left, the main political vehicles of the modern middle and working classes, and an increasingly authoritarian concentration of power in his own hands at the expense of parliament, largely the preserve of the landed oligarchy. To reduce his dependence on the oligarchy and win wider support, he launched a land reform programme but this alienated not only the landed elite but also the Shia religious hierarchy whose *waqf* lands were threatened, both social forces which would otherwise have been natural props of monarchy. The Shah's control of growing oil revenues gave him an autonomy that led him to neglect the class base of his regime, making him increasingly dependent on support in the army and bureaucracy and his main instrument of control, SAVAK, the feared secret police (Cottam 1979: 320–349; Halliday 1996: 53–55; Green 1982: 146–150).

The oil-fuelled economic boom and bust of the late 1970s created the conditions for the mobilisation of discontent among the excluded middle and lower strata. State spending and massive corruption enriched a new bourgeoisie of contractors and intermediaries situated between the state and the external market. At the same time, however, inflation (from massive state spending) eroded fixed incomes, while capital-intensive industrialisation generated insufficient jobs to absorb urbanised job-seekers. The frustration of raised expectation combined with growing inequality, which was de-legitimised by the egalitarian norms preached by both Marxists and oppositionist Islam, stimulated revolutionary sentiment (Halliday 1996: 50–53). At the same time, the Westernisation of Iran associated with oil-based development antagonised those, notably the Islamic clergy, who feared the threat of 'Westoxification' to the integrity of Islamic values and culture (Menashri 1990: 3). The clergy were the natural political leaders of the urban slums and semi-urbanised masses streaming in from the villages; their mobilisation of the urban plebeian strata shifted the balance of power within the opposition from the secular nationalists to Islamic leaders (Halliday 1996: 57–63).

The Shah's insecurity meant that he needed to maximise US commitment to the stability of his regime against nationalist and leftist opposition at home and in the Gulf region. The Shah's strategy was to position his regime, in line with the Nixon Doctrine, as a bulwark against Soviet power and radicalism in the Gulf. This meant such policies as support for Iraqi Kurds against the Iraqi Ba'th and intervention against Marxist insurgency in Oman in the early 1970s. Financing the military build-up needed to play regional gendarme made the Shah a price hawk in OPEC and might have put him at odds with his American patron but the recycling of much of the new oil revenues into arms and capital purchases from the US placated Washington (Cottam 1979: 333–342). However, the American connection only deepened public alienation. Though Iran had become a regional power, nationalists took no pride in this status, believing that the regime was a surrogate for American Middle East interests. Many believed Khomeini's claim that 'the Shah has squandered the oil revenues ... on buying weapons at exorbitant prices' and that Iran's oil money had ended up in the pockets of speculators and arms dealers (Menashri 1990: 28–29). Anti-Americanism was also inflamed by the combination of Washington's support for Israel and the Shah's alliance with Israel, which trained the hatred SAVAK (Cottam 1979: 333).

Gradually, a broad anti-regime coalition came to embrace the liberal nationalist followers of Mossadeq, radical leftist and 'Islamic Marxist' student groups, clergy threatened by Westernisation, bazaar merchants alienated by price controls and foreign competition, leftist unionised workers and the urbanising masses. As opposition mounted, the role of the United States was decisive. President

Carter's urging of the Shah to observe human rights spread the perception in Iran that the US would not necessarily intervene to protect him, emboldening insurgents; during the revolution itself, Carter actually discouraged the massive military repression that would have been needed to turn back the revolution (Halliday 1996: 57–67).

The anti-regime mobilisation was directed from abroad by the charismatic leader, Ayatollah Rouallah Khomeini, who enjoyed the aura of an 'imam' (vice-regent of God) and preached an ideology of Islam mixed with nationalism and hatred of the United States. The beginning of the end for the Shah was when the killing of thousands of unarmed demonstrators in September 1978 led to strikes in the oil fields demanding an end to SAVAK and to the US presence. This caused a dramatic drop in oil production and precipitated a state revenue crisis. Massive street demonstrations that carried on for weeks paralysed the country; the lower ranks of the army refused to fire on demonstrators, military indiscipline spread and the military hierarchy gradually unravelled. None of the props of the Shah's rule – oil, the army, or his American ally – could save him from the non-violent protest of a largely unarmed population alienated by his image as a foreign puppet beholden to the West and hostile to Islam.

The revolutionary roots of foreign policy Islamic Iran epitomises the case of regimes which, arising from revolutionary movements, are initially intensely driven by revisionist ideology that impugns the legitimacy of status quo states and even the regional states system. But, as with other revolutions, Iran's followed the 'natural history' delineated by Brinton (1938): first the radicals pushed the moderates out of power as the masses were increasingly mobilised against external threats to the revolution. Then came a 'Thermidor', in which the economic costs of revolution and the requirements of war and post-war economic reconstruction tilted the balance of power back to pragmatic elements.

The primacy of radical ideology in the formation of Iran's foreign policy under Khomeini had multiple roots. Deepest was the socialisation of the generation that took power in the revolution. Many were Khomeini's students, imbued with his intense hatred of the Shah and his American backers. Many were brought up on the teachings of Ali Shariati, the ideologue of the revolution, whose fusion of anti-imperialism and populism with Islam provided the basis for a coalition between the clergy and militant lay youth. The revolutionary situation itself – that is, the ideological mobilisation of militants and the radicalisation of the population in the revolutionary struggle – raised great expectations for a trans- formation; since the revolution was in part a reaction against the Shah's policy of defending the pro-Western regional status quo, it dictated an absolute reversal of Iran's role. The new regime won widespread support when it withdrew Iran from CENTO, joined the non-aligned movement, broke relations with Israel and turned its embassy over to the PLO. Relations were severed with Sadat's Egypt for its peace with Israel and the asylum given to the Shah. By the end of 1980, Iran had cancelled $9 billion worth of Western arms contracts: it had no intention of continuing the re-cycling of petrodollars that made local control of oil resources acceptable in the West. Instead, Iran would seek to reduce the dependency which reliance on oil dictated and pursue an inward-looking road to development that maximised self-sufficiency.

Reinforcing the 'ideologisation' of foreign policy was its use by the new elites to legitimise the initially unstable revolutionary regime. For a revolution advocating a universalistic (not purely national) ideology such as Islam, legitimation required revolution- ary success abroad. The revolutionary leaders, buoyed by the suc- cess of their revolution, expected that the Muslim masses across the region would similarly respond to their Islamic *da'wa* and rid themselves of client regimes; they were, therefore, ready to embark on dangerous challenges to the regional status quo. At the same time, though, the export of the revolution was meant to overcome the revolution's dangerous isolation amidst status quo states: as Khomeini put it, 'if we remain in a closed environment we shall defi- nitely face defeat'. The revolution actually fed off external threats and sacrifice; the threat from the US and then the sense of siege and the sacrifices, particularly of sons, in the Iran–Iraq war invested ordinary people in the revolution. And, as the revolutionaries split, rivals in the post-revolutionary power struggle had to prove their revolutionary credentials through radical stances in foreign policy, thereby freezing out moderate voices.

Khomeini's worldview and the conflict with the US   Khomeini's worldview was central to revolutionary Iran's foreign policy. For him, the US was a major preoccupation. As he saw it, the world was dominated by 'satanic' imperialist powers – headed by the US, the 'Great Satan' and the USSR, the 'Little Satan' (especially after the Soviet invasion of Afghanistan) – which were enemies of Islam and sought to oppress the weak (*mustaza'fin*) and to plunder their resources (oil). This view, growing out of Iran's modern experience under imperialism and the Shah, was reinforced by Shiism's historic strong sense of being the underdog; but while Shiism has often been quietist, Khomeini's activist version preached a duty of Muslims to struggle against imperialism whose control over the region's oil could never be challenged by quietism (Hunter 1988; Menashri 1990: 71). Iran's revolution, Khomeini declared, would be a role model for the Muslim world, showing that it was possible to stand up against 'world arrogance' (Chubin 1994: 11–16). Khomeini also sought to challenge the regimes of the region, which he saw as Western clients and as illegitimate obstacles to the unity of the Islamic umma. The key to revolution was the mobilisation of the *mustaza'fin* against an oppressive status quo.

After the Shah was given refuge in the US, Khomeini stirred up anti-American feeling, precipitating the seizure of the US embassy in November 1979. While this may initially have been an effort to block any US effort to return the Shah to power, the demand for his extradition and the return of his wealth held abroad as a condition for release of the hostages was also meant to mobilise domestic support and to show the invincibility of Islam over the 'Great Satan'. The struggle with America also became a tool and issue in the post-revolutionary power struggle between the clerical radicals and moderates. The moderates, led by Prime Minister Bazargan, wanting to resume ties with the US, although on a new equal basis, tried to arrange the hostages' release. Bazargan's attempts to normalise Iran's US relations alarmed a public fearful that any this would 'let the US in through the back door', and allowed his enemies to sweep him from power.

The cost of the hostage crisis with the US was Iran's international isolation: general condemnation, hostile UN Security Council resolutions, US-engineered economic sanctions and the seizure of Iranian assets. Iranian relations with the USSR were little better and Iran actually rejected a Soviet offer of protection, warning it against using Iran as a Cold War battleground and condemning the Soviet presence in Afghanistan (Menashri 1990: 155–156). It was this international isolation that enabled Iraq to attack Iran and face virtually no international disapprobation. Thereafter France also became an enemy for its arms deliveries to Iraq in the war. To overcome its isolation, Iran sought alternative friends – radicals or underdogs such as Syria and North Korea – and sought to foster the rise of kindred Islamic states by exporting the revolution.

Exporting the revolution The clerical consolidation of power positioned militant ideologues to use state resources to export the revolution: the revolutionary guards, the Interior Ministry and the Intelligence Ministry each sponsored rival revolutionary networks abroad. They sponsored an Islamic revolutionary council that grouped Iranian-backed and -financed revolutionary organisations like the Supreme Assembly of the Islamic Revolution in Iraq and the Islamic Liberation Movement of Bahrain. The Ministry of Islamic Guidance promoted cultural missions, provided preachers and publications, hosted conferences of *ulama* from outside Iran and broadcast the Voice of the Iranian Revolution. Iran was also able to exploit a ready-made trans-state ideological network, the Shia *ulama* throughout the Muslim world, especially those who had been trained in Iran's holy cities. The hajj was seen as a unique opportunity to convert pilgrims from all parts of the Islamic world (Menashri 1990: 157).

The impulse to spread the revolution encouraged Iranian intervention in Arab politics. If Iran was to export the revolution to the Arab heartland of Islam and overcome the barriers which its Sunni-dominated Arab Gulf neighbours sought to erect, its Islamic *dawa* (call) had to be seen as universal, not specifically Shia. Indeed, the message of Islamic revolution had a powerful trans-state appeal, similar to Nasserism, throughout the Arab world. Responding to similar grievances, that is, Israel, regimes seen to be subservient to the West, corruption, inequality and Westernisation, it exploited domestic discontent prevalent throughout the region. Its demonstration effect stimulated imitative movements in every Middle East state, including Turkey and the Israeli occupied territories (Nahas 1985).

The attempt to export revolution to Iran's traditional Gulf neighbours was a high priority. Khomeini insisted that Islam denied the legitimacy of monarchic rule and deprecated the Gulf states for their 'American Islam'. The Iranian model of Islam, anti-American, mass mobilising, anti-monarchic and appealing to Shia minorities, was especially threatening to these states owing to their own liabilities: ineffective nation-building, reliance on expatriate labour and large deprived Shia communities. The political demonstrations conducted by Iranian hajj pilgrims, attacking the Saudi regime's US alignment, were meant to discredit Saudi Arabia as an alternative (and conservative) centre of Islam in Sunni Muslim opinion.

Iran's message, was, however, obstructed by the Sunni–Shia divide and it found its strongest reception where there were concentrations of Shia, not only because of Shiite connections with Iran but because they were typically deprived communities, often living in states with great oil wealth. Iran inspired and aided Shia Islamic movements in Bahrain, where the Shia were 72% of citizens, Iraq (60%) and Kuwait (23%, plus 14% of Iranian origin). Iran's encouragement of Islamic rebellion against the Soviet presence in Afghanistan found resonance among the Afghan Shia who it backed through the Hizb al-Wahdat militia. The export of revolution was most successful in Lebanon where the Shia were already mobilising in the context of civil war and where a failed state could not protect its borders from massive trans-state penetration. Iran used its Syrian alliance to jump over the 'Sunni Arab barrier', insert revolutionary guards in western Lebanon, sponsor Hizbollah and achieve a front in the Arab–Israeli conflict (Ramazani 1986: 140; Hunter 1987).

The Iran–Iraq War   The war with Iraq appeared to grow out of a (secular-religious) clash of ideologies but if revolutionary ideology was the sole driving force of Islamic Iran's foreign policy there might well have been no war. Ba'thist Iraq was a radical force no less than Ba'thist Syria with which Tehran was forming a close alliance against the American-Israeli *combinazione* in the region. Yet Iran played its full role in the cycle of provocation and counter-provocation that led to war with Iraq. The outlook of Iran's revolutionary elite was, in the case of Iraq, seemingly shaped by inherited Sunni Arab–Persian Shia animosity exacerbated by Iraq's mistreatment of its religious-minded Shiites. Iran calculated that Iraq, because of its majority Shia population, was extremely vulnerable to Islamic revolution and began encouraging Shiite dissidence especially through the Islamic Dawa Party.

From Baghdad's point of view, interests, not ideology, were decisive in its decision to launch a pre-emptive war against Iran. Shiite revolutionary Islam posed a serious subversive threat to a secular regime dominated by Sunnis. But there were certainly less risky ways than war of containing this threat and ambition was at least as important a consideration in Baghdad's decision-making. Iraq and Iran were geopolitical rivals for dominance in the Gulf but Iraq, being smaller, less populous, more vulnerable to subversion by Iran and its oil export lifelines exposed, had a slimmer and less secure base of national power for this contest. However, Iran's revolutionary turmoil had temporarily enervated its military capabilities while Iraq's power potential was simultaneously on the rise as its oil production, exceeding Iran's, reaped it $31 billion in currency reserves (Ramazani 1986: 57). Saddam Hussein believed the fall of the Shah created a power vacuum that he could fill as well as an opportunity to assume the Shah's role by offering the Gulf states protection from the Islamic revolution. He also aimed to reverse the humiliating 1975 Iranian imposition of joint control over the Shatt al-Arab with which he was personally identified. He may even have imagined he could seize and keep Iran's Arabic-speaking, oil-rich Khuzestan province. As such, a classic overlapping of threat, ambition and opportunity from an apparent power imbalance shaped Iraq's decision to go to war.

Yet Iraq was biting off more than it could chew. Saddam Hussein miscalculated that he could quickly knock Iran out of the war and impose a settlement, but the Iraqi army was unable to even seize the border oil town of Abadan and Iran's ideologically mobilised forces proved unexpectedly tenacious. Saddam hoped Iran's fragmented revolutionary regime would collapse but wartime ideological mobilisation consolidated it. Iran managed to seriously reduce Iraqi oil exports in the Gulf and its Syrian ally shut down Iraq's trans-Syria pipeline (Ramazani 1986: 70–85). Iraq also miscalculated its ability to get Soviet arms replenishments, for the Soviets were wooing Khomeini and Iraq had condemned their invasion of Afghanistan. Two years after the war started, Iraq had been expelled from Iran and had expended its currency reserves. By 1983 Iran was on the offensive in Iraqi territory with the aim of overthrowing the regime and spreading the revolution.

Iraq, on the defensive, sought to regionalise and internationalise the war while Iran, enjoying natural superiority and poor relations with most states, tried to contain it to the two parties. Iran and Iraq put competing pressures on the Gulf states but an attempted Shia coup in Bahrain, blamed on Iranian subversion, precipitated a Saudi initiative to promote security co-ordination against Iran, leading to the founding of the Gulf Co-operation Council (GCC).

Iran was in a dilemma: pressure drove the Arab Gulf states into Iraqi arms but relaxing the pressure let them contribute more to the Iraqi war effort (Ramazani 1986: 49). At the 1982 Fez summit, most of the Arab states united behind Iraq. Iraq's escalation of the 'tanker war' which targeted tankers loading from Iranian ports, aimed to force a Western-imposed halt to the war. In 1984–85 Iran retaliated with attacks on Saudi and Kuwaiti tankers and stopped ships to search for Iraq-bound war material. But Iran was deterred from further widening the war by growing US involvement in the Gulf and the need to avoid dissipating its forces (Calabrese 1994: 48–51).

In the event, Iraq was saved by the backing of status quo states against a revolutionary threat. Saudi and Gulf aid poured in, alternative Saudi and Turkish routes for Iraqi oil were established, and military equipment and workers arrived from Egypt. Iran was subject to Western arms embargoes while Saddam Hussein's regime was deliberately built up by the West; Western arms dealers made lucrative deals for Iraqi oil which put Iraq deeply in debt and would be a factor in its later invasion of Kuwait. France, in particular, supplied high-tech arms while US intelligence allowed Iraq to pinpoint and counter Iranian offensive build-ups. The Soviet Union also began to supply Iraq with arms once Iraqi territory was at risk. Iran, by contrast, had to resort to the international black market and seek supplies from other 'pariah' states like North Korea and its only close ally, Syria. The war continued far longer than it might otherwise have done owing to this 'borrowed capacity' (Ramazani 1986: 84).

Iran thought the faith and motivation of its troops would overcome Iraq's superior firepower, but its army's lack of military professionalism eventually weakened its offensives, which ground to a halt in the face of improved Iraqi defensive capabilities (Chubin 1994: 17). Iraq's chemical weapons were effective in its 1988 counter-offensive; the 'war of the cities', in which Iraqi missiles rained on Iranian cities, demoralised the population which began to desert the cities, enervating the legitimacy of a leadership that could not protect its people (Chubin 1994: 21). The economic base of Iranian war capacity was also under threat. Iran needed to expand its oil quota as well as keep up prices but in 1986 Saudi Arabia flooded the market to moderate prices, recover its falling market share and drive down Iran's oil revenues; this, together with Iraqi raids, degraded Iran's economic war-making capacity (Calabrese 1994: 57–62).

As long as it appeared that the war would not disrupt oil supplies, the US and the West were content to merely contain it, arguably pleased that these two potential candidates for Gulf hegemony checked and enervated each other to the benefit of the fragile pro-Western monarchies. However, the escalation of the war of the tankers raised alarms in the West while the US perceived an Iranian threat to close the Straits of Hormuz if its own oil exports were stopped (Chubin 1994: 80–81). The US presence in the Gulf was stepped up during the later stages of the war: Kuwaiti tankers were 'reflagged' to prevent Iranian attacks on them, there were 1987 naval engagements between Iranian and US forces, and the West made tacit threats to blockade Iran if it did not agree to UN conditions to end the war (Chubin 1994: 42). As Iran's forces were driven out of Iraq and Iran increasingly besieged, realists in the Iranian leadership were strengthened. Iran accepted the UN resolution ending the war, with Iraq enjoying the upper hand.

The war and the revolutionary regime   Iran's case shows dramatically the impact of war on domestic politics. The war was provoked by the attempted ideological export of revolution and initially had the effect of consolidating the regime. On the one hand, the revolutionary elite exploited Shiite traditions of martyrdom (*shehadat*) to energise the public and the fighters, especially the *basaj*, volunteers for whom revolutionary zeal substituted for training and arms; on the other hand, Iranian victories beginning in 1982 were exploited to demonstrate the rightness of the Islamic cause. The war diverted attention from troubles at home and wartime success boosted the self-confidence of the regime and the people (Hooglund 1987b; Menashri 1990: 228–230).

The Iranian leadership shared a consensus on the war, namely, that it would continue until Iraq's defeat and the fall of the Ba'th regime. But as the costs mounted, this consensus unravelled. Popular support for the war started ebbing away; a sign of this was the decline of volunteerism and the rise of draft dodging. The Mousavi government's campaign against war profiteering and its provision of rationed subsidised commodities for the poor alienated merchants while its proposals for the nationalisation of foreign trade and land reform were blocked by conservative clerics tied to bazaari interests. Militant 'trans-nationalists' heading revolutionary organisations wanted to continue the export of revolution, notably Interior Minister Ali Akbar Mohteshemi, who was behind Hizbollah's attempt to create an Islamic republic in Lebanon. On the other side, a more pragmatic faction, including parliament Speaker Hashemi Rafsanjani, Prime Minister Mousavi and President Khamenei, put the Iranian state's survival interests over ideological zeal (Hooglund 1987a; Menashri 1990: 305–368; Ramazani 1986: 255). The two sides also split on the role of government-to-government relations. The trans-nationalists held to Khomeini's original line that, since there were no just governments in the region, Iran should aid their overthrow rather than make friends with them. Rafsanjani countered that through deliberate rejection of the legitimacy of the states system and the conventions of diplomacy, Iran had so isolated itself that Iraq was able to mobilise global and regional resources on its side. 'By the use of an inappropriate method', he argued, 'we created enemies for our country' and failed to actively seek allies. His self-criticism was often pointed: 'If Iran had demonstrated a little more tactfulness in its relations with Saudi Arabia and Kuwait, they would not have supported Iraq' (Menashri 1990: 389, 393).

The balance between these shifting factions was fluid and often dependent on Khomeini's stand. In 1984 Khomeini came down against the trans-nationalists, warning that Iran would be annihilated if it did not overcome isolation; when, in retaliation, the trans-nationalists exposed the regime's 'hostage for arms' negotiations with the 'Great Satan', they were curbed (Ramazani 1986: 256, 264). As war reverses, falling oil prices and mounting international pressure, especially the threat of American intervention, closed in on Iran, the internal balance shifted further toward the moderates, whose leader, Rafsanjani, persuaded Khomeini to accept the UN sponsored ceasefire resolution. Khomeini consented to drink the 'poisoned chalice', as he put it, to save the revolution from internal demoralisation and external encirclement (Hooglund 1989). Thereafter, the Iranian Thermidor accelerated as Rafsanjani, in charge after Khomeini's death, subordinated ideology to postwar reconstruction, not only reviving the private sector but even seeking foreign loans and investment. Gradually, the economic self-sufficiency at which the revolution had aimed was abandoned. Each step Iran took in seeking reintegration into the world economy spilled over in the moderation of its foreign policy, without which economic relations to the outside could not be repaired.

An increasingly 'realist' foreign policy re-established relations with Iran's Gulf neighbours and economic links to the West. Export of revolution was replaced with a more conventional attempt to create spheres of influence in Iran's immediate neighbourhood. The imprint of ideology survived only in the continued hostility to Israel and the US (Ehteshami 1995; Harrop 1991).

In the end, the international system tamed the Iranian revolution: it used Iraq to wear Iran down and derail its attempts to restructure its economy; having failed to overcome its dependence on oil exports, and in dire need of resources to reconstruct a war-damaged economy, Iran's now chastened realists pushed the radicals aside and sharply moderated its foreign policy ideology in the face of these realities.

The states system and the periphery wars

The Iranian and Israeli threats on the eastern and western flanks of the Arab world, rather than uniting it, polarised it into two rival coalitions shaped by differential perceptions of the greater threat. A 'moderate' coalition, which came to include Iraq, Egypt, northern Yemen, Jordan, Saudi Arabia and the other GCC states, combined against the Iranian threat. Owing to the Gulf states' intense fear of Iran, massive resources were diverted from the Israeli front to support Iraq's war with Iran while the need for Egyptian arms and manpower on the anti-Iranian front drove Cairo's inter-Arab rehabilitation despite its adherence to its separate peace with Israel. Moreover, the US was allowed to expand its anti-Iranian presence in the Gulf despite its bombing of Libya, complicity in the Israeli invasion of Lebanon and designation of Israel as a US strategic asset. These developments, in turn, drove Syria and Iran into a defensive counter-alliance, with Iran mobilising Lebanese Shia on behalf of Syria's resistance to Israel in Lebanon and Syria obstructing the isolation of Iran in the Arab world. This axis, together with a so-called 'Steadfastness Front' of radical states – Libya, Democratic Yemen, Algeria – saw Israel and the US as the greater threats and sought support in Moscow. This inter-Arab split further 'de-constructed' Arab nationalism: Arab norms did not entirely disappear and the two camps each claimed to represent the Arab interest, but each, in the end, took opposing paths.

At the same time, the alternative basis of regional order, the balance of power, came more fully into being. Two anti-hegemonic alliances, cutting across the ideological and Arab-non-Arab fault-lines, blunted the ambitions of revisionist states on the eastern and western flanks of the Arab world. Iran's revolutionary mobilisation of its superior resource base was countered by the financial aid and arms to Iraq from its Arab and Western allies, generating a stalemate in which the two dominant Gulf powers wore each other down. The Iranian revolution was contained, no state succumbed to Islamic revolution and the Americans were enabled to enhance their presence and influence in the Gulf, quite the opposite of what either of the two parties to the war had intended. On the Western front, Syria, sheltered by a Soviet deterrent, used the Iranian-assisted mobilisation of Lebanese Shia to frustrate the American–Israeli *combinazione* in Lebanon. The 1980s ended with the Middle East having reached a precarious peace as the costs of war exhausted all sides in both conflict arenas. This, however, was only to be the pause before the 'desert storm'.

Conclusion: order without peace?

The search for solutions to regional conflict, for a basis on which to create a secure regional order, has been on-going since the founding of the Middle East states system. There are, indeed, sources of order in the region that have managed to preserve the states system, and, to a much lesser extent, to keep the peace for limited periods. However, each of the major attempts to build regional order proved defective, in varying degrees ameliorating or containing conflict but also either failing to deal with its roots or sometimes actually exacerbating it.

Order and supra-state identity: a Pan-Arab regime

Western efforts to impose an anti-communist security order on the region stimulated an indigenous response, Egypt's attempt to forge a Pan-Arab regime that would ensure Arab collective security against Israel and autonomy of Western penetration. This regime deterred the consolidation of a system of fully Westphalian states, confined inter-Arab conflict to the ideological level and rolled back Western penetration in the interests of a more autonomous Arab world (Barnett 1993, 1995, 1998). However, the threat Nasser posed to other Arab elites precipitated anti-hegemonic balancing, which obstructed his attempt to enforce the Pan-Arab 'regime'; it also stimulated defensive state formation which, in time, made the individual Arab states more immune to ideological penetration. It may be that anti-hegemonic balancing preserved the sovereignty-based states system against the potential imposition of a more integrated Cairo-dominated Pan-Arab order; but the outbidding that came with this balancing also led to the disastrous 1967 war. The consequent much-increased Israeli threat fostered an alternative sort of Pan-Arab regime based on recognition of sovereignty and formally realised through consensus-generating inter-state institutions, notably the Arab summits. In these forums, peer pressures and material inducements helped settle inter-Arab conflicts and unify the Arab states against shared threats. However, the weakening of Pan-Arabism amidst conflicts over the road to peace with Israel increased insecurity and encouraged states' resort to self-help. The Pan-Arab regime also offered no bridge to overcome the security dilemma on the fault-lines with the Middle East's non-Arab states. But the decline of Pan-Arabism, far from making for a more stable Middle East, merely spelled the replacement of Arab ideological conflicts with much more violent and sustained military conflicts on the Arab-non-Arab periphery.

Toward a Westphalian order: war and the balance of power
The growing incidence and cost of war forced states to adapt themselves to the survival imperatives of a threat-drenched system. Thus, in 1967 the radical Arab states, Egypt and Syria, driven by supra-state ideologies to challenge the status quo in defiance of the balance of power, suffered high costs; their leaders were chastened or replaced by realists that built up the autonomy and capacity to more rationally match ends and means. Two decades later revolutionary Iran was similarly brought by the costs of war to adopt less ambitious and ideological foreign policies. War and threat of war also induced the adoption of realpolitik power balancing as states built up deterrent capabilities and combined against threats from ambitious powerful states. The insecurity of an anarchic system was reconstructing the states that made it up and transforming their behaviour.

Despite the socialisation of states into the traditions of balancing, the region nevertheless proved all too vulnerable to power imbalances that provided renewed occasions for war. Power imbalances were built into the regional system by the creation of small super-rich mini states alongside large dissatisfied ones – an ingredient of the Iraqi invasion of Kuwait – and by the unevenness of state formation which positioned early state-builders, notably the non-Arab states, to threaten those where state formation was delayed. 'Buck-passing' frustrated the construction of stable collective deterrents against such powerful threatening states: the most extreme case was the dramatic upset in the power balance resulting from Egypt's opting out of the Arab–Israeli power balance. The security dilemma was also fully operational: as high insecurity drove states to improve their power position, the threat they posed to their neighbours stimulated arms races, jeopardising existing power balances. This was exaggerated by the rapid power advantages achieved by states that enjoyed exceptional oil revenues or foreign aid and hence access to massive arms deliveries from external powers. Arguably, a decade of war, including Israel's 1982 invasion of Lebanon and Iraq's two Gulf wars, was partly the product of such power imbalances. In time, such ambitious states overreached themselves, stimulated anti-hegemonic alliances and incurred high costs that restored the balance of power. The Middle East came, therefore, to exhibit certain of the self-equilibrating features of a Westphalian states system: but if this was enough to preserve the system it was not enough to keep the peace.

8

The Middle East under US hegemony (1990–2010)

While for parts of the world post-Cold War globalisation was associated with growing interdependence and the spread of 'zones of peace', in the Middle East the first decade of globalisation was ushered in by war, was marked by intrusive US hegemony, renewed economic dependency on the core, continuing insecurity and ended with yet another round of war in 2003.

In the early 1990s, prospects looked different to some observers: the end of the Cold War, the Second Gulf War and the advance of economic globalisation seemed to provide a unique opportunity to incorporate the area into a 'New World Order' in which the struggle for power would be superseded by the features prescribed by liberals to promote peace – complex interdependence, democratic peace. The defeat and discrediting of Iraq's militaristic Arab nationalism, the beginnings of the Arab–Israeli peace negotiations and a Washington-imposed Pax Americana were to facilitate creation of the co-operative security arrangements needed to tame the power struggle. The consequent dilution of insecurity, together with the exhaustion of economies from arms races, would allow economic development to push military ambitions off state foreign policy agendas. Access to the global market and investment would both require and encourage policies of peace (Solingen 1998) which, in turn, would foster regional economic interdependence and co-operation in resolving common problems such as water scarcity. This would create vested interests in peace, while public opinion, exhausted by war and acquiring enhanced weight from democratisation, would restrain state leaders. In consequence, the regional system would move, in Korany's words, 'from warfare to welfare'. The final displacement of Pan-Arabism by the doctrine of state sovereignty would allow 'normal' state-to-state relations based on shared interests and accord non-Arab states such as Turkey and Israel legitimate membership in a 'Middle East system' (Barnett 1996–97; Ehteshami 1997; Korany 1997; Tibi 1998).

In fact, few of these benign expectations for regional order were realised in the two decades after the Gulf war. Globalisation proved to be very uneven in its economic impact on the region and seemed to benefit a few at the expense of the many; as such, it was an obstacle to rather than an impetus to democratisation. The Arab–Israeli peace process dead-ended and arms races actually accelerated. While the intractability of regional conflicts and problems helped derail the benign promise of globalisation, an equally important factor was the way the much-intensified penetration of American hegemonic power was applied in the region. There is much debate over whether a world hegemon exercises its power in a largely self-interested way or whether successful hegemony means satisfying the interests of a wide range of lesser powers. In the developed core, where Washington must deal with other major powers and is itself locked into interdependencies, its role may be relatively benign; but in the Middle East its power was applied so systematically on behalf of a minority of privileged clients and so aggressively against others that it was widely perceived as a malign hegemon.

Many regional states sought to use, evade or appease American power but, given the weakness of the region, it was perhaps inevitable that actual resistance would chiefly take a non-state form. The September 11, 2001 attack by Islamic terrorists on the very heart of America led the US into its second Middle East war in a decade. In the aftermath of the 2003 invasion of Iraq, the region, far from entering the 'zone of peace', seemed to become an arena for a 'clash of civilisations'. Yet this attempt at a more robust militarised US hegemony over MENA only deepened resistance, notably inside occupied Iraq, which so raised the costs of Washington's adventurism that, under the Obama administration, the US began pulling back from its excessive regional engagement. What had gone wrong? Such an outcome might have been anticipated given the way globalisation was ushered into the Middle East – namely by a profoundly unequal war whose outcome gave the Western victors excessive power over the region and insufficient incentive to satisfy the interests and values of the region's states and peoples.

The second Gulf war

The second Gulf war (or first Iraq war) of 1990–91 represented a watershed event in the Middle East that sharply underlined how far it is a 'penetrated system', its politics a product of interaction between global and local forces. The war can, as such, only be understood by recourse to multiple 'levels of analysis'; analysis of the war can therefore serve as a model of how such multivariate analysis has superior explanatory power to approaches content to focus on one level to the exclusion of others. Regional level conflicts and Iraqi political economy largely explain the Iraqi choices that unleashed the war. However, there would have been no war without global-level factors, namely, an American attempt to secure global hegemony that was intimately connected to a struggle over the international oil market. Finally, despite the grave issues at stake, it was the peculiarities of the policy process inside the two main protagonist states that made a violent resolution of the conflict unavoidable. Without the interaction of all these levels, there would have been no second Gulf war.

Level one: formation of a 'war state'
Saddam's Hussein's decision to invade Kuwait provoked the Second Gulf war but this was not a purely idiosyncratic choice, for Iraqi state formation produced a certain kind of state which made war possible, in certain circumstances even likely, though not necessary. The very weakness of Iraq at its birth as a state produced a reaction, a drive to overcome this weakness at home and abroad, which turned Iraq, in Mufti's words (1996: 220–230), into a 'war state'.

Iraq's weakness was a function of its formation as an artificial state, arbitrarily carved by Great Britain out of conquered Ottoman domains and combining three communally different regions which shared no history of statehood or common identity – the Sunni Arab centre around Baghdad, a majority Shia Arab south and the Kurdish north. None of Iraq's pre-Ba'th regimes found a viable state-building formula that could stabilise this centrifugal society. The monarchy, resting on a thin stratum of landlords and tribal chiefs and lacking popular support and nationalist legitimacy, was only kept in power by the British; ironically, the one issue which united most of Iraq's disparate politically active population and produced the 1958 revolution was opposition to British tutelage.

The 1958 revolution marked the mobilisation of the masses into politics but the military regimes that emerged from it were too fragmented to build the institutions needed to incorporate the mass public; their attempts to stay in power by balancing competing forces resulted in fragile regimes barely controlling a country seemingly made ungovernable by the rival mobilisation of Shia communists, Arab nationalists, Ba'thists and the Kurdish KDP (Batatu 1978; Bromley 1994: 135–138; Frankel 1991: 18; Mufti 1996: 98–167).

All this only changed after the second Ba'th regime, which seized power in a 1968 coup, finally found a workable power formula. First, the Ba'thist leadership, a product of a decade of unrestrained power struggle, was convinced that only utterly ruthless treatment of opponents could defeat the natural rebelliousness of Iraqi society. Moreover, the man who survived the post-1968 power struggles within the regime, Saddam Hussein, an urban guerrilla turned Stalin-like organiser, was arguably the 'fittest' to survive in this environment. To consolidate his position, he relied on kin and sectarian *assabiya* to construct a patrimonialised power centre while brutally purging rivals and forging new instruments of power. The Ba'thisation of the army and intensive intelligence surveillance rid the officer corps of factionalism and finally put an end to the age of coups; the army's massive increase in size gave the regime, for the first time, thorough control over Iraqi territory. In a burst of organisation building, the Ba'th party expanded from a conspiratorial group into a 500,000 member 'institutionalised and deeply invasive' Leninist apparatus with another million supporters or sympathisers (Miller and Mylroie 1990; Mufti 1996: 204; Norton 1991: 25).

The 1970s nationalisation of the oil industry and the oil boom put soaring oil revenues in the hands of the government: its share of GNP doubled from 39% to 60% and its share of investment from 50% to 70% (Mufti 1996: 202–203). This control of the economy gave the regime massive patronage resources, enabled bureaucratic expansion which recruited nearly a million state workers dependent on the government for their livelihoods, and provided the wherewithal for crash modernisation in which infrastructure – roads, telephones – doubled and state penetration of society increased. Oil relieved the state of the need to extract taxes, giving it considerable autonomy from society. It also allowed the public sector to remain dominant in an age of *infitah*. Although private crony capitalism was encouraged among regime clients, the party and the regime's clientelist networks remained ladders of political recruitment from plebeian strata, diluting the consolidation of state elites into a new bourgeoisie. No bourgeois class formed to balance the state elite or with a stake in economic *infitah* as in Egypt where this class helped subordinate nationalist ambitions to participation in the world economy (Bromley 1994: 139–141).

Lacking a class base, the regime remained threatened by deep-seated sectarian-ethnic cleavages, which, in the absence of a secure Iraqi national identity, could only be contained by extraordinary means. Autonomous civil society was eradicated and citizens incorporated in all-encompassing totalitarian structures of control, co-opted by material benefits and the developmental achievements of the regime, or demobilised by fear enforced by a vast network of informers and a pervasive secret police (Norton 1991: 25). State patronage was used to divide the population, favouring or disfavouring groups on the basis of perceived loyalty (Bromley 1994: 139). All opposition from the Kurdish or Shia communities was brutally repressed; indeed, during the Iran–Iraq war, 250,000 Shia supposedly of Iranian origin were expelled to Iran, Kurdish villages suspected of rebellion were razed and relocated and mass killings were carried out (Khalil 1989; Mufti 1996: 229–230).

At the same time, Arab nationalist ideology was used to legitimise the state, in the first instance to consolidate a Sunni support base, but also to bridge the gap with the Shia Arabs. Many Sunnis felt limited affinity for a separate Iraqi state in which, indeed, they were a minority and found Pan-Arabism a much more attractive identity. Paradoxically, the regime also secured support from Sunnis by exploiting the threat to the integrity of the secular state and its officially dominant Arabism from Kurdish separatism and Islamist Shia groups inspired by Iran. Many Shia Arabs were attracted by upward mobility through state jobs and by their systematic recruitment into the ruling Ba'th party, which promoted the Arab identity they potentially shared with the Sunnis. The Iran–Iraq war was the test of this control strategy. That the majority of the population and the bulk of wartime conscripts were Shiite and hence possibly susceptible to the appeal of Iranian revolutionary Islam against their own Sunni-dominated secular state was the regime's potentially fatal liability. Yet there were no Shia uprisings or defections to Iran during the war even in the face of major defeats (Gause 1991: 17).

Iraq's state formation had several key consequences for its foreign policy. First, the credibility of its state-building Arab nationalist ideology required Iraqi leadership on the Pan-Arab stage. Iraqi leaders, from the very founding of the state, imagined that Iraq had the potential to be the Prussia of Arab politics but for years this role fell to Egypt while Iraq was preoccupied with instability at home. With the rise of the Ba'thists to power an ideological thrust was given to the notion that the arena of political competition was not within a single state, but a contest for Pan-Arab leadership; once they consolidated the state at home, they started to act on these ambitions in the region (Mufti 1996: 194).

Second, if the arbitrary drawing of Iraq's borders had created an artificial state within, it also artificially excluded much as well. In particular, Iraq's southern and south-eastern borders with Iran and Kuwait were forced on it by Britain explicitly to limit its access to and power projection in the Gulf, its economic lifeline. This built a powerful irredentism into Iraq's very fabric. Recurrent Iraqi leaders, from King Ghazi to Abd al-Karim Qasim, contested Kuwait's independence, insisting it had been a part of Iraq under the Ottomans until separated under British tutelage. The disputed and ill-defined Iran–Iraq border along the Shatt al-Arab put Iraq into permanent conflict with a more powerful Iran against which it was mostly on the defensive. Iran under the Shah supported Kurdish insurgency against Baghdad that forced Iraq to accept a 1975 readjustment of the boundary to its disadvantage. This situation both generated considerable insecurity in Baghdad and inflamed irredentist grievances (Frankel 1991: 17–18; Tripp 2001: 168, 170, 179–182).

Third, the regime, which always rested on a military pillar of power, created, during the Iran–Iraq war, an enormous, professionalised military machine with some 4 million soldiers under arms at the end of the war. It was, moreover, well equipped with advanced weapons financed by oil or debt and provided by Western states seeking profits or anxious to see Iran contained. What had once been a defensive Iraq, barely able to control its own territory against Kurdish insurgency, was, by the end of the Iran–Iraq war, in a position to pursue an activist foreign policy against weaker neighbours.

Fourth, the paradox of Iraq's oil-driven development was that the investment of oil revenues in rapid modernisation, education and welfare created what seemed to be the Arab world's most developed state with the most balanced power assets; but, at the same time, oil-fuelled development created a new dependency on imported machinery, food and consumer goods which would make Iraq particularly vulnerable to economic pressures and fluctuations in the price of oil (Mufti 1996: 202–203). Indeed, in the aftermath of the Iran–Iraq war, Iraq, deeply indebted to both Western and Gulf Arab creditors, suddenly discovered its access to foreign imports restricted and the leverage of its rich Gulf funders over it enhanced. Iraq's massive build-up of military power in excess of its own substantial economic base had bankrupted it. For Saddam, the invasion of Kuwait appeared to be a solution to this dilemma. However, additional regional-level factors, specifically Saddam's Pan-Arab ambitions, the Kuwait–Iraq conflict and a regional power imbalance helped create the environment in which this decision could seem rational.

Level two: an unstable region
Regional conflicts, ambitions and power imbalances   Once the Iraqi state was, by the late 1970s, relatively secure at home, it was better positioned to act on its regional grievances and ambitions. Saddam made Iraq into an aggressive actor in inter-Arab politics, seeking to destabilise the rival Ba'thist regime in Syria and to isolate Egypt after Camp David. He promulgated a National Covenant, which, in Nasser style, sought to lay down Pan-Arab standards for the Arab states. While acknowledging the reality of independent Arab states, Saddam insisted that they should not allow foreign bases or troops and that the richer should share their wealth with the poorer (Mufti 1996: 221–229), an overt challenge to the Arab Gulf monarchies. In 1980 the threat from Iran was met, not by appeasement as in 1975, but by aggression. Saddam evidently saw this war as a way of mobilising the Arabs behind his ambitions (Mufti 1996: 220–230). In fact, it forced him to dilute his challenge to the Gulf monarchies whose financial help he needed for the war, but, by contrast to Egypt after its 1967 war, the costs of the war only temporarily moderated Saddam's ambitions.

Indeed, the most salient theme in regional geopolitics in the aftermath of the Iran–Iraq war was Iraq's bid for Pan-Arab leadership.

Iraq saw itself as the victor in a war that had successfully defended the Arab eastern flank against Iran. It saw itself and was widely seen in the Arab world as the Arab state with the greatest power potential that entitled it to Arab leadership. At the same time, Saddam perceived threats and opportunities issuing from the end of the Cold War of which he sought to take advantage to assert this leadership. The decline of the Soviet Union and the tide of Soviet Jewish emigration to Israel threatened to shift the regional balance against the Arabs at a time when, under Likud, Israel was rejecting the latest bid for a negotiated settlement to the Arab–Israeli conflict. Taking advantage of the damage this did to moderate Arab leaders, notably Egypt's Mubarak who promoted his role as Arab–Israeli interlocutor, Saddam proposed a confrontational stand against Israel's American backer, urging the use of the oil weapon, and, in response to Israeli threats, warning that he would burn half of Israel (with chemically armed missiles) if it attacked any Arab country. The enthusiastic mass response to this strengthened and emboldened Saddam. But his bid was rejected by Egypt and Saudi Arabia, which, together with Syria, started forming a new anti-Iraq axis. Invading Kuwait was, in part, a gamble to force his leadership and strategy of confrontation on his rivals, but, in fact, it only strengthened their opposition to him (Khalidi 1991a: 170–171; 1991b: 60–61).

The Kuwait–Iraq dispute was, of course, the immediate occasion of the invasion. Iraq's historic reluctance to accept Kuwait's legitimacy conditioned Iraqi attitudes in the dispute, but a more immediate issue was Iraq's attempts to secure access to the Gulf by either incorporating or leasing the Kuwaiti islands of Warbah and Bubiyan. Kuwait rejected this and sought to use Iraq's economic vulnerabilities to impose a final settlement of the boundaries between the two states to its advantage. The most immediate bone of contention, however, was what Saddam Hussein declared to be Kuwait's 'economic warfare' against Iraq: its 'over-pumping' of oil in excess of its OPEC quota, driving down the price of Iraq's oil exports; its encroaching on the Iraqi share of the jointly held Rumaila oil fields; and its insistence on repayment of loans made to Iraq for the war with Iran – which Iraq interpreted to be a quid pro quo for protecting Kuwait and the Gulf from the Iranian threat (Bahbah 1991; *Christian Science Monitor,* 10 September 1990, p. 8, Khalidi 1991b: 62–65).

Many states have comparable grievances against their neighbours, but few invade them. The relative permissiveness of the
regional environment toward the use of force conditioned Iraq
to opt for such means. To be sure, there was a Pan-Arab norm of
peaceful settlement of disputes, underpinned by a tradition of inter-
Arab mediation; both Egypt and Saudi Arabia tried to mediate the
dispute with Kuwait but this 'Arab solution' failed. Kuwait seemed
to play a reckless out-of-character game, apparently with American
encouragement, of provoking rather than conciliating its powerful
neighbour. Arab political culture also lacks the powerful normative
barrier to the violation of state borders which restrains states elsewhere: Saddam Hussein seemingly believed that he could legitimise
his invasion as a blow for Pan-Arabism against artificial borders
and the approval of segments of the Arab public suggests he was
not wholly wrong (Halliday 1991: 395–398).

In the absence of institutionalised norms, it is the balance of
power that must keep the peace. However, the Gulf region was
afflicted by built-in chronic power imbalances from the contiguous
position of weak rich states and large poorer ones. The build-up of
Iraq's huge military machine in the Iran–Iraq war and the enervation
of Iran as a check on it as a result of the war's outcome exacerbated
these imbalances. Potential Soviet restraints on Iraq – a Cold War
function of preventing local conflicts from escalating into superpower confrontation – had declined as Iraq became less dependent
on Soviet arms and the USSR disengaged from the area under
Gorbachev. In this situation, the map imposed on the region, specifically the Iraqi giant contiguous with the Kuwaiti midget, was a
structural invitation to war (Hiro 1991b; Khalidi 1991b).

Formation of an anti-Iraq Middle East coalition   Without the
creation of an anti-Iraq Arab coalition that could facilitate US
intervention against Iraq, there would have been no war and
possibly a very different kind of 'Arab solution' to the invasion.
Remarkably, however, the US managed to co-opt the three most
pivotal Arab states into a Western-led coalition against another
Arab state. Saudi Arabia, most crucial, provided the territorial
base and a lot of the financing for the US intervention, while
Egyptian and Syrian participation in the coalition were essential to
managing Arab public reaction to it. Saddam's invasion of Kuwait
had violated the norms of sovereignty that had been incorporated

into the Arab elite consensus, but their support for Washington's assault on Iraq was itself such an egregious violation of Arabism that, arguably, they must have had other vital interests at stake to so risk the very bases of their domestic legitimacy. While each had its particular motives, the dependence of all three states, in one way or another, on the US gave Washington crucial leverage over them. This construction of the coalition was both a symptom of – and a major watershed in deepening – the increasing American penetration of the region.

Saudi Arabia's motives for inviting the Americans in were, of course, security-centred. The Saudis probably did not expect an Iraqi invasion, but in an anarchic system one must prepare for the worst-case scenario and if Iraq succeeded in keeping Kuwait, it would be in a position to intimidate Saudi Arabia over the longer term. The driving factor in the Saudis' perceptions was that, being weak and rich in a dangerous neighbourhood, they could not do without an external protector and to deny the US the access to their territory it was demanding could well cost them American protection.

As the Arab world's pivotal state, Egyptian support for the Gulf coalition was crucial. If Saudi Arabia was motivated by its security dependency, Egypt's choice was ultimately motivated by its economic dependency. President Mubarak had worked assiduously to position Egypt as the 'moderator' of the Arab system: enjoying American confidence and Arab leadership, Egypt would be pivotal to resolving or containing regional conflicts, especially the Arab–Israeli conflict. It was in this capacity that Egypt was valuable to the West and entitled to the foreign aid on which its economy had become dependent. However, at a time when Egypt faced a growing debt crisis and the possibility of default, Saddam Hussein's promotion of a confrontational strategy toward the US and Israel threatened Egypt's role. On the other hand, the invasion presented a welcome opportunity to demonstrate to the West Egypt's continued importance to regional stability and thereby win debt relief. In fact, Cairo was promised and given unprecedented debt forgiveness (Abdalla 1991; Haseeb and Rouchdy 1991; Hetata 1991).

Syria was essentially engaged in geopolitical balancing. Iraq under Saddam was a major rival for Pan-Arab leadership and a potential military threat (especially after its war with Iran was over); the war was a chance to cut Saddam Hussein down to size.

More important, however, was Syria's conflict with Israel over the Golan Heights for, with the end to Soviet patronage and protection in the post-Cold War era, Syria was exposed to a power imbalance in Israel's favour and left without the military option needed to credibly threaten war in the absence of an Israeli withdrawal from the occupied Arab territories. Syria had no alternative to a negotiated recovery of the Golan and it could only hope to secure one if the US was prepared to broker an Arab–Israeli settlement that recognised its legitimate interests. Syria's diplomatic dependency on the US meant it had to bring Washington to put aside old animosities and accept Syria as a responsible power on the side of regional stability. The Gulf war was a golden opportunity to do so (Hinnebusch 1997).

Level three: the political economy of oil
The concentrated oil reserves of the Gulf were, of course, the main stake in the war: in one sense, the war was a north–south conflict over resources – specifically over the determination of the north, and especially the US hegemon, to keep control of vital resources located in the Arab Gulf but central to the economic health of the whole world capitalist economy. Direct US control over world oil was declining: its own proportion of world reserves shrunk from 34% in 1948 to 7% in 1972 and its share of production decreased from 20% in 1970 to 10% in 1991. Yet in the same period that its imports had risen from 12% to 50% of its consumption (1970–91), OPEC had diluted the control of US oil companies over oil produced abroad. To be sure, in 1990 only about 12.5% of US oil consumption was from Gulf sources and, in the short run, Iraq and Kuwait together supplied only 7% of world oil demand. However, looking to the longer term, Iraq, Kuwait and Saudi Arabia controlled 40% of world oil reserves. The concentration of oil reserves in such a turbulent region made guaranteed reliable access to them a vital interest that would have to be defended by whatever means (Kubursi and Mansur 1993: 7; Tanzer 1991: 264).

A shorter-term threat was Iraq's influence over the *price* of oil. Some argue that prices are determined by the global oil market, not producers – so there is some debate over the extent to which Iraq would have been able to control prices. However, Saudi Arabia, with a 21% share of world exports, was crucial to moderating prices and had great influence over the price of oil on the 'spot market'. Were Iraq to have retained Kuwaiti fields and remained in a position to intimidate Saudi Arabia, it might have been able to dictate prices, causing major economic headaches for Western governments. However, regardless of who controls the oil fields, they must sell oil on the international market where excessive prices reduce demand, eventually forcing prices down; moreover, even in the short run, Iraq, desperate for revenues (for reconstruction and debt repayment) would likely have needed to maximise production, thus keeping prices at moderate levels. Hence, oil access and price are insufficient explanations for the high US/Western perception of threat from Iraq (*Christian Science Monitor*, 8 August 1990). In any case, if Iraqi intimidation of Saudi Arabia was the main lever by which it could influence oil prices, this could have been neutralised by the deployment of defensive forces there, stopping far short of the war that was actually launched by Washington.

Equally important, however, to the oil relation between the 'core' and the oil-producing 'periphery' was the 're-cycling' of the petrodollars accruing to the oil producers through Western banks and through the purchase of Western arms. The conservative Gulf monarchies moderated prices and re-cycled proceeds on a massive scale without threatening the West. Iraq, by contrast, had not acquired a stake in Western economic health through large-scale investment and, while its arms purchases re-cycled petrodollars, once Iran was defeated, continuing extensive arms sales were bound to overly strengthen Iraq in the Gulf region.

A strengthened Iraq was all the more unacceptable because it was threatening to *politicise* the oil relation. What was most alarming to the US was that Saddam Hussein had explicitly proposed the reactivation of the oil weapon, which meant making Western access to oil conditional on a favourable Western policy in the Arab–Israeli conflict. The West could not afford to have such an independent, even hostile, regime in charge of 'the world's' concentrated oil reserves. Rather, it was crucial that oil remain in the hands of friendly regimes, which, by virtue of their dependence on the US for security and their Western investments, had a shared interest with the West in ensuring stable unpoliticised access to oil at moderate prices. Iraq's power intimidated these regimes and its example threatened to destabilise them. What was at stake, therefore, was not access to oil but access on Western terms.

Level four: the international system and US hegemony

The systemic transformation of the international system at the end of the Cold War and the looming end to US–Soviet bi-polarity provided the global context of the Gulf war. The Iraqi invasion of Kuwait was the precipitant of the conflict but it resulted in a global war partly because the US took it as a challenge to the world order that it wanted to shape and defend. Had such an invasion taken place during the Cold War or in some obscure part of the world where no global interests were at stake, there would have been no comparable global war.

With the end of the Cold War, the US was positioning itself as the unchallenged world hegemon. Wallerstein (1974) argues that, owing to the political fragmentation of the international capitalist system, its maintenance and expansion depends on a hegemon – a state qualitatively different in function from others, which enjoys preponderant economic, political and military power that is used to police challenges to global order. The hegemon also sustains the functioning of the world capitalist political economy by breaking down barriers to international trade and investment, protecting the interests of the international capitalist class (i.e., the multinational corporations) and ensuring the capitalist core's access to vital economic resources in the periphery, above all to cheap energy. The hegemon's success depends in part on the ideological hegemony of liberalism, which generates a measure of consent, but while this ideology dominates the core it is periodically challenged in the periphery and hegemony there is more likely to require the application of military power. Historically Britain played the role of hegemon, providing the main power and capital for dragging the Middle East into the international division of labour. After World War II, however, the US superseded Britain, seeking to absorb most of the Third World into the world capitalist system while militarily containing Soviet or radical nationalist challenges to it.

However, the US ability to play the hegemon was in doubt from the mid-1970s through the 1980s owing to an apparent economic decline attributed to its 'imperial overreach' – excessive military spending and lack of domestic investment combined with rising economic competition from Europe and Japan which were less willing than heretofore to defer to the US. Indeed, a Pentagon planning document in the late 1980s discussed the need for the US to defend its hegemonic power from such competitors. At a time when some of the other ingredients of US economic hegemony, such as financial assets and trading capacity, had declined, control of Middle East oil, including petrodollar re-cycling, was an all-the-more crucial instrument of hegemony and source of leverage over economic competitors.

It is no accident that US foreign policy and its watershed doctrines – from the Truman and Eisenhower Doctrines through those of Nixon, Carter and Reagan – all explicitly identified control of Middle East oil as central to the US national interest (Kubursi and Mansur 1993: 8). In the view of some structuralist analysts, the US orchestration of the Gulf war was used to demonstrate the continuing indispensability of US hegemony to protecting the world capitalist core's control of oil against Third World challenges and restored the US protectorate over global oil resources. The war ensured that Gulf petrodollars would continue to be re-cycled through US institutions and firms and therefore serve US competitiveness. In addition, in the Gulf war the US actually managed to make its imperial policing profitable by inducing its economic competitors (Germany, Japan) and clients (Saudi Arabia, Kuwait) to pay for the service (Aarts 1994; Bina 1993; Darnovsky, Kauffman and Robinson 1991; Kubursi and Mansur 1993).

US hegemony had also been threatened by the perceived decline of the utility of military force. The US needed an opportunity to show the world that American military power was still usable and essential to world order. A Pentagon planning document before the Iraqi invasion identified the main potential threats to Pax Americana as militaristic Third World nationalist regimes. Iraq was fingered as a possible troublemaker owing to its attempt to acquire missiles and 'weapons of mass destruction' and its challenge to Israel. Once Iraq invaded Kuwait the advantages of confronting it came into focus. The Pentagon had wanted enhanced military bases in the Gulf since the mid-1970s, but the Arab Gulf states had demurred for domestic reasons; the invasion was a perfect opportunity to establish a greater Gulf presence and enhance America's ability to project power globally. It was also an opportunity to demonstrate US resolve to protect its regional clients, as a credible hegemon must. The military defeat of Iraq would demonstrate that US military force was effectively usable and send a warning to other potential troublemakers that, as President Bush put it: 'what we say goes' (Klare 1991).

If the US was to retain hegemony, the US public had to support a globalist role but with the end of the Soviet threat, the US military-industrial complex needed a new mission to justify continued military spending. This new mission would be a Pax Americana, the defence of the liberal world order emerging from the defeat of communism against the remaining threat of Third World – especially Islamic – pariah states. Moreover, the Pentagon was determined that the war would be fought with the unrestrained application of its massive firepower and new high-tech military capabilities. Only if fought in this way would a war assure the American public that international policing could be cheap and incur minimal casualties. The Iraqi invasion posed a perfect opportunity to banish the 'Vietnam syndrome' – public reluctance to get involved in wars abroad (Klare 1991).

Whatever the US might have wished to do in the Gulf war, it was the collapse of bi-polarity that gave it the opportunity to act. In the Cold War bi-polar world, the risks of superpower confrontation would probably have restrained it. It was only the USSR's withdrawal from global competition with the US and, specifically, the end of Soviet opposition to the projection of US military power that made it possible for the US to mount an international coalition and to intervene in the Gulf on such a massive scale. The war hastened the collapse of the Soviet Union, as Gorbachev's pro-Western policy was part of the disaffection that produced the failed conservative coup and Soviet collapse. The collapse of Eastern bloc alternatives to capitalism and the end to Soviet patronage of Third World nationalism enormously increased the self-confidence of US elites that a capitalist Pax America could be imposed against lingering resistance in the Third World.

This is not to argue that the US planned the war or even that it was waiting for the opportunity that the Iraqi invasion presented. Indeed, the invasion apparently took Washington by surprise and it was not even initially prepared or seemingly keen to act. But once policy-makers assessed their options and realised the opportunities could outweigh the risks of intervention, they quickly determined on a war and set out to mobilise the support needed to undertake it.

Level five: decision-making

While geopolitical analysis tries to identify the 'objective' interests, threats, opportunities and capabilities of states, analysis of the decision-making process is necessary to understand how and why a country reacts to its geopolitical situation as it does. Analysis of how states choose between conflicting goals and match means with them frequently reveals leadership flaws, such as misperceptions, and domestic pressures, which, to the analyst, distort the geopolitical rationality of decisions. Specifically, in explaining war, analysis seeks to understand why leaders reject compromises that could *satisfice* their interests at less risk and cost than going to war. This is most important in understanding Iraq for which the costs and risks were exceptionally high.

Iraq Regime stability had always been a decisive calculation for Iraqi leaders and, arguably, this was under some threat in the period running up to the war. The end of the Iran–Iraq war was trumpeted as a Pan-Arab victory, but Iraq had paid a high cost and made few tangible gains while Iraqis expected a peace dividend. But repayment of Iraq's economic debt and Kuwaiti over-pumping were perceived to threaten post-war recovery (Bromley 1994: 142; Chaudhry 1991). The invasion of Kuwait, besides realising Saddam's Pan-Arab ambitions, promised to alleviate this dilemma: Saddam sought to reinforce domestic support by giving Iraqis war spoils and portraying the annexation of Kuwait as a Pan-Arab challenge to imperialism.

Yet there were other less risky ways of securing the regime and the decision to opt for the military occupation of Kuwait resulted from a profound leadership miscalculation of the international permissiveness for such a venture. Arguably, Saddam's risk-taking personality made him prone to such miscalculation and his seeming victory over Iran had, no doubt, reinforced his recklessness (see chapter 4). Tripp (2001: 172) argues that Saddam and his inner circle projected their unforgiving view of politics and the ruthless methods which were a product of the internal power struggle on to the external arena, failing to understand that such behaviour was outside the pale of the emerging post-Cold War world order. Moreover, the nature of the decision-making process meant that there were no effective checks on Saddam. The totalitarian state of fear and the boundless cult of personality he had created turned his lieutenants into submissive sycophants who, knowing the cost of opposition, were bound to tell him what he wanted to hear.

As such, Saddam repeatedly miscalculated the situation or misplayed his hand. He underestimated the US and Western reaction to his invasion, perhaps because they had built him up against Iran. He may have thought the US would acquiesce because of US ambassador April Glaspie's remark that Washington considered the dispute with Kuwait to be an inter-Arab matter and the assurances he gave her that Iraq respected US oil interests in the region. On the basis of the Vietnam experience, Saddam believed the US could not sustain casualties and that air power was of limited importance, but the parallel of Vietnam and Iraq was faulty. He either miscalculated the reaction of states like Egypt and Saudi Arabia, which had been recent close allies against Iran, or falsely believed that the pro-Saddam acclaim of the Arab street would deter their timid rulers from taking the side of the US. He also falsely believed the Soviets would block an American intervention and was astonished and outraged that they took the American side against their old ally (*Christian Science Monitor*, 17 January 1991; *Global Research* 2012; Hitchins 1991: 115–117).

In the post-invasion diplomatic contest in which attempts were made to secure Iraqi evacuation of Kuwait without war, Saddam played a poor diplomatic hand. Once it was clear there would be a robust international reaction, he could have bargained withdrawal in return for some Kuwaiti concessions. But the formal annexation of Kuwait, enacted in reaction to the dispatch of American troops, made it impossible to compromise without losing face. Whether this was a rational tactic to show his enemy he had no way back and thus that he would fight any attempt to get him out of Kuwait or a prideful refusal of concessions to what he saw as the arrogance of the UN demand for unconditional withdrawal, such obduracy cost Iraq chances to forestall or divide the coalition (*Christian Science Monitor*, 3 January, 11 February 1991). Later, the decision to withdraw from Kuwait on the eve of the coalition ground offensive only sowed confusion in Iraqi ranks and made for a very poor defence.

The US   There is no doubt that the US could have achieved many of its objectives short of war but domestic politics and the character of its leadership made war inescapable. First, when it comes to the Middle East, the US policy process is uniquely vulnerable to colonisation by pressure groups and in this case the Middle East lobbies, normally in conflict, tended to come together against Iraq. The coalition of conservative Arab state lobbyists, oil companies and arms exporters, including big contributors to the Republican

Party, were for containment of and perhaps action against Iraq, although they feared the effect of the latter on Arab opinion could undermine their Middle East interests. Zionist pressure groups, however, had no such hesitation: since Saddam's speech threatening to burn half of Israel, a campaign of demonisation of Iraq had begun. Zionists were well positioned in the national security bureaucracy as well as the press and congress to argue for action and offending this lobby is dangerous to the political health of American politicians. Public opinion, being split and vulnerable to media manipulation, was largely neutralised as a check on either pressure groups or elite belligerency.

Bush and his inner circle ultimately made the decision for war and the outcome was no accidental war from miscalculation or misperception in Washington. The Bush administration wanted a war, not a diplomatic settlement, and indeed US policy-makers openly feared Saddam might make concessions which could deprive them of this opportunity – the so-called 'nightmare scenario' of a partial Iraqi withdrawal from Kuwait. Saddam had to be beaten because his 'linkage strategy' – offering withdrawal from Kuwait in return for Israeli withdrawal from the occupied territories – dramatically exposed the double standards by which the US exempted Israel from the norms it enforced against others. Any sign of US weakness would, it was believed, encourage Arab nationalists and Islamists to challenge US interests across the region. Were Saddam to retreat with his military assets intact, he would be a future threat needing constant containment and in a position to revive Arab nationalism, and thus threaten both Israel and the Arab clients that ensured US access to oil. It was far better for the US to deal with Saddam while it had the coalition and the UN behind it and before Iraq got the nuclear deterrent that would prevent such action. Thus, the US rejected Iraq's offer to withdraw from Kuwait on the eve of Washington's ground offensive. Moreover, once Iraq was defeated, Washington imposed a victor's diktat meant to destroy the country as a viable power. Yet at the same time, the administration passed up the opportunity to invade Iraq and overthrow Saddam and hence left a wounded but defiant regime still in power. Arguably decision-makers ought either to have done this or alternatively allowed an Iraqi retreat from Kuwait that could avoided the costs of war and would probably have better served regional stability than destroying the country.

This fateful decision would lead to another Iraq war and introduce powerful centrifugal forces that would deepen the long-term instability of the region.

The consequences of the Gulf War: 'New World Order' or disorder?

The main immediate consequence of the Gulf war was the opening of the region to much greater external penetration and to shift the regional balance of power to the advantage of the non-Arab peripheries. While the war opened a window of opportunity to advance a resolution of the Arab–Israeli conflict, Arab weakness, American hegemony and Israeli superiority prevented the equitable distribution of benefits that alone might have issued in a settlement. Without such a settlement, any attempt to shape a new order based on legitimacy rather than force was doomed.

Power politics in a Pan-Arab vacuum

The second Gulf war both reflected and contributed to the further enervation of the remnants of Arab solidarity that had heretofore contained inter-Arab conflict. Saddam Hussein's use of Arabism to justify his invasion of another Arab state discredited the sentiment among Gulf Arabs. The formation of the anti-Iraq coalition showed how decision-making in the Arab states was driven almost exclusively by individual geopolitical interests and Western economic or security dependency and hardly at all by supra-state identity. That a majority of the states of the Arab League voted to invite foreign intervention against Iraq demonstrated that the sanctity of state borders had achieved legitimacy – at least among governments – at the expense of Arab identity and norms against Western intervention (Barnett 1998: 217). Inter-Arab institutions were much weakened: the coalition states, led by Egypt, once the champion of Pan-Arabism, had manipulated the Arab League into facilitating Western intervention against another member of the League at the expense of an 'Arab solution' to the crisis.

In the post-war period, the Arab League was paralysed, with no agreement possible on holding an Arab summit between 1990 and 1996, even though momentous decisions were being taken affecting the common Arab interest, notably in the Arab–Israel peace process. This paralysis reflected, above all, the inability to heal the rift between Iraq (and to a degree its supporters) and the Gulf Arabs, especially Kuwait, which distanced themselves from Arab core concerns such as Palestine. The Arab League Secretary-General, presumably the keeper of the common interest, announced that henceforth no Arab state could interfere in another's definition of its own interest and security. Brief hopes for the creation of a new collective Arab security framework embracing Egypt, Syria and the GCC under the Damascus Declaration failed when the latter chose to rely on Western treaties, further enervating the Arab norm against overt foreign treaties and bases (Barnett 1998: 227–228; Faour 1993: 84–85). While Saddam's arousal of the Arab street in the Gulf war had shown the durability of mass Pan-Arab sentiment, it was contained by authoritarian regimes, receded in the wake of Iraq's defeat and ceased to be a constraint on states in the post-war Arab–Israeli negotiations.

A main effect of Arab fragmentation was the increased ability of hostile periphery states to exploit Arab divisions and their greater engagement in balancing against Arab states. The virtual collapse of Arab collective security was sharply exposed amidst the intensification and cross-border spillover of the Kurdish–Turkish conflict. The conflict not only drew Turkey into punitive expeditions in northern Iraq against PKK guerrillas, but also sharpened disputes with Syria, which gave sanctuary to the PKK. This dovetailed with a conflict over Turkey's control of Euphrates water, on which Iraq and Syria were dependent, in which Syria was trying to use the PKK as counter-leverage against Ankara. For this and other reasons, Turkey and Israel entered a security pact, which, in enabling Israeli forces to use Turkish territory, encircled Syria and threatened Iraq and Iran. The continued paralysis of Arab collective institutions was underlined by the unfolding of the conflict: when, in 1998, Turkey's threats of war against Syria forced it to expel the PKK, not only was Arab support for Syria ineffective but Jordan was actually tacitly aligned with the Israel–Turkish alliance and Egypt's Mubarak underlined to Asad Turkey's determination, bringing him to capitulate. This episode made it clear that, far from a new collective security system taking hold, high-intensity conflict and military power remained central to the region's international relations. This was all the more so because the promise that the post-war Arab–Israeli peace process would resolve the region's most enduring conflict also proved illusory (Carley 1995: 16–19; El-Shazly and Hinnebusch 2001: 78–80; Kirisci 1997).

A flawed peace process

The 1990s did begin with movement, starting with the 1992 Madrid Peace conference, toward resolution of the Arab–Israeli conflict. The peace process had its roots in the rising costs of the conflict in the 1980s and a very gradual and uneven realisation by both sides of the declining utility of force in reaching their goals. For both Israel and the PLO the 1982 Lebanon war was decisive. Israel paid a high cost but failed to reach many of its objectives while the PLO's loss of its south Lebanon military front made armed struggle obsolescent as a method of realising Palestinian national rights. The focus of Palestinian resistance became the *intifada* – an unarmed rebellion in the occupied territories, which the Israelis tried to repress by force and economic deprivation. The *intifada* put Palestine back on the world agenda and brought Israel international opprobrium. Only as the PLO thus achieved international legitimacy could it afford to recognise Israel and in November 1988 it accepted UN Resolution 242, contingent on acquisition of a Palestinian state in the occupied territories. Meanwhile, inside Israel, the two main political parties were drawing apart. The Likud government continued its drive to expand Jewish settlements in occupied territory, 'creating facts' which it expected would put a 'land-for-peace' settlement beyond reach. This stimulated the rise of terrorism by Islamic militants which both pushed Israel toward and away from a negotiated settlement (Smith 1996: 302–308). Inside the Labour party, by contrast, the traditional realist security doctrine stressing the primacy of military power and territorial defence was incrementally being challenged: on the one hand, by the new threat to Israel from the regional spread of weapons of mass destruction (WMDs), against which the occupied territories provided no defence, a reality underlined by Iraq's use of Scud missiles against it during the Gulf war; on the other hand, by the growing effectiveness of sub-state guerrilla warfare (in southern Lebanon), insurgency (the *intifada*) and terrorism which seemed to enervate Israel's ability to translate conventional military superiority into security and political ends. The increasing costs of containing the Palestinian *intifada* raised doubts about the viability of the occupation status quo. At the same time, Labour's constituency, rooted in the new technocratic-entrepreneurial middle class, was embracing an economic strategy of globalisation and viewed peace negotiations as crucial to overcoming Israel's poor record in attracting investment and to breaking out of the international diplomatic isolation which obstructed its access to markets (Solingen 1998).

However, it took global transformation and a watershed election to stimulate a new peace initiative in Israel. The end to the Arabs' Soviet patron, the defeat of Iraq and the grave weakening of the PLO in the Gulf war reduced the conventional security threat to Israel while a peace settlement offered the chance to neutralise both the WMD and the internal Palestinian threats. Some Israelis, moreover, believed the increasing readiness of the Palestinians and the Arabs generally for a settlement presented a new opportunity to end the conflict. The beginning of the Madrid peace talks and, in particular, of Syrian–Israeli negotiations presented Israel with a very real opportunity to finally attain regional acceptance and security. The rejectionist prime minister, Shamir, had no interest in taking up this opportunity, although the US pressured him into going through the motions. Then, in the 1993 Israeli elections, the electorate was given a choice between Likud's rejectionism and the promise of serious peace negotiations. The Israeli public was alarmed by how Shamir's intransigence had brought relations with the US to an unprecedented low, but, equally, his diversion of resources to the expansion of settlements in the occupied territories at the expense of investment and jobs needed by his Sephardi constituency and the new Soviet immigrants turned many of the latter against him; hence, the domestic economic costs of foreign policy intransigence came together with a favourable external situation, to stimulate a shift in Israeli public opinion. The election of the relatively dovish-leaning Labour–Meretz coalition under Rabin produced a government with a unique composition. It incorporated younger, more dovish leaders around Shimon Peres, notably Yossi Beilin, who were prepared to take some risks for peace while Prime Minister Rabin's hard-line credentials gave him the credibility to break Israel's traditional paralysis and seize the new opportunities (Aronoff and Aronoff 1998: 14–15). The immediate outcome of this change in Israeli policy was considerable progress in the peace negotiations. But even this government, still ultimately driven by hard-headed national security priorities, remained determined to extract the maximum and concede the minimum in the negotiations. Given the profound power imbalance in its favour, it was well situated to confront the Arabs with a choice between no settlement and one that would concede them less than the internationally recognised land-for-peace trade they had long considered their bottom line.

This power imbalance was in part global, the disappearance of Soviet backing on the Arab side and the American deployment of its newly hegemonic power largely on Israel's behalf. It was also, however, a result of the decline of Arabism, which, fragmenting the Arab states, put them at a major disadvantage in negotiating a new order. This was sharply exposed by the inability of the Arabs to convene a summit and reach a consensus on a common strategy toward Israel. The US, on Israel's behalf, insisted on and the Arab states conceded separate negotiating tracks between the individual Arab states and Israel rather than an all-Arab team bargaining jointly for a comprehensive settlement. The resulting inability of Syria, the PLO and Jordan to hold to a common front in the negotiations, and the consequent ease with which Israel played them off against each other, weakened the leverage of each individual Arab party. Despite protests by Syria that Israel should not enjoy the fruits of peace before conceding its reality (Barnett 1998: 235), premature normalisation by the Arab Gulf monarchies weakened pressure on Israel to concede a comprehensive settlement. Barnett argues that Arab solidarity, rooted in the we–they fault fostered by threat, weakened as the perceived Israeli threat declined in an environment where peace seemed realistic and attainable; but it was largely the vulnerability of Arab governments now sharply dependent on Washington that precluded a collective Arab stand.

Given the weakness of an Arab collective stance, the Palestinians may have seen no alternative to the unilateral deal reached with Israel at Oslo. The Oslo Accords produced the breakthrough of mutual Palestinian–Israeli recognition and raised the prospect of Palestinian self-determination, even statehood. However, the PLO negotiators, seemingly victims of wishful thinking, appeared to assume Oslo would lead inevitably to a Palestinian state and critically failed to insist that the accords stipulate the minimum condition for confidence-building, namely, an end to further Jewish settlement on the Palestinian land which would potentially constitute such a Palestinian state. The accords merely committed Israel to negotiate with the PLO over a vague set of principles and, given the power imbalance between a regional superpower and a non-state actor, the outcome of such negotiations was bound to be inequitable. To reach an equitable settlement, the more powerful side would have to make the most concessions; only if a mediator had weighed in to right the power imbalance was such an outcome likely but, perversely, the Americans consistently reinforced the more powerful Israeli side (Murphy 1997: 122–123).

Nor did the Arab world add any serious weight to the Palestinian side. The PLO, in striking a separate deal with Israel, assumed full responsibility for the fate of the Palestinians, marking a watershed in releasing remaining constraints from Arab public opinion on Arab leaders to pay even lip service to the Palestinian cause. Oslo thus precipitated Jordanian and Syrian moves toward their own separate agreements with Israel. Subsequently, neither Syrian objections nor domestic opposition deterred King Hussein from reaching a peace treaty and normalisation with Israel despite the lack of a comparable settlement on the Palestinian and Syrian fronts. Most remarkably, Israel and Syria tacitly agreed on the principles of a land for peace settlement over the Golan Heights and made considerable progress in negotiating the details of the necessary security arrangements. The state-to-state conflict between Israel and the Arab states was, thus, largely neutralised: it seemed very unlikely the Arab states would ever again combine against Israel. Israel came to believe that it could have peace with the Arab states without necessarily conceding the minimum to Palestinian self-determination, although most Arab states still felt it the better part of wisdom to refrain from more than incremental moves toward normalisation of relations prior to such a comprehensive settlement.

The development of Israeli–PLO negotiations under the Oslo Accords, including the proposals of Ehud Barak in 2000, pointed toward a grossly inequitable settlement that risked merely legitimising and systematising an indirect form of Israeli rule. To be sure, an autonomous Palestinian Authority (PA), possessing the rudimentary institutions of statehood, was established under PLO leadership on limited parts of West Bank and Gaza territory. However, Israel continued the expansion of Jewish settlements in the occupied territories and by 2000 Israel had seized 42% of Palestinian land on the West Bank for settlement (*Guardian*, 15 May 2002, p. 11; Malley and Agha 2001). Israel made it clear it hoped to satisfy

the Palestinians with autonomy on the remaining parts of this territory without according them sovereign statehood. It seemed likely
that in any final settlement the Palestinian entity would incorporate
perhaps 77% of the West Bank and Gaza while substantial blocks
of settlements around Jerusalem would be incorporated into Israel
(in return for desert land in Israel). Palestinian self-rule areas were
likely to be Bantustans, lacking territorial contiguity, surrounded
by Israeli security roads and settlements, and always vulnerable
to reoccupation. Barak's proposals insisted on Israel retaining 69
Jewish settlements where 85% of the settlers lived – in violation of
the Geneva Convention. The Palestinian entity, reduced to a captive
export market and a source of cheap labour for Israel and deprived
of all but a fraction of the water resources that had been mostly
appropriated by Israel, was unlikely to be economically viable and
certain to remain financially dependent on Western donors for the
foreseeable future; in the Gaza strip alone, 1.2 million Palestinians
were penned into a tiny area with few economic prospects. Needing
to appease Israel, the Palestinian Authority was reduced to the role
of enforcing Israeli security demands against its own people, saving
Israel the costs of direct occupation. The emerging Palestinian
entity would enjoy few of the attributes of true sovereignty, including control of its airspace, seacoast and borders, but in return for
self-rule would be required to forfeit the rights of return or compensation of the exiled Palestinian Diaspora which are enshrined in UN
resolutions (Hagopian 1997; Karmi 1999; Kubursi 1999; Murphy
1997: 123–130; Zunes 2001).

Indicative of the precarious grounding of this elite-led peace
process in domestic society was its abrupt halt in the mid-1990s.
Continued Israeli settlement activity inflamed Islamic terrorism by
Palestinians against Israelis and led to the election of the hard-line
Netanyahu government, which tried to renege on the implementation of Oslo, and pushed a Syrian–Israeli settlement off the agenda.
This finally precipitated an Arab summit, the first since the Gulf
war, which resolved to make normalisation of relations with Israel
dependent on implementation of the peace process (Barnett 1998:
221–226). The Ehud Barak government elected in 1999 briefly
revitalised the peace process. Syria and Israel, between whom there
was a rough power balance, came very close to a settlement, but
each, playing realist hardball, missed the chance and much the same
happened in Barak's negotiations with Arafat. The failure of the

latter negotiations precipitated the second and much more violent al-Aqsa *intifada* in 2000, which coincided with the rise of the ultra-rightist Ariel Sharon to power in Israel and the resurrection of militant Islamic alternatives to Arafat's PLO among the Palestinians. The failure of the moderates to reach an equitable agreement had allowed the rejectionists on both sides to escape their early 1990s marginalisation and to reclaim the dominant ground.

The collapse of the Arab–Israeli peace process was the nub of the failure of US policy and suggests that it is not hegemony but symmetry in power that facilitates peace building. At the Arab–Israeli level, conflict resolution was more likely to succeed when a relative power balance inflicted a certain symmetry of costs on the parties, giving each the incentive to accommodate the other's interests. At the global level, while the end to bi-polarity seemed to give America the power to shape the Middle East order, it had removed much of the incentive to make it an equitable one.

Failed liberal designs
The peace process was promoted as an opening wedge to regional economic integration and globalisation. The multilateral talks held within the Madrid framework on water and economic co-operation between Israel and the Arabs were expected to build confidence, while economic normalisation was to be an incentive and guarantor of peace. A Middle East Common Market was advocated by Shimon Peres in which Israel would contribute technology, the Arab oil states capital and markets and the non-oil states labour. The resulting economic interdependence would arguably create cross-national business interests with a stake in peace. However, in the absence of a satisfactory political settlement, this was perceived by most Arabs as an Israeli bid to conquer through market power what it could not do militarily. Given that Israel's GNP equalled that of Egypt, Syria and Jordan combined, economic integration would likely make Israel the core of the regional economy, enabling it to exploit cheap Arab labour and energy and turning neighbours such as Jordan and the Palestinian entity into economic satellites (Aarts 1999; Korany 1997).

An alternative argument (Solingen 1998) envisioned globalisation advancing regional peace, not because regional partners were economically integrated but because individual states were tied into the global economy by economic liberalisation. In this scenario, influence would flow away from the military and toward liberal internationalist elements in ruling coalitions that understood that regional access to global investment and markets was dependent on regional peace and Western alignment. Indeed, an early precursor of this route was Sadat's Egypt where economic liberalisation, Western alignment and peace with Israel went hand in hand; Jordan likewise opted for peace with Israel to restore the economic aid it had lost for siding with Iraq in the Gulf war and to revitalise a depressed economy badly needing foreign investment. Iran's postwar need for investment was paralleled by the moderation of its foreign policy.

But these developments were far from creating the 'complex interdependence' that makes war unthinkable, as the record of the region's most 'globalised' states makes clear. It was Israel that most successfully pursued globalisation as an alternative to regional integration, using Oslo to end the Arab secondary boycott which had effectively limited its regional economic relations and the peace process to attract high-tech MNCs which would export to East Asia and Europe (Murphy 1997: 132–134); yet this did not prevent the election of the ultra-nationalist Sharon, an ex-military commander prepared to jeopardise Israeli prosperity in defence of Likud's irredentist project. Moreover, the notion that globalisation spreads the zone of peace rests, in part, on the expectation that it delivers economic prosperity which populations will not wish to sacrifice in conflicts; but in the Arab states globalisation merely stimulated a massive export of capital, continuing debt and dependency and very limited economic development amidst high population growth (Guerrieri 1997). The spearheads of globalisation, notably the IMF, harnessed regional states to enforce their neo-liberal agenda against recalcitrant populations, splitting societies between new crony bourgeoisies who benefited and the marginalised masses that turned to radical Islam as a vehicle of protest (Abdel-Fadil 1997; Farsoun and Zacharia 1995). The Euro-Mediterranean initiative, designed to consolidate and accelerate globalisation in the region by systematically imposing the core's liberal order on each of the regional states made breakthroughs in Morocco and Tunisia. But this scheme, in opening Middle East industries to ruinous European competition while maintaining the protection of Europe's agricultural markets from Middle Eastern exports, merely reflected the profound power imbalance between Europe and the Middle East

(Joffe 1999; Owen 1999). Ehteshami (2007) observed that the Western agenda being forced on the region was a threat to social stability, with structural adjustment and de-industrialisation from the ending of tariff barriers to foreign competition coming at a time when MENA states were ill-equipped to provide a social safety net and had little of the legitimacy needed to enforce austerity; ruling elites were caught between external demands that they conform to international economic norms and the indigenous moral economy which demanded social justice.

Nor did globalisation stimulate the political democratisation and 'democratic peace' its advocates expected. While economic liberal-isation was accompanied by limited political liberalisation experi-ments, these were stalled and even reversed by the rise of Islamic political movements, fuelled by the damaging impact of struc-tural adjustment on marginal populations and by the Westward foreign policy alignments and accommodations with Israel that accompanied economic liberalisation. Egypt's Mubarak, whose government's IMF-imposed structural adjustment was reversing the populist social contract and who portrayed his fight against political Islam as a stand on behalf of the Western world while pursing closer links with Israel, could hardly afford democrati-sation and reversed his previous halting steps toward it. Intense though peaceful domestic opposition to Jordan's separate peace with Israel forced King Hussein to put Jordan's democratisation on hold. Generally, externally driven peace agreements and economic liberalisation were obstacles to rather than facilitators of democ-ratisation in the Middle East. The region's 'internationalist coali-tions', thus, remain dependent on Western support, not domestic legitimacy. At the end of the century, the liberal design showed little sign of generating a new political order in the Middle East.

The failure of Pax Americana

American attempts to substitute a Pax Americana for an indigenous order were also failing. To be sure, the Middle East was exception-ally impacted by the rise of US hegemony for, unlike other regions, there was no regional great power, comparable to China or India, which could balance it. The defeat of Iraq and the much-enhanced American military presence in the Gulf seemed to effectively deter any future challenges to Washington. Its manipulation of the UN Security Council sanctions against Iraq demonstrated its ability to punish recalcitrant actors as never before. The US sponsorship of the Arab–Israeli peace process also made it pivotal to the interests of all regional actors, including Arab nationalist Syria, and fostered a potential Israeli regional hegemony working in concert with Washington. US influence was also exercised indirectly through the other most powerful states in the region – Egypt, Turkey and Saudi Arabia. The dependence of the Arab Gulf, especially Saudi Arabia, on American protection from a resurgent Iraq and Iran abetted US determination to maintain its enhanced military presence. Those regional powers not yet fully resigned to American hegemony – Syria, Iraq, Iran – were surrounded and contained or co-opted.

However, if there ever was a chance for the US to use its unrivalled power to foster a stable regional security order, Washington missed it, and instead, in certain ways, it actually exacerbated the insecurity of the region. First, massive arms sales to the Arab Gulf monarchies and Israel, largely by the US, threatened the military balance and spurred a counter-build-up by the Syro-Iranian axis and hence an increased level of regional militarisation. The expectation of a decline in the utility of military force after the Cold War hardly applied to the Middle East where weapons proliferation continued, with all its repercussions for the 'security dilemma'. Insecurity also fuelled a drive by regional states to acquire non-conventional deterrents. Of the 25 countries having or developing ballistic missile capabilities, 11 were in the Middle East (Norton, 1991: 20–21). Again, the US passed up a chance to check the non-conventional arms race by backing Israel's refusal to sign the Nuclear Non-Proliferation Pact; inevitably, despite US efforts to prevent it, when one side acquires non-conventional weapons and delivery systems, other states will seek the capability to deter the threat they pose.

Washington's policy of designating and isolating 'pariah states' was also ultimately destabilising. The 'Dual Containment' of Iran and Iraq obstructed the moderation and normalisation of Iran's role in the region. But it was the American exacerbation of the problem of Iraq that was the main source of regional instability. In the wake of the Gulf war, the American-dominated Security Council imposed unprecedented demands on Iraq – to dismantle its chemical and biological weapons and missiles, to recognise a Kuwaiti border imposed without consultation on Iraq, to pay reparations from oil exports and forgo claims to compensation, to seek permission for all imports, and to submit to international inspection. Later, no-fly zones were unilaterally imposed and enforced by an on-going US–UK air campaign against Iraq. A decade after the Gulf war, Washington continued to obstruct all initiatives to lift economic sanctions on the country.

The aim was not just to strip Iraq of non-conventional weapons, but to impose sufficient suffering that Saddam would be toppled from within or, that failing, to keep Iraq permanently weak. While the limits imposed on imports of food and medicine by the sanctions regime were an irritant, the major damage was its use to prevent the reconstruction of Iraq's infrastructure, preventing the restoration of irrigation and industry and the repair of disease-controlling sanitation systems. The consequences were devastating for Iraq. Around 6,000 to 7,000 children a month were dying of embargo-related causes according to Denis Halliday, the UN humanitarian co-ordinator for Iraq, who argued that the Washington imposed sanctions regime 'amounted to genocide' (*Middle East International,* 12 February 1999, p. 23). Radiation from the depleted uranium weapons used by the US was reported to have contaminated wide areas. Yet Washington remained oblivious to the human costs of its policies, which Secretary of State Madeline Albright notoriously declared to be 'worth paying'. Keeping Iraq as a pariah state, however, only postponed and exacerbated the unavoidable problem of rehabilitating and readmitting it to the regional system. The sanctions – making Iraqis more dependent on state rations for daily survival – actually strengthened Saddam Hussein's hold on power while his external ambitions could easily have been contained without the intrusive and punitive measures that constantly inflamed Iraqi–Western relations. The refusal to let Iraq get on with post-war reconstruction deterred it from what would otherwise likely have been a natural turning inward to its own problems (Graham-Brown 1999; Niblock 2001; Simons 1996).

There were, however, recessive but important counterforces to US hegemony. Its ability to lead in the Gulf war had been a function of the broad threat Saddam Hussein posed to a variety of actors – both the economic interests of the industrialised states and the sanctity of borders so dear to Third World states – but this threat had been largely neutralised (Norton 1991: 23). US hegemony depended, in good part, on the acquiescence of other world powers and major regional powers. This could only be readily sustained if the hegemon consulted with and satisfied the interests of these partners and if it was effective in dealing with the two main threats to regional stability, Iraq and the Arab–Israel conflict. Yet the special relation with Israel, which was supposed to allow the US to broker a resolution of the Arab–Israeli conflict, had failed to deliver an equitable or permanent solution ten years after the start of the Madrid peace process. As for the Iraqi threat, US policy, in keeping the conflict going, actually exacerbated regional instability and was pursued in increased disregard of the interests of other states. Washington's inability to mobilise the UN Security Council in the 1998 Iraq inspections crisis indicated an erosion in its hegemony that allowed Iraq to exploit conflicts of interest between the core states. The attempt of the US to impose, through extra-territorial legislation, the isolation of Iran also aroused impatience with its unilateralism. US policy provoked a similar dissatisfaction and an increased independence among even its closest regional allies. Egypt proved a disappointment to Washington by its campaign to force Israel into the Nuclear Non-proliferation Treaty in the late 1990s; Saudi Arabia refused the use of its bases to stage air attacks on Iraq.

At the popular level revulsion against American hegemony was much more advanced. The Middle East was the one region where Western ideological hegemony remained contested: to this extent Huntington's (1993) 'clash of civilisations' thesis, though exaggerated, had a core of truth, for Western penetration did stimulate a resurgence of cultural and religious resistance: 'Islamic jihad' reacting to 'McDonaldisation' (Barber 1992). However, the West was not chiefly resisted for its supposedly antithetical values, many of which were actually shared by local people, or for its material superiority, the products of which were widely embraced in the region. Rather, the West was resented because it was seen to pursue an agenda targeting the Muslim and Arab worlds. The Western-identified enemies of the New World Order, the 'terrorist' groups and the 'pariah states', were exceptionally concentrated in the Middle East – Iran, Iraq, Libya, Sudan. The double standards of the US – its on-going attacks against a virtually defenceless Iraq and the victimisation of the Iraqi people by an unending sanctions regime in the name of UN resolutions juxtaposed to its approval of similar Israeli violations of UN resolutions regarding the occupied territories – were blatant in the eyes of Middle Eastern publics (Salem 1997: 32). To the considerable extent US hegemony therefore lacked ideological legitimacy in the region, American influence was always on the verge of 'deflating' to the threat and use of crude military force which is much more costly to employ. Laura Guazzone (1997: 237–258) pointed out the paradox of US hegemony in the region: while at the military level, it apparently stabilised the Middle East against revisionist states, its biased and inequitable application continually stimulated the nationalist and Islamic reaction at the societal level that kept the regional pot boiling. Failing to deliver the stability expected of a hegemon, the US could not legitimise its hegemonic presence in the region.

Magnet for terrorism to war on terror

In this situation, indigenous resistance increasingly took the form of small group terrorism, the weapon of the weak. It is no accident that the Middle East, the most penetrated regional system, was the source of by far the greatest number of international terrorist incidents or that the US was increasingly the target. The September 11, 2001 attacks by Osama bin Laden's terrorist network on the World Trade Center and the Pentagon raised this to a new level. While some saw the attacks as a symptom of a 'clash of civilisations', they were better interpreted as 'blowback' from previous US involvement in the region: Osama bin Laden and his following of 'Arab Afghans' were partly a US creation, fostered against the Soviets in Afghanistan (Johnson 2000). They were turned against the US, not by religious or cultural differences, but by its continued presence in Saudi Arabia, 'home of the two mosques', its perceived control over Arab oil, its siege of Iraq and its support for Israeli oppression of the Palestinians. The attacks were also a reflection of globalisation in that Bin Laden's Al-Qaida was a function of the acceleration of global transportation, communications and immigration; multi-national in composition, it was a 'post-modern' terrorist network. In a globalised, intensely interdependent but anarchic world, every US action now produced a multitude of unanticipated reactions.

Middle East public opinion, while shocked at the loss of life in the September 11 attacks, widely believed that US policy bore major responsibility for having stirred up the deep animosity on which terrorism flourished. However, Washington denied that it was, itself, part of the problem. Rather, the US sought to punish uninvolved groups, such as Hizbollah, which were perceived in the region as liberation movements, and to act against the states on its 'terrorism list', including Iran, Libya, Syria and Iraq, thus initiating an offensive against the Arab–Islamic world, not just the terrorist groups targeting the US. This further inflamed populations across and beyond the region, making the 'clash of civilisations' a self-fulfilling prophecy. This was intensified by the creation of an Arab public sphere with the spread of Arab satellite TV which revived consciousness of a common Arab community and of the threats to it. The effect on Iraqis of the US sanctions and the massive Israeli repression of the al-Aqsa *intifada* were beamed by Al-Jazeera TV into Arab households, reviving deep-seated grievances against both states. Yet the Arab regimes, rather than standing up for Arab causes, instead took advantage of the US 'war on terror' to target Islamist opposition at home and, needing to head off the new US discourse that blamed Arab authoritarianism for 9/11, sought individual security by appeasing Washington.

The 2003 Iraq War[1]

The failure of the US to translate its 1991 military victory over Iraq into a stable Pax Americana in the region, followed by the 9/11 terrorist attacks, set the stage for the next two watershed regional events, the US invasions of Afghanistan in 2001 and of Iraq in 2003. These events again reshuffled the cards in the Middle East deck. Abandoning the role of stabilising 'off shore balancer', the US now massively entered the region as an occupying power and dominant player; while Washington's professed goal was to create a new democratic order in the region, the means it employed, its doctrine of 'creative destruction' and regime change, destabilised the very order it sought to impose. Indeed, the resistance to the US project generated two new theatres of 'asymmetric warfare' and globalised Middle East conflicts.

The drivers of war

A war to complete the unfinished business of overthrowing Saddam Hussein had been urged by right-wing hard-liners on the Clinton administration throughout the 1990s; with the election of the Bush administration, many of them were appointed to the levers of power. However, it was only the 9/11 events, which legitimised a US 'war on terrorism', that gave them the opportunity to realise their ambition for a war against Iraq. While much of the world supported America's attack on the Afghan Taliban that had harboured Osama Bin Laden, Washington launched its war on Iraq despite having failed to gain UN endorsement and against the views of major world powers and of world opinion. As with the first war on Iraq in 1990–91, so this second one can only be understood as the outcome of factors at multiple levels of analysis.

The cause of the Iraq war is a matter of considerable controversy perhaps because of the unusual gap between the justifications offered for it by its proponents and what appear to have been their actual motives. To legitimise a war that was on almost nobody's agenda, the Bush administration had to claim that Saddam Hussein was linked to Al-Qaida and was actively developing weapons of mass destruction, hence representing an imminent threat to the US. These claims have not only been discredited but, additionally, there is strong evidence that the US hawks deliberately exaggerated unreliable claims and knew Iraq was no threat to the US. At any rate, the threat was never that WMDs would be used against the US, but that they might constrain its freedom of action in the Middle East.

The international level: the Middle East, oil and US hegemony
Indeed, the war arguably had less to do with Iraq, per se, than with US global ambitions. Under Bush, the US was determined to assert global hegemony, as frankly acknowledged by the so-called 'Project for a New American Century'. The Bush doctrine and the 2002 National Security Strategy make explicit a coercive turn to US policy: the reach for 'full spectrum dominance' in military power, the unilateralism, the assertion that those not with the US in the war on terrorism were against it, the insistence that the US liberal model was the only legitimate one, and the change in strategy for dealing with putative threats from traditional containment to 'preventive wars'.

Reshaping the Middle East was pivotal to the success of this project. On the one hand, one of the main pillars of US global hegemony was its protectorate over 'world oil' in the Persian Gulf, a strategic commodity that everybody needs and which is crucial to military power; yet the main resistance to US world hegemony was also concentrated in the Muslim Middle East. While oil was just one, albeit pivotal, factor driving the war, without it the war is hardly conceivable. Vice President Cheney's report on energy security projected US dependence on oil imports rising in an ever-tighter oil market, with global production projected to peak while demand, particularly from Asia, skyrocketed; this made the US potentially vulnerable to an oil shock, historically fatal for US presidents. At some point, Iraq began to be seen as a solution. It had the world's second largest reserves and very low production costs; but as long as Saddam Hussein was in power, it could not be used for US benefit; seizure of Iraq's oil would give Washington a strategic lever for controlling the oil market and enhance US structural power over its economic competitors in Europe and Asia and its emerging global rival, China.

The targeting of Iraq must, however, also be seen in the context of the growing threats to the US strategic position in the Middle East which, after the 1990 Gulf war, had come to rest on three pillars: the 'dual containment' of Iran and Iraq, the peace process and the US–Saudi alliance – but all of these pillars were visibly wobbling. Iraq and Iran were gradually escaping from the isolation dual containment had sought to impose of them. While US sanctions kept its own companies out of their oil fields and markets, Europe and Japan were competing to do business with Iran and Iraq was selling oil concessions to other countries, notably Russia, China and France; moreover, the sanctions on Iraq had increasingly been discredited for the humanitarian damage they caused. Invading Iraq would transform this situation.

Second, the breakdown of the peace process amidst continued Israeli settlement activity in the Palestinian territories and the Islamic terrorism it precipitated drove an increasing wedge between the US and the Arabs who had been promised a peace settlement in reward for their support of the US in the 1990–91 Gulf War. Since the 1980s, ever-rising Zionist influence had led Washington to accept, even fund, Israel's colonisation of the very occupied land that had to be the basis of a compromise peace settlement. Nevertheless, all US presidents sustained the policy of pursuing the peace process until George W. Bush effectively abandoned it (famously discarding official US policy that Israeli settlements in occupied territory were illegal): the alternative to hegemony based on delivering peace had to be military predominance and the invasion of Iraq would establish incontestable American military dominance in the region.

Third, Saudi Arabia had traditionally played an effective 'swing' role in securing oil for the West and moderating oil prices at the US behest, but the US was dissatisfied with its dependence on Saudi

Arabia. As demand soared and Saudi production capabilities stagnated, Riyadh's ability to play a swing role was called into question. Dependence on the Saudis' swing role placed some constraints on US Middle East policy; in parallel, US forces based in Saudi Arabia were a source of discontent there that made the US high command look for alternative basing. The participation of Saudi citizens in the 9/11 attacks and in funding Al-Qaida gave pro-Israeli pressure groups the opportunity to demonise the Saudis in American public opinion. For its part, Saudi Arabia, feeling the US ignored its interests – notably in abandoning a resolution of the Arab–Israel conflict – began looking for alternative security solutions to ease its total US dependence by conciliating Iran and Iraq. US Middle East hegemony rested on its unique ability to balance special relationships with *both* Israel and Saudi Arabia, but this balance was being destabilised. In conquering Iraq, the US would acquire a new compliant swing producer to substitute for Saudi Arabia and an alternative basing platform.

The war on Iraq was expected to decisively assert the *military* dimension of US hegemony. Smashing Saddam Hussein, who had famously defied American power, would send the message that the limits of American military power had been overcome; the Bush administration wanted to establish the right to pre-emptively attack countries it deemed threats and Iraq, being both weak and easily demonised, was an exemplary case to establish the precedent. An easy victory in Iraq followed by images of Iraqis welcoming US troops as liberators would demoralise Arab/Islamic opposition to US hegemony. From the new bases acquired in Iraq, the US could intimidate remaining resistance from nationalist states like Syria and Iran and impose a pro-Israeli Pax Americana in the region.

The domestic level: the war party in Bush's ruling coalition   Yet obviously, a war on Iraq carried grave risks, not least of a destabilisation of the oil market that could damage the US and world economies. Hence US national interests cannot wholly explain the war and why these risks were accepted. The extra needed ingredient was the *special interests of the ruling coalition* because a different coalition would probably not have made war. The Bush Jr government was an exceptional coalition of extreme Zionists (the 'neo-conservatives') and the most belligerent wing of the arms/oil lobbies. The mainstream oil and Zionist lobbies were traditionally opposed over Middle East policy but under Bush leading elements of the former dropped their traditional concern to appease the Arab regimes and embraced the Zionist agenda. That they did so can only be explained by a decision to bandwagon with rather than balance against the Zionists and the expectation that a war would serve their interests; thus, Vice President Cheney, representative of oil interests, who had been frustrated by the Zionist lobby's blocking of US companies' access to oil fields in Iran under Clinton, evidently calculated that since he could not beat the lobby he would join it. But additionally, conflict in the Middle East leads to high oil prices – especially needed for high-cost Texas producers – hence, to high oil company profits and also to renewed arms spending by Middle East states, one of the main sources of profit for US arms exporters. The war also presented a chance, through the privatisation of Iraqi oil, to restore some of the direct ownership over Middle East oil that had been curtailed by the rise of OPEC. And the occupation of Iraq was expected to – and did – provide very good pickings for the arms, construction, security and oil interests associated with the ruling coalition.

Nevertheless, without the role of the neo-cons, the group that most determinedly pushed for war in the belief that it would serve Israel's interests, it would not have happened. The neo-cons, intimately tied to Israel's right-wing Likud party, supported Israel's policy of colonisation in the occupied Palestinian territories; but this obstructed a peace settlement and endangered the Arab relations on which oil access depended (particularly with Saudi Arabia). The neo-con nightmare was that the US would subordinate Israel's ambitions to appeasement of the Arab oil producers, especially Saudi Arabia (as Bush Sr had done). However, seizure of Iraq's pivotal oil fields would make appeasement superfluous; indeed control of Iraqi oil could be used to break OPEC and destabilise unfriendly regimes in the region. It would allow the US to secure access to Arab oil without Arab alliances and consent (Fawn and Hinnebusch 2006: 283–323).

Consequences for the Middle East: deepening destabilisation
The Bush administration expected that the conquest of Iraq would decisively transform the Middle East, empowering pro-US currents, marginalising radical forces and reinforcing the power of Israel. The US was warned by Middle East leaders and area experts that the war would have unpredictable, disastrous consequences for the Middle East. President Mubarak feared it would 'open the gates of

hell' and Bashar al-Asad predicted the US would not be able to control Iraq. They proved to be right, with the immediate consequences seemingly the opposite of those intended.

The deconstruction of Iraq The aim of regime change in Iraq was presumably to create a state that would be stable and legitimate, yet also friendly to the United States. Yet instead of consolidating a client state, the US created a failed state plagued by prolonged insurgency verging on civil war, in which the main beneficiary appeared to be pro-Iranian Shia groups. This outcome was predictable and predicted by Iraq specialists. Since its creation by Britain, Iraq had been a fragile artificial state, with communal cleavages and instability built in. Only over several decades of struggle was a formula for stability found under Saddam Hussein: a brutal strongman ruling through a semi-totalitarian party and relying on one of Iraqi's communities against the others. The US in effect deconstructed this state without having – or even planning for – a viable replacement for it (if such a thing was ever going to be possible).

The particular way the Bush administration went about regime change greatly increased the chances of failure. According to Anthony Cordesman (2005), the foremost American expert on Gulf security, the US made multiple 'strategic mistakes'. It only planned the war it wanted to fight – against the debilitated Iraq army, not against an insurgency; expecting a quick painless war, the US went in undermanned and under-resourced, aiming to skim off the top layer of Iraqi leadership, take control of a functioning state, install imported pro-Western exiles, be out after six weeks and get the oil funds to pay for it (Packer 2005). Defence Secretary Rumsfeld forced his generals to accept a fraction of the 400,000 troops they said would be needed for the occupation. Famously and inexplicably, US proconsul Paul Bremer exacerbated a dire situation through his dissolution of the Iraqi army, creating at a stroke tens of thousands of experienced and armed fighters that would join the resistance, and failed for almost a year to start reconstructing an Iraqi security force, leaving sectarian militias to fill the vacuum. Similarly, the purge and de-Ba'thification of the bureaucracy and other state institutions deprived the state of experienced officials and created massive numbers of disaffected unemployed.

The original sin of the Iraq war was, perhaps, the neo-con belief that the invasion would be welcomed as liberation and a pro-US 'democracy' readily imposed. It was never likely the invaders would be welcomed as liberators since Iraqis were nationalistic and harboured deep distrust of the US and UK, owing to the colonial experience, the decades of sanctions they imposed on the country and America's near-total support for Israel. But the conduct of the occupation multiplied powerful new grievances, which created an insurgency that might not have been inevitable had the US acted differently in Iraq (Dodge 2006). As it was, the invasion resulted in the breakdown of security, infrastructure and public health, and the death of perhaps 100,000 people, mostly civilians, in the first year of war and occupation. The failure to make the security of Iraqis a priority; the initial imposition of a puppet government of mostly exiles without popular bases in Iraq; the mass unemployment inflicted by the dissolution of the army and purge of the bureaucracy; the halving of GNP/capita compared to 2001; the flooding of the country with foreign mercenaries and contractors; the near-absence of post-war reconstruction (compared unfavourably by Iraqis to the performance of the Saddam regime after the 1991 war); the expenditure of reconstruction money outside Iraq or its dissipation through massive corruption, war profiteering and enormous salaries for foreign contractors; the open US avowal of its intention to acquire permanent military bases in Iraq – all this ensured Iraqis would see the invaders as occupiers, not liberators. The US attempt, in violation of the Geneva Convention, to privatise and sell off Iraq's oil assets to Western buyers was another powerful grievance mobilising opposition.

On top of this, however, the heavy-handed US approach to counter-insurgency arguably helped fuel it. Symptomatic of the US approach, a US commander infamously declared: 'With a heavy dose of fear and violence, and a lot of money for projects, I think we can convince these people that we are here to help them' (*Christian Science Monitor*, 11 December 2003). The US used tactics pioneered by Israel in occupied Palestine (*Time Magazine*, 8 December 2003): bombing and firing on densely populated urban areas, demolishing homes, collective punishment of villages, herding thousands into detention camps, food blockades of suspected insurgent areas, the abuses revealed at Abu Ghraib, not to mention the 'daily humiliations and occasional brutalities that come with the presence of an occupying army' (*New York Review of Books*, 18 December 2003). US troops were widely seen as 'lacking in respect for the country's people, religion and traditions' and 'indiscriminate in their use of force when civilians are nearby'. Inevitably, this approach only inflamed resistance which mushroomed into a potent force of up to 20,000 fighters equipped with explosives capable of knocking out even heavily armoured vehicles. America's inability to pacify the country shattered its aura of military invincibility, showing that asymmetric warfare can checkmate the strongest military power in the world.

Iraqi disaffection came very rapidly. Western polls in the year after the invasion showed that 82% of Iraqis opposed the occupation and 57% wanted foreign troops to leave immediately; 5% or less of Iraqis believed the US invaded 'to assist the Iraqi people', destroy WMDs or establish democracy, while 43% said the aim was 'to rob Iraq's oil'. More than 50% said attacks on US troops were 'justified' or 'sometimes justified' (*Washington Post*, 13 May 2004). Over the years of occupation, Iraqi opinion only hardened against the occupiers.

On top of this, the reconstruction of Iraq proceeded in a flawed way that was, perhaps, bound to create a failed state. The destruction of the secular Ba'thist state centre left a vacuum in which sectarian/ethnic leadership took over. US policies of relying on the Kurds against the Arabs and the Shia against the Sunnis and the institutionalisation of ethnic/sectarian politics in the ruling bodies the US co-opted reinforced sectarian divisions. Constructing security forces by relying on the Shia and Kurds made Sunnis perceive the US-fostered 'national' army as a sectarian force. Elections merely reflected this environment: sectarian groups voted in elections as blocs, creating what looked like permanent triumphant (Shia) majorities and disaffected (Sunni–Arab) minorities. The proposed 'federalist' constitution would weaken central government and precipitate inter-communal struggle over oil resources. This created fertile ground for extremist insurgents who tried to provoke civil war as a way of preventing consolidation of what they saw as a collaborationist sectarian regime. While many of these outcomes are commonly critiqued as unintended mistakes, the destruction of Iraq's power, identity and collective purpose was compatible with the neo-cons' pro-Israeli goals of debilitating the main potential Arab power. If there is one underlying explanation for why US policy produced results the opposite of what Washington intended, it is that military force, when lacking in legitimacy, stimulates resistance rather than compliance.

Nevertheless, the mistakes of Washington's opponents allowed it to make the best of a bad situation; notably, the extremist behaviour of Al-Qaida linked resistance to the US in Iraq, targeting Shias with suicide bombings and even alienating their own putative constituents in anti-American Sunni bastions such as Falluja, allowed US commanders to co-opt both Shia and Sunni tribal militias and thus sustain the survival of what seemed to be a compliant Iraqi regime. While this regime was dependent on the US, it was at least as much also dependent on Iranian support and therefore, at Iranian urging, was unwilling to accept conditions the US demanded for permanent bases – immunity of US troops from accountability in Iraqi courts. Obama, therefore, evacuated US troops, leaving behind an unstable and beleaguered Shia-based Iraqi government that could not be depended upon to follow US dictates, as became clear when prime minister Nour al-Maliki opted, after the start of the Syrian uprising, to support the Asad regime against US wishes.

The US deconstruction of Iraq also left behind the seeds of a 'clash within civilisations': Sunni–Shia civil war in Iraq started to spill over to the wider region, and was paralleled by a regional struggle in which Saudi Arabia, alarmed at Iranian/Shia gains in Iraq, unleashed an anti-Shia sectarian discourse that would play a major role in the deconstruction of neighbouring states in the next decade. In 2014, the vulnerability of a weak Iraqi government, based on the Shia Arabs, but having failed to sufficiently include the Sunni Arabs and Kurds, was exposed by its loss of control over both the Kurdish regions and the Sunni west where Sunni militants led by the Islamic State of Iraq and Syria (ISIS) seized power and proclaimed a 'caliphate' straddling the borders.

Regional repercussions   At the beginning of the Iraq war, Iran, surrounded by US forces or proxies and the next likely target of the neo-cons, seemed slated to be a big loser. Indeed, the threat to Iran from the US invasions of Iraq and Afghanistan was a key factor in its possible drive for a nuclear deterrent and in the 2005 rise of the militantly anti-Western Ahmadinejad administration at the expense of Iran's moderate reformers. However, the tables were turned and Iran was actually empowered by the war. The rise in oil prices accompanying the war benefited it while the rise of Shia power in Iraq gave Iran great influence in the country. Syria also seemed a likely loser in the Iraq war, demonised by Washington for its opposition to the invasion and thereafter sandwiched between US forces to the east and Israel in the west. However, US pressure to isolate Syria curtailed domestic reform, strengthened the regime's national-ist credentials, and pushed Syria into the arms of Iran; by demonis-ing Syria, the US gave it an incentive to see America fail in Iraq and to try to tighten its grip in Lebanon. American and French efforts to punish Syria for opposition to the Iraq war and its role in Lebanon sparked off a struggle for Lebanon. It probably precipitated the killing of Rafiq al-Hariri, which was then used by the West to force Syria out of Lebanon. But Syria and Iran still had their trump card in Lebanon – Hizbollah. This set the scenario for the Israeli war in the summer of 2006 when Israel tried to destroy Hizbollah and instead devastated Lebanon's economic recovery and precipitated a struggle for power there between pro-Syrian/Iranian forces and a Lebanese government that had become dependent on US/French patrons for survival. However, the outcome was a violent 2008 showdown in which Hizbollah defeated Hariri's forces, enabling it to dictate a new national unity government in which it could veto any move to make Lebanon a base for US moves against Syria.

The Bush administration thought that invading Iraq would sub-stitute for brokering a peace process in Palestine or, by demor-alising all resistance to Israel, enable a US–Israeli dictated peace settlement. A major mistake, rooted in the belief that the con-quest of Iraq would allow a diktat in Palestine, was the George W. Bush administration's demonisation of moderate PLO leader Yasir Arafat, and the full backing it gave to the coercive policies of the Sharon government. These sought to systematically destroy and discredit the Palestinian Authority while expanding illegal Israeli settlements that were likely to make a Palestinian state non-viable. Israel's apartheid policies, with their interminable checkpoints, Bantustans and separation walls, would have been impossible with-out US financing and support. The electoral victory of Hamas was the consequence of failing to deal with Palestinian moderates. The effective empowering of the rejectionists on both sides by Bush's policy made a settlement of the conflict in Palestine all the harder, with all the attendant negative consequences for regional stability.

Indeed, on the face of it, Israel appeared initially to be a big winner from the Iraq war. The destruction of Iraq as a power in the Arab–Israeli power balance, the connections Israel built with Iraqi Kurds and the diminution of Syria's strategic stature were to its advantage. However, Israel's inability to destroy Hizbollah in its summer 2006 war or to subdue Hamas and the Palestinians, plus the enhanced stature of Iran, meant that there was no positive transformation in Israel's strategic situation.

A further unintended consequence of the Iraq war was to generate a 'New Arab Cold War' between a militant 'resistance axis' and pro-Western Sunni powers such as Egypt and Saudi Arabia. The former included Shiite Iran, some of Iran's Shia supporters in Iraq and Hizbollah. However, this axis reached beyond the Shia to embrace Syria, which is majority Sunni, the Sunni insurgency in Iraq and Hamas. Indeed, the cleavage between this bloc and its opponents was less a sectarian one than one between those who resisted US hegemony, which the Iraq war was meant to consolidate, and those who accepted it. Pro-US Arab states feared this force because it de-legitimised their alignment with Washington, especially as neither the US nor Israeli power seemed able to destroy it.

Indeed, pro-US Arab regimes were weakened by the war on Iraq. The war caught all the pro-US Middle East regimes between their US alignments and their populations who widely opposed it; hence it further eroded their already precarious legitimacy. If the Iraq war was meant to deter terrorists through 'shock and awe', it had the opposite effect, stimulating sub/trans-state resistance to American hegemony. As studies have demonstrated, the single most potent generator of 'terrorism' is foreign occupation: now, to the occupation of Palestine was added that of Afghanistan and Iraq, which, according to former CIA anti-terrorist expert Michael Scheuer, was 'completing the radicalisation of the Islamic world'. According to former US anti-terrorism czar Richard Clarke, the invasion of Iraq 'delivered to Al-Qaida the greatest recruitment propaganda imaginable' (Munson 2006: 243). Iraq became a training ground for terrorism, giving rise to a new generation of fighters, as the Afghan conflict did, carrying bin Laden's vision and new skills in asymmetric warfare that would find new opportunities in the regimes that collapsed in the Arab Uprising. Moreover, the war resulted in a dramatic increase in Muslim hostility to the US, and hence in jihadist recruits. What is most striking in this regard is how Bush managed to alienate the publics of allied states in which America had invested over decades: Turkey, Jordan, Egypt and Saudi Arabia.

Indeed, not just Middle Eastern publics but also their ruling elites became much more wary of American intentions and competence even if, for some of them, there was no seeming alternative patron-state. Just at this time of vulnerability, the Bush administration, in an attempt to deflect blame for 9/11 from US policy in the Middle East, declared that the root of terrorism was authoritarian regimes and that it would expect its non-democratic allies to start democratising. Its programme for regional democratisation, the Greater Middle East Intiative, was launched without regional consultation, prompting Egyptian President Husni Mubarak to complain that the US acted as if regional states had no sovereignty (Ehteshami 2007). In parallel Saudi Arabia was pressured to change its education system, also blamed for 9/11, even as Saudi elites were increasingly disillusioned with Washington by the empowering of Iran that resulted from the US invasion of Iraq.

Worse yet, the war greatly advanced the prospects of a 'clash of civilisations'. This most intense American intervention in the Middle East spread and deepened Muslim hostility to the US. If two decades ago this was largely over Palestine and concentrated in the Arab heartland, US policy spread it to Iran in the 1980s (revived by US spurning of Khatami's dialogue of civilisations) and to Afghanistan and Pakistan in the 1990s; with the Iraq war, it pervaded the wider Muslim world and even the Muslim Diaspora in the West. The Iraq war was, indeed, the occasion for empowering those on *both* sides who advocated a 'clash of civilisations'. On the one side, the neo-cons, Christian fundamentalists and pro-Israeli lobby around the Bush administration, and on the other the disparate Islamic forces clustering around the Al-Qaida networks together generated an action/reaction spiral of hostility in which Muslim terrorist acts inspired by grievances over Iraq reinforced Islamophobia in the West.

Parallel to this faltering in US hegemony over the region, other trends emerged which started to shift the balance of power against Washington. The war helped precipitate another oil boom, although the tightening oil market was the underlying cause of sustained high prices. The boom accompanied and intensified a growing economic interdependence that increasingly linked the Middle East and East Asia. For example, in the decade of the 2000s, about 60% of oil movements from the Middle East were eastward, compared to 13% to the US and 21% to western Europe, a total reversal of the trend of the previous hundred years (Ehteshami 2007). Most East Asian energy needs were met by Middle East hydrocarbon producers and, as a result, massive revenues flowed into the region from East Asia. At the same time, US hostility to the Islamic world made Middle East investors and governments increasingly wary of putting their money in the US. Instead, they started investing a growing part of their new surplus capital in East Asia, especially in Japanese and Chinese downstream energy industries. Parallel to this, East Asian states, increasingly concerned about the security of their energy supplies, developed strategic oil relations with the Middle East, including investment in joint oil production and other projects (Ehteshami 2007). Moreover, frictions between Asia and the US rose as the US tried to assert the right to dictate to Asian countries that they could not have normal relations with states like Iran (and before Iran, with Iraq and Libya) by using extra-territorial sanctions on non-US companies investing in these states. As the first, second and third largest oil consumers, the US, China and Japan were inevitably locked into a triangular competitive relationship over Middle East oil. This potentially could have restored to Middle East states some of the autonomy they lost when the Soviet check on US power collapsed had not the region self-destructed in the Arab Uprising.

Conclusion

Outcomes of the Iraq wars

The Iraq wars and their aftermath massively heightened Western penetration of the region in a way the architects of the Baghdad Pact could only dream of. If this had been the price of increased regional security and prosperity, many people in the Middle East might have considered it worth paying. But American hegemony, far from increasing either individual or collective security, proved to be counter-productive for regional order.

Indeed, the US demolished all the requisites of regional order. Not only did its destruction of Iraq upend the regional power balance, relatively empowering both Israel and Iran, but it also undermined Arabism as a normative basis of regional order, yet failed to replace it with an effective liberal substitute based on a regional peace settlement and instead opened the door to the spread of virulent sectarian wars. While Washington and key regional elites may have believed there was no viable alternative to US hegemony, significant parts of indigenous society retained visions of an Arab–Islamic order free of Western and Israeli dominance. There remained a gap between the pro-Western and state-centric behaviour of Arab state elites, which privileged sovereignty, and the persisting normative expectation among the Arab masses that states should act on behalf of the shared (Arab) community against the West and Israel. This gap tainted the legitimacy of regimes and encouraged challenges to the regional order by sub-and trans-state movements and 'terrorist' networks.

To a very considerable extent, therefore, the regional status quo, lacking indigenous popular legitimacy, was erected on hegemonic external force and on economic and security relations that benefited a relative few. The continued application of American force in the region was thus essential to maintain the status quo but, paradoxically, further undermined its legitimacy, and so raised the costs for America that it started to withdraw from its ambition to control the region.

Theoretical implications of the Iraq wars

The US reach for MENA hegemony via two wars on Iraq had implications for our theoretical understanding of the region. The superior power of structuralism's core–periphery paradigm in explaining the IR of the Middle East appeared underlined: not only in the determination of an imperial hegemon to re-assert its indisputable control over the region and its resources, but the impotence of fragmented periphery states to resist. What other than the dependency and clientage of ruling elites in most of the Arab states can explain their failure not only to combine to oppose, except verbally, the invasion of a fellow Arab state (Iraq) but, in the case of a few of the most dependent ones (Bahrain, Kuwait, Qatar), to allow their territory to be used to launch it. While realism's story of rival states carries some power in explaining this, the Arab regimes were aware that Iraq posed far less threat to them than the instability the US invasion threatened to unleash: their dependence on the US appears to have been the decisive factor. It cannot be a coincidence that the only Arab state to oppose the invasion, Syria, was also the only one that was not dependent on the hegemon.

The aftermath of the invasion, of course, sharpened inter-state rivalries, but that these were seemingly identity-driven (the Shia–Sunni cleavage) underlined the relevance of constructivism. So did the fact that it was at the sub/trans-state level that the role of identity was most intensified: the Islamic resurgence precipitated by the hegemon's ever increasing penetration of the region, took ever more intense forms and ever wider geographical scope. It is hard to see any material interest a movement like Osama bin Laden's Al-Qaida can be said to champion; rather, it is a response to the perceived assault on the identity and autonomy of the region. It, together with the identity-based neo-con-Likud trans-state connection and the Islamophopia unleashed among Christian fundamentalists in the US, threatened to make Huntington's 'clash of civilisations' a reality. But these developments were neither the inevitable outcome of anarchy, nor of identity, but the direct consequences of the actions of the US hegemon in the region.

Finally, this episode has some relevance for theories of global order and specifically the arguments of liberal 'hegemonic stability theory' (HST) that the US global hegemon had created an 'international regime' that delivered global 'public goods' such as order and free trade. In the Middle East the US hegemon claimed to deliver order and also to guarantee the flow of hydrocarbons to the world economy; however, Washington failed in the former and arguably, in so doing, put the latter potentially at risk. Alternatively, the 'realist' version of HST acknowledges that the international regime created by the hegemon chiefly services the interests of its creator but claims that other key states also benefit from it and to the extent this ceases to be the case, they will increasingly challenge it; the resultant need to coercively police an order declining in legitimacy induces imperial overreach and undermines the economy of the hegemon. Certainly there is evidence of this in the resistance of key allies to the US invasion of Iraq, the high costs of the occupation of Iraq and the subsequent US withdrawal to a less costly off-shore balancing in the region. However, the whole notion that a global hegemon delivers public goods is cast into doubt by the enduring consequence of the US adventure in Middle East hegemony: it left behind a much less viable regional states system that soon showed signs of fracturing and implosion, and which threatened to billow outwards into a global level crisis (Hinnebusch 2006).

Note

1 See Hinnebusch 2007 for evidence and documentation of this section.

9

The Arab Uprising:
consequences for state and system

What effect did the Arab Uprising having on the MENA regional states system? Some believed that revolution and democratisation would transform the region. States would be strengthened as authoritarian elites gave way to representative leaders and publics could therefore identify with states as their own. Public opinion would become a newly empowered factor in foreign policy-making. The narrative of democratic peace led some to anticipate that the overthrow of authoritarian elites presaged a democratised, hence more pacific Middle East. Also widespread was the expectation, particularly after the fall of Egypt's Mubarak, that revolutions against Western clients would bring more regional autonomy. Whatever the longer-term effect of the Uprising, in the immediate following years such expectations of benign change were utterly unrealised; rather, the region became afflicted by failed states, sectarian conflict and economic debilitation that made many states more dependent than ever on external financing.

The drivers of the Uprising

The Uprising was driven by the way global forces magnified the region's special vulnerabilities. Widespread socio-economic conditions came together to produce strong grievances against regimes: demographic explosion, producing large numbers of unemployed – and educated – youth, spreading water scarcities and drought propelling urbanisation, and soaring international prices driving up the cost of food. This was accompanied by growing inequality and declines in social mobility as the crony capitalism unleashed on the region by global neo-liberalism enriched a few while debilitating public services and the welfare of the masses. Just as socialism during the Cold War years had promoted a norm of equality that restrained personal wealth accumulation in both developed and developing world, so leaders in the Arab republics inevitably tried to follow the examples set by the luxurious lifestyles of the Gulf oil sheikhs and the unrestrained wealth accumulation by Western financial elites under globalisation; in less developed economies without oil wealth, this was, however, unsustainable.

While social mobilisation – the spread of education, urbanisation, media exposure – had inexorably deepened, political incorporation had stalled. Rather, the availability of rent enabled clientelist practices that incorporated privileged minorities as regime constituents to the exclusion of others; post-Cold War experiments in limited political liberalisation in states such as Egypt had regressed by the end of the 2000s, while in Syria, Libya and Tunisia they had remained rudimentary. If the sovereignty of fragile states had heretofore been protected by their Cold War patrons and by rent from the oil boom, now neo-liberal globalisation both reduced the ability of regimes to satisfy the welfare of mass publics while also promoting a discourse of democracy and human rights that encouraged anti-regime political mobilisation by educated middle-class youth who had absorbed Western liberal ideology and mastered Internet technology. The latter, combined with the continuing existence of an almost unique trans-state Arab public sphere, magnified the contagion effect of protests starting in Tunisia, which quickly encouraged imitative protests elsewhere. Also important in encouraging this was the Western promoted doctrine of 'responsibility to protect' through humanitarian intervention which spread the illusion among protestors that the West would constrain regimes from resort to mass coercion should they take to the streets.

Such structural (material and global) factors do not negate the importance of local *agency* in explaining the suboptimal outcomes of the Uprising. Thus, the repressive responses of leaders such as Qadhafi and Asad to peaceful protests stimulated violent opposition. A cycle of violence empowered hard-liners and marginalised moderates in both regime and opposition – just the opposite of the pact between soft-liners on both sides required for a democratic transition – and therefore led, in the worse cases, to civil wars and failed states.

Dimensions of the Uprising

State reformation or deconstruction?

While the Arab Uprising, insofar as it led to more politically inclusive institutions, could, in principle, strengthen states, in the short term the result was a further state weakening, especially in the more fragmented societies. This was most obvious in Syria where the outcome was civil war, but in Yemen and Libya central government capacity fell precipitously while states' monopoly of violence and territorial control was damaged by the rise of armed groups and unruly protestors unleashed by revolution. Even in the cases of more peaceful political transfer, Tunisia and Egypt, the state was weakened because, while the Uprising unleashed considerable political mobilisation, none of the Uprising states, in spite of holding relatively free elections to parliaments and executives, developed stable institutions that were able to incorporate it, with the possible exception of Tunisia. This is partly because publics became sharply divided along sectarian and Islamist vs. secular lines and between remnants of the old state establishment and radicals wanting more thorough revolution, producing a three-sided struggle over the very rules of political order. This renewed 'praetorianism' was manifested in continued street violence and crime that threatened public order. Instability also damaged public services, economic capacity, including tax collection, and deterred investment. As a result, successor regimes lacked the capacity to incorporate unemployed youth who were the major tinder of revolutionary conflagration. State immunity to trans-state penetration also plummeted, exposed to the social media and the Internet used by revolutionary youth, the flow of funds via trans-state networks from the Arab Gulf to Islamist movements, and the increased smuggling of arms, some of them looted from state stockpiles, notably in Libya and Syria. Amidst economic decline, dependency on outside powers, IMF loans or Gulf funders also rose. 'Thermidors' – conservative backlashes – and a yearning for the 'man on horseback' to restore order became palpable; even in Tunisia, the best-case outcome, considerable nostalgia for Ben Ali reflected disillusionment with the exaggerated promises of democracy (Ghribi 2014).

In short, the weakening of the Arab states meant forces at the other levels – trans-state networks and the core great powers – were better enabled to penetrate them, a regression to the early post-independence period of state formation. On the other hand, regional state weakening was very *uneven:* specifically, the non-Arab states, Iran, Israel and Turkey, and the Arab monarchies did not suffer state deconstruction, which profoundly tilted the regional balance of power in their favour.

The trans-state ideological struggle

MENA states had always been exceptionally penetrated by supra-state identities and trans-state networks that competed with loyalties to the territorial states; while the effect of this was muted with the consolidation of the states through the 1980s, the supra-state public arena was reinvigorated by Arab satellite TV from the 1990s. In the 'New Arab Cold War' of the late 2000s, there was a battle for public opinion which the 'resistance axis' was winning, with its leaders Ahmadinejad, Asad and Nasrallah, far more popular than their counterparts in US-aligned regimes which suffered substantial de-legitimisation owing to their Western alliances.

The Arab Uprising both manifested and deepened the trans-state level via the proliferating networks of cyberactivists. It also re-opened contests over identity, between sub-state, state (*watani*) and supra-state (the Arab nation (*qaumi*) or Islamic *umma*) loyalties, hence over enemies and appropriate allies of regional states. But this was no equal contest: on the one hand, state weakening in the republics exposed them to trans-state penetration; on the other hand, control of the Pan-Arab media was disproportionately concentrated in the Gulf Co-operation Council (GCC) states and reflected their agenda, with al-Arabiyya founded by Saudi and Al-Jazeera by Qatari money. Trans-state networks using the social media were dominated by the Western-educated middle classes and Arab expatriates and Western foundations played a role in funding and organising Arab cyberactivists.

Partly owing to this, the content of the post-Uprising regional discourse shifted away from the resistance axis narrative. Thus, Bush's regime change in the name of democratisation, by unleashing civil war in Iraq and Lebanon, had seemingly discredited the notion in the 2000s; yet after 2010 the demands of the youth protestors were chiefly for democracy and freedom and in their *own states*, at the expense of the traditional Pan-Arab, anti-imperialist or anti-Zionist concerns that had dominated the 'New Arab Cold War' (Tamlali 2011b). Moreover, Arab nationalism suffered from association with the repressive republics the Uprising was targeting, notably the Syrian regime. And while previously regimes and nationalist-minded publics had agreed on sovereignty as a defence against Western imperialism, in the discourse wars over Libya and Syria, a major portion of Arab opinion embraced the Western norm, 'responsibility to protect', legitimising Western intervention, although majorities had second thoughts after casualties soared in Libya (Telhami 2011). Moreover, to the extent the Uprising preoccupied activists with their individual states, Pan-Arab issues, notably Palestine, became less salient as issues for Arab publics; in the short run at least, states that legitimised themselves with the discourse of resistance, notably Syria and Iran, lost soft power. The reframing of the regional struggle from one of a resistance axis against imperialism and its regional clients to one between Sunni and Shia shifted the balance of soft power from the anti- to pro-Western blocs.

Another salient outcome of the Uprising was the increased transstate power of Islamic discourses and movements. However, there were many variants of Islam and they were not uniformly empowered by the Uprising. The main initial beneficiaries were the Muslim Brotherhood from its electoral prowess and the salafis (Islamic purists) funded by GCC money – which, respectively, had affinity to the Turkish and Saudi Islamic models, and both of which legitimised incorporation of the region into the global capitalist market. These movements mostly sought to culturally Islamise the individual states, but they were nevertheless linked by trans-state networks and their simultaneous rise toward the levers of power in several states initially seemed to strengthen Pan-Islamic sentiments. In parallel, anti-imperialist Islamic movements were initially weakened. Hizbollah's support for the Asad regime made it vulnerable to accusations that it followed a Shia sectarian, rather than an Arab nationalist, agenda and cost it its former popularity on the Arab street. Al-Qaida's anti-imperialist Pan-Islamism targeting the Western 'far enemy' that had seemed so potent in the 2000s suffered reversals when its new leader, Ayman Al-Zawahiri, denounced the principle of majority rule, thus defying the yearning of Muslim populations for democracy. However, it also enjoyed new opportunities to establish a presence in the failing states of Libya, Yemen, Iraq and Syria where it and similar jihadists promoted a trans-state Islamic identity hostile to both the West and secular or non-Sunni regimes; yet, in attacking the Syrian regime, its interests in practice coincided with those of the West. Finally, salafi fundamentalist currents mobilised by Riyadh against Iran as part of their geopolitical struggle deepened the sectarian character of Islamic identity, empowering Sunni militants against the Shia. Syria and Iraq were the most violent battlegrounds of this conflict, with Saudi Arabia/Qatar and Iran promoting the warring sides. Sectarian discourses were overtly utilised by embattled minority regimes in Syria (anti-Sunni discourse) and Bahrain (anti-Shia discourse) to rally their core supporters while Sunni jihadists across the Levant increasingly demonised Shiites. Militant secularists also joined the fray, demonising Islamists, notably in Egypt after the fall of Islamist president Morsi. As the conflict continued, rival actors appeared to be constructing a new fractured inter-subjective normative universe in which Sunni–Shia–secularist differences increasingly defined political enmity and amity; this, in turn, incentivised actors to further manipulate sectarian discourse in their conflicts. As Dergham put it, 'The smell of sectarian wars is becoming ever more redolent across the whole region' (*al-Arabiyya*, 1 January 2012), increasing insecurity and defensive sectarian solidarity in Lebanon, Syria, Bahrain, Yemen and Iraq.

The regional level: the inter-state power struggle
The Uprising both intensified the regional struggle for power and shifted the balance between the antagonists. The major immediate effect of the Uprising was to consign two previous major players, Egypt and Syria, to the category of battleground states, making them the main prizes in the contest, but lesser prizes included Tunisia, Libya, Bahrain and Yemen; also battlegrounds were Iraq and Lebanon, where unconsolidated regimes and fragmented societies were highly vulnerable to spillover of the conflicts unleashed by uprisings in their neighbours. Three rival regional powers, Turkey, Iran and Saudi Arabia, had enough power resources and enough immunity to the Uprising to be in contention to shape the post-Uprising regional order. They each sought to shift the domestic balance and bring to power (or prevent the fall of) friendly forces in states undergoing the Uprising, hence to expand (or protect) their spheres of influence.

Over four years into the Arab Uprising, the main cleavage remained that between the pro and anti-Western coalitions, but their struggle was increasingly framed in sectarian terms and took an ever more violent form. Expressive of sectarianisation, Sunni Turkey, Qatar and Hamas had de-aligned from the resistance axis, which lost its soft power but still survived. The balance between the two sides had not, however, been decisively transformed for Egypt and Iraq had been loosened from their American moorings and avoided full alignment with either side, with Iraq split on sectarian lines.

Of the three rival contending powers, Iran – hence the resistance axis – was initially most weakened. Iran's rulers suffered from greater domestic vulnerabilities, having just turned back the challenge of the Green uprising. Iran's economy was being constricted by international sanctions and it lost soft power from support for the Asad regime and the limited attractiveness of the Iranian model, compared to Turkey, for the emergent democracies. It suffered from the decline of Hizbollah's regional standing and the break of Hamas from the resistance axis. The drive of Sunni protestors and later armed insurgents to overthrow its most important ally, Syria's Asad, put Tehran on the defensive, for if Asad were to be replaced by Western-installed expatriates or a hostile salafi regime aligned with Saudi Arabia, Iran's ability to support Hezbollah and be a player in the Arab–Israeli arena – important to the regime's legitimacy – would be damaged. On the defensive, Iran sought to create via Iraq (where, post-US occupation, the move of the Maliki regime against Sunni rivals made it more dependent on Iran), a corridor linking Iran to Syria and the Lebanese coast, allowing Iran to supply Hizbollah and providing the Asad regime with a two-sided buffer that could help it survive.

From the viewpoint of the pro-Western monarchies, the loss of Mubarak's Egypt, state collapse in Yemen and the potentially contagious Shia uprising in Bahrain offered many opportunities for Iran. But the monarchies proved more resilient than the republics in dampening the domestic threat of the Uprising via a combination of repression, most obvious in Bahrain; political concession, most obvious in Morocco; and economic blandishments to citizens, most obvious in Saudi Arabia where $97 billion worth of jobs and benefits were promised, the equivalent to $5,000/citizen. The GCC was proposed to be upgraded into a 'Holy Alliance' to contain the democratic threat, with the richer monarchies transferring billions to the poorer ones (Morocco, Jordan, Oman and Bahrain) and using petrodollars to promote salafism, for example against the democratic youth in Egypt. For the Saudis, Yemen's descent into turmoil posed the threat of a failed state on their soft underbelly where Al-Qaida and pro-Iranian elements found space to operate; however, they managed a controlled transfer of power in Sana that preserved their influence in the country, which, however, continued to verge on a failed state. The GCC also took advantage of the vacuum left by the marginalisation of the key Arab republics and of its bloc vote in the Arab League to bid for pan-Arab leadership: it used the League to legitimise Western intervention against Qaddafi, an old monarchic foe, and then against Syria, where it aimed to break the resistance axis, which had repeatedly attacked the legitimacy of its Western alignments, notably during the wars in Lebanon (2006) and Gaza (2008). Saudi Arabia and Qatar put their media assets, money and arms at the disposal of the Syrian opposition, but the tenacity of the Asad regime frustrated their ambitions, as did the unwillingness of the US to intervene militarily against Damascus. Yet they were not entirely united: in Egypt, Qatar backed Morsi and the Muslim Brotherhood while Saudi Arabia backed his ousting. Nor would they necessarily remain immune to 'blowback' from the empowerment of radical jihadists in Syria and Iraq that their sectarian discourse and financing had unleashed.

Turkey, a third regional pole, had, prior to the Uprising, situated itself as balancer between the two rival pro- and anti-Western blocs, even tilting toward the resistance axis in reaction to the US destabilisation of Iraq, which empowered Kurdish separatism. Its zero-problems policy of good relations and business deals with non-democratic neighbours was a bid to assert regional leadership. The Uprising initially threatened Ankara's standing in the region. The Libya crisis, where Turkey opposed Western intervention, angered the eventually triumphant opposition; the uprising in Syria, the showcase of its zero-problems policy, cost Turkey economic opportunities, the anti-Kurdish alliance with Damascus and good relations with Iran, as the two backed opposing sides. But as Turkey shifted its stance to back the 'people' against authoritarian governments, it seemed to recover the initiative: Prime Minister Erdoğan was welcomed in Egypt as a hero (where he was by far the most popular world leader). The congruity of Turkey's political system – a democracy that incorporated Islamic forces – with regional popular aspirations; its alignment with rising business/Islamist coalitions similar to the AKP in the new Sunni democracies (Egypt, Tunisia); and the economic prowess which enabled it to build interdependences with the Uprising states were factors empowering Turkey's bid for regional leadership. Yet as the Syrian uprising deepened into intractable conflict, Turkey looked impotent to control the turmoil on its own borders, much less to bid for regional leadership and was forced to turn back to the West to deal with the fallout. The removal of the AKP's Egyptian ally, President Morsi, by a military coup in 2013 put Turkey at odds with the new military-dominated regime in Cairo. As such, four years into the Arab Uprising, weaknesses had been exposed in each of the three contending regional powers, with none able to take decisive advantage of the Uprising to establish hegemony.

The global level: MENA in the core–periphery hierarchy
After an attempt starting in the 1990s to impose a Pax Americana on the region, US power appeared, by the mid-2000s, to be receding owing to the failure of the peace process, the regional perception that the war on terror was a war on Islam and the invasion of Iraq, which inadvertently empowered Iran and provoked counter-balancing even by US ally Turkey. Rival powers were penetrating the region, with Russia and China developing stakes in arms sales, energy and trade.

The Uprising had an ambiguous impact on US standing. The fall of close ally Mubarak, and Washington's uneasy relation with his successors, seemed a setback. Yet the US hegemon potentially benefited from the relative empowerment of the GCC, and where US-friendly regimes fell (Egypt, Tunisia, Yemen) their successors proved too dependent to turn against Washington. The historic ideological resistance to the West of Arab nationalism collapsed as opposition groups called for foreign intervention against their own governments. The uprising in Libya presented an opportunity for the US to reverse perceptions that US power in the region was declining (in the face of the resistance axis) and Washington demonstrated its ability to promote regime change at little initial cost to itself, and this time in concert with supportive European allies. If the main struggle in the region was over the competing bids of the US and Iran for regional hegemony, the uprising in Syria provided the former with an opportunity to debilitate the resistance axis. Indeed, as the Syrian civil war made the country a

battleground between Hizbollah and Al-Qaida, the US could anticipate its two most formidable trans-state enemies might debilitate
each other at very little cost to itself. Yet, generally speaking, the US
seemed remarkably impotent to control or influence an increasingly
turbulent region. For example, the regime change it promoted in
Libya, as formerly in Iraq, left a mess behind, including a power
vacuum in which radical Islamists, armed from looted Libyan army
depots, emerged empowered in the northern part of Africa.

In the Arab Uprising, by contrast to the US invasion of Iraq, the
US and the West acted in concert, no longer split. But the West
was still not able to fully capitalise on regional disarray to revive
hegemony over the region. To be sure, Washington's main global
competitors in the region, China and Russia, lost soft power for
their opposition to interventions against Arab governments that
repressed protestors. But Russia started actively contesting Western
intervention in the region, with Syria the showcase of this 'New
Cold War'. Second, economic crisis in the West constrained the
interventionist impulse, while in the US, in particular, fatigue at
highly costly interventions led the Obama administration to retreat
to off-shore balancing, 'leading from behind', and particularly
reluctant to fully involve itself in the Syrian quagmire.

Notwithstanding this, key regional states become even *more* economically vulnerable to Western penetration owing to the economic
collapse resulting from the Uprising. While the Uprising was stimulated by grievances rooted in global neo-liberalism and its crony
capitalist manifestations in MENA, Western IFIs reframed it as a
revolt against the intrusive state and rentier monopolies; this was to
be addressed by enhancing competition through *further opening* of
regional states to global finance capital; exploiting the post-Uprising
economic crises, IFIs made loans conditional on such openings
(Hanieh 2011). This had implications for regional democratisation: since the dominance of global finance capital tends to hollow
out democracy, the outcome of the MENA uprisings risked turning out, at best, to be what Robinson (1996) called 'low intensity
democracy', limited to the political sphere, with countries locked
into international agreements that remove the big socio-economic
issues from democratic accountability and with all political parties pursuing similar economic policies, much as in the West itself.
This quickly produced a certain disillusionment with democracy as
elections failed to deliver governments responsive to the electorate

on issues of wealth distribution. Politicians, unable to decide on or deliver the big issues of who gets what, fell back on identity politics for mobilising their constituents, deepening sectarian and secular–Islamist cleavages; or else their inability to manage faltering economies was used by the remnants of the deep state to discredit them, as most dramatically happened to President Morsi of Egypt.

Repercussions of the Uprising

Regional consequences of the Uprising, four years after it began, were exemplified in three pivotal cases: (1) the persistence of dependence, seen in constraints on Egyptian foreign policy; (2) the failure of liberal peace, seen in Turkey–Syria relations; (3) the debilitation of the state and spread of trans-state sectarianism, most apparent in Iraq and Syria.

Egypt: the persistence of dependency

With the fall of Mubarak in Egypt's revolution, the country became the potential swing power where a major change in foreign policy would be decisive for the regional power balance. Indeed, Cairo early signalled its intention to disengage from the rival pro- and anti-Western alliances inherited from the pre-Uprising period and to pursue an independent foreign policy aimed to restore its traditional leadership position in the Arab world. Moreover, the revolution was widely seen as Egypt's chance to reassert its independence from the United States and to break the close relations with Israel, which appeasing Washington had dictated and which had disqualified Egypt from Arab leadership. Yet despite widespread expectations in Egypt, the post-revolutionary change in leadership produced neither a move toward greater foreign policy independence nor toward restoring Egypt's Arab leadership.

Most central for Egypt was its relationship with the United States, which was widely seen as the main constraint on Egypt's autonomy. In the post-Mubarak period, public pressures to restructure the US relationship – making it less asymmetric and less conditional on serving Israel's interests – required all rival Egyptian politicians to rhetorically eschew Mubarak's perceived submissiveness to Washington. But actually pursuing a foreign policy independent of the US was another matter. Indeed, Egypt's politicians were caught between the pervasive anti-Americanism of their constituents and inherited dependencies on the US, which could withhold crucial resources: the arms that sustained the bloated military, the economic aid that Egypt needed to overcome the worsening economic crisis. The military itself swung between its material stake in the US relationship and its need for legitimacy by occasionally playing the anti-US card in public discourse; the Muslim Brotherhood, the main organised political alternative to military rule, was also caught between the expectations of its rank-and-file followers and its need, exemplified in Muhammad Morsi's short-lived presidency, for IMF support to satisfy the rich businessmen in the Muslim Brotherhood's inner core and power an economic recovery needed to satisfy the electorate.

The issue that made US dependency most explosive was Washington's support of Israel. Mubarak, rather than balancing against Israel, had instead bandwagoned with the US at least partly to contain the Israeli threat. His complicity in Israel's blockade of Gaza was a major cause of his legitimacy deficit. Israel's much more powerful military, the constraints on Egypt's sovereignty in the Sinai from the peace treaty with it, and the fact that Israel was seen by most Egyptians as an enemy state despite the treaty all made the close relations with Israel inherited from Mubarak a domestic liability for post-Uprising governments. Democratisation and Egypt's Arab role conception both generated pressures to reverse the normalisation of relations; yet aid from Washington was contingent on sustaining it. Moreover, Cairo's drive to reassert sovereignty over Sinai against trans-state Islamist militants who could drag Egypt into conflict with its more powerful neighbour gave Egypt's security elites a shared interest with Israel in stabilising their common border.

The Gaza conflict of November 2012 between Israel and Hamas, an offshoot of the Muslim Brotherhood, was a test of whether the Brotherhood-backed President, Muhammad Morsi, could change Egyptian foreign policy. He was pulled between the expectations of the West and of his constituency: thus, while the US warned that Egypt would sacrifice US aid if it did not clamp down on Hamas, Egyptian political parties, activists, the media and his own supporters in the Brotherhood called on him to sever relations with Israel. Morsi sent his prime minister to Gaza, recalled the Egyptian ambassador from Israel, met with Hamas leaders and organised anti-Israeli demonstrations. Yet he offered little material support and, rather, assumed a Mubarak-like attempt to broker between Hamas and

Israel; and the outcome of the ceasefire negotiations, while supposedly easing Israel's blockade of Gaza, also committed Egypt to intensify its own efforts, on Israel's behalf, to stop arms deliveries via Sinai into Gaza.

Asserting regional leadership and diversifying dependences potentially would allow Egypt to increase its bargaining power in dealing with the US and Israel. Post-revolutionary Egypt, with its new democratic legitimacy, was potentially well positioned to recover a regional role. President Morsi had a particular incentive to forge a more independent foreign policy, which, if successful, would win him the needed legitimacy to marginalise his rivals, the secularists and generals, as the AKP had done in Turkey. In his post-election visit to Washington, he suggested that Egypt's continued peace with Israel was conditional on whether the US would 'live up to its own Camp David commitment to Palestinian self-rule' (*New York Times*, 23 September 2012). Post-revolutionary Egypt's jettisoning of Mubarak's anti-Iran enmity and Morsi's attempt to broker a settlement of the Syrian crisis via a contact group that would include Iran appeared harbingers of an independent foreign policy.

Yet, as Salem (2012) observed, Morsi's Egypt was not that of Nasser's day. The bi-polarity that had allowed Nasser to diversify dependency was a thing of the past. Then Egypt was the strongest state and largest economy in the Arab world; in 2012, Egypt's economic troubles made it extremely vulnerable to the demands of its funders. The imbalance of power with Israel, combined with dependency on the US, constrained Egypt's ability to soft-balance against Israel, hence stunting the capacity to defend Arab–Islamic causes that was needed for regional leadership.

Egypt as a foreign policy actor was also debilitated by the ongoing three-cornered internal struggle for power among the revolutionary youth (in coalition with, notably, leftists and secularists), the Islamists and the military (together with the remnants of the old regime), each of which differed on the identity of the state and hence on its appropriate foreign policy and alignments. Further, Egypt's political process was penetrated and its power struggle distorted by outside financial flows: the US funded the liberals and the military, Qatar the Muslim Brotherhood and Saudi Arabia the salafis, giving all of them leverage over Egypt's foreign policy. President Morsi had to move cautiously, negotiating between his MB constituency and the security establishment, which defended continuity in foreign policy, often deferring to the latter, and eschewing decisive choices.

In consequence, the results were meagre. Morsi's Syrian initiative went nowhere, with the Saudis rejecting co-operation with Iran. Full diplomatic relations were not even re-established with Tehran. And Morsi's most high-profile foreign policy initiative, the Gaza ceasefire, kept Egypt embroiled in defending Israel against Gaza militants, as under Mubarak. Thus, alterations in Egypt's policy were mostly symbolic and aimed at domestic audiences. Even here Morsi ultimately failed: his verbal encouragement of Islamist rebels in Syria and his attempt to establish amicable relations with Hamas in Gaza were held against him by the generals and were a main motive for his overthrow. With Morsi's removal, and the re-empowerment of the 'deep' state establishment, Egypt seemed to revert to 'Mubarakism without Mubarak'. Public opinion, which, in the aftermath of the revolution, had been expected to be empowered, was by 2013 too disunited and readily manipulated to matter. The expectations of realists that external constraints would sharply dilute pressures issuing from revolution and democratisation for a foreign policy transformation in Egypt appeared validated, but the zero-sum domestic struggle was, as realists might not have anticipated, at least as important in deterring such change.

Failure of liberal peace: Turkey–Syria relations

The year 2000 rise of the AKP government to power in Turkey initiated a transformation in Turkey's Middle East policy. 'Zero problems' with its neighbours and solutions to the region's interminable conflicts were now sought by exporting to the region the liberal practices of the zone of peace (Murinson 2006). The primary instrument of this policy was economic, transport and energy integration with Turkey's neighbours, which would enable the export, as well, of Turkish business in need of new markets. At the political level, Turkey now had the ambition to fill what it saw as an enduring post-Ottoman power vacuum; it tried to legitimise this bid for hegemony in the ethnically different Arab world by appeal to shared Islamic civilisation (with Turkish and Arab brothers said to have been artificially severed by Western-imperialist imposed borders at the time of Ottoman collapse), and through Erdoğan's high-profile discourse in defence of the Palestine cause (accompanied by clashes with Israel).

Turkey's ambitions made good relations with contiguous Syria of first importance and, indeed, Syria became the showcase of its zero-problems strategy. As relations improved, the trans-state issues that had hitherto been occasions of conflict, notably the disputed Turkish annexation of Iskanderun and Kurdish separatism that Syria had supported, were quickly resolved. The issue of Euphrates river water sharing, over which previously both sides had taken rigid positions based on rights or sovereignty, was now de-securitised, allowing trans-state links between irrigation bureaucracies to facilitate co-operation over water-management. Historic trade ties ruptured at the breakup of the Ottoman empire began to be re-established. A free trade agreement was signed in December 2004 and trade rapidly increased. Turkey was seeking to build a regional economic belt extending towards the Arab Gulf area and Syria, as a member of the Greater Arab Free Trade Area (GAFTA), provided a conduit to this larger Arab market; Syria, for its part, sought access via Turkey to European markets. The opening of borders to passage without visas was meant to blur the territorial demarcations between the states. Infrastructure and energy pipeline projects were proposed that would make the two states a joint international energy hub. These growing interdependences were accompanied by explicit discourse, notably from Turkey, claiming that the partners were constructing a security community, expected in Ankara to pull Syria into the orbit of the liberal peace; in Damascus, the stress was put on the partnership as a counter-balance to the destabilising intervention of the US in the Middle East.

However, this project came to an abrupt halt amidst the Syrian uprising. When Asad dismissed Turkey's calls to carry out political reforms and instead continued repressing protestors, Turkey sacrificed its ties with his regime, helped organise the Syrian opposition, and gave it safe haven to operate an insurgency from Turkish territory. Sunni Islamic identity became an element in Turkey's armoury against the secular/Alawi regime in Damascus. With renewed Turkey–Syria hostility, mutual threat perceptions escalated. Asad's new enmity to the AKP was driven by the existential threat from Ankara's support for the uprising. Turkey's anti-Asad stance requires more explanation since it was sacrificing not only economic ties but also security co-operation against the PKK, hitherto the major threat to Turkey. However, the AKP was convinced that repressive dictatorships had become a serious threat to its ambition for a pacific neighbourhood; certainly Asad's use of violence against unarmed protestors would have been seen as incompatible with a liberal peace. The Turkish government apparently also miscalculated that the Asad regime could not long survive the uprising. Ankara also saw the stimulus given to both democracy and to political Islam by the Arab Uprising as a unique opportunity for Turkey to translate soft power into regional hegemony and this required supporting the Syrian opposition. Were the Muslim Brothers to come to power in Damascus, the AKP could expect to enjoy special influence there. Turkey was positioning itself to become the big brother of the fledgling Arab democracies.

In the immediate term, however, the earlier achievements of the fledgling 'liberal peace' were rapidly lost as each side sacrificed the shared benefits of co-operation and resumed the use of trans-state interdependencies *against the other*. Turkey imposed economic sanctions on Syria, which responded by ending the free trade arrangements that had favoured Turkey, ousting Turkish investors and obstructing Turkey's transit links to the Gulf. The Syria–Turkey border, which had been open during the rapprochement, allowing dense family and trade ties, was now re-militarised and the border areas suffered economic losses. Foreign Minister Davutoğlu announced the suspension of the High Level Strategic Council that had facilitated co-operation over issues such as water. Syria threatened to retaliate by reviving support for the Kurdish PKK and indeed it allowed a PKK-affiliated party to take over much of its Kurdish border zone with Turkey. Turkey tried to head off this threat by striking an alliance with Iraq's KDP to restrain the PKK and later by entering into peace negotiations with the PKK. However, the inability of Turkey to affect the ever escalating turmoil in Syria, which periodically spilled across its border, seemed to cast doubt on Turkey's capacity to act as a regional liberal hegemon.

In retrospect, the security community the two country's leaderships had envisioned as the end goal of intensified co-operation was exposed, at least from a liberal perspective, as lacking the solid foundation of common liberal political systems. The costs of abandoning it were, however, high: Turkey's attempt to export democracy to its neighbour had much the same effect as the earlier US attempt in Iraq: collapse of the target into a failed state (Hinnebusch and Tur 2013).

State deconstruction and trans-state sectarianisation:
Syria and Iraq

Post-Uprising deconstruction of the state and the resulting empowerment of the trans-state level was most exaggerated in Syria and Iraq. Iraq had already been deconstructed by the US invasion and occupation, which decapitated the central government and institutionalised sectarianism. The constitution, electoral arrangements and the party system fostered sectarian solidarities producing permanent Shia governing majorities, while the military and police were filled with the clients of Shia factions. Prime Minister Nouri al-Maliki used appointments to the army, clientelism, sectarian solidarity and, ironically, both US and Iranian support to establish semi-patrimonial governance in Baghdad. The alienated Sunnis became the backbone of the insurgency against the US occupation and its client regime. In parallel, the Kurdish north was separated under an autonomous government with its own militias and oil resources. A debilitated Iraqi state lacked full control over its territory, was incapable of maintaining security or delivering services and faced separatist tendencies in each of its three major regions. A decade after the US invasion, the country was increasingly balkanised, with people afraid to venture into areas affiliated with the opposing identity, and sectarianism the main tool by which politicians mobilised their communal constituencies. It appears that, once deconstructed, a state cannot easily be put back together.

The Syrian uprising led to a similar deconstruction of the state in Syria. Although anti-government protests in Syria began with a cross-sectarian discourse, they took on an ever more Sunni Islamist cast against an Alawi-dominated regime. The mostly Sunni protestors felt empowered by the rising influence of Sunni movements across the region and particularly that of the Muslim Brotherhood whose Syrian branch was the historical alternative to the Ba'th regime. Initial centres of the uprising were mixed areas where Alawis and Sunni lived adjacent to each other, as in Latakia, Banias and Homs, or areas of concentrated Sunni religiosity, such as Hama. Fatally, the regime also played the sectarian card to rally its minority core by depicting the opposition as Islamist terrorists and unleashing violent Alawi militias against it. The regime discourse of Islamist terror became a self-fulfilling prophecy: government violence radicalised Sunnis and, in time, led to Sunni defections from the army and an armed resistance to the regime, the Free Syrian Army. Escalating violence led to massive exit of the secular upper middle and middle classes, leaving a vacuum filled by radical Islamist fighters from the countryside or who flooded in from around the region. Only two years into the uprising, the country had become a failed state, split between government-controlled areas, such as Damascus and the western coast, a countryside under a fragmented patchwork of local Islamist insurgencies, the north-east under Kurdish control, and parts of the east under control of Islamist jihadists and of tribes with links to the Sunni tribal areas of Iraq.

The Arab Uprising unleashed forces that threatened to further destabilise the fragile Iraqi regime as well. Regular mass Sunni protests in the western provinces started against Maliki's use of anti-terrorism laws to target Sunni politicians, with tribal leaders defying the Baghdad government and raising the discourse of separatism. The conflict in Syria soon spilled over into Iraq, symptomatic of the trans-state tribes and identity groups that Western-imposed boundaries had cut across, but which were now increasingly porous as state power collapsed. During the US occupation of Iraq, the tribes and mosques of Deir al-Zur had provided significant numbers of fighters and weapons to Iraqi insurgents in Anbar province; now the situation was reversed as Euphrates Valley tribes in Iraq sent money, weapons and fighters to support their Syrian cousins in Deir al-Zur. They attacked Sadrist Shia militias travelling to Syria to support the Asad regime (Wieland 2012: 206). Anbar province became an arms supply route from Saudi Arabia to the Syrian insurgents. Violence by Al-Qaida insurgents in Iraq increased in parallel with their presence in Syria. Syrian insurgents crossed the Iraqi border to attack Syrian regime forces taking refuge on Iraqi soil, even killing Iraqi troops. An Al-Qaida avatar, ISIS, promoted the idea of a caliphate nullifying the boundaries that divided Sunni areas in both countries. A 'Free Iraqi Army', mimicking the Free Syrian Army, was formed and Syrian activists called for a revolution in Syria and Iraq that would 'quench the fire of Magi' (a derogatory reference to Shiites and Alawis).

In parallel, Kurdish national ambitions were strengthened by the state weakening issuing from the US invasion of Iraq and by the Syrian uprising. Syria's north-west Kurdish regions, effectively autonomous since Damascus lost control of its territory, had trans-state links to the Kurdish regional government controlling

Iraqi Kurdistan and which competed with the PKK to influence Syrian Kurds. In parallel, Turkey played a dangerous balancing game of strengthening, in order to co-opt, the KRG, hence separating it from Baghdad. If Syrian Kurds extract legal autonomy from a post-Asad government, alongside a virtually independent Kurdish regional government in Iraq, the demonstration effect may be hard to contain among Kurds in Turkey and Iran. Multiple autonomous Kurdish regions would be a first step toward carving a new united Kurdistan out of the MENA states system.

A 'new struggle for Syria' linked to the already existing struggle for Iraq carried implications for the regional balance of power. While the Syrian uprising was essentially indigenous, external forces sought to use it to their advantage, making Syria a regional battleground of a conflict framed in Sunni–Shia terms quite similar to that in Iraq. On one side of the struggle was Saudi Arabia which had never accepted a Shia-governed Iraq and sought to extirpate Iranian influence in Damascus and destroy the 'resistance axis'; the Saudis funnelled money and arms to anti-Asad tribes while Qatar's Al-Jazeera amplified the voices of Syrian protestors and later the insurgents. Turkey gave sanctuary to Sunni rebels and allowed jihadist fighters to transit its territory to Syria, while also supporting Iraqi Sunni Arab and Kurdish politicians against al-Maliki's Shia regime.

The Asad regime's only chance of slipping out of this tightening stranglehold lay in its links to Hezbollah in the west and, in the east, to Iran and Iraq, both Shia powers. It increasingly relied on Iran for financial and counter-insurgency support, on Hizbollah fighters and on Iraqi oil. The al-Maliki government, fearing the rise of a Sunni-dominated government in Damascus would strengthen the alienated Sunnis in Iraq's western provinces, and perceiving a Saudi–Qatari–Turkish plot to spread Syria's Sunni insurgency to Iraq, defensively aligned with Asad. Indeed, the seizure of Mosul by ISIS in summer 2014, with the support of Sunni tribes and ex-Saddam supporters, exposed both the fragility and excessively Shia character of the Iraqi regime. Both Arab regimes drew closer to Iran for protection, which committed substantial resources to the defence of the Asad regime and latter the embattled Maliki government.

The unmaking of the Versailles-imposed Westphalian system which, a hundred years ago, denied Kurdish national aspirations and imposed boundaries in violation of Arab identities was no longer unthinkable. Moreover, ISIS, as it seized cities, oil fields, arms depots and wide swathes of territory bridging eastern Syria and western Iraq, acquired statehood attributes that made its proclamation of a caliphate more than fanciful. As Barkey (2012) pointed out, Syria and Iraq were both at the 'cusp' of Arab–Kurdish, Persian–Kurdish and Turkish–Kurdish divisions: 'Before it has run its course [the Syrian uprising] could undo multiple existing regimes and even alter the region's post-World War I territorial boundaries'.

Conclusion

Most liberal expectations about the democratising effect of the Arab Uprising were not realised *in the short run*. Rather than moves toward democratisation strengthening the Arab republics, they were weakened, more so in the more identity-fragmented states, Syria and Iraq, but to a lesser degree also even in more coherent ones like Egypt and Tunisia. In the former, the rapidity with which the weakening of secular regimes empowered sectarian identities and allowed a growing merging of Sunni–Shia conflicts and of Kurdish separatism in Syria and Iraq indicated that, almost a century after their arbitrary creation by Western imperialism, in what Fromkin (1989) appropriately named a 'peace to end all peace', these states remained 'artificial'. Across the region, trans-state forces, whether discourse, finance or arms and fighters, penetrated states losing control of their borders. The trans-state public space had deepened but the pre-Uprising Pan-Arab discourse that had been promoted by Arab satellite TV now gave way to the broadcast of sectarian discord within and between states.

Rather than the uprisings making for a more autonomous region, they opened new fissures that outside powers exploited. While most revolutions enhance nationalism, the Arab protestors invited Western intervention, notably in Libya and Syria. Egypt shows how dependency on external patrons increased, rather than diminished. While public opinion may matter more in states where leaders must face election, as realists anticipated, external constraints – the balance of power with neighbours, dependences on external patrons – substantially diluted its effect.

As for the narrative of democratic peace, the immediate consequence of the Uprising was the *intensification* of the regional power struggle, nowhere more evident than in Turkey–Syria relations where pre-Uprising progress in establishing a zone of peace regressed into a zone of war. The new regional power struggle was similar to that in the early post-independence period in that it took the form of competitive interference in the domestic affairs of other states, but rather than the financing of rival officer factions to mount bloodless coups, the competitors now funnelled arms to rival militias engaged in internal wars.

Indeed, the region's turmoil closely replicated Mary Kaldor's (1999) scenarios regarding 'New Wars', which, she argued, were a function of the weakening of the state under globalisation. States suffered a loss of capacity and legitimacy, caught, in Barber's (1992) metaphor, between *both* 'McWorld' – global level forces, such as the IMF, and Westernised and Western-funded Internet empowered youth – *and* 'jihad', denoting a intensified revival of fragmenting ethnic and religious particularisms at the sub/trans-state level. In this scenario, which spread to the Middle East as states were debilitated first by the US destruction of Iraq and then under the Arab Uprising, trans-national state/non-state actors were relatively empowered – irregular militias, 'terrorists' and warlords fighting with regime forces, often sustained by funding from diasporas and trans-national arms trafficking. Sliding into identity wars, distinctions between military and civilian opponents broke down, hence civilian casualties became enormous, 'ethnic cleansing' typical and refugee flows massive. Thus, more than 100,000 had been killed in Iraq since the 2003 US invasion, followed by 30,000 in Libya and 100,000 in Syria, with refugee displacements in the millions.

The Uprising also shifted the balance of power among the contenders in the regional struggle. It weakened the Arab world generally by debilitating the historically key Arab powers, Egypt, Syria and Iraq (in the last case, this dates to the US invasion). Within the Arab world, the republics were weakened while the oil monarchies remained unscathed and well positioned to penetrate the republics through use of their petrodollars and support for Islamists. But none of the three main regional powers seeking to exploit the Uprising, Turkey, Saudi Arabia and Iran, were able to gain a decisive advantage. Similarly at the global level, in a throwback to the Cold War, the US and Russia checkmated each other in the region. All of the attempted prescriptions for order in the region – Arabism, the balance of power between coherent states, US hegemony – had failed. The region was further from peace, much less a *democratic* peace, than ever before.

10

Conclusion: between IR theory and the Middle East case

The introduction to this book surveyed the main IR theories that have been used by scholars to understand the MENA area. Each of these examined important aspects, none of which could be neglected without damage to our grasp of regional politics. Bearing in mind the framework and the empirical evidence in the subsequent chapters, we are in a position to summarise the lessons of the Middle East case for IR theory.

A multivariate framework

The MENA region has been described as a graveyard of IR theories, since none seems to adequately capture its dynamics. It seems more war-prone than other regions, hence amenable to realist analysis. But it also has features that realism does not address, such as the concentration of hydrocarbon resources and rentier states, authoritarian governance, exceptionally powerful supra-state identities (Arabism, Islam) and exceptional penetration by global powers.

The special features of the region do not, however, mean that IR theories invented elsewhere and purporting to capture universal tendencies have no leverage in MENA; MENA is distinguished chiefly by the particular configuration in which universal factors come together. Since the problem with IR theories is that each captures only *one* aspect of regional IR to the neglect of others, arguably only a *multivariate* synthetic approach can adequately guide analysis of the region's complexity. The MENA case can both expose the strengths and weaknesses of each theory and show us how to creatively upgrade and combine them to get enhanced explanatory power.

First cut: realism and the regional struggle for power

A synthetic framework would have to depart from knowing what we seek to explain. The focus of study of international *politics* is arguably *power* and the relative intensity of the struggle for power in MENA makes this an appropriate starting point for understanding the region. We can ask what factors drive and mitigate this struggle and what forms it takes. It is, of course, realism that most directly focuses on the struggle for power and identifies the underlying factor that is a necessary – but not sufficient – condition of it, namely anarchy-induced insecurity. MENA certainly fits the realist scenario: with two of the world's most intractable (the Arab–Israeli and Gulf) conflict zones, high levels of militarisation and a high expectation of war, MENA foreign policy-makers' first priority is security. Realism also captures and describes recurring universal regularities that do occur in MENA – power balancing against threats, alliance-making, the struggle for hegemony – and assesses their consequences for regional stability.

For neo-realism, states are caught in security dilemmas that they have little ability to control or modify. The national interest is assumed to be security, indeed survival, which trumps all other goals, such as ideology or wealth, that are only pursued insofar as security is secure or they contribute to it. Security requires following realist rules, notably the accumulation and prudent use of power, via military build-ups or alliances to balance against threats, or, when state weakness makes this unrealistic, 'bandwagoning'. Leaders are socialised into realist rules by imitation of the practice of successful states that play by these rules and by the bad experiences of those that violate them (Waltz 1979). MENA leaders do appear to be obsessed by security and to be well versed in realist rules; moreover, where they have ignored them, whether in pursuit of Pan-Arabism (Nasser) or Pan-Islam (Khomeini), and suffered lost wars, they were succeeded by chastened realist rulers (Sadat, Rafsanjani).

Although all states have to cope with anarchy, there is considerable variation in the realist canon regarding how they respond to it. The defensive vs. offensive realist debate acknowledges that states might seek merely a sufficiency of power to secure themselves or, alternatively, that bigger powers, locked in rivalry, would only feel secure by seeking hegemony. The distinction between balancers, typical of larger powers, and bandwagoners, typical of weak powers, similarly differentiates kinds of responses to anarchy. Classical realism made a key distinction between revisionist (dissatisfied) and status quo states; for Organski (1968) and the *power transition* variants of realism, relative power position determined this, with the state on top of the global order satisfied and its proximate rivals among other great powers likely to mount revisionist challenges to it.

While power-balancing, bandwagoning and hegemony-seeking are all recognisable in the Middle East, realism provides little explanation for states' choices among these strategies other than their relative power position. Some MENA states have, indeed, been revisionist, reaching for hegemony while others are status quo defensive realists but the correspondence of ambition and power is far from exact and the same large states have alternated between status quo and revisionist stances (e.g. Iran, Iraq, Egypt, Turkey) while some smaller powers (Syria) have had durable revisionist ambitions.

The neo-realist paradigm is, as its proponents admit, 'thin', with the state-system level leaving much state behaviour indeterminate, predicting long-term tendencies but not *why* particular states react to the system via one or the other sort of behaviour, since, as Waltz admits, it has to be supplemented by a theory of foreign policy. Thus, to explain why some states are revisionist and others status quo requires looking to other traditions, such as Foreign Policy Analysis or neo-Gramscian forms of structuralism (Cox and Sinclair 1996).

Walt's (1987) notion of *balance of threat* was meant to upgrade neo-realism since the aggregate power and proximity of other states was not enough to produce power balancing unless other states were *seen* as threatening, an ideational element. Neo-classical realism (Lobell 2009) addressed why states adopt revisionist or status quo orientations and why they miscalculate threats and respond suboptimally, over- or under-balancing, by bringing in domestic variables: leadership perceptions of threat and regimes' institutional capacity to mobilise resources to counter them. However, accounting for threat perceptions requires understanding the way identity is constructed, the domain of constructivism, while variations in states' ability to mobilise power is a function of state formation, the domain of historical sociology.

A particular weakness of neo-realism when applied to the Middle East is that it assumes a Westphalian states system, with domestic hierarchy sharply distinguished from external anarchy. Similarly, its presumption that states pursue a national interest assumes a congruence of state territory with a national identity, i.e. the nation-state model that proved so effective in the core and ostensibly was spread to the post-colonial periphery. Waltz believed the dynamics of the international power struggle stimulated ruling elites to create states in the Weberian model, thus pushing all regions toward a Westphalian states system. The Middle East provides evidence both of a pervasive 'defensive modernisation' by which regional state-builders attempted to replicate Western nation-building (famously Ataturk in Turkey) but also of cases where such projects were never attempted or failed, notably where imperialist-created states were particularly unviable, with fragmented identities or minuscule territories (city-states).

Steven David (1991), a precursor of neo-classical realism, adapted realism to the pre-Westphalian Third World, arguing that the distinction between anarchy without and hierarchy within did not hold there: in fragmented states with weak institutions and capabilities, opposition within was actually more potent than the threats posed by such weak states to each other. Moreover, because these states lacked a secure national identity, foreign policy did not defend a *national* interest but rather the *regime* interest, one possibly at odds with that of a state's people, and rather than balancing against eternal threats, *omni-balanced* – typically, appeasing a stronger external power, less threatening because more remote, to get the material resources to deal with more proximate internal threats. Conversely, in what might be called 'reverse omni-balancing', regimes could rhetorically 'balance' against external threats (imperialism) in order to get the nationalist legitimacy to contain opposition within.

Omni-balancing has been widely applied in explanations of MENA states' foreign policies. What is lacking is an explanation of why regional states are so weak and prone to omni-balancing. Moreover, in assuming a uniform weakness of states, this model ignores the agency of state-builders and its effect on variable levels of state consolidation, which in MENA differ widely over time and across states, accounting for variations in state behaviour: thus, the weak states of the immediate post-independence period were likely to omni-balance while the militarised bureaucratised regimes that populated the region in the 1980s created a world of realist balancing.

Despite its advance in explaining variable regime responses to the international system, neo-classical realism still assumes the states system is a realm of undifferentiated insecurity outside of the control of most states, when, as constructivist Alexander Wendt (1999) showed, states, through their interactions, have the agency to construct *different versions* of anarchy. Realism, insensitive to *variations* in *kinds* of anarchy, is not well equipped to explain the relatively greater tendency toward Hobbesianism in MENA compared to other regions. This Hobbesianism cannot, indeed, simply be explained by anarchy and, rather, originates, as structuralism shows, in the external construction of an extremely flawed states system with irredentism, grievances and revisionism built into it, even if the malign interactions of regional states have subsequently continued to reproduce this Hobbesianism.

Realism is also not well-equipped to assess the extent to which MENA insecurity can be mitigated. For classical and defensive neo-realists, states are caught in security dilemmas that can only be mitigated by a balance of power; when it breaks down, the door is open to war. By contrast (realist) hegemonic stability theory (Gilpin 1982) attributes greater agency to great powers, seeing hegemony – just the opposite of a power balance – as capable of establishing stability. However, the experience of MENA indicates that bids for regional hegemony, whether by regional or global actors, are destabilising while, by contrast, states that have played by 'defensive realist' rules have sustained power balances that have arguably kept the peace for long periods on various fraught fault-lines, such as the Syrian–Israeli one. Bids for hegemony have regularly upset the power balance and although anti-hegemonic counter-balancing has blunted such bids, it has taken costly wars to do so. The balance of power has preserved the system but not the peace.

Realism effectively identifies the anarchic logic of the inter-state structure and recurring patterns of behaviour that it induces. The Middle East seems to support realist pessimism about world order and the region remains part of the 'zone of war' where realism remains realistic. But realism's highly parsimonious, ahistorical and static view of structure ignores the deep forces that account for structural variations and the effect of agency on it; and its sole focus on the inter-states system ignores the complexity of structure in MENA. Thus, we need to bring in other theories that account for *variation* in both agent and structure over time and space. The role of identity and norms has to be brought in via constructivism and the English School (the International Society approach); political-economy via Marxist-inspired structuralism and liberalism; and history via historical sociology.

Agent-structure dynamics and variations in anarchy I: constructivism, liberalism and international society

One of constructivism's main contributions is to show that the interests and threats said to motivate states are constructed, hence *variable*. Stressing identity-driven agency, it takes seriously what the actors say the power struggle is about. Interests and threats are not given by material factors but are shaped by actors' identity, which, however, is not fixed and is itself constructed, often against an 'other'. If states construct their identities against each other, enmity, other things being equal, is more likely than amity, a view congruent with realism; indeed, in MENA identity does shape pervasive perceptions of threats and enemies: rival identities, especially Zionism, against which the rest have constructed themselves, but also Arab vs. Persian or Turk, and Shia vs. Sunni, define recurring conflict fault-lines in MENA, often taking Hobbesian forms. Within an identity, by contrast, chances for amity should be much greater.

If international anarchy for neo-realism is undifferentiated and constant, constructivist Alexander Wendt (1999), affirming agency, has shown that anarchy is *what states make of it* and this can vary from Hobbesian to Lockean and even Kantian versions (a 'zone of peace'). While anarchy, reinforced by identity conflicts, may make international politics a power struggle, it is not necessarily conducted solely with realist material power and violence, but may be prosecuted via symbols, discourse (soft power) and contests over legitimacy, with the mix of instruments varying according to the *kind* (Hobbesian or not) of anarchy constructed.

Michael Barnett, the main constructivist scholar working on the Middle East, has argued that inter-Arab (intra-identity) politics has largely taken the form of discourse wars, not wars of hard power (Barnett 1993; 1995; 1998). Moreover, while realists see identity as just another tool in power struggles, Barnett shows that discourse has been deployed to construct Pan-Arab identity, which shapes conceptions of common Pan-Arab interests and normative structures that facilitate co-operation among Arab states and constrain the unfettered pursuit of individual state interests. This is because, as constructivists and area specialists agree, the Arab core of the regional states system is embedded in a supra-state public space (Lynch 1999) grounded in the exceptional power of supra/trans-state identities, Arabism and Islam. It is the existence of this trans-state public space that made possible projects by aspirant regional hegemons, classically Nasser's Egypt, to construct, via soft power, a normative 'Pan-Arab regime' that constrained other states, even though Egypt lacked the material (military and economic) power to enforce these norms.

However, rival norms or conflicting interpretations of the same norm exist in MENA, stimulating discourse wars, in which states and trans-state movements seek to promote different norms. Barnett saw two norms competing in the Arab world, the regional norm of Arabism and the global norm of sovereignty, with regional states competing to construct rival versions of Arabism, more or less sovereignty-friendly, as it suited their interests and with the balance shifting over time toward sovereignty as a result of Arabism's failures. As Arabism declined, Islam arguably filled the vacuum, becoming the main counter-hegemonic ideology against global neo-liberalism (Murden 2002), and, some argued, an agent in a 'clash of civilisations' with the West.

Strikingly, even though partly responsible for triggering disasters such as the 1967 Arab–Israeli and Iran–Iraq wars, and while constantly mutating and paralleled by identity fragmentation, supra-state identities remain powerful in MENA, indeed, strong enough to prevent the emergence of a classical nation-state system in which territorial states correspond to a distinct and exclusive identity. Supra-state identities are kept alive, periodically inflamed by the residues of imperialism, the conflict with Israel and recurrent Western interventions, especially the two Iraq wars. In showing that the regional inter-state system is embedded in a powerful overarching supra-state regional public space, and that the individual regional states are penetrated by trans-state identity movements – both of which affect state behaviour – constructivism exposes a dimension of regional politics missing from realism.

Constructivism, however, struggles to explain why some norms and identities triumph over others. It apparently sees this as a function of the persuasive power of the discourses wielded by rival identity entrepreneurs and discourse is, indeed, the focus of analysis by

constructivist scholars. But why are some discourses more persuasive than others? Nor can constructivists readily explain why the
existence of the most powerful shared super-state identities that
exist in any region have failed to generate durable co-operative
behaviour; rather, identities increasingly became, in the period of
state consolidation, tools of states rather than constraints on them
and, especially after the Arab Uprising, spurs to conflict. Why is
the outcome of actors' interaction norm fragmentation instead of
normative consensus? Whether enmity or amity, Hobbesian or
Kantian, how anarchy is constructed largely depends, in constructivism, on agents' volition.

Yet variations in anarchy are not purely a matter of agency but
depend also on the material structural conditions in which agency
is undertaken, with some more conducive to Hobbesian kinds of
anarchy and some to diluting anarchy. In a Westphalian system,
states reproduce security dilemmas, in MENA much intensified
by the way irredentism was built into the regional system at its
founding through the arbitrary imposition of territorial boundaries
that tended to frustrate rather than satisfy identities, left stateless
nations (Palestinians, Kurds) bound to be irredentist, and created
artificial states with many warring sub-state identities (Lebanon,
Iraq). Structuralism's analysis of the impact of imperialism in
MENA explains the origin of the scenarios constructivism attributes to regional agency.

Conversely, liberalism shows how Hobbesian anarchy can be
diluted by trans-state economic ties among states, generating
shared material interests, notably from the economic interdependencies typical of market capitalism (Keohane and Nye 1977). If,
therefore, trans-state identities have failed to engender co-operation
in MENA, it is in good part because the imposition of the states
system snapped trans-state economic ties and reoriented them to
the Western core, as in Galtung's (1971) structuralist narrative;
subsequently, petrodollars tied the oil monarchies to the West
rather than the regional economy. As such, Pan-Arab norms had
no underlying material infrastructure.

Moreover, the balance between states' interests and supra-
state identity is not constant but *varies with material conditions*:
thus, in the 1980s oil rent, used to co-opt populations and inflate
bureaucratic and security apparatuses, made states less permeable by trans-state movements while in the 1990s rent decline and

enhanced communication technology (satellite TV) again made states permeable.

Thus, if realism exaggerates the constraints of material structure, constructivism exaggerates agency, especially in the Middle East where the system was imposed and is defended by superior global power from without, to which regional actors either submit or revolt. Thus, constructivism makes a mistake realism and structuralism would never do: it ignores that agency, dependent on material capabilities, is very unequally distributed: global hegemons may have considerable agency to make anarchy as they will, but weak states of the periphery are caught in a system largely created by others.

Because realism and constructivism are two complementary (material and ideational) sides of the same coin, bringing them together has seemed a promising way to redress the one-sidedness of each. Thus, Buzan and Weaver's (2003) study of regions defined them in terms of both a realist distribution of power among states and *also* patterns of enmity and amity among them. The English School also bridges the two traditions. In its original form, pioneered by Bull (1995), it saw 'International Society' as constituted by norms, but the dominant norms were 'realist' – sovereignty, nationalism and power balancing; the balance of power itself was not a mechanical tendency, as neo-realism sometimes implies, but an *institution* that leaders were socialised into following, a view close to classical realism. Importantly, however, norms were operative only when they were *congruent with material conditions*: thus power balancing required hard power assets and a realist system in MENA required consolidated states with military capabilities. Sovereignty, the norm most compatible with the equal autonomy of all states, was most observed when a material *power balance* obstructed global hegemony and MENA states' actual sovereignty varied inversely with the level of hegemonic penetration of the region. Later versions of international society identified (and advocated) counter-norms qualifying sovereignty, such as humanitarian intervention, that were empowered by material globalisation and, in MENA, increased hegemonic penetration.

International Society (IS) is also more history- and region-sensitive than realism and constructivism. First, it shows how the 'Third World' was historically constituted via the export of Westphalian norms from the core to the periphery, where, ironically, sovereignty and nationalism were embraced by late developers as tools against imperialism (Bull and Watson 1984). Only its intimate link to material power adequately explained the outcome of the normative battle between imperialism and nationalism in MENA: nationalism's capacity to mobilise mass resistance is what made imperialism too costly to be profitable and, thus, sovereignty realisable.

Additionally, IS applied to the Middle East by Buzan and Gonzalez-Palaez (2009) showed that the particular mix of norms and institutions is *region-specific*, with the Middle East having its own distinctive *regional society*. Its main feature, the normative conflict of sovereignty and Arabism, was linked to material conditions, with the former more comparable with a multipolar regional power balance and the latter requiring a regional hegemon.

Thus, IS occupies a middle ground between neo-realism and constructivism, more amenable to agency by norm entrepreneurship than realism but more cognisant than constructivism that norms can only endure when congruent with material power, and more sensitive to history than either of them. However, IS still tends to be static, very good at providing snapshots of the system at various points, sensitising us to whether norms/identity and material power/ interests are congruent, hence stable or not, but still neglecting the *deep structures* that determine normative change and continuity.

Structuralism: variations in systemic anarchy II: the impact of hierarchy

Historical sociology (Hobson and Sharman 2005) has argued that the contemporary states system mixes elements of anarchy and hierarchy and this is clearly the case in the Middle East where a regional anarchy is incorporated into a global hierarchy. It is the varieties of Marxist-inspired 'structuralism', including World Systems theory (Wallerstein 1974), Dependency theory (Alnasrawi 1991; Galtung 1971) and neo-Gramscianism (Cox and Sinclair 1996), that best captures this further dimension of MENA IR. This tradition is the only one that sees world politics from the point of view of the periphery and explains the phenomenon of imperialism. It is essential to explain key features of regional politics that other approaches take for granted, namely how the region was subordinated to imperialism, its special vulnerability to Hobbesian forms of anarchy and the sustained core penetration of the region that tends to hollow out the sovereignty that regional states theoretically enjoy.

For structuralism, imperialism originates in uneven capitalist development, in which the early capitalist developers acquired increased appetites for markets, raw materials, cheap labour and investment outlets, and the material (military) capacity to forcefully open up and reshape the non-Western world, reducing it to a primary-product exporting periphery of the global core. In imposing a Western-style states system on the region after World War I, fragmenting the Ottoman area regional market, snapping regional economic interdependencies and subordinating the economies of the individual states to the core powers, imperialism economically consigned MENA to underdevelopment. Agency for this project was spearheaded by a hegemonic state, initially the UK, with the French junior partners in MENA, both heading the world's greatest maritime empires; they were later superseded by the US hegemon which created an informal empire of client elites, treaties, bases and intervention.

The vulnerability of the region to Hobbesian versions of anarchy is difficult to explain without an appreciation of imperialism's fragmentation of the region into a multitude of weak states, creation of a colonial settler state, Israel, in their midst, and imposition of arbitrary borders that generated multiple occasions of inter- and intrastate conflicts, while leaving two peoples, Kurds and Palestinians, stateless and imbued with irredentism. This is also a main origin of the identity conflicts in the region: not only are enduring enmities rooted in it, but the frustration by arbitrary border drawing of larger pre-existing or emergent identities, such as Arabism, Pan-Islam and Pan-Syrianism, explains much of the regional revisionism that has inspired bids for hegemony. Imperialism, in creating artificial states, when the identity of most people remained with bigger or smaller units, also afflicted the states with legitimacy deficits that made them insecure within and dependent on great power protection. The security dilemma inherent in anarchy was also greatly exaggerated by the creation of buffer states (Jordan) or mini/city states around oil wells (Gulf states) attracting the envy or exciting the revisionism of contiguous more powerful neighbours. Unable or unwilling to ensure their own security through self-help and threatened both from within and without, such states naturally sought protection by omni-balancing with a global patron.

Moreover, as Lustik (1997) argued, Western intervention systematically defended such unviable or artificial states (whether Lebanon, Jordan or Kuwait) from absorption by larger regional powers, thus preventing the emergence of a Middle East great power, which, as he argues, would constitute an 'oil hegemon' threatening Western control of MENA's concentrated hydrocarbons. The very possibility of omni-balancing and systematic intervention by Western hegemons presupposes a global hierarchy consistent with Galtung's feudal-like system in which periphery states are strongly linked to the core but set against each other, facilitating divide and rule of the region; and in which the core hegemon is the natural patron of client regimes (and policeman against revisionist ones). While in some parts of the post-colonial world, Western intervention has been muted over time, in the Middle East, penetration has actually *increased* over several decades, with the combination of oil, Israel and instability being unique magnets.

In the structuralist narrative, subordination naturally provokes resistance and this is certainly so of the Middle East where it has been paralleled by recurring anti-imperialist resistance movements championing Arabism and political Islam, which have given rise to revisionist states seeking to challenge the region's place in the periphery. Hence also the persisting drive of the global hegemon to co-opt the regional clients it needs to help control the region. It is this dynamic, observed but inadequately explained by realism, that underlies the struggles for regional hegemony between revisionist regional aspirant hegemons seeking to throw off the control of the global hegemons and the counter-interventions of the latter to head off these challenges and preserve the core's global control over regional hydrocarbons.

No more than anarchy is hierarchy a static structure and, indeed, the relative subordination of regions to the global core varies. Structuralism's version of hegemonic stability theory sees such variations resulting from cycles in the role of the hegemon in the capitalist world economy; hegemony is based on the economic supremacy of the hegemonic state, particularly as a centre of finance capital and in playing the key role of penetrating and opening up the non-capitalist world to such capital; but imperial overreach and the diffusion of technology, together with defensive modernisation, nationalism and resistance to imperialism in periphery states, tends, over time, to raise the economic costs of hegemony, undermining the hegemon's economic dominance, forcing a geopolitical retreat, and paving the way, after an interregnum, for the rise of a new hegemon. The decline of the UK and its withdrawal from MENA ushered in an interregnum – the Cold War – in which the emerging new US hegemon and the Soviet counter-hegemon contested for the region, in the process sufficiently checking each other's power projection that regional powers achieved some regional autonomy. This, in overlapping with Nasser's ability to deploy the power of Arabism to enforce exceptional regional unity, diluted the power of the global hierarchy over the region. While the subordination of the region in the global hierarchy is a function of the 'normal' situation described by Galtung – relative unity of the core and fragmentation of the periphery – under bi-polarity the situation was briefly reversed, with consequences for regional politics. Even after Pan-Arabism declined, bi-polar rivalry, issuing in growing delivery of arms and aid to regional states by their Cold War patrons, contributed to state consolidation and militarism, pushing a certain Westphalianisation of the states system. This regional experience suggests that structuralism would profit from appreciating how the realist variable of global *polarity* affects the *extent* of core hierarchy over the periphery.

However, even before the end of the Cold War, the US hegemon was actively attempting to reassert hegemony over the region, in particular because control of its concentrated oil reserves was crucial to world hegemony. US success, particularly in reinforcing an alliance with Saudi Arabia, the swing producer on the global oil market and in establishing a re-cycling of petrodollars from the Gulf to its financial institutions, was the key to reviving Washington's economic hegemony: empowering its use of globalised finance capital to assert dominance over the periphery and head off challenges in the core to its economic hegemony, from, for example, Europe and Japan. The fall of the USSR further empowered the US reach for hegemony, with the 1990 Gulf war against Iraq sealing US global and regional hegemony and re-invigorating hierarchy. Under a unipolar world, in which US penetration of the Middle East was unchecked, regional states had far fewer options and bandwagoning/omni-balancing became the modal state strategy, returning the region to something akin to its pre-World War II subordination to British hegemony. Filling the vacuum left by states' submission to the West was the rise of trans-state Islamic resistance (including 'terrorism') to Western penetration.

Structuralism alone helps us to appreciate the forces that constructed the core–periphery system in which the region is embedded. Also, it shows us why the security strategies of regional states have tended to divide between omni-balancing and reverse omni-balancing – using nationalist mobilisation against imperialism to get domestic legitimacy – rather than the self-help power balancing realism expects to be the modal behaviour. It provides some insights into how, over time, the region has shifted, as a whole, from omni-balancing (before Nasser) to its reverse (under Nasser) and back (after the defeat of Saddam) in parallel to the rise and decline of bi-polarity at the global level.

However, it is Cox and Sinclair's (1996) neo-Gramscian paradigm that explains *variations among regional states* in their choice of omni-balancing or reverse omni-balancing: the composition of the ruling coalition (plebeian or privileged in origin) is decisive, with regional states' ruling coalitions dividing historically in their origins between those implanted or co-opted by imperialism – the status quo omni-balancers – and those that came to power in revolts against imperialism's clients – the revisionist reverse omni-balancers. Similar factors explain, too, where such revolts happen: in those where the impact of imperialism was most prolonged or damaging, notably frustrating identity by boundary drawing and creating landed oligarchies, which generated dissatisfied peasantries and middle classes that became the constituents of social revolutionary nationalist movements (Iraq, Syria). By contrast, where imperialism was light-touch and left tribal structures in place, conservative pro-Western monarchies were more likely to survive (the Gulf).

However, structuralism, in neglecting state formation, does not explain why the region moved from a weak pre-Westphalian system toward a realist-like Westphalian system of relatively consolidated states before regressing again into a region of weak states: this is the domain of historical sociology.

Historical sociology

Critics of realism have effectively demonstrated that the realist world describes a historically specific situation that emerged in the early modern West, hence that, insofar as neo-realism universalises its model in time and space, it is ahistorical. Taking the international system for granted as a universal constant, realists do not bother to explain its origins, its variation or its evolution, how it was constructed and its long-term historical transformations.

Historical sociology, while accepting key elements of the realist narrative, has shown how the nation-state and inter-state anarchy in its starkest form was historically constructed. Ruggie (1983), attacking the ahistorical character of realism, showed that in the medieval period supra-state identities (Christianity) and hierarchies (Pope, Roman emperor) as well as sub-state ones (city states, tribes) constrained states. Tilly (1975) showed how the West's Westphalian states system was a product of war and capitalism, with the construction of Weberian rational-legal bureaucracies and mass nationalism, hence nation-state formation, driven by the competitive dynamic of realist inter-state competition; this realist dynamic only fully holds to the extent that a Westphalian states system is consolidated, namely, one in which states have the cohesion and capabilities to threaten each other and throw off the authority of trans-state norms or supra-state hierarchies. The story is carried forward by the argument that in the post-Cold War period, the world is divided into a core and periphery: in a West-centred 'zone of peace' (Goldgeier and McFaul 1992; Singer and Wildavsky 1996) liberal norms, economic interdependence and globalisation have led to a sharing of jurisdictions between states and supra-state institutions constituting a 'new medievalism' (Friedrichs 2001); while the 'export' of Westphalian states capable of waging war has displaced the 'zone of war' to the periphery. This is congruent with the argument of Buzan and Weaver (2003) that realist states systems are composed of 'modern' states, as distinguished from 'pre-modern' ones (in which weak states lack the military capacity to threaten each other) and post-modern ones (wherein nationalism is diluted by new supra-state identities).

The Middle East states system's origin is quite historically specific. It was born in a 'pre-Westphalian' region with a universalistic empire and religion and a heterogeneous mosaic of sub/trans-state communities similar to medieval Europe. This neo-medievalism remains relevant to the Middle East since states remain constrained by supra-state identity and the global hierarchy. As Ayoub has pointed out, the 'defensive modernisation' of late developers, by which they sought to overcome their severe power disadvantage in a world dominated by early developers in the core, has been very uneven, with many states still suffering from both internal opposition and dependency on the core. This state weakness has been facilitated by MENA's unique hydrocarbon-fuelled rentierism that allows many states, particularly the monarchies, to avoid Westphalian state-building, eschewing tax-extraction bureaucracies and substituting Western protection for nationalism and mass conscription armies. Moreover, even where 'stronger' states were relatively consolidated, it was not via Weberian legal-rational rule but rather *neo-patrimonialism*, mixing elements of pre-modern patrimonial leadership based on personal loyalties, *asabiyya* (group solidarity) and clientelism, with centralising modern bureaucracy and also reinforced by rentierism (Bank and Richter 2010); however, while not wholly overcoming internal vulnerabilities, this formula, when employed in the region's large population states, such as Iran, Iraq, Egypt and Syria, forged states sufficiently Westphalian to help construct a zone of war. The Middle East therefore arguably has features of *both* neo-medieval and Westphalian states systems.

The uneven and incomplete consolidation of states in the region means, therefore, that the neo-medieval scenario still holds, with the states embedded in a multiple layered system – global, regional, trans-state and domestic, with which they 'share' power. However, the *relative weight*s of the different levels of the system have *varied over time*, and with them the kind of states and state systems. The level of state strength has varied according to a bell-shaped curve of rise and decline, in which the greater the level of state consolidation, the less penetrated and vulnerable both states and state system have been to pressure from the other – global, trans-/supra-state and domestic – levels and the more the Westphalian realist model (and the less neo-medievalism) has been approximated. The rise and fall of Westphalian states corresponded to alterations at the domestic level, with the evolution in ruling coalitions from old oligarchies to populist inclusionary (nationalist-statist) regimes associated with state consolidation; while the move toward post-populist exclusionary ones was paralleled by an erosion in state consolidation, ending in the Arab Uprising that threw many states back to their pre-consolidation starting points. At the global level, a contraction of Western hegemony corresponded to increased state-ness and sovereignty and its expansion with their decline; at the trans-state level the rise, decline and rise again of supra-/trans-state movements was inversely related to state consolidation.

These factors intervene between the logic of anarchy, state foreign policies and the outcomes of the power struggle. Thus, variations in the *states system* corresponded to variations in the chief *determinants* of state behaviour. *Identity* was most important in the period of Pan-Arab hegemony (1950s–1960s) and global bi-polarity, with Egypt, the strongest state, constructed via populist revolution against the landed oligarchy, exporting its revolution to mostly weak Arab oligarchies which, for a period, bandwagoned with Cairo under the pressures of trans-state Arab identity movements, enabling Nasser's formation of a regional coalition to balance against external (Western) interference. However, as Egypt's hegemony sparked balancing against it, the Arab coalition declined, although briefly reconstructed as Israeli power became more threatening after 1967, with the most effective Pan-Arab alliance formed to fight the 1973 war (and pursue the potential peace) reflective of the combined weight of identity and security in Arab state foreign policy calculations.

The 1980s marked a low point of Arabism, as the US clientelisation of Egypt and Saudi Arabia and the Iran–Iraq war fragmented the Arab world; in parallel, rent-enabled consolidation and militarisation of states, accompanied by rising inter-state threats, drove an eclipse of Arab identity as a foreign policy determinant by *security*, resulting in realist power *balancing* among regional states. The predominantly symbolic contestation of the Pan-Arab period was eclipsed by increased militarisation and war, with norms tilting from Arabism toward sovereignty; even in this period, however, identity continued to shape the *perception* of threat, reflected in Arab alliances to counter the threats from Israel and Iran, although some regional alliances also cut across identity fault-lines, driven by realist geopolitics, notably the counter-balancing Syrian–Iranian and Turkey–Israeli alliances which blocked Israeli and Iraqi bids for regional hegemony.

Subsequently, the movement of the international system away from bi-polarity and the socio-economic weakening of Arab regimes revived dependencies not seen since before Nasser, and, together with the destruction of Iraqi power in two wars, ended in US hegemony over the region. *Dependency* drove bandwagoning with the US by most of the Arab states in order to balance against more proximate 'interrelated' threats (from trans-state identity movements supported by regional rivals); bandwagoning was over-determined by both realist threats and dependency. Then, in the mid-2000s, US hegemony overreached itself and also stimulated counterbalancing, notably by Syria, Iran (and partly Turkey) in alliance with trans-state movements. Finally, with the Arab Uprising, a relative deconstruction of states, and the increased power of sub- and trans-state movements relative to the state, led to paralysis of foreign policy in most of the Arab republics and a regional power struggle via trans-state discourses and penetration of the republics by the relatively empowered Arab monarchies and non-Arab states.

The states and the states system have, as HS argues, co-constituted each other: state consolidation has depended, to a great extent, on globally provided resources – arms, rent – while the *level of state consolidation* has determined the dominant foreign policy determinants, hence the dynamics of the region. In periods of state consolidation, classic realist balancing was pervasive. In periods of state weakness omni-balancing dominated but whether it was with a great power patron to counter domestic opposition *or* 'reverse omni-balancing' with regional trans-state movements to counter global penetration depended on the inversely related power of these two levels: the former behaviour dominated when external penetration and clientelisation of regional states by a global hegemon were maximised (as in 1990–2010); the latter when this was minimalised but also when unconsolidated states remained permeable to trans-state penetration (as in 1950–70).

Foreign policy analysis: determinants and process

The foreign policy of any given state is the product of an *interaction* between the system-level and internal processes. The system-level cannot therefore predict or explain foreign policy behaviour, especially because the *different* levels of the system tend to push states in opposing directions. Indeed, state foreign policies – behaviour – can be seen as efforts to negotiate these ever changing levels, typically with the aim of accessing *resources* at one level to cope with *threats* or pursue *ambitions* at another.

The foreign policy *orientations* of MENA states toward the system have historically fallen along a continuum between *revisionist* and *status quo* poles. At one end, recurring bids for hegemony have been made by the larger states with sufficient material and soft power resources, facilitated by bi-polarity, and in the wake of revolutions that brought to power ruling coalitions led by nationalist middle-class elements – army officers and secular or religious intellectuals – with plebeian (peasant, worker) constituencies; they assume a foreign policy role championing supra-state identity (Arabism, Islam) against 'imperialism'. At the other pole are status quo states, weaker in territory and population, with ruling coalitions led by client elites with 'pre-national' tribal constituencies co-opted via hydrocarbon rent which seek to construct state-centric identities and omni-balance with the hegemon. Between these two extremes, there are many intermediate possibilities wherein defensive realist strategies are most likely to dominate.

Whatever a state's general orientation, only by opening the 'black box' of decision-making, in the tradition of foreign policy analysis, can we understanding specific decisions. Decisions will reflect the way regime structures distribute power in the policy process, determining the roles of leadership, 'bureaucratic politics', interest group pressures and public opinion. The rise and decline of the role of the military (leading statist-nationalist coalitions) and the opposing tangent of economic – landed or trading – interests (internationalist coalitions) has biased regimes' policy processes in opposing directions. In a region under authoritarian governance, the roles of individual leaders have been particularly salient, with the impact left by the contrasting personalities of Nasser and Sadat or Hafiz al-Asad and Saddam Hussein exposing the considerable scope for such agency.

Particularly important for *outcomes* – the regional balance of power – are states' *alliance choices*, which vary depending on where decision-makers see the location of threats and resources. Such perceptions have varied according to such factors as global polarity (determining e.g. availability of resources) and level of regime consolidation (are threats within managed?), filtered through the prism of identity (which defines allies or enemies). However, identity itself – as it shapes foreign policy *role* – while normally reflecting external factors such as geopolitical position and interactions with other states, is contested and constructed internally, with dominant interpretations normally reflecting the interests of the ruling coalition.

Conclusion

The encounter of the Middle East with IR theory clearly exposes the virtues of eclecticism. Each theory surveyed, operating on a different level or focusing on a different aspect of IR, makes a contribution to understanding the region. The multiple and ever changing layers of the system and the great variance in the states cannot be captured without a synthetic multivariate approach that tries to maximise the compatibilities between rival theories. While this means we must deal with many 'moving parts', ignoring any of them for the sake of parsimony only sacrifices explanatory power. The Middle East is not so exceptional that this approach cannot be transferred to the study of international politics elsewhere. It arguably lends weight to the arguments of those who, dismayed by the sectarianism of the discipline, call for synthetic and complex approaches to the study of international relations (Barkin 2010; Buzan 1993; Sil and Katzenstein 2005).

Bibliography

Aarts, Paul (1994), 'The new oil order: built on sand?', *Arab Studies Quarterly*, 16:2, 1–12.

—— (1999), 'The Middle East: a region without regionalism or the end of exceptionalism?', *Third World Quarterly*, 20:5, 911–925.

Abdalla, Ahmad (1991), 'Mubarak's gamble,' *Middle East Report*, 168, January–February, 18–21.

Abdel-Fadil, Mahmoud (1997), 'Macroeconomic tendencies and policy options in the Arab region,' in Laura Guazzone, ed., *The Middle East in Global Change*, London, Macmillan Press, 119–134.

Abu Khalil, As'ad (1992), 'A new Arab ideology: the rejuvenation of Arab nationalism', *Middle East Journal*, 46:1, 22–37.

Adib-Moghaddam, Arshin (2009), *The International Politics of the Persian Gulf: A Cultural Genealogy*, London, Routledge.

Ahmad, Feroz (1993), *The Making of Modern Turkey*, London, Routledge.

Ajami, Fouad (1977–78), 'Stress in the Arab Triangle,' *Foreign Policy*, 29, 90–108.

—— (1981), *The Arab Predicament: Arab Political Thought and Practice since 1967*, Cambridge, Cambridge University Press.

Allison, Graham and Morton Halperin (1972), 'Bureaucratic politics: a paradigm and some policy implications', *World Politics*, 24 (Supplement), 40–79.

Alnaşrawi, Abbas (1991), *Arab Nationalism, Oil and the Political Economy of Dependency*, New York and London, Greenwood Press.

Altunışık, Meliha (2009), 'Worldviews and Turkish foreign policy in the Middle East,' *New Perspectives on Turkey*, 40, 169–192.

Amin, Samir (1978), *The Arab Nation: Nationalism and Class Struggles*, London, Zed Press.

Anderson, Lisa (1986), *The State and Social Transformation in Tunisia and Libya, 1830–1980*, Princeton, NJ, Princeton University Press.

—— (1987), 'The state in the Middle East and North Africa,' *Comparative Politics*, 20:1, 71–79.

—— (1991), 'Legitimacy, identity and the writing of history in Libya,' in E. Davis and N. Gavrielides, eds, *Statecraft in the Middle East*, Miami, FL, Florida International University Press.

Aronoff, Myron J. and Yael S. Aronoff (1998), 'Domestic determinants of Israeli foreign policy,' in Robert O. Freedman, ed., *The Middle East and the Peace Process: The Impact of the Oslo Accords*, Gainesville, FL, University Press of Florida, 11–34.

Ayoob, Mohammed (1995), *The Third World Security Predicament, State Making, Regional Conflict and the International System*, Boulder, CO, Lynne Rienner Press.

Ayubi, Nazih (1988), 'Arab bureaucracies: expanding size, changing roles,' in A. Dawisha and I. W. Zartman, eds, *Beyond Coercion: The Durability of the Arab State*, London, Croom-Helm, 14–34.

—— (1995), *Overstating the Arab state: Politics and Society in the Middle East*, London, I. B. Taurus.

Ayubi, Shaheen (1994), *Nasser and Sadat: Decision-Making and Foreign Policy, 1970–1972*, University Press of America, Lanham, MD, New York and London.

Bahbah, Bishara (1991), 'The crisis in the Gulf: why Iraq invaded Kuwait,' in Phyllis Bennis and Michel Moushabeck, eds, *Beyond the Storm: A Gulf Crisis Reader*, New York, Olive Branch Press, 50–54.

Bank, Andre and Thomas Richter (2010), 'Neopatrimonialism in the Middle East and North Africa: overview, critique and alternative conceptualization,' presented at the GIGA Workshop, 'Neopatrimonialism in various world regions', Hamburg, 23 August, www.researchgate.net/publication/258325694_Neopatrimonialism_in_the_Middle_East_and_North_Africa_Overview_Critique_and_Alternative_Conceptualization, accessed 7 October 2014.

Barber, Benjamin (1992), 'Jihad v. McWorld,' *Atlantic Monthly*, March, 53–63.

Barkey, Henri (2012), 'Spinoff: the Syrian crisis and the future of Iraq,' *American Interest*, 26 December.

Barkin, J. Samuel (2010), *Realist Constructivism: Rethinking International Relations Theory*, Cambridge and New York, Cambridge University Press.

Barnett, Michael (1993), 'Institutions, roles and disorder: the case of the Arab states system,' *International Studies Quarterly*, 37:3, 271–296.

—— (1995), 'Nationalism, sovereignty, and regional order in the Arab states system,' *International Organization*, 49:3, 479–510.

—— (1996–97), 'Regional security after the Gulf war,' *Political Science Quarterly*, 111:4, 597–617.

—— (1998), *Dialogues in Arab Politics: Negotiations in Regional Order*, New York, Columbia University Press.

Batatu, Hanna (1978), *The Old Social Classes and the Revolutionary Movements of Iraq*, Princeton, NJ, Princeton University Press.

—— (1981), 'Some observations on the social roots of Syria's ruling military group and the causes of its dominance,' *Middle East Journal*, 35:3, 331–344.

—— (1982), 'Syria's Muslim Brethren,' *MERIP Reports*, 110, November–December, 12–20.

Battah, Abdullah and Yehuda Lukas, eds (1988), *The Arab-Israeli Conflict: Two Decades of Change*, Boulder, CO, Westview Press.

Beblawi, Hazem and Giacomo Luciani (1987), *The Rentier State*, London, Croom-Helm.

Berberoglu, Berch (1989), *Power and Stability in the Middle East*, London, Zed Books.

Bina, Cyrus (1993), 'The rhetoric of oil and the dilemma of war and American hegemony,' *Arab Studies Quarterly*, 15:3, 1–20.

Brand, Laurie (1995), *Jordan's Inter-Arab Relations: The Political Economy of Alliance Making*, New York, Columbia University Press.

Brecher, Michael (1972), *The Foreign Policy System of Israel*, London, Oxford University Press.

Brinton, Crane (1938), *An Anatomy of Revolution*, New York: Norton.

Bromley, Simon (1990), *American Hegemony and World Oil: The Industry, the State System and the World Economy*, Oxford, Polity Press.

—— (1994), *Rethinking Middle East Politics*, Oxford, Polity Press.

Brown, L. Carl (1984), *International Politics and the Middle East: Old Rules, Dangerous Game*, Princeton, NJ, Princeton University Press.

—— (1988), 'The June 1967 war: a turning point?' in Yehuda Lukas and Abdalla M. Battah, eds, *The Arab-Israeli Conflict*, Boulder, CO, Westview Press, 133–146.

——, ed. (2001), *Diplomacy in the Middle East: The International Relations of Regional and Outside Powers*, London and New York, I. B. Tauris.

Bull, Hedley (1995), *The Anarchical Society: A Study of Order in World Politics*, 2nd edn, London, Macmillan.

Bull, Hedley and Adam Watson (1984), *The Expansion of International Society*, Oxford, Clarendon Press.

Buzan, Barry (1991), 'New patterns of global security in the twenty-first century,' *International Affairs*, 67:3, 246–247.

Buzan, Barry (1993), 'From international system to international society: structural realism and regime theory meet the English School,' *International Organization*, 47: 3, 327–352.

Buzan, Barry and Ole Weaver (2003), *Regions and Powers: The Structure of International Security*, Cambridge, Cambridge University Press.

Barry Buzan and Ana Gonzales-Palaez, ed. (2009), *International Society and the Middle East: English School Theory at the Regional Level*, New York and Basingstoke, Palgrave-Macmillan.

Calabrese, John (1994), *Revolutionary Horizons: Regional Foreign Policy in Post-Khomeini Iran*, New York and London, St Martins/Macmillan.

Callinicos, Alex (2009), *Imperialism and Global Political Economy*, Cambridge, Polity Press.

Calvert, Peter (1986), *The Foreign Policies of New States*, Sussex: Wheatsheaf Books.

Cantori, Louis J. and Steven L. Spiegel (1970), *The International Politics of Regions: A Comparative Approach*, Englewood Cliffs, NJ, Prentice Hall, 192–207.

Carley, Patricia (1995), *Turkey's Role in the Middle East*, Washington, DC, US Institute of Peace.

Chatelus, Michel (1993), 'From the mirage of rent to the burden of debt: adjustment and insecurity in Arab economies,' in B. Korany, P. Noble and R. Brynen, eds, *The Many Faces of National Security in the Middle East*, New York, Macmillan, 145–168.

Chaudhry, Kiren Aziz (1991), 'On the way to the market: economic liberalization and Iraq's invasion,' *Middle East Report*, 170, May–June, 14–23.

—— (1997), *The Price of Wealth*, Ithaca, NY, Cornell University Press.

Chubin, Shahram (1994), *Iran's National Security Policy, Capabilities, Intentions, Impact*, Washington, DC, Carnegie Endowment for International Peace.

Clapham, Christopher (1977), *Foreign Policymaking in Developing States*, Saxon House Westmead, Farnborough.

Clawson, Patrick (1989), *Unaffordable Ambitions: Syria's Military Buildup and Economic Crisis*, Washington, DC, Washington Institute for Near East Policy.

Cobban, Helena (1991), *The Superpowers and the Syrian–Israeli Conflict*, New York, Praeger, Washington Papers, no. 149.

Cordesman, Anthony H. (1984), *The Gulf and the Search for Strategic Stability*, Boulder, CO and London, Westview Press and Mansell Publishing.

—— (2005), *Iraq's Evolving Insurgency*, Washington, DC, Center for Strategic Studies, 23 June.

Cottam, Richard (1979), *Nationalism in Iran*, Pittsburgh, PA, University of Pittsburgh Press.

Cox, Richard with Timothy Sinclair (1996), *Approaches to World Order*, Cambridge, Cambridge University Press.

Cremeans, Charles (1963), *The Arabs and the World: Nasser's Arab Nationalist Policy*, New York, Praeger.

Crystal, Jill (1991), *Oil and Politics in the Gulf: Rulers and Merchants in Kuwait and Qatar*, New York and London, Cambridge University Press.

David, Steven (1991), 'Explaining Third World alignment,' *World Politics*, 43:2, 233–256.

Darnovsky, Marcy, L. A. Kauffman and Billy Robinson (1991), 'Warring stories: reading and contesting the New Order,' *Socialist Review*, 91:1.

Dawisha, Adeed (1976), *Egypt in the Arab World: The Elements of Foreign Policy*, New York, Wiley.

—— (1978a), 'Syria under Asad, 1970–1978: the centres of power,' *Government and Opposition*, 13:3, 341–354.

—— (1978b), 'Syria's intervention in Lebanon, 1975–1976,' *Jerusalem Journal of International Relations*, 3:2–3, 245–264.

—— (1979), *Saudi Arabia's Search for Security*, International Institute for Strategic Studies, London, Adelphi Papers, no. 158.

—— (1990), 'Arab regimes: legitimacy and foreign policy,' in Giacomo Luciani, ed., *The Arab State*, London, Routledge, 284–299.

Dawisha, Adeed and I. William Zartman (1988), *Beyond Coercion: The Durability of the Arab State*, London, Croom-Helm.

Dekmejian, R. Hrair (1971), *Egypt under Nasir: A Study in Political Dynamics*, Albany, State University of New York Press, 1, 105–108.

Dergham, Raghida (2012), 'Dangerous Upcoming Year After the Arab Spring,' *al-Arabiya*, 1 January, http://english.alarabiya.net/views/2012/01/01/185692.html?PHPSESSID=tf100ia5sumf4g26s3kc76b9u4, accessed 9 June 2012.

Dessouki, Ali ad-Din Hillal (1982), 'The new Arab political order: implications for the eighties,' in Malcolm Kerr and El Sayed Yassin, eds,

Rich and Poor States in the Middle East, Boulder, CO, Westview Press, 319–347.

—— (1991), 'The primacy of economics: the foreign policy of Egypt,' in Bahgat Korany and Ali E. Hillal Dessouki, eds, *The Foreign Policies of Arab States: The Challenge of Change*, Boulder, CO, Westview Press, 156–185.

Devlin, John (1976), *The Ba`th Party: A History from Its Origins to 1966*, Stanford, CA, Hoover Institution Press.

—— (1992), 'Leadership style and oil policy: Syria and Iraq,' *Energy Policy*, November, 1048–1054.

Diab, Zuheir (1994), 'Have Syria and Israel opted for peace?,' *Middle East Policy*, 3:2, 77–90.

Dorraj, Manochehr (1993), 'Will OPEC survive?', *Arab Studies Quarterly*, 15:4, 19–32.

Dodge, Toby (2006), 'War and resistance in Iraq: from regime change to collapsed state,' in Fawn and Hinnebusch, *The Iraq War*, 211–224.

Doyle, Michael (1995), 'On the democratic peace,' *International Security*, 19:4, 164–175.

Drysdale, Alasdair (1979), 'Ethnicity in the Syrian officer corps: a conceptualization,' *Civilisations*, 29:3–4, 359–373.

Ehteshami, Anoushiravan (1995), *After Khomeini: The Iranian Second Republic*, London, Routledge.

—— (1997), 'Security structures in the Middle East: an overview,' in ed. Haifaa Jawad, *The Middle East in the New World Order*, London, Macmillan, 97–109.

—— (2007), *Globalization and Geopolitics in the Middle East*, London, Routledge.

Ehteshami, Anoushiravan and Hinnebusch, Raymond A. (1997), *Syria and Iran: Middle Powers in a Penetrated Regional System*, London, Routledge.

Eickelman, Dale F. (1998), 'From here to modernity: Ernest Gellner on nationalism and Islamic fundamentalism,' in John A. Hall, ed., *The State of the Nation: Ernest Gellner and the Theory of Nationalism*, Cambridge, Cambridge University Press, 258–271.

El-Shazly, Nadia and Raymond Hinnebusch (2001), 'The challenge of security in the post-Gulf war "Middle East System"', in Raymond Hinnebusch and Anoushiravan Ehteshami, eds, *The Foreign Policies of Middle East States*, Boulder, CO, Lynne Rienner Press, 71–90.

Evron, Yair (1973), *Nations, Superpowers and Wars*, London, Elek Books.

—— (1987), *War and Intervention in Lebanon: The Syrian–Israeli Deterrence Dialogue*, Baltimore, MD, Johns Hopkins University Press.

Fahmy, Ismail (1983), *Negotiating for Peace in the Middle East*, MD, Baltimore, Johns Hopkins University Press.

Faksh, M. (1993), 'Withered Arab nationalism', *Orbis*, 37:7, 425–438.

Faour, Muhammed (1993), *The Arab World after Desert Storm*, Washington, DC, US Institute of Peace Press.

Farah, Tawfiq and Feisal Salam (1980), 'Group affiliations of children in the Arab Middle East (Kuwait),' *Journal of Social Psychology*, 111.

Farsoun, Samih (1991), 'A new balance of forces,' *Middle East Report*, 168, January–February.

Farsoun, Samih & Christina Zacharia (1995), 'Class, economic change, and political liberalization in the Arab World,' in Rex Brynen, Bahgat Korany and Paul Noble, eds, *Political Liberalization and Democratization in the Arab World*, vol. 1, Boulder, CO, Lynne Rienner Press, 261–280.

Fawn, Rick and Raymond Hinnebusch (2006), *The Iraq War: Causes and Consequences*, Boulder CO, Lynne Rienner Publishers.

Frankel, Glenn (1991), 'Lines in the sand,' in Micah Sifry and Christopher Cerf, eds, *The Gulf War Reader*, New York, Times Books, 16–29.

Friedrichs, Jörg (2001), 'The meaning of New Medievalism,' *European Journal of International Relations*, 7: 4, 475–501.

Fromkin, David (1989), *A Peace to End All Peace: Creating the Modern Middle East: 1914–1922*, London and New York, Penguin Press.

Fuller, Graham (1997), 'Turkey and the Middle East northern tier,' in Laura Guazzone, ed., *The Middle East in Global Change*, London, Macmillan, 43–57.

Furia, P. and Lucas, R. (2006), 'Determinants of Arab public opinion on foreign relations', *International Studies Quarterly*, 50:3, 585–605.

Galtung, Johan (1971), 'A structural theory of imperialism,' *Journal of Peace Research*, 8:2, 81–98.

Gause, F. Gregory III (1991), 'Revolutionary fevers and regional contagion: domestic structures and the export of revolution in the Middle East,' *Journal of South Asian & Middle East Studies*, 14:3, 1–23.

—— (1992), 'Sovereignty, statecraft and stability in the Middle East,' *Journal of International Affairs*, 45:2, 441–467.

—— (1994), *Oil Monarchies: Domestic and Security Challenges in the Arab Gulf States*, New York, Council on Foreign Relations Press.

—— (1997), 'Arms supplies and military spending in the Gulf,' *Middle East Report*, 204, July–September, 12–14.

—— (2010), *The International Relations of the Persian Gulf*, Cambridge and New York, Cambridge University Press.

George, David (1996), 'Pax-Islamica: an alternative New World Order?', in A. Sidahmad and A. Ehteshami, eds, *Islamic Fundamentalism*, Boulder, CO, Westview Press, 71–90.

Gerges, Fawaz (1994), *The Superpowers and the Middle East: Regional and International politics, 1955–1967*, Boulder, CO, Westview Press.

Gerner, Deborah (1991), *One Land, Two Peoples: The Conflict over Palestine*, Boulder, CO, Westview Press.

Ghali, Boutrus Boutrus (1963), 'The foreign policy of Egypt,' in J. E. Black and K. W. Thompson, eds, *Foreign Policy in a World of Change*, New York, Harper and Row.

Ghribi, Asma (2014), 'What Tunisians miss about Ben Ali,' *Transitions*, 14 January, http://transitions.foreignpolicy.com/posts/2014/01/17/what_tunisians_ miss_about_ben_ali, accessed February 2014.

Gilpin, Robert (1982), *War and Change in World Politics*, Cambridge, Cambridge University Press.

Global Research (2012), 'Gulf War Documents: meeting between Saddam Hussein and US Ambassador to Iraq April Glaspie', 30 June, www.global research.ca/gulf-war-documents-meeting-between-saddam-hussein-and-ambassador-to-iraq-april-glaspie/31145, accessed 11 October 2014.

Goldgeier, James M. and Michael McFaul (1992), 'A tale of two worlds: core and periphery in the post-Cold War era,' *International Organization*, 46:2, 467–491.

Graham-Brown, Sarah (1999), *Sanctioning Saddam: The Politics of Intervention in Iraq*, London, I. B. Taurus.

Green, Jerrold (1982), *Revolution in Iran: The Politics of Countermobilization*, New York, Praeger Publishers.

Guazzone, Laura (1997), *The Middle East in Global Change: The Politics and Economics of Interdependence versus Fragmentation*, London, Macmillan.

Guerrieri, Paulo (1997), 'Globalism and regionalism in the world economy and the Middle East,' in Laura Guazzone, ed., *The Middle East in Global Change*, London, Macmillan, 153–73.

Hagopian, Elaine (1997), 'Is the peace process a process for peace?: a retrospective analysis of Oslo,' *Arab Studies Quarterly*, 19:3, 1–28.

Halliday, Fred (1988), 'The great powers and the Middle East,' *Middle East Report*, 151, March–April, 3–6.

—— (1991), 'The crisis of the Arab world,' in Micah Sifry and Christopher Cerf, eds, *The Gulf War Reader*, New York, Times Books, 395–401.

—— (1994), *Rethinking International Relations*, London, Macmillan.

—— (1996), *Islam and the Myth of Confrontation*, London and New York, I. B. Taurus.

Halperin, Morton and Priscilla Clapp (2006), *Bureaucratic Politics and Foreign Policy*, Washington, DC, Brookings Institution.

Halpern, Manfred (1963), *The Politics of Social Change in the Middle East and North Africa*, Princeton, NJ, Princeton University Press.

Hanieh, Adam (2011), 'Egypt's orderly transition: international aid and the rush to structural adjustment,' *Jadaliyya*, May 29, www.jadaliyya.com/pages/index/1711/egypts-'orderly-transition'-international-aid, accessed 6 October 2014.

Harik, Iliya (1987), 'The origins of the Arab state system,' in Ghassan Salame, ed., *The Foundations of the Arab State*, London, Croom-Helm.

Harknett, Richard J. and Jeffrey A. VanDenBerg (1997), 'Alignment theory and interrelated threats: Jordan and the Persian Gulf crisis,' *Security Studies*, 6:3, 112–153.

Harrop, William Scott (1991), 'Iran's emerging World Order,' *Middle East Insight* 8:2, 46–49.

Haseeb, Dina and Malek Rouchdy (1991), 'Egypt's speculations in the Gulf crisis: the government's policies and the opposition movements,' in Haim Bresheeth and Nira Yuval-Davis, eds, *The Gulf War and the New World Order*, London, Zed Books, 70–76.

Heikal, Muhammed Hassanein (1975), *The Road to Ramadan*, New York, Reader's Digest Press.

—— (1978a), *The Sphinx and the Commissar: The Rise and Fall of Soviet influence in the Middle East*, London, Collins.

—— (1978b), 'Egyptian foreign policy', *Foreign Affairs*, 56:4, 714–727.

—— (1983), *The Autumn of Fury: The Assassination of Sadat*, London, Corgi Books.

Hetata, Sherif (1991), 'What choice did Egypt have?', in Phillis Bennis and Michel Moushabeck, eds, *Beyond the Storm: A Gulf Crisis Reader*, New York, Olive Branch Press, 241–247.

Hinnebusch, Raymond (1982), 'Children of the elite: political attitudes of the westernized bourgeoisie in contemporary Egypt,' *Middle East Journal*, 36:4, 535–561.

—— (1985), *Egyptian Politics under Sadat*, Cambridge, Cambridge University Press.

—— (1993), 'Revisionist dreams, realist strategies: the foreign policy of Syria,' in Bahgat Korany and Ali E. Hillal Dessouki, eds, *The Foreign Policies of Arab States: The Challenge of Change*, Boulder, CO, Westview Press, 374–409.

—— (1997), 'Syria's role in the Gulf war coalition,' in Andrew Bennett, Joseph Lepgold and Danny Unger, eds, *Friends in Need: Burden Sharing in the Gulf War*, New York, St Martin's Press, 219–240.

—— (2001), *Syria: Revolution from Above*, London, Routledge.

—— (2006), 'Hegemonic stability theory reconsidered,' in Fawn, and Hinnebusch, *The Iraq War*, 283–322.

—— (2007), 'The US invasion of Iraq: explanations and implications,' *Critique: Critical Middle Eastern Studies*, 16:3, 209–228.

—— (2011), 'The Middle East in the world hierarchy: imperialism and resistance', *Journal of International Relations and Development*, 14:2, 213–246.

Hinnebusch, Raymond and Anoushiravan Ehteshami (2001), *The Foreign Policies of Middle East States*, Boulder, CO, Lynne Rienner Publishers.

Hinnebusch, Raymond and Ozlem Tur, eds (2013), *Turkey–Syria Relations: Between Enmity and Amity*, Abington, Ashgate.

Hiro, Dilip (1991a), *The Longest War: The Iran-Iraq Military Conflict*, London and New York, Routledge.

—— (1991b), 'A few of our favorite kings', in Micah Sifry and Christopher Cerf, eds, *The Gulf War Reader*, New York, Times Books, 408–411.

—— (1992), *Desert Shield to Desert Storm: The Second Gulf War*, New York, Routledge.

Hitchins, Christopher (1991), 'Realpolitik in the Gulf', in Micah Sifry and Christopher Cerf, eds, *The Gulf War Reader*, New York, Times Books, 107–118.

Hobson, John and J. C. Sharman (2005), 'The enduring place of hierarchy in world politics: tracing the social logics of hierarchy and political Change,' *European Journal of International Relation*, 11:1, 63–98.

Holsti, Kal (1970), 'National role conception in the study of foreign policy,' *International Studies Quarterly*, 14, 233–309.

Hooglund, Eric (1987a), 'The search for Iran's moderates,' *Middle East Report*, 144, January–February, 5–6.

—— (1987b), 'Iran and the Gulf War,' *Middle East Report*, 148, September–October, 12–18.

—— (1989), 'The Islamic Republic at war and peace,' *Middle East Report*, 156, January–February, 4–12.

Hourani, Albert (1970), *Arabic Thought in the Liberal Age, 1798–1939*, London, Oxford University Press.

Hudson, Michael (1977), *Arab Politics: The Search for Legitimacy*, New Haven, Yale University Press.

—— (1999), *Middle East Dilemmas: The Politics and Economics of Arab Integration*, London and New York, I. B. Taurus.

Hunter, Shireen (1987), 'Islamic Iran and the Arab world,' *Middle East Insight*, 5:3, 17–25.

—— (1988), 'Islam in power: the case of Iran,' in Shireen Hunter, ed., *The Politics of Islamic Revivalism*, Bloomington, IN, Indiana University Press, 265–280.

Huntington, Samuel (1968), *Political Order in Changing Societies*, New Haven, CT, Yale University Press.

—— (1993), 'The clash of civilizations,' *Foreign Affairs*, 72:3, 22–49.

Hussein, Ahmad (1973), *Class Conflict in Egypt, 1945–70*, New York, Monthly Review Press.

Ibrahim, Saad ad-Din (1997), 'From Taliban to Erbakan: the case of Islam,' in Elizabeth Ozdalga and Sune Persson, eds, *Civil Society and Democracy in the Muslim World*, Swedish Research Institute in Istanbul, Transactions, vol. 7, distributed by Curzon Press, 33–44.

Ionides, Michael (1960), *Divide and Lose: The Arab Revolt of 1955–1958*, London, Geoffrey Bles.

Ismael, Jacqueline (1993), *Kuwait: Dependency & Class in a Rentier State*, Gainsville, FL, University Press of Florida.

Ismael, Tareq Y. (1986), *International Relations of the Contemporary Middle East: A Study in World Politics*, Syracuse, NY, Syracuse University Press.

Issawi, Charles (1982), *An Economic History of the Middle East and North Africa*, New York, Columbia University Press.

Joffe, George, ed. (1999), *Perspectives on Development: The Euro-Mediterranean Partnership*, London, Frank Cass.

Johnson, Chalmers (2000), *Blowback: The Costs and Consequences of American Empire*, New York, Henry Holt.

Jones, Clive (2001), 'The foreign policy of Israel' , in Raymond Hinnebusch and Anoushiravan Ehteshami, *The Foreign Policies of Middle East States*, 115–139.

Jourjati, Murhaf (1998), 'Syrian foreign policy: an institutional perspective on why Asad did not emulate Sadat,' Ph.D. dissertation, University of Utah.

Kaldor, Mary (1999), *New and Old Wars: Organized Violence in a Global Era*, Oxford, Polity Press.

Karasapan, Omar (1986), 'Turkey's super-rich,' *Middle East Report*, 142, September–October, 30–34.

Karawan, Ibrahim (1994), 'Sadat and the Egyptian-Israeli peace revisited,' *International Journal of Middle East Studies*, 26:2, 249–266.

Karmi, Ghada (1999), 'A binational state in Palestine,' *Middle East International*, 7 May, 20–22.

Keohane, Robert and Joseph Nye (1977), *Power and Interdependence: World Politics in Transition*, Boston, Little, Brown.

Kerr, Malcolm (1971), *The Arab Cold War: Jamal Abd al-Nasir and His Rivals, 1958–1970*, London, Oxford University Press.

—— (1975), 'Hafiz al-Asad and the changing patterns of Syrian politics,' *International Journal*, 28:4, 689–707.

Keyder, Caglar (1987), *State and Class in Turkey*, London, Verso.

Khadduri, Majid (1970), *Political Trends in the Arab World*, Baltimore, MD, Johns Hopkins University Press.

Khalidi, Walid (1991a), 'Why Some Arabs Support Saddam,' in Micah Sifry and Christopher Cerf, eds, *The Gulf War Reader*, New York, Times Books, 161–171.

—— (1991b), 'Iraq vs. Kuwait: claims and counterclaims,' in Micah Sifry and Christopher Cerf, eds, *The Gulf War Reader*, New York, Times Books.

Khalil, Samir (1989), *The Republic of Fear: The Politics of Modern Iraq*, London, Radius.

Khouri, Rami (1998), 'Tyranny, dependence, power and the rule of law,' *A View from the Arab World*, 29 December, www.dailystar.com.lb/Opinion/Commentry/1998/Oct-29/101612-dependency-and-the-rule-of-law.ashx#axzz3FxN9MYBr, accessed 11 October 2014.

Kienle, Eberhard (1990), *Ba'th vs. Ba'th: The Conflict between Syria and Iraq*, London, I. B. Taurus.

Kimsche, David and Dan Bawly, (1968), *The Sandstorm: The Arab Israeli War of June 1967: Prelude and Aftermath*, New York, Secker and Warburg.

Kirisci, Kemal (1997), 'Post Cold-War Turkish security and the Middle East,' *MERIA Journal*, 2, June, Begin–Sadat Center for Strategic Studies, Bar-Ilan University, www.gloria-center.org/1997/07/kirisci-1997-07-06, accessed 11 October 2014.

Klare, Michael (1991), 'The Pentagon's new paradigm,' in Micah Sifry and Christopher Cerf, eds, *The Gulf War*, New York, Times Books, 466–479.

Knightly, Philip (1991), 'Imperial legacy,' in Micah Sifry and Christopher Cerf, eds, *The Gulf War Reader*, New York, Times Books, 3–15.

Korany, Bahgat (1986), *How Foreign Policy Decisions Are Made in the Third World*, Boulder, CO, Westview Press.

—— (1987), 'Alien and besieged yet here to stay: the contradictions of the Arab territorial state,' in Ghassan Salame, ed., *The Foundations of the Arab State*; London, Croom Helm 1987, 47–74.

—— (1988), 'The dialectics of inter-Arab relations, 1967–1987', in Abdullah Battah and Yehuda Lukas, eds, *The Arab-Israeli Conflict: Two Decades of Change*, Boulder, CO, Westview Press, 164–178.

—— (1997), 'The Old/New Middle East', in Laura Guazzone, *The Middle East in Global Change*, London, Macmillan, 135–149.

Korany, Bahgat and Selma Akbik (1986), 'Decision-making in a non-state actor: OPEC,' in Bahgat Korany, ed., *How Foreign Policy Is Made in the Third World*, Boulder, CO, Westview Press.

Korany, Bahgat and Ali E. Hillal Dessouki, eds (1991), *The Foreign Policies of Arab States: The Challenge of Change*, Boulder, CO, Westview Press.

Korany, Bahgat, Paul Noble and Rex Brynen, eds (1993), *The Many Faces of National Security in the Middle East*, New York, Macmillan.

Kubursi, Atif (1999), 'Prospects for Arab economic integration after Oslo,' in Michael Hudson, ed., *Middle East Dilemmas*, London and New York, I. B. Taurus, 299–319.

Kubursi, Atif and Salim Mansur (1993), 'Oil & the Gulf war: an American century or a "New World Order"?', *Arab Studies Quarterly*, 15:4, 1–18.

Lobell, Steven (2009), 'Threat assessment, the state, and foreign policy: a neoclassical realist model', in Steven Lobell, Norrin M. Ripsman and Jeffrey W. Taliaferro, eds, *Neoclassical Realism, the State and Foreign Policy*, New York and Cambridge, Cambridge University Press, 42–74.

Love, Kenneth (1969), *Suez: The Twice-Fought War*, New York, McGraw-Hill.

Luciani, Giacomo, ed. (1990), *The Arab State*, London, Routledge.

Lustik, Ian (1997), 'The Absence of Middle Eastern great powers: political "backwardness" in historical perspective,' *International Organization*, 51:4, 653–683.

Lynch, Marc (1999), *State Interests and Public Spheres: The International Politics of Jordan's Identity*, New York, Columbia University Press.

Maddy-Weitzman, Bruce (1993), *The Crystallization of the Arab State System, 1945–1954*, Syracuse, NY, Syracuse University Press.

Malley Robert and Hussein Agha (2001), 'Camp David: the tragedy of errors,' *New York Review of Books*, 9 August.

Mansfield, Edward and Jack Snyder (1995), 'The dangers of democratization,' *International Security*, 20:1, 5–38.

Mansfield, Peter (1991), *A History of the Middle East*, London and New York, Penguin Books.

Ma'oz, Moshe (1972), 'Attempts at creating a political community in modern Syria,' *Middle East Journal*, 26:4, 389–404.

—— (1988), *Asad, the Sphinx of Damascus: A Political Biography*, New York, Grove Weidenfeld.

Marr, Phebe (1985), *The Modern History of Iraq*, Boulder, CO, Westview Press.

Mearsheimer John (2001), *The Tragedy of Great Power Politics*, New York, W. W. Norton.

Menashri, David (1990), *Iran: A Decade of War and Revolution*, New York, Holmes & Meier.

Miller, Judith and Laurie Mylroie (1990), *Saddam Hussein and the Crisis in the Gulf*, New York, Times Books.

Moon, Bruce (1995), 'Consensus or compliance? Foreign-policy change and external dependence,' *International Organization*, 39:2, 297–329.

Morgenthan, Hans (1978), *Politics among Nations*, New York, Knopf.

Mufti, Malik (1996), *Sovereign Creations: Pan-Arabism and Political Order in Syria and Iraq*, Ithaca and London, Cornell University Press.

—— (1998), 'Daring and caution in Turkish foreign policy,' *Middle East Journal*, 52:1, 33–50.

Munson, Henry (2006), 'Islamic militancy,' in Fawn and Hinnebusch, *The Iraq War*, 235–246.

Murden, Simon (2002), *Islam, the Middle East, and the New Global Hegemony*, Boulder, CO, Lynne Rienner Publishers.

Murinson, A (2006), 'The strategic depth doctrine of Turkish foreign policy,' *Middle Eastern Studies*, 42:6, 945–964.

Murphy, Emma (1997), 'The Arab-Israeli conflict in the New World Order,' in Haifa Jawad, ed., *The Middle East in the New World Order*, Basingstoke, Macmillan, 110–139.

Nahas, Maridi (1985), 'State systems and revolutionary challenge: Nasser, Khomeini and the Middle East,' *International Journal of Middle East Studies*, 17:4, 507–527.

Niblock, Tim (1990), 'The need for a new Arab order,' *Middle East International*, 12 October, 17–18.

—— (2001), *'Pariah States' and Sanctions in the Middle East: Iraq, Libya, Sudan*, Boulder, CO, Lynne Rienner Press.

Noble, Paul (1991), 'The Arab system: pressures, constraints, and opportunities,' in Bahgat Korany and Ali E. Hillal Dessouki, eds, *The Foreign Policies of Arab States: the Challenge of Change*, Boulder CO, Westview Press, 41–78.

Norton, Augustus R. (1991), 'The security legacy of the 1980s in the Third World,' in Thomas Weiss and Meryl Kessler, eds, *Third World Security in the Post-Cold War Era*, Boulder and London, Lynne Rienner Press, 19–33.

Organski, A. F. K. (1968), *World Politics*, New York: Knopf.

Owen, Roger (1981), *The Middle East in the World Economy, 1800–1914*, London and New York, Methuen.

—— (1992), *State, Power and Politics in the Making of the Modern Middle East*, London, Routledge.

—— (1999), 'Inter-Arab economic relations during the twentieth century: world market vs regional market?', in Michael Hudson, ed., *Middle East Dilemmas*, London and New York, I. B. Taurus, 217–232.

Packer, George (2005), *Assassin's Gate: America in Iraq*, New York: Farrar, Straus and Giroux

Padoan, Piercarlo (1997), 'The political economy of regional integration in the Middle East,' in Laura Guazzone, ed., *The Middle East in Global Change*, Basingstoke, Macmillan, 174–200.

Parker, Richard (1993), *The Politics of Miscalculation*, Bloomington, IN, Indiana University Press.

Paul, James (1986), 'The new bourgeoisie in the Gulf,' *Middle East Report*, 142, September–October, 18–22.

Peleg, Ilan (1988), 'The impact of the Six-Day War on the Israeli right: a Second Republic in the making?,' in Yehuda Lukas and Abdalla M. Battah, eds, *The Arab-Israeli Conflict*, Boulder, CO, Westview Press, 54–66.

Peretz, Don (1988), 'Israeli policies toward the Arab states and the Palestinians since 1967,' in Yehuda Lukas and Abdalla M. Battah, eds, *The Arab-Israeli Conflict*, Boulder, CO, Westview Press, 26–40.

Peri, Yoram (1983), *Between Battles and Ballots: Israeli Military in Politics*, Cambridge, Cambridge University Press.

—— (1988), 'From political nationalism to ethno-nationalism: the case of Israel,' in Yehuda Lukas and Abdalla M. Battah, eds, *The Arab-Israeli Conflict*, Boulder, CO, Westview Press, 41–53.

Perlmutter, Amos (1969), 'From obscurity to rule: The Syrian army and the Ba'th Party,' *Western Political Quarterly*, 22:4, 827–845.

Perthes, Volker (1995), *The Political Economy of Syria under Asad*, London, I. B. Taurus.

Petran, Tabitha (1987), *The Struggle for Lebanon*, New York, Monthly Review Press.

Phillips, Christopher (2011), 'Arabism after the Arab Spring', http://cjophillips.wordpress.com/2011/07/31/arabism-after-the-arab-spring/, accessed 10 October 2014.

Picard, Elizabeth (1988), 'Arab military in politics: from revolutionary plot to authoritarian state,' in Adeed Dawisha and I. William Zartman, eds, *Beyond Coercion: The Durability of the Arab State*, London, Croom-Helm, 116–146.

Quandt, William (2001), 'The United States', in Leon Carl Brown, ed., *Diplomacy in the Middle East: The International Relations of Regional and Outside Powers*, London and New York, I. B. Tauris, 59–74.

Rabinovich, Itamar (1972), *Syria under the Ba'th, 1963–1966: The Army-Party Symbiosis*, New York, Halstead Press.

—— (1987), 'Controlled conflict in the Middle East: The Syrian–Israeli rivalry in Lebanon,' in Gabriel Ben-Dor and David B. DeWitt, eds, *Conflict Management in the Middle East*, Lexington, MA, Lexington Books, 97–111.

Rahim, A. H. (2011), 'Whither political Islam and the Arab Spring?', *Hedgehog Review*, 13:3, 8–22.

Ramazani, Rouhollah (1986), *Revolutionary Iran: Challenge and Response in the Middle East*, Baltimore, MD, Johns Hopkins University Press.

Riad, Mahmoud (1982), *The Struggle for Peace in the Middle East*, London and New York, Quartet Books.

Richards, Alan and John Waterbury (1996), *A Political Economy of the Middle East*, Boulder, CO, Westview Press.

Roberts, Samuel J. (1990), *Party and Policy in Israel, the Battle between Hawks and Doves*, Boulder, CO, Westview Press.

Robins, Philip (1991), *Turkey and the Middle East*, London, Pinter RIIA.

Robinson, William I. (1996), *Promoting Polyarchy: Globalization, US Intervention, and Hegemony*, Cambridge, Cambridge University Press.

Rubinstein, Alvin Z. (1977), *Red Star on the Nile: The Soviet–Egyptian Influence Relationship since the June War*, Princeton, NJ, Princeton University Press.

Ruggie, John (1983), 'Continuity and transformation in the world polity: toward a neo-realist synthesis,' *World Politics*, 35:2, 261–285.

Rustow, Dankwart (1984), 'Realignments in the Middle East,' *Foreign Affairs*, 63:3, 581–601.

Sadat, Anwar (1978), *In Search of Identity: An Autobiography*, New York, Harper and Row.

Sadowski, Yehia (1991), 'Arab economies after the Gulf War,' *Middle East Report*, 170, May–June, 4–13.

Salame, Ghassan (1989), 'Political power and the Saudi state,' in B. Berberoglu, *Power and Stability in the Middle East*, London, Zed Books, 70–89.

Salem, Paul (1997), 'Arab political currents, Arab–European relations and Mediterraneanism', in Guazzone, Laura, ed., *The Middle East in Global Change*, London, Macmillan, 23–42.

—— (2012), 'Mursi moves to rebuild Egypt's mideast leadership role,' *Al-Monitor*, October 5, www.al-monitor.com/pulse/originals/2012/al-monitor/morsi-egypt-regional-role.html#ixzz2EI3bQyZF2012, accessed 6 December 2012.

Salloukh, Bassel (1996), 'State strength, permeability, and foreign policy behavior: Jordan in theoretical perspective,' *Arab Studies Quarterly*, 18:2, 39–66.

Sayigh, Yezid (1993), 'Arab military industrialization: security incentives and economic impact,' in Korany, Noble and Brynen, *The Many Faces of National Security in the Middle East*, 214–238.

Sayigh, Yusuf (1999), 'Arab economic integration: the poor harvest of the 1980s,' in Michael Hudson, *Middle East Dilemmas*, London and New York, I. B. Taurus, 233–258.

Schiff, Zeev and Ehud Ya'ari (1984), *Israel's Lebanon War*, New York, Simon & Schuster.

Schulze, Kirstin (1999), *The Arab-Israeli Conflict*, London, Longman.

Seale, Patrick (1965), *The Struggle for Syria*, London, Oxford University Press.

—— (1988), *Asad: the Struggle for the Middle East*, Berkeley, University of California Press, 1988.

Sela, Avraham (1998), *The End of the Arab-Israeli Conflict: Middle East Politics and the Quest for Regional Order*, Albany, NY, State University of New York Press.

Shafiq, Nemat (1999), 'Labour migration and economic integration in the Middle East,' in Michael Hudson, ed., *Middle East Dilemmas*, London and New York, I. B. Taurus, 279–298.

Sharabi, Hisham (1970), *Arab Intellectuals and the West: The Formative Years, 1875–1914*, Baltimore, MD, Johns Hopkins University Press.

Shazli, Saad al- (1980), *The Crossing of the Suez*, San Francisco, American Mideast Research.

Sheehan, Edward (1976), 'How Kissinger did it: step by step in the Middle East,' *Foreign Policy*, 22, 3–71.

Sifry, Micah (1991), 'U.S. intervention in the Middle East: a case study,' in Micah Sifry and Christopher Cerf, eds, *The Gulf War Reader*, New York, Times Books, 27–33.

Sil, Rudra. and Katzenstein, Peter, (2005), 'What is analytic eclecticism and why do we need it? A pragmatic perspective on problems and mechanisms in the study of world Politics', Paper presented at the annual meeting of the American Political Science Association, www.allacademic.com/meta/p41957_index.html, accessed 5 January 2012.

Simons, Geoffrey (1996), *The Scourging of Iraq: Sanctions, Law and Natural Justice*, London, Macmillan.

Singer, Max and Aaron Wildavsky (1996), *The Real World Order: Zones of Peace, Zones of Turmoil*, Chatham, NJ, Chatham House Publishers.

Sirriyeh, H. (2000), 'A new version of Pan-Arabism?', *International Relations*, 15:3, 53–56.

Smith, Charles D. (1996), *Palestine and the Arab-Israeli Conflict*, New York, St Martin's Press.

Smith, Pamela Ann (1986), 'The exile bourgeoisie of Palestine,' *Middle East Report*, no. 142, September–October, 23–27.

Solingen, Etil (1998), *Regional Orders at Century's Dawn: Global and Domestic Influence on Grand Strategy*, Princeton, NJ, Princeton University Press.

Spero, Joan Edelman (1990), *The Politics of International Economic Relations*, 4th edn, New York, St Martins.

Spiro, David E. (1999), *The Hidden Hand of American Hegemony: Petrodollar Recycling and International Markets*, Ithaca, NY, and London, Cornell University Press.

Springborg, Robert (1989), *Mubarak's Egypt: The Fragmentation of the Political Order*, Boulder, CO, Westview Press.

Stein, Janet (1993), 'The security dilemma in the Middle East: the prognosis for the decade ahead,' in Bahgat Korany, Paul Noble, Rex Brynen, eds, *The Many Faces of National Security in the Middle East*, London, Macmillan, 56–75.

Stork, Joe and Martha Wenger (1991), 'From rapid deployment to massive deployment,' *Middle East Report*, no. 168, January–February, 22–26.

Tachau, Frank (1975), *Political Elites and Political Development in the Middle East*, Cambridge, MA, Schenkman/Wiley.

Talhami, Ghada (1997), 'An interview with Sadiq al-Azm', *Arab Studies Quarterly*, 19:3, 124.

Tanzer, Michael (1991), 'Oil and the Gulf crisis,' in Phyllis Bennis and Michel Moushabeck, eds, *Beyond the Storm: A Gulf Crisis Reader*, New York, Olive Branch Press, 263–267.

Taylor, Alan (1982), *The Arab Balance of Power*, Syracuse, NY, Syracuse University Press.

Telhami, Shibley (1990), *Power and Leadership in International Bargaining: The Path to the Camp David Accords*, New York, Columbia University Press.

—— (2011a), '2010 Annual Arab Public Survey,' Brookings Institute, 5 August, www.brookings.edu/~/media/research/files/reports/2010/8/05%20arab%20opinion%20poll%20telhami/0805_arabic_opinion_poll_telhami.pdf, accessed 3 March 2012.

—— (2011b), The striking Arab openness to intervention', *The National Interest'* 4 April.

Telhami, Shibley and Zogby International (2007), *2006 Annual Arab Public Opinion Survey*, Washington, DC, Saban Center for Middle East Policy at the Brookings Institute, February.

Temlali, Yassine (2011), 'The "Arab Spring": rebirth or final throes of Pan-Arabism?', *Perspectives*, Heinrich Boll Stiftung, 6:2, 46–9, http://lb.boell.org/downloads/Perspectives_02-06_Yassine_Temlali.pdf, accessed January 2012'

Thompson, William R. (1970), 'The Arab sub-system and the feudal pattern of interaction: 1965,' *Journal of Peace Research*, 7, 151–167.

—— (1981), 'Delineating regional subsystems: visit networks and the Middle East case,' *International Journal of Middle East Studies*, 13:2, 213–235.

Terzian, Pierre (1985), *OPEC: The Inside Story*, London, Zed.

Tibi, Bassam (1998), *Conflict and War in the Middle East: From Interstate War to New Security*, London, Macmillan.

Tilly, Charles (1975), *The Formation of National States in Western Europe*, Princeton, NJ, Princeton University Press.

Torrey, Gordon (1964), *Syrian Politics and the Military, 1945–1958*, Columbus, Ohio State University.

Trimberger, Ellen Kay (1978), *Revolution from Above: Military Bureaucrats and Development in Japan, Turkey, Egypt and Peru*, New Brunswick, NJ, Transaction Books.

Tripp, Charles (1996), 'Islam and the secular logic of the state in the Middle East', in A. Ehteshami and A. S. Sidahmad, eds, *Islamic Fundamentalism*, Boulder, CO, Westview Press, 51–69.

—— (2001), 'The foreign policy of Iraq,' in Hinnebusch and Ehteshami, eds, *The Foreign Policies of Middle East States*, 167–192.

Valbjørn, Morten and Andre Bank (2007), 'Signs of a new Arab Cold War: the 2006 Lebanon war and the Sunni–Shi'i divide,' *Middle East Report*, 242, Spring.

Van Dam, Nikolaos (1981), *The Struggle for Power in Syria: Sectarianism, Regionalism and Tribalism in Politics, 1961–1980*, London, Croom-Helm.

Van Dusen, Michael (1975), 'Downfall of a traditional elite,' in Frank Tachau, ed., *Political Elites and Political Development in the Middle East*, Cambridge, MA, Schenkman/Wiley, 115–155.

Vassiliev, Alexi (1998), *The History of Saudi Arabia*, London, Saqi Books.

Vatikiotis, P. J. (1978), *Nasser and His Generation*, New York, St Martin's Press.

—— (1987), *Islam and the State*, London, Routledge.

Vitalis, Robert (1997), 'The closing of the Arabian oil frontier and the future of American-Saudi relations,' *Middle East Report*, 204, July–September, 15–21.

Waldner, David (1995), 'More than meets the eye: economic influence on contemporary Syrian foreign policy,' *Middle East Insight*, 11:4, 34–37.

Wallerstein, Immanuel (1974), *The Modern World System*, New York, Academic Press.

Walt, Steven (1987), *The Origin of Alliances*, Ithaca, NY, Cornell University Press.

Waltz, Kenneth (1979), *Theory of International Politics*, Boston, MA, Addison-Wesley.

Wendt, Alexander (1999), *Social Theory of International Politics*, Cambridge and New York, Cambridge University Press.

Weulersse, Jacques (1946), *Paysans de Syrie et du Proche-Orient*, Paris, Gallimard.

Wieland, Carsten (2012), *Syria – A Decade of Lost Chances: Repression and Revolution from Damascus Spring to Arab Spring*, Seattle, WA, Cune Press.

Yaniv, Avner (1986), 'Syria and Israel: the politics of escalation,' in Moshe Ma'oz and Avner Yaniv, eds, *Syria under Assad: Domestic Constraints and Regional Risks*, London, Croom-Helm, 157–177.

—— (1987), 'Alliance politics in the Middle East: a security dilemma perspective,' in Auriel Braun, ed., *The Middle East in Global Strategy*, Boulder, CO, Westview Press.

Yavuz, M. Hakan and Mujeeb Khan (1992), 'Turkish foreign policy toward the Arab Israeli conflict,' *Arab Studies Quarterly*, 14:4, 69–94.

Yergin, Daniel (1991), 'Oil: the strategic prize,' in Micah Sifry and Christopher Cerf, eds, *The Gulf War Reader*, New York, Times Books, 21–26.

Zartman, I. William, et al. (1982), *Political Elites in Arab North Africa*, New York and London, Longman.

—— (1993), 'State-building and the military in Arab Africa,' in Korany, Noble and Brynen, *The Many Faces of National Security in the Middle East*, 239–257.

—— (1999), 'The ups and downs of Maghrebi unity,' in Michael Hudson (ed.), *Middle East Dilemmas*, London and New York, I. B. Taurus, 171–86.

Zunes, Stephen (2001), 'The United States and the breakdown of the Palestinian-Israeli peace process,' *Middle East Policy*, 8:4, 66–85.

Glossary of terms

Agency: In IR, agency refers to the capacity of states (and leaders) to act autonomously and affect their environment; structure, by contrast, refers to the preexisting context that constrains agent choices.

Anarchy: The absence of government, seen by realism as the main distinction between domestic and international politics.

Balance of power: A key realist concept referring to a balance between the power of states or alliances of states, and seen as the main way of preventing dominance and establishing order. Classical realists see it as the result of artful statesmanship, while structural realists view it as a natural or probable response to the insecurity of the system.

Bandwagon: The opposite of balancing against a threat, bandwagoning seeks to appease a superior, potentially threatening power, in order either to help balance against a more proximate threat or to share in the spoils of a winning coalition.

Bureaucratic politics: According to this concept, policy is seen as a product of struggle within governments by rival branches of the bureaucracy, each defending its own interests, possibly at the expense of coherent, rational policy-making. See Halperin and Clapp (2006) See also *Rational actor*.

Complex interdependence: The result of the multiple trans-national and inter-state ties, often economic, that bind states together and potentially mute conflict. See Keohane and Nye (1977). See also *Pluralism*.

Complex realism: the author of the book uses this term to refer to varieties of realism which accept that several levels of analysis, notably the internal (domestic) as well as the international systemic level, have major impacts on state behaviour and international politics.

Constructivism: According to this concept, the state system is an intersubjective (cultural, not material) set of norms and expectations created by the interactions of states. The system, in turn, shapes (constitutes) the identities of states, and it is this, not simply power considerations, that explains their behaviour. See the work of Alexander Wendt (1999) and Michael Barnett (1998).

Democratic peace theory: The claim that the spread of democracy will lead to greater international security because democratic processes predispose states to resolve conflicts peacefully rather than through war. See also *Liberalism* and *Pluralism*.

Dependency theory: A branch of Marxist-inspired structuralism, dependency theory argued that the dependency of developing countries on the developed economies allows the latter to exploit the former, thereby keeping the Third World underdeveloped.

Globalisation: The acceleration and intensification of worldwide social relations, driven by the internationalisation of business and communications. Globalisation both partly by-passes states and ties them into a mutually interdependent world society that reduces their self-sufficiency and sovereignty.

Hegemony: Dominance by a leading state (e.g., the United States and the United Kingdom, at different times) that supposedly maintains order and economic stability in the world system, usually in the name of an *Ideology,* such as liberalism.

Historical sociology: A school of thought that, when applied to international relations, focuses on how states and states systems mutually consititute each other over time; in Charles Tilly's (1975) famous aphorism, 'war makes the state and the state makes war'. HS disputes what it sees as neo-realism's view of an unchanging international system and argues that changes in the kind of states shape changes in the kind of states system.

Ideology: Refers to a comprehensive belief system which purports to both describe the world and to prescribe how it can be changed for the better. While claiming to promote a universal good, it expresses the interests of a particular social force (such as a class). Ideology is widely deployed by movements and parties to attract followers and by ruling regimes and classes to legitimise their dominance.

Irredentism: Refers to dissatisfaction with state borders where they are incongruent with, cut across and frustrate identity groups' (such as putative nations) aspirations for self-determination or for inclusion in a state coterminous with their identity. It is a major source of conflict within and between states.

Liberalism: in International Relations refers to claims that capitalist economics affects international politics by creating trans-state interdependencies that shape more pacific state behaviour (see *Democratic peace theory*). Scholars in this tradition also argue that international regimes (or institutions) and international organisations can facilitate co-operation and mute the power struggle of states in anarchic world systems.

Level of analysis: Refers to the possible alternative foci for explaining international behaviour. The system level refers, in realism, to the anarchic structure of the states system and, in structuralism, to the hierarchic core–periphery global division of labour. The system level is seen by these approaches to shape behaviour at the unit level (the states). Other levels of analysis may refer to substate phenomena, including individual leaders, government (executives, interest groups, bureaucracies) and civil society (political culture, public opinion), which, according to pluralism, equally affect states' international behaviour.

Neo-liberalism: Refers to the ideology promoting de-regulation and a rollback of state intervention in economies. Promoted by Reagan and Thatcher in the West and imposed on the Third World by the IMF, it has advanced economic globalisation to the advantage of international finance capital.

Neo-realism (or structural realism): A version of realism that stresses the predominant influence of the state system (especially insecurity from anarchy) in shaping states and their behaviour. See Waltz 1979. See also *Realism*.

Pluralism: The school of International Relations theory that sees a plurality of forces as shaping relations between states, notably supra-state actors (international organisations), trans-state actors (trans-national corporations) and non-state actors (professional associations, social movements). The resulting complex interdependence constrains states, especially deterring warlike behaviour. Seeing states as less than unitary actors, pluralism also focuses on the role of sub-state domestic actors, such as competing bureaucracies, interest groups and public opinion, as determinants of a state's behaviour. It also stresses the role of leadership beliefs and images, including the irrationality caused by misperceptions. Pluralism is subsumed within the broader school of liberalism. See Keohane and Nye (1977).

Polarity: Refers to the number of great powers in the international system at a given time; for example, bi-polarity refers to the Cold War period of two superpowers while multi-polarity describes nineteenth-century Europe. Neo-realists see the polarity of international systems as their most important distinguishing feature but disagree over which pattern of polarity is more stable (and least war-prone).

Rational actor: The notion that states, ideally, act as unitary actors, making decisions after collecting full information, surveying all feasible options, weighing costs and benefits and matching ends and means. See also *Bureaucratic politics* and *Realism*.

Realism: The traditionally dominant school of International Relations theory. States are seen as unitary rational actors advancing their national interests amid the insecurity of the anarchic international arena. International politics is a struggle for power, war is an ever-present possibility, and order depends on a balance of power. Decision-maker rationality means careful 'realistic' matching of goals and resources (the more commonsense use of the word *Realism*). See Morgenthau 1978. See also *Neo-realism*. Realists come in many varieties, but one main intra-realist debate is over the dominant response of states to insecurity: 'defensive realists' believe states seek a sufficiency of deterrent power to balance against threats while 'offensive realists' believe great powers are different and seek hegemony.

Regime: In the domestic context, *regime* refers to an existing governmental order. In international politics, *regime* refers to the set of voluntarily agreed principles, norms and procedures that restrain the behaviour of states.

Security dilemma: The notion, conceptualised by John Herz, that, in an anarchic system, each state increases its power for defensive purposes but, in doing so, is seen as more threatening by its neighbours, who respond in kind, setting off arms races, with the result that all states end up less secure.

Structuralism: The broad view, inspired by Marxism, that the hierarchical structure of the international capitalist system determines state options. Specifically, in the international economic division of labour, the core (developed) states subordinate and exploit the peripheral (less developed) states, whose function is to supply the developed states with primary products. The system is maintained by trans-state alliances between dominant classes in the core and the periphery and by the economic dependency of the peripheral states. Dependency theory and world systems theory are varieties of structuralism. See Wallerstein (1974). Not to be confused with 'structural realism'; see *Neo-realism*.

Trans-national (or trans-state): Refers to ties and non-state groups that cross state boundaries.

World systems theory: refers to the work of Immanuel Wallerstein and his followers, which analyses the long-term evolution of the world capitalist system, seen as the most important determinant of world politics. The international division of labour divides the globe into the core advanced economies, the underdeveloped periphery and the intermediate semi-periphery. Over time hegemons rise and fall in the core of the system, their function to stabilise and expand the capitalist market. See *Structuralism*.

Index